CW01661953

Bar Training Courses Revision

Prepare to Pass

Civil Litigation and Evidence

from 2020

Gillian Woodworth

Bar Training Courses Revision

Prepare to Pass

Civil Litigation and Evidence

from 2020

Copyright ©2020 by Gillian Woodworth

All rights reserved. This book or any portion thereof may not be reproduced or used in any manner whatsoever without the express written permission of the publisher except for the use of brief quotations in a book review or scholarly journal.

ISBN: 978-1-716-44630-6

Upfish Business Services Ltd
Park Street Lane
St Albans

Ordering Information:
Special discounts are available on quantity purchases by corporations, associations, educators, and others. For details, contact the publisher at gwoodworth.upfish.law@gmail.com

As part of your learning, or revision, you may photograph the MOCS if you have purchased your own copy of this book. You would then have created a portable set of flashcards to peruse on your phone "on the go".

You may photograph once only and you may not share these, your personal photographs of the MOCs with anybody else, in any way, on any platform or otherwise or elsewhere, even if you change them in any way or annotate them or print them or copy them by hand or by any other method. This would put you in breach of copyright.

Contents and Syllabus

for the centrally set assessments in Civil Litigation and Evidence from 2020 for the BTC curriculum as set by the Bar Standards Board Central Examination Board

You can access a copy of the BTC syllabus on the BSB website as well as here below.

The details of examinable CPR, Commentary and PDs found in the syllabus as displayed on the BSB website are not reproduced in the table below for reasons of space and clarity. Rather, I have copied them across from the BSB website and set them out in bold at the beginning of the Chapter in which they appear.

(The author has added sub-section numbers for ease of reference in this book)

	Norwich Pharmacal	**3, after 16,**	**37, 229**
15.	**Interim applications**	**3,4, before17**	**25, 41, 230**
15.1	with notice and without notice applications;	3,4, before17	
15.2	documentation required in interim applications;	3,4	
15.3	periods of notice in interim applications;	3	
15.4	duty of full and frank disclosure in without notice applications.	4	
16.	**Interim Payments and Security for Costs**	**16, 15**	**223, 217**
16.1	interim payments	16	
16.2	security for costs	15	
17.	**Interim injunctions**	**4,17**	**41, 283**
17.1	interim injunctions	4,17	
17.2	***American Cyanamid*** principles	17	
17.3	exceptions and variations to ***American Cyanamid***	17	**236**
17.4	usual undertakings and cross-undertakings	17	
18.	**Settlement (including offers to settle)**	**7**	**103**
18.1	negotiation and joint settlement meetings	7	
18.2	Calderbank offers and offers to settle under Part 36	7	
18.3	consequences of accepting Part 36 offers	7	
18.4	withdrawing, reducing and increasing offers to settle	7	
18.5	consequences of failing to obtain judgment more advantageous than offer to settle	7	
19.	**Evidence of Fact**	**11, 20, 21**	**161, 269, 281**
19.1	evidence of fact in civil proceedings	21	
19.2	witness statements and witness summonses	21	
19.3	notices to admit facts and notices to prove documents	11, 20	165,
20.	**Expert Evidence**	**22**	**291**
20.1	the general exclusionary rule in relation to evidence of opinion	22	
20.2	the main exceptions to the rule	22	
20.3	expert opinion evidence in civil proceedings	22	
21.	**Civil Trial and Evidence**	**23**	**301**
21.1	the trial of civil cases	23	
21.2	hearsay evidence in civil proceedings	23	
21.3	convictions as evidence in civil proceedings	23	
22	**Judgments, Orders and Enforcement**	**24, 25**	**311, 319**
22.1	judgment and orders, including Tomlin orders	24	
22.2	enforcing money judgments	25	
22.3	recording and enforcement of settlements following ADR	24, 25	
23.	**Costs**	**6, 18**	**75, 243**
23.1	summary and detailed assessment of costs	6	

Thank you from the author

I would like to thank you for buying this book.

Thank you also to those who bought the editions of "BPTC Revision Prepare to Pass Civil Litigation and Evidence" over the past six years and for the feedback from those who provided it. I have made many of the amendments you suggested in preparing this book for the new Bar Training Courses from 2020. I trust that students this year will further benefit from your helpful input.

Any feedback to help enhance future editions will again be gratefully received. Please email gwoodworth.upfish.law@gmail.com

I hope that this book helps you on your way towards an enjoyable and successful career at the Bar or as a lawyer in your home jurisdiction.

Gillian Woodworth

The author, Gillian Woodworth, transferred from full-time professional practice to working in full-time legal education in 1995. Since then she has spent over 25 years training students on both academic and professional legal courses and as a regulator of those courses. She worked for 10 years at BPP as a tutor, Course Director and Director of Staff Training and Development; she has worked as a visiting lecturer at what is now the University of Law; she then worked in the Education and Training department of the Solicitors Regulation Authority prior to moving to what is now The City Law School, City University of London.

Gillian worked for over 6 years full-time at City, teaching and assessing initially on the on the Bar Vocational Course and latterly on the BPTC course where she also had a responsibility for ensuring The City Law School's compliance with Bar Standards Board requirements.

Now retired from City, Gillian's motivation in writing this book is to provide assistance so that all students can enter the Bar Standards Board centrally set civil litigation and evidence assessments on the Bar Training Courses from 2020 with confidence.

In addition to writing and marking final assessments for LLB, GDL, LPC, BVC and BPTC programmes and supervising dissertations at LLM level, Gillian has also trained professional legal course external examiners. She is therefore well placed to provide advice and guidance on how to pass assessments at all levels of legal education.

Praise for the predecessor to this book

"BPTC Revision Prepare to Pass Civil Litigation and Evidence" from 2014 to 2020.

There is reproduced below feedback, without amendment, and with the kind permission of each of the individuals who provided it, other than reviews quoted from the internet.

THANK YOU GILLIAN. This book helped me to pass Civil Litigation! This was my main revision resource and I used it every single week. It sets out the whole process from lodging a claim to appeals in a really easy way to understand. A lot of things that I didn't understand in BPTC classes were clearly explained in this book and I could always rely on it. Part 36 offers is explained so clearly and the best chapter in my opinion. This book makes understanding the White Book seem like a piece of cake.

I advise buying this book at the start of your Bar course and reading it as you go along because Civil Lit is something you learn slowly and you need to build on it each week. Then read it all again for revision and again and again! I made flashcards on the key points and by the time I took the exam I felt confident in my knowledge of Civil Lit.

Couldn't have done it without you Gillian!

Thank you so much for all your help which made me pass first time. Even though we never met, I felt like you taught me the whole of civil litigation from start to finish. Whenever I was confused by the White Book and it seemed too complex, your book always explained it in a simple way for me to understand and remember. I had some very frustrating weeks on the BPTC where Civil Litigation seemed like a mountain to climb in order to understand but then I would read your book and understand it. Aside from understanding the material, your book really did make me feel like I was on the right path to becoming a barrister and that I was clever enough to pass this course. I just needed someone else to explain it in another way, which you always did. It was much more than a book to me

- *5.0 out of 5 stars* The greatest asset to passing Civil Litigation
  Verified Purchase

This was an extremely helpful book and helped me to secure a VC in the Bar Professional Training Course this year. Thank you so much for your amazing work Gillian Woodworth.

- *5.0 out of 5 stars* A Life Saver

The Best in the Business.
I have bought all the books - and this one saved the day.
Clear, accessible, with lots of handy tips.
I passed on my final 'last chance' sit because of this book.

- A life saver!
  Verified Purchase

I've had the pleasure of meeting Gillian personally for private tuition, and she is absolutely brilliant and worth every penny. If this book was double the price I would still consider this fantastic value for money - and at circa £ it is an absolute steal. Every page is really well considered, and the aim of the book is to distill very complex areas into more accessible chunks with clear explanations. I have bought pretty much every available book on for BPTC Civil litigation revision - many are little more than pages upon pages of tedious bullet points and some are in dire need of update. Long review short - Gillian is an educator at heart and genuinely wants everybody to do the best they can. I know every year she is at pains to revise the book to make sure it is the best reflection of the current curriculum, so to this end if you are wavering then please purchase as it will ensure the future cohorts to come will also have access to this delight. Part 36 is done particularly well (an area I oft struggled with!)

*** Edit - the proofs in the pudding - I passed!

A BPP student

❖ Excellent revision manual

The author has broken down the curriculum very well for this subject and covers every minute detail.

❖ Verified Purchase

Phenomenal revision guide. Bought it just to supplement my own notes and make sure I'd covered everything. it was well worth the money and what a fantastic woman. Amazing revision guide.

❖ Excellent book

Without exaggeration this book on it's own helped me secure an outstanding in the Civil Litigation paper. It is very cleverly written, covers all the main points

❖ I passed because of Gillian. This book helps to cut through the overwhelming volume of material that is presented in the BPTC Civil Lit syllabus. It is set out in a logical order (from pre-litigation to appeal), which I felt helped everything to slot into

A BPP student

❖ I am so grateful for your wonderful book.

A Bar Transfer Test candidate

❖ Gillian is known by students and members of the Bar as one of the best BPTC tutors out there. She taught me in 2011 and I was awarded an Outstanding in the examination. Her knowledge of the White Book is unparalleled, as is her ability to teach complex topics in a way that is easy to understand. Her new book reflects her teaching style and is a perfect revision guide for trainee barristers (and for qualified barristers who like to have a refresher to-hand). A very senior member of the bar recently remarked that her description of the Norwich Pharmacal Order in the book is the most concise and easy to understand description he has ever come across. I would strongly recommend this book (and anything else Gillian writes) as a revision guide

A City student

❖ Everything you write is clear, the diagrams are great and I like the structure of it as everything sticks in your memory.

A University of Law student

Abbreviations

A	Applicant
AC	Appeal Court; the higher court in relation to a lower court
ADR	Alternative Dispute Resolution (ReDOC); see also the definition in GL
AETO	Authorised Education and Training Organisation is the new acronym for the Provider with whom you are studying the new Bar Training Courses from 2020. The list of AETOs from September 2020 taken from The BSB website as at 6 November 2020 is BPP University Cardiff University Manchester Metropolitan University Northumbria University Nottingham Trent University The City Law School, City, University of London University The Inns of Court College of Advocacy The University of Law The University of the West of England (UWE)
AN	Appellant's notice
AOS	Acknowledgment of Service of a document by the party on whom it was served
BPTC	Until 2019-2020, the predecessor to the Bar Training Courses, the Bar Professional Training Course.
BTC	The Bar Training Course(s) is the umbrella term for the courses which will train you for the vocational component of training for the Bar that lead to Call to the Bar.
BSB	Bar Standards Board
C	Claimant
CA	Court of Appeal
CC	County Court
CF	Claim Form
CPR	The Civil Procedure Rules (set out in the White Book)
CUR	Shorthand for Curriculum in this book; e.g. a reference in this book to CUR 1.3 is a reference to the third bullet point of section 1 of the curriculum for the centrally set assessments in civil litigation and evidence and hence to the duty of the court to manage cases
D	Defendant
D1	First Defendant
D2	Second Defendant
EM	Examinable material as set out in the syllabus

GL	The Glossary in Section F, Volume 1 of the White Book; this abbreviation is used as a helpful indicator within the text of the White Book to alert you to the fact that there is a definition in the glossary
He	All masculine nouns and pronouns should be construed as if they were alternatively feminine nouns and pronouns
Jackson	The Jackson ADR Handbook (Second Edition, 2016)
LC	Lower Court
MOCS	**MO**st **C**oncise **S**ummary (distillation of main points to the most basic in order to aid preliminary understanding; found at the end of most Chapters)
MCQ	Multiple Choice Questions. This question format tests your knowledge of the examinable elements of the CPR rules, Commentary and Practice Directions. There are one correct choice and three incorrect ones.
NOCR	No Other Compelling Reason (summary judgment)
NRPOS	No Real Prospect of Succeeding (summary judgment)
PD	Practice Direction (usually found at the end of each part of the CPR)
PI	Personal Injury
POC	Particulars of Claim; a statement of case setting out the details (particulars) of the claim being brought
Provider	Synonym for AETO
QOCS	Qualified One-Way Cost Shifting
R	Respondent
RCJ	Royal Courts of Justice
ReDOC	**RE**solution of **D**isputes **O**ut of **C**ourt (ADR)
RN	Respondent's Notice
RP	Relevant Period for Part 36 offers. (in the Chapter on "offers to settle").
RPOS	Real Prospect Of Success (setting aside default judgment); (Appeals)
RTA	Road Traffic Accident
S.	Section number (of an Act)
SBA	Single Best Answer. This question format tests your understanding and application of your knowledge in practical situations. At least three of the four options are possible in the real world and you must select the one which best suits the given scenario.
She	All feminine nouns and pronouns should be construed as if they were alternatively masculine nouns and pronouns
SOCR	Some Other Compelling Reason (Appeals)

SOGR	Some Other Good Reason (setting aside default judgment)
TP	Third Party
W	Witness
WB	The White Book; references are to Volume 1 unless otherwise stated.
X	A party named X
XIC	Examination In Chief (questioning your own witness); see also the definition in GL
XX	Cross examination (questioning a witness for the other side); see also the definition in GL
Y	A party named Y

Further publications that you may find helpful for the Bar Training Courses are listed here with supplementary information in the final pages at the back of this book.

10 Reasons you didn't write an outstanding opinion	Suzanne Reece
LLM Dissertation. How to maximise marks for your Practice Focused Dissertation	Suzanne Reece

The White Book.

When a party wishes to make a civil claim against another party, the procedure to be followed in England and Wales is set out in the White Book. This is the colloquial term for the volumes called Civil Procedure, published by Sweet and Maxwell. It is very likely that your Provider will furnish you with a copy of this for your Bar Training Course.

The White Book is made up of 2 volumes and both volumes are renewed each year around April. During the course of any one year cumulative supplements are produced, updating the rules as the year progresses. We must all therefore ensure that we are following the current rules by using the White Book printed for the current year together with any cumulative supplements to date. Your Provider/AETO will confirm to you the date relevant to your assessment. This book was completed at the end of October 2020.

The principal volume for the Bar Training Course will be Volume 1 which sets out in section A the civil procedure rules (usually abbreviated to CPR). In turn, these rules in section A are divided into 89 parts. You will therefore hear reference to "Part 1 of the CPR" which sets out the overriding objective or "Part 23" when dealing with general rules about applications for court orders.

Once you have access to the White Book, take a look at 1.1, 1.2, 1.3,1.4 and 1.5. You will see that these form the entirety of the CPR in Part 1, dealing with the overriding objective and that the **CPR rules** themselves are printed in **bold type**.

Before we reach CPR 1.4, there is lots of very small type. This is **Commentary** on the rules and not the rules themselves. The syllabus for the centralised assessments sets out which Commentary will be assessed. In this book they are highlighted in boxes in between two stars. The commentary is just that: a commentary, setting out comments on the way that each of the CPR rules has been applied.

Next please turn to Part 2 of the CPR, "Application and interpretation of the Rules". At the end of the section of this Part, as with all other Parts, you will find a series of pages beginning with the title, "**Practice Direction**". These practice directions are important and give directions as to how the rule operates in practice. You will need to know and be able to apply the contents of the practice directions set out as assessable on the syllabus as well as the CPR rules and Commentary which are on the syllabus for your assessments and beyond. In this book the CPR rules and the PDs contained in each Chapter are set out in bold at the beginning of the Chapter.

The first practice direction in Part 2 is called "Practice Direction 2A-court offices". You will see that on the right-hand side of the page in bold are the numbered practice directions for this section. Although these are now set out to read, for example 2APD.1, you may often hear them referred to as practice direction 2A, paragraph or note 1. Do not let this confuse you; it is two ways of saying exactly the same thing.

Continuing on through practice direction A Part 2, you will see that there is also a section 2B containing the various elements making up PD 2B (2BPD.1 etc.).

You are not expected to learn the individual numbering of the elements of the CPR for your assessment although you are expected to know their content. For this reason and because from year-to-year it is not unheard of for the numbering of paragraphs in each part of the CPR to change, even if only slightly, then, unless I feel that it is helpful for explanatory purposes in this book, I will not be referring to the internal numbering of each Part, but only to each Part in its entirety in the heading of each Chapter.

Most importantly, there can be no substitute for getting to know your way around the White Book and getting to grips with its content. Please do not defer referring to it. Start to become conversant with it from day one. You will have it with you in the second of the centralised assessments for civil litigation and evidence and you will need to be able to refer to it in the assessment.

You can access the Civil Procedure rules in electronic form from the UK government website www.justice.gov.uk by clicking on 'procedure rules' under the heading 'most popular' at the top right hand side of the homepage. This will not give you the commentary from the White Book but it is a useful source of the rules, practice directions and pre-action conduct and protocols themselves. Should you choose to refer to this website, do be alert to the fact that it will be updated, possibly beyond the date as which you will be assessed. Thus if, say, you were to be assessed on the CPR as it stood at the end of July, then should you consult it in, say November prior to the December assessments, it will be showing any changes made which may not be assessable for you. It has not been unknown, albeit relatively rare, in the past for important rule changes whilst you are studying to become assessable. Where this has been the case in the past that the Bar Standards Board have contacted Providers to inform them of this. You Provider in turn would pass that information on to you.

The DO NOTS of approaching the assessment

(however tempting they may be)

The DO-NOT list

I have several suggestions as to how the understanding you need to be successful in this assessment may be achieved. Unusually, rather than advising you on what to do, I have chosen to advise you on what not to do.

- DO NOT treat each area of the syllabus as a self-contained item.

- DO NOT choose to learn only some areas of the syllabus, leaving others out, in the hope that what is tested is what you have learnt.

- DO NOT borrow notes from any student who was previously on a BPTC course as the law may have changed since then, the CPR may have changed since then (there are several supplements every year), the syllabus for the new Bar Training Courses from 2020 has been modified and supplemented.

- DO NOT use practice MCQ or SBA questions that you have obtained from a previous year's BPTC students or from students at a different provider as they may now be out of date, even more so now that the new pathways for Bar Training Courses leading to the centralised assessments are in place.

- DO NOT use practice MCQ or SBA questions unless you have received them from your Bar Training Course AETO for the specific sit of assessments that you are taking or unless they are in any BSB mock that may be available to you through your AETO. That is the only way you can be guaranteed that they are of sufficient rigour to prepare you for the assessment.

- DO NOT choose to wait until a few weeks before the civil litigation and evidence assessments before you begin to "revise" for them. Remember these are not a "learn and churn" assessments: you need to understand it in order to be able to answer the questions. That understanding should come from your own work throughout the year (and this can include work that you undertake in self-appointed study groups with your colleagues), not only from a few weeks of "revision".

- DO NOT work from any contracted down notes prepared by somebody else. You need to do all the work yourself so that the memory jogger notes that you use have meaning because you understand the expanded knowledge that lies behind them.

- DO NOT miss the opportunity of sitting any mock assessments provided to you by your AETO or via your AETO from the Bar Standards Board. It would be madness not to organise your time so that you give yourself the opportunity of sitting the assessment in conditions as close to that of the actual assessments as possible. It would be madness to sit the real assessments and only then meet the format and timing of the real assessments for the first time.

FLOW CHART

The progress of a claim in the civil courts from pre-action through to trial and beyond

This flow chart reflects procedural situations and considerations at the first possible point in the process that they may occur or are likely to occur.

a) Introductory / General matters / The court's general powers of case management

↓

The matter in dispute takes place; consider ADR before contemplating litigation

↓

b) Counsel may be instructed to write an opinion (also known as an advice)

↓

c) Pre- Action disclosure

↓

d) Interim application for urgent [prohibitory] injunction

↓

e) Alternative Dispute Resolution/Resolution of Disputes Out of Court

↓

f) Costs

↓

g) Settlement (including offers to settle)

↓

h) Limitation

↓

i) Pre-Action Conduct

↓

Commencing proceedings

↓

j) Claim Form issued and served; Particulars of Claim served

↓

k) Defendant Acknowledges Service of the above mentioned statements of case and/or serves her Defence or

l) D fails to serve a defence so that C can apply for default judgment against her

and then

If C is successful, D may want to get the default judgment against her set aside so she gets the chance to properly defend herself in court.

↓

m) D or another party may want to amend a statement of case;
n) D may want to add an additional claim to the original main claim, passing on liability to someone else

   a. Counterclaim against C
   b. Ask for contribution or indemnity against, e.g. D2
   c. "some other remedy" additional claim, e.g. D bringing her own claim against a third party

   ↓

Next there may be the "what-ifs" – interim applications – set out "in the rim" of the frame on the next page; if any of these are applicable, this will be signalled as part of the directions questionnaire which happens in o) track allocation on the page following the "what-ifs".

The "what-ifs" – interim applications

The Defendant

i. **What if D thinks there are no reasonable grounds for bringing the claim?**

- Apply for strike out (there are further alternative grounds too); and/or
- Apply for summary judgment if the grounds for it are met
- (both are also available to C)

ii. **"What if" (ii); D (or any party) needs more clarification or information about a matter in dispute, whether or not the matter is contained or referred to in a statement of case, so, e.g when she sees the Claim Form and the Particulars of Claim or other papers provided by C?**

- Request further information

iii. **What if D has concerns that C will not be able to afford to pay D's costs when/if D wins? (Also applies to a person in a defendant position e.g. a claimant when a defendant is counterclaiming against that claimant)**

- Apply for security for costs

The Claimant

iv. **What if C wants to claim an advance payment of what he believes he will win in damages?**

- Apply for an interim payment

v. **What if, during proceedings, C becomes aware of the need to find out the identity of another potential D?**

- Apply for a Norwich Pharmacal Order

vi. **What if, during proceedings, C wants an injunction either to stop the defendant doing something or to require the defendant to do something?**

- Apply for prohibitory injunction
- Apply for mandatory injunction

↓

o) <u>Track allocation and case management; notice of proposed allocation, directions questionnaire which includes setting out intended interim applications; sanctions for failing to comply with directions</u>

↓

p) <u>Disclosure and inspection of documents (and Privilege)</u>

↓

q) <u>Evidence</u>

I. <u>Evidence of Fact - Witness statements, Witness summaries, Witness summonses, Depositions,</u>
II. <u>Expert evidence</u>
III. <u>Civil Trial and Evidence - hearsay,</u>

↓

r) <u>Judgments and Orders and Enforcement of them</u>

↓

s) <u>Appeals</u>

This concludes the civil litigation process. We are now ready to follow a claim through from conception to conclusion, including possible appeals.

Chapter 1

GENERAL MATTERS

a) Introductory

THIS CHAPTER CONTAINS THE ITEMS PRINTED IN BOLD IN THE FOLLOWING BOXES

CURRICULUM ("CUR")

1.1 Allocation of business between the High Court and County Courts

1.2 The overriding objective of the Civil Procedure Rules

1.3 The duty of the court to manage cases

1.4 General principles of Alternative Dispute Resolution (ADR)

1.5 Timing the use of ADR

3.3 ADR prior to the issue of proceedings

SYLLABUS

Examinable material will consist of where to start proceedings, the overriding objective, application by the court of the overriding objective, the duty of the parties to help the court further the overriding objective and the court's duty to manage cases, general principles of ADR, roles and responsibilities of lawyers and parties in ADR, timing the use of ADR in relation to the progress of a case, the approach of the courts to ADR, and sanctions for refusing to engage in ADR

ADR prior to the issue of proceedings from CUR 3

confidentiality in ADR from CUR 14

(Each of the above has its own subheading in this Chapter, flagged by EM:)

- **CPR 1.1-1.3**
- **CPR 7.1**
- **PD7A paragraphs 1 and 2.1-2.5**
- **Paragraphs 4, 4A, 5, 8 and 9 of the High Court and County Courts Jurisdiction Order 1991 (SI 1991/724), at section 9B of Volume 2 of 'Civil Procedure' (the White Book) 2020 from CUR 6**
- **Commentary is incorporated in context in this Chapter, highlighted in an Activity box between two stars**
- **Relevant ADR references to The Jackson ADR Handbook (Second Edition, 2016) are incorporated in context in this Chapter, highlighted in an Activity box between two lightning flashes**

- ***Halsey***

Chapter 1 MOst Concise Summary (MOCS)

- ***Assessing the quantifiable value of a money claim***
- ***Amount reasonably expected to be recovered***
  What to include
  What to disregard
  Reductions

❖ ***Whether a claim is to be in the County or High Court***

❖ ***Overriding objective – duties of courts and parties***

❖ ***Court duty to manage cases***

❖ ***Introduction to Alternative Dispute Resolution ("ADR")***

GENERAL MATTERS [CURRICULUM 1]

The sessions dealing with this area of the syllabus on my BTC course are	

CUR 1.1 **ALLOCATION OF BUSINESS BETWEEN THE HIGH AND COUNTY COURTS**

EM: Where to start proceedings

Assessing the value of an action

The value of an action is

- ***the amount of money***
  - **C or A reasonably expects to recover**;
  - **Including**
    - sums which, by virtue of section 22 of the Social Security Act 1989(**2**), are required to be paid to the Secretary of State
    - any amount which C or A could reasonably state to be the financial worth of the claim to him, where the relief sought is not monetary

        - any amount which is the aggregate of the values of the claims as determined above, where an action includes more than one claim.

    - **Disregarding**
        - any sum not in dispute
        - interest [other than interest pursuant to a contract]
        - costs
        - unspecified further or other relief
        - a possible finding of contributory negligence, except to the extent, if any, that such negligence is admitted;
        - that D may make a counterclaim or that the defence may include a set-off
        - the possibility of a future application for further damages where C seeks an award of provisional damages

    - **Reduced by**
        - the amount of any debt which C admits that he owes to a D in that action and which arises from the circumstances which give rise to the action;

- ***an unquantifiable value***;

    - where the action includes more than one claim and one is an unquantifiable value, the value of the action also unquantifiable

- Where an action is brought by more than one C or A regard shall be had to the aggregate of the expectations or interests of all the claimants or applicants.

<u>Where to start proceedings</u>

Remember that we bring a claim (sometimes called an action) by starting proceedings.

We start proceedings by issuing a claim form at the correct court. How to decide which court is the correct one continues on the next page.

Depending on the value of the claim, which court?

County Court	High Court[1]
Subject to the remainder of this table, may start in either, where both have the jurisdiction. Here that means in England and Wales.	
Where the values of an action for a **money** claim is [note that another way of saying this is "non-PI money claims"] ≤ £100k.	Where the values of an action for a **money** claim is [note that another way of saying this is "non-PI money claims"] **Only if** > £100k.
If PI is included in the claim < £50k **County Court**	If PI is included in the claim only if ≥ £50k **High Court**
PI means personal injuries to the claimant or any other person, and includes disease, impairment of physical or mental condition, and death.	
If an enactment so requires	If an enactment so requires

[1] Not on your syllabus this year, but useful to know is that the High Court consists of 3 Divisions.

Queen's Bench Division for mainly contract and tort; in turn this is split into these courts - Administrative Court- Admiralty Court - Commercial Court - Mercantile Court - Planning Court - Technology and Construction Court;

Chancery Division which in turn is split into Bankruptcy and Companies Courts - Intellectual Property Enterprise Court (IPEC) - Patents Court.

Family Division

A claim in the County Court[2] under Part 7 (dealt with in Chapter 10) may be made at any County Court hearing centre, unless any enactment, rule or practice direction provides otherwise. Please see also Money Claims on Line in the footnote below and in footnote 4 in Chapter 10. If a claim which is required to be made at a particular County Court hearing centre is made at the wrong hearing centre, a court officer will send the claim to the correct hearing centre before it is issued. A claimant should consider the potential delay which may result if a claim is not made at the correct County Court hearing centre in the first instance.	Should start in High Court where C believes the claim is • high value and/or • complex and/or • in the public interest. Thus even if the claim is for in excess of £100k, it may be started in the County court if C believes it is not high value / not comp / not likely to have any great bearing on the public.

Chancery claims, unless subject to an enactment, rule or PD may begin in either; as may

Claims relating to Business and Property work which includes any of the matters specified in paragraph 1 of Schedule 1 to the Senior Courts Act 1981.

Paragraph 1 of Schedule 1 to the Senior Courts Act 1981

To the Chancery Division are assigned all causes and matters relating to—

(a) the sale, exchange or partition of land, or the raising of charges on land;

(b) the redemption or foreclosure of mortgages;

(c) the execution of trusts;

(d) the administration of the estates of deceased persons;

(e) bankruptcy;

(f) the dissolution of partnerships or the taking of partnership or other accounts;

(g) the rectification, setting aside or cancellation of deeds or other instruments in writing;

[2] Once in legal practice you may like to be aware that there are currently two pilot schemes running which have recently been extended until 30 November 2021.

Online civil money claims

This scheme offers a digital service for specified money claims not exceeding £10k. Claimants who could otherwise make their claim through the main Money Claim Online system (see Footnote 4 in Chapter 10) may use the pilot to make their claim, if their claim is suitable for the pilot. Details are in PD 51R which is not on your syllabus this year.

County Court online

This scheme offers a digital service for specified and unspecified money claims for use only by legal professionals. Details are in PD 51S which is not on your syllabus this year.

(h) probate business, other than non-contentious or common form business; (i) patents, trade marks, registered designs copyright or design right; (j) the appointment of a guardian of a minor's estate, and all causes and matters involving the exercise of the High Court's jurisdiction under the enactments relating to companies.	
For Chancery claims, the claim form should, if issued in the County Court, be marked in the top right hand corner 'Chancery **Business**'.	For Chancery claims, the claim form should, if issued in the High Court, be marked in the top right hand corner "Chancery **Division**".
For Business and Property work, the claim form should, if issued in the County Court, be marked in the top right hand corner 'Business and Property work' [unless it is one of the following exceptions which do not form part of the specialist work undertaken in the Business and Property Courts. (a) Claims for possession of domestic property and rent and mesne profits, or in respect of domestic mortgages; (b) Claims for possession of commercial premises or disputes arising out of business tenancies that are routine in nature; (c) Claims falling under the Trusts of Land and Appointment of Trustees Act 1996, unless combined with other specialist claims; (d) Hearings of applications to set aside statutory demands, unopposed creditors' winding-up petitions or unopposed bankruptcy petitions; (e) Building claims, other than adjudication claims, of a value under £75,000; (f) Invoice and other straightforward business claims of a value under £75,000; (g) Boundary and easement disputes involving no conveyancing issues; (h) Claims to enforce a charging order; (i) Applications under the Access to Neighbouring Land Act 1992; (j) Proceedings under the Inheritance (Provision for Family and Dependants) Act 1975.]	For Business and Property work, the claim form should, if issued in the High Court, be marked in the top right hand corner "Business and Property Courts'

CUR 1.2 THE OVERRIDING OBJECTIVE

EM: The overriding objective,

The overriding objective of the CPR is **to enable the court to deal with cases justly and at proportionate cost**, so that matters are conducted in a quick, cheap and proportionate way. Briefly put, cases must be dealt with in ways which are proportionate with regard to

- parties being on an equal footing
- money (the amount involved and the financial position of each party)
- importance
- complexity.

Matters are to be dealt with expeditiously and fairly, allotting to court resources appropriately, complying with rules, practice directions and orders.

It is imperative, however, that you fully appreciate the importance of this overriding objective and that you address your mind to it constantly from now on. Therefore you are advised to complete this activity.

Activity

In the White Book, read CPR 1.1 – 1.4 inclusive (just the bold bits);

Note here the exact words that the CPR uses to express the overriding objective in CPR 1.1.

EM: Application by the court of the overriding objective

The court **must seek to give effect to the overriding objective** when exercising powers it gets from the rules, (or interprets any rule subject to rules 76.2, 79.2 and 80.2, 82.2 and 88.2 – none of which are on your syllabus this year).

The latter are mirror provisions of each other in respect of proceedings under

- The Prevention of Terrorism Act 2005
- The Counter-Terrorism Act 2008 and Part 1 of the Terrorist Asset-Freezing etc. Act 2010
- The Terrorism Prevention and Investigation Measures Act 2011
- Closed Material Procedure for applications made in respect of the Justice and Security Act 2013
- The Counter-Terrorism and Security Act 2015

These CPR rules modify the overriding objective and any other relevant rule so that they must be read and given effect to in a way compatible with the court's duty to ensure that information is not disclosed contrary to the public interest. The court must still be satisfied that the material available to it enables it properly to determine the proceedings.

EM: The duty of the parties to help the court further the overriding objective

Parties are required to do this.

Activity

Remember to make notes on the relevant case law authorities in paragraphs
1.4.4
1.4.9
1.4.11
in the commentary in the White Book.

You may find it useful to add in references to the case law NOW at the appropriate points of this Chapter.

When approaching final revision time, remember to add in the salient findings of the cases at the relevant point in any 'mental crib sheet' into which you have distilled the main points of your learned knowledge.

CUR 1.3 THE DUTY OF THE COURT TO MANAGE CASES

EM: ***The court's duty to manage cases***

The court must actively manage cases
by

- encouraging party co-operation, ADR, helping settlement
- identifying issues early
- making prompt decisions, giving directions to aid swift and efficient proceedings
- deciding the order of issues, fixing timetables
- considering whether the costs of taking actions can be justified
- using technology, avoiding court attendance where possible

CUR 1.4 *GENERAL PRINCIPLES OF ALTERNATIVE DISPUTE RESOLUTION (ADR)*

Activity

You may find it useful to copy the definition of ADR from GL here:-

Activity

Explanatory material which will NOT be assessed
To complement understanding of the examinable material set out above, students may find it helpful to be familiar with paragraphs

1.01-1.08;

2.02-2.24; 2.27; and

11.01-11.03
of The Jackson ADR Handbook (Second Edition, 2016)

EM: ***General principles of ADR***

Parties are encouraged both before the road to litigation has started as well as after a claim has been initiated, to try to a find a resolution to a dispute between them and another party with the aim of avoiding continuing on to litigation.

Your course covers a range of ADR options:

- Adjuducative
  - Arbitration Expert
  - Expert Neutral Determination
- Non- Adjuducative
  - Early (or Neutral) Evaluation
  - Conciliation
  - Mediation
  - Negotiation and Joint Settlement Meetings

Activity

Remember to incorporate the relevant paragraphs from The Jackson ADR Handbook (Second Edition, 2016):-

1.20
2.30-2.61

You may find it useful to make your notes here, below this box.

General Principles (your notes)

Range of ADR options (your notes)

EM: ***Roles and responsibilities of lawyers and parties in ADR***

Activity

Remember to incorporate the relevant paragraphs from The Jackson ADR Handbook (Second Edition, 2016)

4.02-4.03
4.07-4.08

You may find it useful to make your notes here, below this box.

Roles and responsibilities of lawyers and parties in ADR (your notes)

EM: *Confidentiality Clauses in ADR*

Activity

Remember to incorporate the relevant paragraphs from The Jackson ADR Handbook (Second Edition, 2016):-

Paragraphs 5.15-5.26

You may find it useful to make your notes here, below this box.

Confidentiality in ADR (your notes)

CUR 1.5 TIMING THE USE OF ADR

EM: ADR Prior to the Issue of Proceedings

Please see Chapter 9 of this book for further reference to this.

Activity

Explanatory material which will NOT be assessed

To complement understanding of the examinable material, students may find it helpful to be familiar with paragraphs

8.01-8.02 (from CUR 3)

of The Jackson ADR Handbook (Second Edition, 2016)

Activity

Remember to incorporate the relevant paragraphs from The Jackson ADR Handbook (Second Edition, 2016)

8.03
8.07
8.23
8.24-8.25

You may find it useful to make your notes here, below this box.

ADR prior to the issue of proceedings (your notes)

EM: ***Timing the use of ADR in relation to the progress of a case***

Interplay between ADR, CPR, and Litigation

Activity

Remember to incorporate the relevant paragraphs from The Jackson ADR Handbook (Second Edition, 2016)

3.04-3.11
3.14-3.16
3.24-3.34

You may find it useful to make your notes here, below this box.

Timing the use of ADR in relation to the progress of a case (your notes)

EM: ***The approach of the courts to ADR***

Activity

Remember to incorporate the relevant paragraphs from The Jackson ADR Handbook (Second Edition, 2016)

9.05
9.06-9.07
9.11-9.12
9.20
9.22-9.25

You may find it useful to make your notes here, below this box.

The approach of the courts to ADR (your notes)

EM: ***Sanctions for refusing to engage in ADR***

Activity

Explanatory material which will NOT be assessed

To complement understanding of the examinable material, students may find it helpful to be familiar with paragraphs

11.01-11.03 (from CUR 3)

of The Jackson ADR Handbook (Second Edition, 2016)

Halsey

The most succinct way to summarise the relationship between ADR and Civil Litigation is to say that there will be costs sanctions against a party who refuses to engage in ADR before pursuing litigation through the courts. There are overt references to that in the White book, for instance:

CPR 1.4 (2) (e) regarding the court's duty to manage cases sets out that active case management includes

"(e) encouraging the parties to use an alternative dispute resolution (GL) [You should have copied this out in the Activity box at the beginning of this Chapter[3]] procedure if the court considers that appropriate and facilitating the use of such procedure"

And CPR 3.1 (2) (m) regarding the court's general powers of management sets out that

"(2) Except where these Rules provide otherwise, the court may –

(m) take any other step or make any other order for the purpose of managing the case and furthering the overriding objective, including hearing an Early Neutral Evaluation with the aim of helping the parties settle the case" (Early Neutral Evaluation appears in Chapter 5 of this book.)

In ***Halsey v Milton Keynes General NHS Trust*** [2004] EWCA Civ 576 it was reaffirmed that the court

- **may encourage the use of ADR,** but not compel the parties to engage in ADR. ADR is supposed to be voluntary!
- You will learn in the first few pages of Chapter 6 of this book that when a court exercises its discretion as to who pays whose costs and in what amount, the court must have regard to all the circumstances including how the parties have conducted themselves; If the successful party **unreasonably refused to participate in ADR** it may be that as a result of that, the successful party will have a smaller amount of its costs paid by the losing party than would otherwise have been the case; i.e**. costs sanctions can be imposed**. It is for the **losing party to demonstrate that the successful party's refusal was unreasonable.**

---

[3] Content in square brackets added by author.

The *Halsey* decision includes a non-exhaustive list of examples of **what the court will consider when deciding** whether a refusal to engage in ADR was unreasonable:-

- The nature of the dispute
- The merits of the case; any reasonable prospect that ADR would be successful. Yet case law in 2020 includes a couple of decisions where it was held that it is unreasonable to refuse to engage in ADR on the basis that a party believes it has a strong case. (Perhaps the circumstances are such that the party believing they have a strong case, should instead have applied for summary judgment (Please see Chapter 13 of this book) rather than pursue the case to a full trial). Thus the strength of the case must, it appears, be so, so ,so compelling before a court will consider it to be a reasonable to refuse ADR for that reason.
- Whether there had been any other attempts to settle the case
- Would ADR have been costly and/or have led to more delay?

Halsey was a refusal to engage in mediation. Please see Chapter 5 of this book, although these principles have since been used a benchmark for **all types of ADR**, to the extent that the Court of Appeal in 2013 that **no response at all** to a suggestion (here to go to mediation) does amount to an unreasonable refusal to engage in ADR, even where the reason for the silence is a good one

Activity

Remember to incorporate the relevant paragraphs from The Jackson ADR Handbook (Second Edition, 2016)

11.05-11.06 and 11.60 from CUR 3

11.07-11.23
11.34-11.37
11.59-11.61
11.62- 11.63

You may find it useful to make your notes here, below this box.

<u>Sanctions for refusing to engage in ADR (your notes)</u>

Sanctions for refusing to engage in ADR (your notes continued.)

Chapter 1

Elements of the syllabus which you have now covered for **civil litigation and evidence**

- A cell with heavy outlining means that that area of the syllabus was covered in this Chapter;
- A darkly shaded cell with a tick √ means that the whole of that syllabus element has now been covered;
- A lightly shaded cell means that part of that element of the syllabus has been covered in a previous Chapter; and
- An unshaded cell means that element of the syllabus has not yet been covered.

1.1 √	1.2 √	1.3 √	2.1	2.2	3.1	3.2	6.1	6.2	6.3
6.4	7.1	7.2	8.1	8.2	8.3	9.1	9.2	9.3	9.1
9.2	11.1	11.2	11.1	12.2	12.3	13.1	13.2	13.3	13.4
13.5	13.6	13.7	13.8	14.1	14.2	14.3	14.4	14.5	14.6
15.1	15.2	15.3	15.4	16.1	16.2	17.1	17.2	17.3	17.4
18.2.	18.3	18.4 18.5	19.1	19.2	19.3	20.1	20.2	20.3	21.1
21.2	21.3	22.1	22.2	23.1	23.2	23.3	23.4	24.1	

Elements of the syllabus which you have now covered for **ADR**

1.4 √	1.5√	3.3	4.1	4.2	5.1	5.2	18.1	22.3	

Chapter 2

THE BEGINNINGS OF CASE MANAGEMENT [CURRICULUM 13].

The Court's general powers of case management

THIS CHAPTER CONTAINS THE ITEMS PRINTED IN BOLD IN THE FOLLOWING BOXES

CURRICULUM ("CUR")

13.3 Case management

(additions to this appear in later Chapters -see syllabus box below. It is not necessary for you to refer to them at this point.)

(We will deal with sanctions and striking out in Chapters 13 and 19).

SYLLABUS

Examinable material will consist of the court's case management powers, court's power to make orders of its own initiative, *power to strike out statements of case, sanctions, relief from sanctions,* ***power of court to rectify where there have been errors of procedure,*** *costs management, case management, directions questionnaires, stays to allow for settlement, referrals to mediation, scope of the small claims track, fast track and multi-track, allocation, directions in fast track cases and case management in multi-track cases.*

(Each of the above has its own subheading in this Chapter, flagged by EM:)

- CPR 2.8 appears in context in Chapter 3 under CUR 15.3 Periods of notice in interim applications and in Chapter 10 under CUR 6.3 Service of other court documents within the jurisdiction.
- **CPR 2.11**
- **CPR 3.1, 3.1A, 3.3, 3.10**
- CPR 3.4 is dealt with in Chapter 13 on striking out
- CPR 3.5, 3.8 and 3.9 are dealt with at the end of Chapter 19
- CPR 3.12-3.18; PD 3E paragraphs 1-7 are dealt with in Chapter 6 on costs
- CPR 26.1 and 26.3-26.10; PD 26 paragraphs 7 and 9 are dealt with in Chapter 19 on case management, sanctions and striking out
- CPR 28.3-4 directions are also in Chapter 19near the beginning
- CPR 29.1-29.9; PD 29 paragraphs 3-10 -multi track are also in Chapter 19
- CPR 38.1-7 are also in Chapter 19

- The following specific leading case authority (which students should be able to refer to by name): *Denton*, is in Chapters 13 and 19

- Commentary is incorporated in context in this Chapters 13 and 19, highlighted in an Activity box between two stars

Chapter 2 MOst Concise Summary (MOCS)

- ***Court's General Powers of case management***
  - they help those acting without representation
- ***Court may make orders on its own initiative***
  - without the need for a court application to have been made
- ***Courts may rectify errors in procedure.***

The sessions dealing with this area of the syllabus on my BTC course are	

This Chapter introduces the general case management powers of the court as set out **in bold** above. The remainder, (i.e. those not in bold above), on specific case management powers, are dealt with in future Chapters as listed above.

EM: case management powers

In addition to any powers given to the court by any other rule or PD or by any other enactment or any powers it may otherwise have, and except where the CPR provides otherwise, CPR 3.1 lists the court's general powers of management. I have not listed them all here to save space. You should take a look at them in the White Book.

Remember also that the court may require that any proceedings in the High Court be heard by a Divisional Court of the High Court.

These general powers of management do apply **where at least one party is unrepresented** and the **court must**

- have regard to the fact that there is an unrepresented party
- adopt such procedure at any hearing as it considers appropriate to further the overriding objective. At any hearing where the court is taking evidence, this may include ascertaining from an unrepresented party the matters about which the witness may be able to give evidence or on which the witness ought to be cross-examined and putting, or causing to be put, to the witness such questions as may appear to the court to be proper.

Both the parties and the court must, when drafting case management directions in the multi-track and fast track, take as their starting point any relevant standard directions which can be found online at www.justice.gov.uk/courts/procedure-rules/civil/standard-directions and adapt them as appropriate to the circumstances of the case.

EM: court's power to make orders of its own initiative

Except where a rule or some other enactment provides otherwise, the court may exercise its powers on an application (i.e. part 23 applications, explained in the next Chapter) or of its own initiative.

Where the court proposes to make an order of its **own initiative** and there is to be a

hearing to decide whether or not to make the order

- it **may** give any person likely to be affected by the order an **opportunity to make representations**, **specifying** the **time** by **and** the **manner** in which the representations must be made
- it **must** give each party likely to be affected by the order **at least 3 days' notice** of the hearing.

However, the court may make an order of its own initiative, **without hearing** the parties

or giving them an opportunity to make representations. The order must contain a statement of the right of a party affected by the order may apply to have it set aside, varied or stayed/temporarily suspended (these three actions are dealt with in context as appropriate throughout this book).

An application to set aside, vary or stay the order must be made in any period specified by the court, or if there is no such period specified, then not more than 7 days after the date on which the order was served on the party making the application.

If the court of its own initiative strikes out a statement of case (see Chapter 13) or dismisses an application and it considers that the claim is totally without merit

- the court's order must record that fact; and
- the court must at the same time consider whether it is appropriate to make a civil restraint order.

EM: power of court to rectify where there have been errors of procedure

The court has a general power to rectify matters where there has been an error of procedure.

Where there has been an error of procedure such as a failure to comply with a rule or PD, the error does not invalidate any step taken in the proceedings unless the court so orders, and the court may make an order to remedy the error.

Time limits may be varied by parties

If a rule/PD court order states that something must be done within a time limit and sets out the consequences of failing to comply, it can only be extended by prior written agreement between the parties by up to 28 days[4] (if the court has not ordered that it cannot be extended in this way) as long as no hearing date is put at risk.[5]

---

[4] CPR 3.8:- In Chapter 11 you will find a further footnote to remind you that the 28 days referred to in the relevant diagram has its roots here; similarly in the "striking out a claim" section of Chapter 19.

[5] The Coronavirus Act 2020 received Royal Assent on 25th March 2020 and is initially in force for 2 years, whilst incorporating powers to alter that expiry date. PD 51ZA was updated on 2nd April 2020, initially until 30 October 2020. The

Note, however, that in areas of specific case management to be dealt with in Chapter 19 there are in the CPR some time limits that cannot be varied by agreement between the parties.

- CPR 28.4 (variation of case management timetable – fast track)
  - A party must apply to the court if he wishes to vary the date which the court has fixed for
    - the return of a pre-trial check list under rule 28.5
    - the trial or
    - the trial period.

- CPR 29.5 (variation of case management timetable – multi-track),
  - A party must apply to the court if he wishes to vary the date which the court has fixed for
    - a case management conference;
    - a pre-trial review;
    - the return of a pre-trial check list under rule 29.6;
    - the trial; or
    - the trial period.

We will take up case management again when we deal with costs management in Chapter 6.

Chapter 2

Elements of the syllabus which you have now covered for **civil litigation and evidence**

- A cell with heavy outlining means that that area of the syllabus was covered in this Chapter;
- A darkly shaded cell with a tick √ means that the whole of that syllabus element has now been covered;
- A lightly shaded cell means that part of that element of the syllabus has been covered in a previous Chapter; and
- An unshaded cell means that element of the syllabus has not yet been covered.

1.1 √	1.2 √	1.3 √	2.1	2.2	3.1	3.2	6.1	6.2	6.3
6.4	7.1	7.2	8.1	8.2	8.3	9.1	9.2	9.3	9.1
10.2	11.1	11.2	12.1	12.2	12.3	13.1	13.2	13.3	13.4
13.5	13.6	13.7	13.8	14.1	14.2	14.3	14.4	14.5	14.6
15.1	15.2	15.3	15.4	16.1	16.2	17.1	17.2	173	17.4
18.2	.18.3	18.4 18.5	19.1	19.2	19.3	20.1	20.2	20.3	21.1
21.2	21.3	22.1	22.2	23.1	23.2	23.3	23.4	24.1	

result is that CPR 3.8 has effect as if in substitution for the reference to 28 days there was a reference to 56 days. You are strongly recommended to check with your Provider whether you will be assessed on the 28 days rule or the initially temporary 56 days rule for agreeing extensions; and whether the 56 day reference has been extended in real life to cover what you will be assessed on.

↓

The matter in dispute takes place

↓

b) Counsel may be instructed to write an opinion (also known as an advice)

Chapter 3

DISCLOSURE AND INSPECTION OF DOCUMENTS BEFORE A CLAIM IS COMMENCED [CUR 14]

INTERIM APPLICATIONS [CUR 15]

c) Disclosure before proceedings are issued; i.e. pre-action disclosure and how to apply for it

THIS CHAPTER CONTAINS THE ITEMS PRINTED IN BOLD IN THE FOLLOWING BOXES

CURRICULUM ("CUR")

First section of the Chapter

14.1 Disclosure and inspection of documents ***(This Chapter deals with the position BEFORE a claim is commenced.)*** *(The position AFTER a claim has been commenced appears in Chapter 20.)*

Second section of the Chapter

15.1 Interim applications WITH NOTICE ***15.2 Documentation required for with notice applications*** ***15.3 Periods of notice in interim applications***

(Other curriculum areas appear alongside this. These are interim payments are in Chapter 16.

(Look out for the slightly different timeframes), security for costs is in Chapter 15 and interim injunctions in Chapters 4 and 17. You do not need to look at these yet. They are simply other types of interim applications).

There are further types of interim applications which also have their own Chapter in this book.

SYLLABUS

The first section of this Chapter (CUR 14)

***Examinable material will consist of: disclosure** and inspection, right of inspection of disclosed documents, the meaning of document, standard disclosure, duty of search, disclosure of documents in party's control, disclosure of copies, procedure for standard disclosure, disclosure lists, disclosure statements, withholding disclosure or inspection, specific disclosure or inspection, disclosure in stages, documents referred to in statements of case, inspection and copying of documents, **pre-action disclosure, disclosure against non-parties**, and **other powers of the court to order disclosure, (**privacy, legal professional privilege and confidentiality in ADR; the 'without prejudice' principle were dealt with or signposted in Chapter 1).*

(Each of the above has its own subheading in this Chapter, flagged by EM:)

(Please refer to the above curriculum boxes should you wish to know where in this book the other elements of examinable material appear in this book).

- **CPR 31.16 (disclosure before proceedings start)**
- **Senior Courts Act 1981 section 34, County Courts Act 1984 section 53 at paragraphs 9A115 and 9A506 of Volume 2 of 'Civil Procedure' (the White Book) 2020.**
- **Commentary relevant to this Chapter is incorporated in context in this Chapter, highlighted in an Activity box between two stars**
- Paragraphs 5.15-5.26 of The Jackson ADR Handbook (Second Edition, 2016) are referred to in Chapter 1
- The following is the specific leading case authority with which students should be familiar (and should be able to refer to by name): *Norwich Pharmacal* (the first reference to this from CUR 14 is in the second section of this Chapter).

The second section of this Chapter contains ***(CUR 15)***

Examinable material will consist of how to apply for an interim remedy, *applicant's disclosure duties in applications made without notice or on short notice, consequences of material nondisclosure,* ***where to make an application, content of application notice, filing and serving application notice,*** *applications made without notice,* ***applications dealt with without a hearing,*** *setting aside or varying orders made without notice,* ***proceeding in absence of a party, dismissal of applications totally without merit, pre-action applications, evidence in interim applications, and supply by the applicant of a draft order.***

other powers of the court to order disclosure (CUR 14)

(Please refer to the above curriculum box should you wish to know where in this book the other elements of examinable material appear in this book).

- **CPR 23.1-12; PD 23A paragraphs 2-5, 9, 12.1, 13;**
- CPR 25.1 is in Chapter 4
- **CPR 25.2**
- **CPR 25.3 (how to apply for an interim remedy)**
- **PD 25A paragraphs 4 and 5.**

We will return for more on the rules in Chapter 4.

- **Commentary relevant to this Chapter is incorporated in context in this Chapter, highlighted in an Activity box between two stars**

- **The following is the specific leading case authority with which students should be familiar (and should be able to refer to by name): *Norwich Pharmacal* (from CUR 14).** There is more on *Norwich Pharmacal* between Chapters 16 and 17.

Chapter 3 MOCS

Before proceedings are issued

- ***to discover whether you have a viable case, apply for pre action disclosure***
  make a Part 23 application:-
  - *application notice*
  - *written evidence*
  - *draft order*

- ***to discover the identity of a defendant apply for a Norwich Pharmacal Order** to get their identity disclosed to you if the requirements are met: initiate Part 8 proceedings – (please see Chapter 10);*

  [for an NPO when a Part 7 claim has started, make a Part 23 application].

THIS FIRST SECTION OF THIS CHAPTER CONTAINS

c) **Disclosure before proceedings are issued; i.e. pre-action disclosure**

The sessions dealing with this area of the syllabus on my BTC course are	

DISCLOSURE BEFORE CLAIM

BSB 14.1 DISCLOSURE AND INSPECTION OF DOCUMENTS

There are situations where an intended claimant will need documents to be disclosed to him before he issues proceedings to start the litigation process.

[Only the examinable material **highlighted in bold in the BSB syllabus box above** will be dealt with in this Chapter. The remainder of the examinable material will be dealt with in Chapter 20 “Disclosure and Inspection of Documents”, in the context of disclosure of documents between parties *during* the litigation process.]

EM: pre-action disclosure

An application to the court for an order for pre-action disclosure is made when a potential claimant needs to look at documents belonging to a potential defendant, **to decide whether or not there is a viable case** to bring against that potential defendant.

For example if a patient wishes to make a claim against a hospital for poor surgery or care, that patient can apply to court for pre-action disclosure.

The requirements are

- Both the applicant (potential claimant) (“A”) and the respondent (potential defendant) (“R”) must be **likely to be a party** (i.e. may well be a party), to the ensuing proceedings. There is no need to show that proceedings are likely, though.

  Please note in addition the position under the **Senior Courts Act 1981 etc** set out below where proceedings are for personal injury or death.

- The papers must be likely to be or must have been in the **possession, custody or power** of the potential defendant and **relevant to an issue** likely to arise in the claim.

- It must be **desirable to see** these documents **now** so that
  - proceedings can be avoided,
  - any proceedings will be dealt with fairly,
  - costs can be saved.

- The documents that C is now applying to have disclosed to him must be documents that **D would have to disclose to him under standard disclosure** during the litigation process.

  Standard disclosure is set out in CPR 31.6.

Activity

Note here and then learn which documents are disclosed to the other side by each party under standard disclosure. “Standard disclosure requires a party to disclose only….

Powers of High and County Court exercisable before commencement of action.

At an application for pre-action disclosure, the court may make **an order for R to disclose** those documents in her possession custody or power to A / A's legal advisers/ A's medical or other professional adviser.

The court may make **an order for the inspection**, photographing, preservation, custody and detention of property

- which appears to the court to be property which *may become the subject-matter* of subsequent proceedings, or
- as to which *any question may arise* in subsequent proceedings
- The court may order the taking of samples of any such property and the carrying out of any experiment on or with any such property.

The actual written court order, where the order is made under this rule **must counterclaim against**

- the documents which must be disclosed and
- require the respondent to specify any which are no longer in his control or
- require the respondent to specify any in respect of which he claims a right or duty to withhold inspection.

The meaning of 'control' and 'right or duty to withhold inspection' are set out in the later Chapter on disclosure, Chapter 20.

The written court order, where the order is made under this rule **may specify** that the respondent is to indicate what has happened to any documents no longer in his control. The order may specify the time and place for disclosure and inspection.

Activity

Remember to make notes on the relevant case law authorities in paragraphs
31.16.3
31.16.4
31.16.5
in the commentary in the White Book.

You may find it useful to add in references to the case law NOW at the appropriate points of this Chapter.

When approaching final revision time, remember to add in the salient findings of the cases at the relevant point in any 'mental crib sheet' into which you have distilled the main points of your learned knowledge.

Statute provides that the court will **not make an order** for pre-action disclosure if it is likely to be **injurious to the public interest.**

Unless the court otherwise directs, the costs of obtaining the order are usually payable by the party requesting it.

EM: other powers of the court to order disclosure

- The court's power to order pre-action disclosure as set out above does not limit any other power it may have to do so.

- **Senior Courts Act 1981 section 34, County Courts Act 1984 section 53 at paragraphs 9A115 and 9A506 of Volume 2 of 'Civil Procedure' (the White Book) 2020**

  Where proceedings are for **personal injury or death,** the courts have the power to order disclosure of documents, inspection of property etc. in proceedings for personal injuries or death **by a person who is not a party to the proceedings** and who appears to the court to be likely to have in their possession, custody or power any documents which are relevant to an issue arising out of the claim.

  As above, the court may make **an order for R to disclose** those documents in her possession custody or power to A / A's legal advisers/ A's medical or other professional adviser.

  As above, the court may make **an order for the inspection**, photographing, preservation, custody and detention of property

  - which appears to the court to be property which *may become the subject-matter* of subsequent proceedings, or
  - as to which *any question may arise* in subsequent proceedings.
  - The court may order the taking of samples of any such property and the carrying out of any experiment on or with any such property.

THIS SECOND SECTION OF THIS CHAPTER CONTINUES WITH

c) Disclosure before proceedings are issued; i.e. pre-action disclosure and HOW TO APPLY FOR IT

INTERIM APPLICATION BEFORE CLAIM

Or in plain English

HOW TO APPLY FOR (here as an example of such a claim) AN ORDER FOR PRE-ACTION DISCLOSURE

Or to put it another way

HOW TO APPLY FOR THIS ORDER, AN ORDER FOR PRE-ACTION DISCLOSURE, WHICH IS AN EXAMPLE OF

'WITH NOTICE' INTERIM APPLICATIONS [BSB 13]

The sessions dealing with this area of the syllabus on my BTC course are	

BSB 15.1 WITH NOTICE ~~(and without notice~~ – see Chapter 4) APPLICATIONS

EM: pre-action applications
EM: How to apply for an interim remedy

These applications are not classed as urgent ones. They will therefore be 'with notice' applications. (Urgent applications will be dealt with in the next Chapter for when the urgency arises before any proceedings have started and again in Chapter 17 for when the urgency arises after proceedings have started. Urgent applications will be 'without notice' applications.)

Although "interim" means "in the middle of" proceedings, applications for an order for pre-action disclosure is an interim application that needs to be made before proceedings start.

An order may be granted **if it is desirable to do so in the interests of justice.**

BSB 15.2 DOCUMENTATION REQUIRED IN INTERIM APPLICATIONS

Most non-urgent interim applications (so in addition, those dealt with in the "What if" Chapters of this book, although there are a few twiddles with, e.g. summary judgments and interim payments, dealt with in context later in this book) are made under **Part 23** of the CPR. **The required documentation must be served on each respondent for interim applications**

- **(i) Application notice** (An application is known as a **with notice** application if this notice and the documents in (ii) and (iii) are served on the other side, thus giving them notice of the application).
- **(ii) Evidence** (unless the court orders otherwise)
- **(iii) A draft of the requested order**

(These 3 basic requirements will be modified and added to, where the application is an urgent one in the way we shall see in the next Chapter. Here we will introduce without notice applications and this will be referred to again in Chapter 17).

The required detail for each of the 3 basic requirements is as follows.

(i) APPLICATION NOTICE

EM: where to make an application

- Applications for an order for pre-action disclosure, or for any other interim application made **before** a claim has been started, may be made at **any County Court hearing centre**, **unless** any enactment, rule or practice direction provides otherwise.

- (For interim applications being made after proceedings have started, the general rule is that the application must be made to the County Court hearing centre where the claim was started).

- (For interim applications being made after proceedings have finished, in order to enforce the judgment, that application must be made to the County Court hearing centre dealing with the enforcement unless any enactment, rule or practice direction provides otherwise – see Chapter 25 for details of enforcement).

EM: content of application notice

- **For all types of non-urgent interim applications, in the application notice**

  - **state the order sought and state why it is sought**

  - It must **include**
    - the title of the claim
    - the reference number of the claim
    - the full name of the applicant
    - where the applicant is not already a party, his address for service, including a postcode
    - either a request for a hearing and if so, whether a telephone hearing (or a request that the application be dealt with without a hearing – this is dealt with in the next Chapter.)
  - It must be **signed**
  - ***EM: Statements of Truth,*** It must contain a **statement of truth** if A wishes to rely on its contents as evidence. This is serious and is what gives the document its legal weight/gravitas as it verifies the factual basis of the case.

BSB 15.3 PERIODS OF NOTICE IN INTERIM APPLICATIONS

EM: filing and serving application notice

So **complete the application notice (and evidence and draft order). File it** at the court where proceedings in this matter are **likely to be started**, unless there is good reason to apply to different court.

An applicant may apply without filing an application notice if a rule or PD allows, or if the court dispenses with the need for an application notice.

The court inserts the date of the hearing, which must be **at least 28 days after the date of the notice.**

Serve the notice and other documentation on each respondent as soon as practicable after it has been filed, unless the court orders otherwise, **at least 3 clear days before the hearing** of the interim matter (5 clear days before a telephone hearing); here, the hearing to decide whether or not the interim application for an order for pre-action disclosure will be granted. [Remember that this is a with - notice application i.e. with service of a copy of the application notice to the other side.]

If shorter notice is given it is possible for a court to direct that the application be heard anyway.

Where there is to be a telephone hearing the application notice must be served as soon as practicable after it has been issued and in any event at least 5 days before the date of the hearing.

If the court is doing the serving, a copy of any written evidence in support must be filed as well.

A copy of the application notice need not be served if a rule or PD or court order so allows.

Calculating periods of notice in interim applications

- clear days
    - Do not include the beginning day or, where relevant, the day on which an end event occurs

      At least 28 days after the date of the notice.
      Where the date of the notice is the 1st of the month, do not count that date; then count 28 days which takes you to 29th of the month, so the earliest date for the hearing is 30th of the month.

      At least 3 clear days before a Friday hearing.
      Do not count Friday, so not Thursday, not Wednesday, not Tuesday. The last date for service is Monday.

    - Where the specified period is 5 days or less and includes any of the following, then do not count them in the working out; Saturday, Sunday, a bank holiday, Christmas day or Good Friday.

      At least 3 clear days before a Monday hearing.
      Do not count Monday; Sunday and Saturday do not count; then not Friday, not Thursday, not Wednesday, so the last date for filling is Tuesday.

- If the court office is closed on the date for filing, doing it on the next day the court is open keeps you within the rules.

EM: applications dealt with without a hearing

The court may deal with an application without a hearing if
- The parties agree to this and to the terms of the order sought or
- The court does not consider that a hearing would be appropriate.

(ii) EVIDENCE

EM: evidence in interim applications

Provide with the application notice **written evidence** which
- must include all material facts
- can be in the application notice itself if it is verified by a statement of truth
- can be in a statement of case which is verified by a statement of truth
- is often a witness statement verified by a statement of truth

Activity

Remember to make notes on the relevant case law authorities in paragraphs 25.3.3 in the commentary in the White Book.

You may find it useful to add in references to the case law NOW at the appropriate points of this Chapter.

When approaching final revision time, remember to add in the salient findings of the cases at the relevant point in any 'mental crib sheet' into which you have distilled the main points of your learned knowledge

(iii) A DRAFT OF THE REQUESTED ORDER

EM: supply by the applicant of a draft order

- Attach it to the application notice
- Take a copy of it to the hearing on a disk/digital stick.

  The order **must** set out clearly what the respondent must do or not do and **must** include an undertaking to the court by A to pay any damages sustained by R which the court considers A should pay, unless the court orders otherwise.

  There follows on the next page a summary of this section of the Chapter so far in table form

<table>
<tr><td colspan="2"><u>With notice interim applications</u>
<u>Always used for applications for orders for:-</u>

• Pre-action disclosure

• Some <u>but not all</u> non urgent interim applications i.e. some of the 'what ifs' in this book. Some interim applications modify the Part 23 timeframes set out in this table. Please refer to each of these in context as they arise in this book</td><td rowspan="3"></td></tr>
<tr><td><u>Pre requisites for making the application</u></td><td>• Desirable to do so in the interests of justice</td></tr>
<tr><td rowspan="3"><u>Documents to be filed and served</u>
(This is a Part 23 application)</td><td rowspan="2">• Application notice
i. Set out the order sought
ii. Why you want it
iii. Must be signed
iv. Must contain statement of truth

When filed at court, the court inserts the date of the hearing on it; a date at least 28 days after the date of the notice.

Serve this and the other two sets of documentation below on R at least 3 clear days before the hearing.</td></tr>
<tr><td>This box to be completed when reading ch 13 and 16.
<table><tr><td></td><td></td></tr></table></td></tr>
<tr><td>• Evidence
i. Written (often a Witness Statement or affidavit)
ii. May be part of the application notice or attached to it
iii. Must contain a statement of truth</td><td rowspan="2"></td></tr>
<tr><td></td><td>• Draft of the Order you seek
i. Must contain an undertaking by A that A will pay any damages sustained by R which the court considers A should pay, unless court orders otherwise</td></tr>
</table>

EM: proceeding in absence of a party

Where A or any R fails to attend this or any other hearing, the court may proceed in their absence. Where the court then makes an order it may, on application or on its own initiative, re-list the application. So the court may set aside such an order and the matter could thus even be reheard in full. This is, however, unlikely if there is no real prospect of changing the original order or if it would be unjust to change it.

Activity

Remember to make notes on the relevant case law authorities in paragraphs 25.3.4 in the commentary in the White Book.

You may find it useful to add in references to the case law NOW at the appropriate points of this Chapter.

When approaching final revision time, remember to add in the salient findings of the cases at the relevant point in any 'mental crib sheet' into which you have distilled the main points of your learned knowledge.

EM: dismissal of applications totally without merit

If the court dismisses the application, the court's order must record that fact. At the same time the court must consider whether it is appropriate to make a civil restraint order.

Next we look at another **with notice** interim application that can be made **before** proceedings have been issued - **a Norwich Pharmacal Order.**

EM: The following is the specific leading case authority with which students should be familiar (and should be able to refer to by name): Norwich Pharmacal.

Norwich Pharmacal orders (Norwich Pharmacal Co v Commissioners of Customs and Excise [1974] AC 133)

A potential claimant can apply to court for one of these orders where they want to discover the **identity of the potential defendant.** This is possible where C wants an order for the **facilitator of the wrong doing** to identify the wrong doer, where the facilitator has refused a request for the information.

For example in an RTA, if one of the drivers does not stop after the accident, yet is driving a car clearly marked as rented from a particular car - hiring company, then C can apply to court for a Norwich Pharmacal Order ("NPO") to compel the car hire company to tell him and/or provide him with **documents or other relevant information** regarding who they rented the car to on that day. C will then have discovered the identity of the defendant.

Note that you can**not** get such an order against a **mere witness** as they did not facilitate the wrong doing.

The procedure for making an application for an NPO depends how far the claim has got, certainly in the Chancery division; it is likely that the other divisions will adopt a similar view. If there is no claim yet in the court system, then the procedure for making an application for an NPO is to bring a **Part 8 claim** (see Chapter 10).

(In some circumstances, an NPO can be applied for without notice – please see next Chapter for more detail on how to apply for without notice applications – where for example it is urgent or there is a need for secrecy in e.g. a fraud case. Note from the next Chapter that the need for full and frank disclosure applies here too. If full and frank disclosure is not given there is a risk that any NPO obtained may be set aside.) This method allows R 14 days to respond.

Activity

Remember to make notes on the relevant case law authorities in paragraphs
31.18.2
31.18.3
31.18.4
31.18.5
31.18.6
31.18.7
in the commentary in the White Book.

You may find it useful to add in references to the case law NOW at the appropriate points of this Chapter.

When approaching final revision time, remember to add in the salient findings of the cases at the relevant point in any 'mental crib sheet' into which you have distilled the main points of your learned knowledge.

Norwich Pharmacal applications will appear again after Chapter 16 of this book, setting out the procedure for applying for one after proceedings have started.

Chapter 3

Elements of the syllabus which you have now covered **for civil litigation and evidence**

- A cell with heavy outlining means that that area of the syllabus was covered in this Chapter;
- A darkly shaded cell with a tick √ means that the whole of that syllabus element has now been covered;
- A lightly shaded cell means that part of that element of the syllabus has been covered in a previous Chapter; and
- An unshaded cell means that element of the syllabus has not yet been covered.

1.1 √	1.2 √	1.3 √	2.1	2.2	3.1	3.2	6.1	6.2	6.3
6.4	7.1	7.2	8.1	8.2	8.3	9.1	9.2	9.3	10.1
10.2	11.1	11.2	12.1	12.2	12.3	13.1	13.2	13.3	13.4
13.5	13.6	13.7	13.8	14.1	14.2	14.3	14.4	14.5	14.6
15.1	15.2	15.3	15.4	16.1	16.2	17.1	17.2	17.3	17.4
18.2	18.3	18.4 18.5	19.1	19.2	19.3	20.1	20.2	20.3	20.1
21.2	21.3	22.1	22.2	23.1	23.2	23.3	23.4	24.1	

Chapter 4

INTERIM APPLICATIONS WITHOUT NOTICE [CUR 15.1]

INTERIM INJUNCTIONS ("one") [CUR 17.1 and 17.4]

Applying urgently for this interim remedy before any proceedings have been issued:

the pre-hearing mechanics

THIS CHAPTER CONTAINS THE ITEMS PRINTED IN BOLD IN THE FOLLOWING BOXES

CURRICULUM ("CUR")

15.1 Interim applications WITHOUT NOTICE

15.2 Documentation regarding without notice applications

15.4 the duty of full and frank disclosure in without notice applications

17.2 American Cyanamid principles are in Chapter 17

SYLLABUS

Examinable material will consist of *how to apply for an interim remedy,* ***applicant's disclosure duties in applications made without notice or on short notice, consequences of material nondisclosure,*** *where to make an application, content of application notice, filing and serving application notice,* ***applications made without notice,*** *applications dealt with without a hearing,* ***setting aside or varying orders made without notice*** *proceeding in absence of a party, dismissal of applications totally without merit, pre-action applications, evidence in interim applications, and supply by the applicant of a draft order.*

(Each of the above has its own subheading in this Chapter, flagged by EM:)

- **CPR 23.1-12; PD 23A paragraphs 2-5, 9, 12.1, 13**
- **CPR 25.1 (orders for interim remedies**
- **CPR 25.2**
- **CPR 25.3 (how to apply for an interim remedy)**
- **PD 25A paragraphs 4 and 5.**
- **Commentary is incorporated in context in this Chapter, highlighted in an Activity box between two stars**

Chapter 4 MOCS

- ***Urgent prohibitory injunctions may be granted in the pre-action stage***
- ***The procedure for applying for these without notice applications, undertakings to give.***
- ***Remember the duty of full and frank disclosure.***

A further

INTERIM APPLICATION BEFORE CLAIM

Depending on what the matter in dispute is, C may want to make an

d) e.g. Interim application for an urgent [prohibitory] injunction before proceedings are issued

Or in plain English

HOW C APPLIES (so he is the Applicant) BEFORE PROCEEDINGS ARE ISSUED FOR AN ORDER FOR AN

URGENT [PROHIBITORY] INJUNCTION, (against an intended Defendant, known in these circumstances as the Respondent to the application) WHICH IS AN EXAMPLE OF A

'WITHOUT NOTICE' APPLICATION [BSB 13]

The sessions dealing with this area of the syllabus on my BTC course are	

BSB 17. INTERIM INJUNCTIONS

The first rule in Part 25 of the CPR sets out the **interim remedies** for which a party may need to apply. The first interim remedy on the list is interim injunctions and it is this that the remainder of this Chapter deals with.

Other interim remedies listed in CPR 25.1 include

- Interim declarations
- Orders relating to property including search orders
- Orders to deliver up goods

- Freezing injunctions to stop removal of assets from the jurisdiction or to stop any dealing with any assets
- Interim payments (see Chapter 16)

The related syllabus commentary to this appears at the end of Chapter 17, the continuation and completion in this book of interim injunctions where the author feels the commentary may be more appropriate and more easily understood..

Now back to the first interim remedy in the list in CPR 25.1 – interim injunctions.

BSB 15.1 ~~with notice and~~ WITHOUT NOTICE APPLICATIONS

EM: applications made without notice

This Chapter deals with applications for interim remedies which are urgent and so made without notice to the other side. We are using the example of the interim remedy of an injunction, applied for before proceedings have started with the issue of a claim form, because they are urgent.

The matters set out in the previous Chapter are also relevant here. There is simply more to add in when a without notice application is being made. Therefore the examinable material in this Chapter is that which is in bold on the previous page.

I have repeated just the headings from the previous Chapter in context, referring back to it where appropriate, so that you can see how it all fits together.

~~EM: pre-action applications~~
~~EM: How to apply for an~~ interim remedy
~~E,g, Interim Injunctions; EM: applying for interim injunctions~~

The court may grant an interim remedy following a without notice application if it appears to the court there are good reasons for not giving notice.

Following on from our treatment of two examples of interim applications that may need to be made **before proceedings start** in the previous Chapter, (applications for an order for pre-action disclosure or for a Norwich Pharmacal Order), we turn now to our third example of an application that can be made before proceedings start.

An order for the interim remedy of an injunction applied for before proceedings start may be made **only if it is urgent** OR **it is otherwise desirable to do so in the interests of justice**.

An intended claimant could apply to stop a party from doing something by applying for an **urgent** prohibitory injunction; (or he could apply to make a party do something by applying for an urgent mandatory injunction, although these latter are very difficult to get). Please see more towards the end of Chapter 17.

This Chapter details applications for the interim remedy of an urgent prohibitory injunction and is placed here to make the point that interim remedies can be granted in the pre-action stages as an order for an interim remedy may be made at any time, including before proceedings are started; and also after judgment has been given.

Preparing for your advocacy at a hearing for an injunction will be fully and further dealt with in Chapter 17 called "interim injunctions ("two")", as will applications for mandatory injunctions.

It may be necessary to apply for an urgent prohibitory injunction before any proceedings have been started as in the following example. In the final week of revision for your civil litigation assessment, you need to study at home as you are also a carer for an immobile relative who lives with you. Your landlord has engaged builders who are drilling in the flat below you for 15 hours a day. You are told that such work is likely to go on for months. This noise breaches a covenant in your lease. You need to get the drilling stopped or limited to fewer hours a day and you need that now.

You do have a potential **substantive cause of action** for breach of covenant, possibly also for nuisance, but it is important that the noise is abated now as your exam will be over before the substantive cause of action gets to court. The solution is therefore to apply for an urgent prohibitory injunction.

You will recall from your previous studies that an injunction is an equitable remedy and so it must appear **just and convenient** to the court to grant it.

Do remember that if this particular interim application is successful it is likely to dispose finally of the action; so in making its decision whether or not to grant the injunction, the court will take into account the merits of the case.

BSB 15.2 DOCUMENTATION REQUIRED IN INTERIM APPLICATIONS

EM: where to make an application

See Chapter 3.

EM: content of application notice

First, see Chapter 3. You will recall from the previous Chapter that interim applications are made under **Part 23** of the CPR and that **the required documentation for non urgent interim applications is**

- **Application notice**
- **Evidence**
- **A draft of the requested order**
- These 3 basic requirements will now be modified and added to, as the application is an urgent one.

Those **MODIFICATIONS** are now set out on the next pages. Towards the end of this Chapter the modifications are shown in a table alongside the one in the previous Chapter. This may make it easier to understand the differences between and the reasons for the differences between the two types of application.

APPLICATION NOTICE

EM: filing and serving application notice

The rule is that the application notice **need not be served** on the respondent (and so would be a 'without notice' application) **where any of the following 6 things is the case.** The firsts of these is

- there is exceptional urgency;
  - Where the urgency renders it impossible to serve the application notice on the respondent giving the usual 3 clear days' notice -there will not be time to file and serve the application notice within the timeframes set out in the previous Chapter. However,
  - the applicant must still **notify** the respondent informally that the application is being made
  - The application notice, evidence in support and a draft order should be **filed** at court **two hours before** the hearing for the urgent prohibitory injunction wherever possible.
  - If not, the applicant will have to make a solemn and binding promise, known as giving an undertaking, to the court to file the application notice at court on the same day as the hearing or to file it on the next working day following the hearing, or to file it as ordered by the court. This undertaking will be set out in the draft order.
  - The draft order should also include an **undertaking by A** to serve the application notice, evidence and order on the respondent within a time frame set by the court.

The remaining 5 are

- the overriding objective is so furthered;
- all parties consent;
- the court gave permission;
- Where a date for a hearing has been fixed and a party wishes to make an application at that hearing but he does not have sufficient time to serve an application notice he should inform the other party and the court (if possible in writing) as soon as he can of the nature of the application and the reason for it. He should then make the application orally at the hearing; or
- a court order, rule or PD so provides

EM: evidence in interim applications

EVIDENCE

- Show why there was no time to issue the claim form for the substantive cause of action
- Show good reasons why the interim application is a without notice application
- State what informal notice has been given to the respondent

Activity

Remember to make notes on the relevant case law Authorities for applying for an interim remedy in paragraphs 25.3.2 – 25.3.8 in the commentary in the White Book.

You may find it useful to add in references to the case law NOW at the appropriate points of this Chapter.

When approaching final revision time, remember to add in the salient findings of the cases at the relevant point in any 'mental crib sheet' into which you have distilled the main points of your learned knowledge.

CUR 15.4 THE DUTY OF FULL AND FRANK DISCLOSURE IN WITHOUT NOTICE APPLICATIONS

EM: applicant's disclosure duties in applications made without notice or on short notice

- As the court is wholly reliant on the information provided by A,
    - A has a duty to investigate the facts and to present fairly the evidence on which he relies
    - A must disclose fully all matters relevant to the application including all matters, whether of fact or law, which are, or maybe, adverse to his application
    - If A is proven not to have made full and frank disclosure, the order made for an interim injunction may be discharged.

Remember that as set out in the previous Chapter, the evidence is **written evidence** which
- must include all material facts
- can be in the application notice itself if it is verified by a statement of truth
- can be in a statement of case which is verified by a statement of truth
- is often a witness statement verified by a statement of truth

A DRAFT OF THE REQUESTED ORDER

EM: supply by the applicant of a draft order

The draft order should state in the title after the names of A and R "the Claimant and Defendant in an Intended Action".

- The order **must** set out clearly what the respondent must do or not do and **must** include the following **undertakings** (mostly to do what he has not had time to do!)

  - an undertaking to the court by A to pay any damages sustained by R which the court considers A should pay unless the court orders otherwise
  - if made without notice to any other party, an undertaking by A to the court to serve on R the application notice, evidence in support and any order made as soon as practicable
  - if made before filing the application notice, an undertaking to file and pay the appropriate fee on the same or next working day or as ordered by the court
  - if made before issue of a claim form an undertaking to issue and pay the appropriate fee on the same or next working day. (Detail on claim forms appears in Chapters 10 and 11 of this book. It is with such a form that a claim is started – how proceedings are commenced)

  The interim injunction will be **discharged if A fails to comply** with the undertakings in the order.

- When the court makes an order for an injunction, it should consider whether to require an undertaking by the applicant to pay any damages sustained by a person other than the respondent, including another party to the proceedings or any other person who may suffer loss as a consequence of the order

- An order for an injunction made in the presence of all parties to be bound by it or made at a hearing of which they have had notice, **may** state that it is effective until trial or further order.

- As this is an urgent and so without notice application, the order states the **return date** for a further hearing at which the other party can be present

- If made before the issue of a claim it must contain directions for the commencement of the claim

- There is set out a statement of R's **right to apply to set aside or vary** the order within 7 days of its service on her ***EM: setting aside or varying orders made without notice***

- A penal notice is included - CPR 81.9 and PD 81. [Service will be by personal service so that the penal notice can be enforced by committal]. The effect of non-compliance with the terms of an order amounts to contempt. The standard of proof is the criminal one, Beyond Reasonable Doubt. Contempt is punishable by fine – prison - sequestration. Application for committal can be to any single Judge of the High Court.

A **skeleton** argument should be provided.

The hearing for the urgent interim prohibitory injunction can be **by telephone.** Injunctions will be heard by telephone only where A is acting by counsel or solicitors.

Where it is not possible to arrange a hearing, application can be made between 10.00 a.m. and 5.00 p.m. weekdays by telephoning the Royal Courts of Justice on 020 7947 6000 and asking to be put in contact with a High Court Judge of the appropriate Division available to deal with an emergency application in a High Court matter. The appropriate district registry may also be contacted by telephone. In county court proceedings, the appropriate County Court hearing centre should be contacted,

Where an application is made outside those hours the applicant should either

- telephone the Royal Courts of Justice on 020 7947 6000 where he will be put in contact with the clerk to the appropriate duty judge in the High Court (or the appropriate area Circuit Judge where known), or
- the Urgent Court Business Officer of the appropriate Circuit who will contact the local duty judge.
- Where the facility is available it is likely that the judge will require a draft order to be faxed to him, or her.

The application notice and evidence in support must be filed with the court on the same or next working day or as ordered, together with two copies of the order for sealing.

You will now appreciate that an interim injunction may be granted before any proceedings have started as well as during proceedings or after judgment has been given.

In the table on the following pages, the left hand column is the same as the one in Chapter 3 – with notice applications. In parallel is what you have now met in Chapter 4 – without notice applications.

With notice interim applications Always used for applications for orders for:- • Pre-action disclosure (Part 23) • Norwich Pharmacal when application made after a part 7 claim has commenced. (Part 23). Otherwise for a 'pre-action application' start using a Part 8 claim form. • Some **but not all** non urgent interim applications i.e. some of the 'what ifs' in this book. Some interim applications modify the Part 23 timeframes set out in this table. Please refer to each of these in context as they arise in this book		*Without notice interim applications* *Always used for URGENT applications for orders or where a Norwich Pharmacal needs to be without notice (e.g. fraud cases)* ~ ~ • *Most often found in the context of applications for* ***urgent [prohibitory] injunctions, as in the rest of this table,*** *and so BEFORE a claim has been started* *Also used for, and* • *Most often found in the context of applications for* ***urgent [prohibitory] injunctions, as in the rest of this table,*** *when applied for ALONGSIDE a claim for a substantive cause of action (See Chapter 17)*
Pre requisites for making the application	• Desirable to do so in the interests of justice	• *Desirable to do so in the interests of justice or Urgent* • *Need a substantive cause of action (e.g. nuisance or breach of covenant)* • *It must appear to the court just and convenient that an injunction is granted*
Documents to be filed and served (This is a Part 23 application)	• **Application notice** i. Set out the order sought ii. Why you want it iii. Must be signed iv. Must contain statement of truth When filed at court, the court inserts the date of the hearing on it; a date at least **28** days after the date of the notice. Serve this and the other two sets of documentation below	• *File it at court 2 hours before the hearing wherever possible* • *If not, A must undertake to file it same day/next working day after the hearing/or as ordered by the court* • *Application notice need not be served on D if any one of the following is the case* *i. Exceptional urgency, though you must still*

	on R at least **3** clear days before the hearing.	*give the other side informal notice* *ii. Overriding interest is so furthered* *iii. All parties consent* *iv. The court gave permission* *v. Court order/rule/PD so provides* *Still need to notify R informally of application and its contents*
	• **Evidence** i. Written (often a Witness Statement or affidavit) ii. May be part of the application notice or attached to it iii. Must contain a statement of truth	*Set out in the advocacy for the application* i. *Why there is no time to serve an application notice on the other side (i.e.no time to give them notice)* ii. *The good reason for there not being time to give notice to the other side (e.g. that the nuisance needs to stop now)* iii. *Set out the way in which you still gave the other side informal notice* iv. *Fulfil your duty of full and frank disclosure* v. *Court order/rule/PD so provides*
	• **Draft of the Order you seek** **i.** Must contain an undertaking by A that A will pay any damages sustained by R which the court considers A should pay, unless court orders otherwise	*i. Same* ***ii.*** *Undertaking by A to serve on R* ***<u>as soon as practicable</u>*** • ***Application notice*** • ***Evidence*** • ***The order the court made*** ***iii.*** *If the application notice was not filed at court two hours before the hearing, an undertaking to file it and pay the appropriate fee on the same or next working day* ***iv.*** *If this application is being made BEFORE a claim has been started, an undertaking to issue it and pay the appropriate fee the same or next working day* *The actual order will contain directions for the commencement of the claim.* *The interim injunction will be discharged if A fails to comply with the undertakings in the order.* *The actual order will state the return date* *The actual order will set out R's right to apply to set aside or vary the order within* ***7*** *days of its service on her; and contain a penal notice.*

Chapter 4

Elements of the syllabus which you have now covered for **civil litigation and evidence**

- A cell with heavy outlining means that that area of the syllabus was covered in this Chapter;
- A darkly shaded cell with a tick √ means that the whole of that syllabus element has now been covered;
- A lightly shaded cell means that part of that element of the syllabus has been covered in a previous Chapter; and
- An unshaded cell means that element of the syllabus has not yet been covered.

1.1 √	1.2 √	1.3 √	2.1	2.2	3.1	3.2	6.1	6.2	6.3
6.4 SI √	7.1	7.2	8.1	8.2	8.3	9.1	9.2	9.3	10.1
10.2	11.1	11.2	112.1	12.2	12.3	13.1	13.2	13.3	13.4
13.5	13.6	13.7	13.8	14.1	14.2	14.3	14.4	14.5	14.6
15.1	15.2 √	15.3 √	15.4 √	16.1	16.2	17.1	17.2	173	17.4
18.2	18.3	18.4 18.5	19.1	19.2	19.3	20.1	20.2	20.3	21.1
21.2	21.3	22.1	22.2 22.3	23.1	23.2	23.3	23.4	24.1	

Chapter 5

ALTERNATIVE DISPUTE RESOLUTION: ADJUDICATIVE OPTIONS [CUR 4]

ALTERNATIVE DISPUTE RESOLUTION: NON-ADJUDICATIVE OPTIONS [CUR 5]

THIS CHAPTER CONTAINS THE ITEMS PRINTED IN BOLD IN THE FOLLOWING BOXES

e) Alternative dispute resolution/resolution of disputes out of court

CURRICULUM ("CUR")

Alternative dispute resolution: adjudicative options

4.1 Arbitration
4.2 Expert (or Neutral) Determination

Alternative dispute resolution: non-adjudicative options

5.1 Early Neutral Evaluation
5.2 Conciliation and Mediation

SYLLABUS

Arbitration

Examinable material will consist of fundamental concepts in arbitration, arbitration requirements, stay of legal proceedings, commencement, procedure in arbitrations, privacy and confidentiality, awards, enforcement, and appeals

(Each of the above has its own subheading in this chapter, flagged by EM:)

- **CPR 62.2-62.4 in Section 2E of Volume 2 of 'Civil Procedure' (the White Book) 2020**
- **62.8 in Section 2E of Volume 2 of 'Civil Procedure' (the White Book) 2020**
- **Relevant ADR references to The Jackson ADR Handbook (Second Edition, 2016) are incorporated in context in this chapter, highlighted in an Activity box between two lightning flashes**
- **Commentary is incorporated in context in this chapter, highlighted in an Activity box between two stars**

Expert (or Neutral) Determination

- **Relevant ADR references to The Jackson ADR Handbook (Second Edition, 2016) are incorporated in context in this Chapter, highlighted in an Activity box between two lightning flashes**

Early Neutral Evaluation

Examinable material will consist of: early neutral evaluation

- **Relevant ADR references to The Jackson ADR Handbook (Second Edition, 2016) are incorporated in context in this Chapter, highlighted in an Activity box between two lightning flashes**

Conciliation and Mediation

Examinable material will consist of conciliation, general principles of mediation, preparation for mediation, and the mediation process.

(Each of the above has its own subheading in this chapter, flagged by EM:)

- **Relevant ADR references to The Jackson ADR Handbook (Second Edition, 2016) are incorporated in context in this Chapter, highlighted in an Activity box between two lightning flashes**

Chapter 4 MOst Concise Summary (MOCS)

- ***Alternative dispute resolution: adjudicative options***
  - ***Arbitration***
    - ***General principles***
    - ***Arbitration requirements***
    - ***Stay of legal proceedings***
    - ***Commencement procedure in arbitrations***
    - ***Privacy and confidentiality***
    - ***Awards***
    - ***Enforcement***
    - ***Appeals***
  - ***Expert (or Neutral) Determination***
- ***Alternative dispute resolution: non-adjudicative options***
  - ***Early Neutral Evaluation***
  - ***Conciliation and Mediation***

The sessions dealing with this area of the syllabus on my BTC course are	

Adjudicative options

CUR 4.1 ARBITRATION

Arbitration is binding mini trial, commenced as a claim pursuant to agreed clauses in an arbitration agreement. It is common in business scenarios. Formal rules of evidence generally do not apply at an arbitration. The arbitrator is a neutral third party who comes to a decision, known as an award, on the settlement at the end of the process.

Activity

Explanatory material which will NOT be assessed:

To complement understanding of the examinable material set out above, students may find it helpful to be familiar with the Arbitration Act 1996

The Arbitration Act 1996[6]

EM: fundamental concepts in arbitration

S1 General principles.

The provisions of this Part [of the Act] are founded on the following principles, and shall be construed accordingly—

(a) the object of arbitration is to obtain the fair resolution of disputes by an **impartial tribunal without unnecessary delay or expense;**

(b) the parties should be **free to agree how their disputes are resolved**, subject only to safeguards as are necessary in the public interest; [once the parties have a **written agreement** to resolve the dispute in this way.]

(c) in matters governed by this Part [of the Act] the court should not intervene except as provided by this Part.

[6] The following sections of this Act were copied from the legislation.gov.uk website at the end July 2020. Where they are cited verbatim they are recognisable for being in a smaller font than the remainder of this book. In this chapter the relevant CPR rules are also in the slightly smaller font. All bold highlighting has been added by the author, as has anything which appears in square brackets.

EM: arbitration requirements

SS2 and 3

This Act applies when the judicial seat of the arbitration is in England and Wales or Northern Ireland. This will have been designated by the parties to the arbitration agreement or by an arbitral or similar institution having the power to decide the seat or by the arbitral tribunal if the parties have authorised it to do so.

S4

(1) This sets out which sections of it are mandatory. The list below, taken from Schedule 1, has been shortened by the author to include only those mandatory sections which are specifically mentioned in your syllabus.

(2) The other provisions of this Part (the "non-mandatory provisions") allow the parties to make their own arrangements by agreement but provide rules which apply in the absence of such agreement.

Schedule 1

This sets out a list of sections of the Act which is mandatory to include in an arbitration agreement. Any mandatory sections contained in this chapter are designated s such in square brackets by the author.

EM: stay of legal proceedings

s.9 [mandatory provision in arbitration agreements]

(1) **A party to an arbitration agreement against whom legal proceedings are brought** (whether by way of claim or counterclaim) in respect of a matter which under the agreement is to be referred to arbitration **may (upon notice to the other parties to the proceedings) apply to the court** in which the proceedings have been brought **to stay the proceedings** so far as they concern that matter.

(2) An application may be made notwithstanding that the matter is to be referred to arbitration only after the exhaustion of other dispute resolution procedures.

(3) An application may **not** be made by a person **before** taking the appropriate procedural step (if any) to **acknowledge** [see the first few pages of Chapter 11 of this book] the legal proceedings against him **or after he has taken any step in those proceedings to answer the substantive claim**. [also Chapter 11]

(4) On an application under this section the court **shall grant a stay unless** satisfied that the **arbitration agreement is null and void, inoperative, or incapable of being performed.**

(5) **If the court refuses to stay** the legal proceedings, any provision that an award is a condition precedent to the bringing of legal proceedings in respect of any matter is of no effect in relation to those proceedings.

Activity

Remember to make notes on

section 9 of the Arbitration Act 1996 at paragraphs

2E-107 (first three paragraphs)
2E-111 (first two paragraphs) and
2E-112 (first paragraph)

of Volume 2 of 'Civil Procedure' (the White Book) 2020

You may find it useful to add in these references NOW, above this box.

<ins>How to apply for a stay under s.9 (CPR 62.8)</ins>

(1) **An application notice** seeking a stay of legal proceedings under section 9 of the 1996 Act[6] must be **served on all parties** to those proceedings **who have given an address for service**.

(2) **A copy** of an application notice under paragraph (1) **must be served on any other party** to the legal proceedings (whether or not he is within the jurisdiction) **who has not given an address** for service, **at**

(a) his **last known address**; or

(b) a **place where it is likely to come to his attention**.

(3) Where a question arises as to whether –

(a) an arbitration agreement has been concluded; or

(b) the dispute which is the subject-matter of the proceedings falls within the terms of such an agreement,

the court may decide that question or give directions to enable it to be decided and may order the proceedings to be stayed pending its decision.

<ins>EM: commencement procedure in arbitrations</ins>

The CPR includes rules regarding the commencement of claims procedure in Arbitrations. They do not apply to the enforcement of the awards (see later in this Chapter).

CPR 62.2

(1) In this Section of this Part [62] **'arbitration claim'** means –

(a) **any application** to the court **under the 1996 Act**;

(b) a claim to determine –

(i) **whether there is a valid arbitration agreement**;
(ii) whether an arbitration **tribunal is properly constituted**; or
what matters have been submitted to arbitration in accordance with an arbitration agreement;

(c) a claim to **declare** that an **award** by an arbitral tribunal is **not binding on a party**; and

(d) **any other application affecting** –
(i) arbitration proceedings (whether started or not); or
(ii) an arbitration agreement.

CPR 62.3 – starting a claim

(1) Claims under the Act must be started by the issue of an **arbitration claim form** in accordance with the **Part 8** procedure (See the end of Chapter 10).

(2) **An application under section 9 of the 1996 Act to stay legal proceedings must be made by application notice to the court dealing with those proceedings.**

(3) The courts in which an arbitration claim may be started are set out in Practice Direction 62.

(4) Is unlikely to be important for the purposes of this assessment on the Bar Training Courses, in the author's opinion.

CPR 62.4 - Arbitration claim form

(1) An **arbitration claim form must** –

(a) include **a concise statement** of –
(i) the **remedy claimed**; and
(ii) **any questions on which the claimant seeks the decision of the court;**

(b) **give details of any arbitration award challenged by the claimant, identifying which part or parts of the award are challenged and specifying the grounds for the challenge;**
(c) show that any statutory requirements have been met;

(d) specify under which section of the 1996 Act the claim is made;

(e) identify against which (if any) defendants a costs order is sought; and

(f) specify either –
(i) the persons on whom the arbitration claim form is to be served, stating their role in the arbitration and whether they are defendants; or
(ii) that the claim is made without notice under section 44(3) of the 1996 Act and the grounds relied on.

(2) Unless the court orders otherwise an arbitration claim form must be served on the defendant within 1 month from the date of issue and rules 7.5 [methods of service of a claim form and steps required] **and 7.6** [extension of time for serving a claim form] (both are in the middle of Chapter 10 of this book) **are modified accordingly.**

Arbitration Act

ss. 12 [mandatory provision], 13 [mandatory provision], 14

S 12 Power of court to extend time for beginning arbitral proceedings, &c [mandatory]

(1) **Where** an arbitration agreement to refer future disputes to arbitration provides that a claim shall be **barred**, or the claimant's right extinguished, **unless the claimant takes within a time fixed by the agreement some step—**

(a) **to begin arbitral proceedings**, or

(b) **to begin other dispute resolution procedures which must be exhausted before arbitral proceedings can be begun,**

the court may by order extend the time for taking that step.

(2) Any **party** to the arbitration agreement may **apply** for such an order **(upon notice** to the other parties), **but only after a claim has arisen and after exhausting any available arbitral process for obtaining an extension of time.**

(3) The court **shall make an order** only **if** satisfied—

(a) that **the circumstances** are such as were **outside the reasonable contemplation** of the parties when they agreed the provision in question, **and** that it would be **just** to extend the time, or

(b) **that the conduct of one party makes it unjust to hold the other party to the strict terms** of the provision in question.

(4) The **court** may extend the time for such period and on such terms **as it thinks fit,** and may do so **whether or not** the time previously fixed (by agreement or by a previous order) has expired.

(5) An order under this section does **not affect** the operation of the **Limitation Acts** (see section 13) [See Chapter 8 of this book].

(6) **The leave of the court is required for any appeal** from a decision of the court under this section.

S 13 Application of Limitation Acts [mandatory]

13 (1) The Limitation Acts **apply** to arbitral proceedings as they apply to legal proceedings

(2) The court may order that in computing the time prescribed by the Limitation Acts for commencement of proceedings (including arbitral proceedings) in respect of a dispute which the was the subject matter—

(a) of an award which the court orders to be set aside or declares to be of no effect, or

(b) of the affected part of an award which the court orders to be set aside in part, or declares to be in part of no effect,

the period between the commencement of the arbitration and the date of the order referred to in paragraph (a) or (b) shall be excluded.

(3) In determining for the purposes of the Limitation Acts when a cause of action accrued, **any provision that an award is a condition precedent to the bringing of legal proceedings in respect of a matter to which an arbitration agreement applies shall be disregarded**

S 14 Commencement of arbitral proceedings

(1) The parties are **free to agree when arbitral proceedings are to be regarded as commenced** for the purposes of this Part and for the purposes of the Limitation Acts.

(2) If there is **no such agreement** the following provisions apply.

(3) Where the **arbitrator is named or designated** in the arbitration agreement, arbitral proceedings are commenced in respect of a matter when **one party serves** on the other party or parties a **notice in writing requiring him or them to submit that matter to the person so named or designated.**

(4) Where the arbitrator **or arbitrators are to be appointed by the parties**, arbitral proceedings are commenced in respect of a matter **when one party serves on the other party or parties notice in writing requiring him or them to appoint an arbitrator or to agree to the appointment of an arbitrator in respect of that matter.**

(5) Where the arbitrator or **arbitrators are to be appointed by a person other than a party to the proceedings,** arbitral proceedings are commenced in respect of a matter **when one party gives notice in writing to that person requesting him to make the appointment in respect of that matter.**

EM: privacy and confidentiality

- These should be dealt with in context of your reading of The Jackson ADR Handbook (Second Edition, 2016)

EM: awards

Activity

Please read and make notes on the following sections of the Arbitration Act 1996, as directed by your Provider.

46. Rules applicable to substance of dispute.
47. Awards on different issues, &c.
48. Remedies.
49. Interest.
50. Extension of time for making award.
51. Settlement.
52. Form of award.
53. Place where award treated as made.
54. Date of award.
55. Notification of award.
56. Power to withhold award in case of non-payment_[mandatory]
57. Correction of award or additional award.
58. Effect of award.

EM: enforcement

Please recall

- 'Stay of legal proceedings' CPR 62.8 above
- CPR 62.3 above that an applicaton to stay legal proceedings must be made by application notice to the court dealing with those proceedings.
- CPR 62.8 that the application notice must be served on all parties to the legal proceedings to be stayed.

S 66 Enforcement of the award [mandatory].

(1) **An award** made by the tribunal pursuant to an arbitration agreement **may, by leave of the court, be enforced in the same manner as a judgment or order of the court to the same effect.**

(2) **Where leave is so given, judgment may be entered in terms of the award**.

(3) **Leave to enforce** an award shall **not** be **given where**, or to the extent that, **the person against whom it is sought to be enforced shows that the tribunal lacked substantive jurisdiction** to make the award.

The right to raise such an objection may have been lost (see section 73) [mandatory]. (For instance by acquiescing in the lack of jursidiction or missing agreed time limits for objecting)

(4) Nothing in this section affects the recognition or enforcement of an award under any other enactment or rule of law, in particular under Part II of the Arbitration Act 1950 (enforcement of awards under Geneva Convention) or the provisions of Part III of this Act relating to the recognition and enforcement of awards under the New York Convention or by an action on the award.

S 67 Challenging the award: substantive jurisdiction [mandatory].

(1) A **party** to arbitral proceedings may (**upon notice** to the **other parties** and to **the tribunal**) apply to the court—

(a) **challenging any award** of the arbitral tribunal **as to its substantive jurisdiction**; **or**

(b) for an order **declaring an award** made by the tribunal on the merits to be **of no effect**, **in whole or in part**, **because** the tribunal **did not have substantive jurisdiction.**

A party may lose the right to object (see section 73) [mandatory] (as above) and **the right to apply is subject to the restrictions in section 70(2) and (3) [mandatory].**

70 (2) An application or appeal may not be brought **if the applicant or appellant has not first exhausted—**

(a) any available arbitral process of appeal or review, and

(b) **any available recourse under section 57** (correction of award or additional award).

(3) Any application or appeal **must be brought within 28 days of the date of the award or, if there has been any arbitral process of appeal or review, of the date when the applicant or appellant was notified of the result of that process.**

(2) The arbitral tribunal **may continue the arbitral proceedings and make a further award while** an application to the court under this section is pending in relation to an award as to jurisdiction.

(3) On an application under this section challenging an award of the arbitral tribunal as to its substantive jurisdiction, **the court may by order—**

(a) confirm the award,

(b) vary the award, or

(c) set aside the award in whole or in part.

(4) The **leave of the court is required** for any appeal from a decision of the court under this section.

S 68. Challenging the award: serious irregularity [mandatory].

(1) A party to arbitral proceedings **may (upon notice to the other parties and to the tribunal) apply to the court challenging an award** in the proceedings **on the ground of serious irregularity** [see definition in s 68 (2) below] affecting the tribunal, the proceedings or the award.

A party may lose the right to object (see section 73) [mandatory] and the right to apply is subject to the restrictions in section 70(2) and (3) [mandatory].

(2) **Serious irregularity means** an irregularity of one or more of the following kinds which the court considers has caused or will cause substantial injustice to the applicant—

(a) failure by the tribunal to comply with section 33 (general duty of tribunal);

(b) the tribunal exceeding its powers (otherwise than by exceeding its substantive jurisdiction: see section 67);

(c) failure by the tribunal to conduct the proceedings in accordance with the procedure agreed by the parties;

(d) failure by the tribunal to deal with all the issues that were put to it;

(e) any arbitral or other institution or person vested by the parties with powers in relation to the proceedings or the award exceeding its powers;

(f) uncertainty or ambiguity as to the effect of the award;

(g) the award being obtained by fraud or the award or the way in which it was procured being contrary to public policy;

(h) failure to comply with the requirements as to the form of the award; or

(i) any irregularity in the conduct of the proceedings or in the award which is admitted by the tribunal or by any arbitral or other institution or person vested by the parties with powers in relation to the proceedings or the award.

(3) **If there is shown to be serious irregularity** affecting the tribunal, the proceedings or the award, **the court may**—

(a) remit the award to the tribunal, in whole or in part, for reconsideration,

(b) set the award aside in whole or in part, or

(c) declare the award to be of no effect, in whole or in part.

The court shall not exercise its power to set aside or to declare an award to be of no effect, in whole or in part, **unless it is satisfied that it would be inappropriate to remit** the matters in question to the tribunal for reconsideration.

(4) **The leave of the court is required** for any appeal from a decision of the court under this section.

<u>EM: appeals</u>

S 69 Appeal on point of law

(1) Unless otherwise agreed by the parties, **a party to arbitral proceedings may (upon notice to the other parties and to the tribunal) appeal** to the court **on a question of law arising out of an award made in the proceedings.**

An agreement to dispense with reasons for the tribunal's award shall be considered an agreement to exclude the court's jurisdiction under this section.

(2) An appeal shall not be brought under this section except—

(a) with **the agreement of all the other parties** to the proceedings, **or**

(b) **with the leave of the court**.

The right to appeal is also subject to the restrictions in section 70(2) and (3 [mandatory] (as above).

(3) **Leave to appeal shall be given only if the court is satisfied—**

(a) that the determination of the question will substantially affect the rights of one or more of the parties,

(b) that the question is one which the tribunal was asked to determine,

(c) that, on the basis of the findings of fact in the award—

(I) the decision of the tribunal on the question is obviously wrong, or

(ii) the question is one of general public importance and the decision of the tribunal is at least open to serious doubt, and

(d) that, despite the agreement of the parties to resolve the matter by arbitration, it is just and proper in all the circumstances for the court to determine the question.

(4) An application for leave to appeal under this section shall **identify the question of law to be determined and state the grounds on which it is alleged that leave to appeal should be granted.**

(5) The court shall determine an application for leave to appeal under this section **without a hearing unless it appears to the court that a hearing is required.**

(6) **The leave of the court is required for any appeal from a decision of the court under this section to grant or refuse leave to appeal.**

(7) On an appeal under this section **the court may by order—**

(a) confirm the award,

(b) vary the award,

(c) remit the award to the tribunal, in whole or in part, for reconsideration in the light of the court's determination, or

(d) set aside the award in whole or in part.

The court shall **not exercise** its power to set aside an award, in whole or in part, **unless** it is satisfied that it would be **inappropriate to remit** the matters in question to the tribunal for reconsideration.

(8) The decision of the court on an appeal under this section shall be treated as **a judgment of the court** for the purposes of a further appeal.

But no such appeal lies without the **leave** of the court which shall not be given **unless the court considers that the question is one of general importance or is one which for some other special reason should be considered by the Court of Appeal.**

S 70 Challenge or appeal – supplementary provisions

(1) The following provisions apply to an application or **appeal under section 67, 68 or 69**.

(2) An application or appeal may **not** be brought **if** the applicant or appellant has **not first exhausted—**

(a) any available arbitral process of appeal or review, and

(b) any available recourse under section 57 (correction of award or additional award). [You saw this above]

(3) **Any application or appeal must be brought within 28 days of the date of the award or, if there has been any arbitral process of appeal or review, of the date when the applicant or appellant was notified of the result of that process.** [You saw this above]

(4) If on an application or appeal it appears to the court that the award—

(a) does not contain the tribunal's reasons, or

(b) does not set out the tribunal's reasons in sufficient detail to enable the court properly to consider the application or appeal,

the court may order the tribunal to state the reasons for its award in sufficient detail for that purpose.

(5) Where the court makes an order under subsection **(4), it may make such further order as it thinks fit with respect to any additional costs** of the arbitration resulting from its order.

(6) **The court may order** the applicant or appellant to provide **security for the costs** [see chapter 15 of this book) of the application or appeal, and may direct that the application or appeal be dismissed if the order is not complied with.

The power to order security for costs shall **not** be exercised **on the ground that** the applicant or appellant is—

(a) an individual **ordinarily resident outside the United Kingdom**, or

(b) **a corporation or association incorporated or formed under the law of a country outside** the United Kingdom, or whose central management and control is exercised outside the United Kingdom.

(7) The **court may order** that **any money payable under the award shall be brought into court or otherwise secured pending the determination** of the application or appeal, and **may direct** that the **application or appeal be dismissed if the order is not complied with.**

(8) The **court may grant leave to appeal subject to conditions** to the same or similar effect as an order under subsection (6) or (7).

This does not affect the general discretion of the court to grant leave subject to conditions.

S 71 Challenge or appeal: effect of order of court [mandatory]

(1) The following provisions have effect **where the court makes an order under section 67, 68 or 69** with respect to an award.

(2) Where the award is varied, **the variation has effect as part of the tribunal's award**.

(3) Where the award is **remitted** to the tribunal, in whole or in part, for reconsideration, the **tribunal shall make a fresh award in respect of the matters remitted within three months of the date of the order for remission or such longer or shorter period as the court may direct.**

(4) Where the award is **set aside** or declared to be of no effect, in whole or in part, the court may also order that any provision that an award is a **condition** precedent to the bringing of legal proceedings in respect of a matter to which the arbitration agreement applies, is of no effect as regards the subject matter of the award or, as the case may be, the relevant part of the award.

Remember to incorporate the relevant paragraphs from The Jackson ADR Handbook (Second Edition, 2016)

25.01-25.26

You may find it useful to make your notes here, below this box.

<u>Paragraphs 25.01-25.26 (your notes)</u>

Paragraphs 25.01-25.26 (your notes continued)

CUR 4.2 EXPERT (OR NEUTRAL) DETERMINATION

Activity

Remember to incorporate the relevant paragraphs from The Jackson ADR Handbook (Second Edition, 2016):-

24.01-5
24.07
24.09-24.10
24.15
24.19
24.24-24.25
24.30
24.52-24.53

You may find it useful to make your notes here, below this box

Expert (or Neutral) Determination (your notes)

***Expert (or Neutral) Determination** (your notes continued)*

Non-Adjudicative options

CUR 5.1 EARLY NEUTRAL EVALUATION

Early Neutral Evaluation ("ENE") takes place completely within the court system. An objective evaluation of the arguments on each side is made at a meeting with neutral third party who is an expert on the subject matter of the case, e.g. in Family Law. Issues will be identified and settlement options explored whilst the merits are being evaluated. The parties will have freely agreed to adopt this form of ADR. The evaluation is confidential and not binding. If there is a resolution a written agreement will be submitted to the court for approval.

Activity

Remember to incorporate the relevant paragraphs from The Jackson ADR Handbook (Second Edition, 2016):-

22.01-22.07
22.10-22.13
22.15

You may find it useful to make your notes here, below this box

Early neutral Evaluation (your notes)

CUR 5.2 CONCILIATION AND MEDIATION

EM: conciliation

A conciliator plays a more active role in a conciliation than does a mediator in a mediation. A conciliator will suggest ways in which a compromise could be reached between two parties in dispute. You may have heard of ACAS, the Advisory Conciliation and Arbitration Service often used in Employment disputes - matters such as unfair dismissal claims and where trade unions are involved. The results of conciliations are not legally binding.

Activity

Remember to incorporate the relevant paragraphs from The Jackson ADR Handbook (Second Edition, 2016):-

2.27
23.03

You may find it useful to make your notes here, below this box

Conciliation (your notes)

Mediation

EM: general principles of mediation

In the world of mediation you will come across mediation services such as the Centre for Effective Dispute Resolution ("CEDR").

Mediation is likely to be the choice for resolving a dispute out of court where a future relationship between the disputing parties is important, perhaps e.g. in business, perhaps e.g. in Family Law.

A mediator is a neutral third party who facilitates a potential resolution of the dispute, rather than opining on the stance of the parties. A mediator's role is often to shuttle back and forth between the different rooms in which each of the parties and their legal team members are separately gathered, relaying offers and the position of each party to the other as the day progresses. The idea is that parties who have agreed to a mediation will be ready to work collaboratively to find resolution of the dispute. The preferred outcome of a mediation is a mutually agreed compromise freely entered into by each party. The outcome of a mediation is not legally binding.

Notice also that there is further reference to mediation, in CUR 13 in Chapter 19 of this book; this is the examinable material "referrals to mediation" under the heading "the small claims track" in Chapter 19.

Activity

Explanatory material which will NOT be assessed
To complement understanding of the examinable material set out above, students may find it helpful to be familiar with paragraphs

13.22-13.23
13.29-13.31

of The Jackson ADR Handbook (Second Edition, 2016)

EM: preparation for mediation
EM: the mediation process.

Activity

Remember to incorporate the relevant paragraphs from The Jackson ADR Handbook (Second Edition, 2016):-

13.08-13.10
13.11-13.15
13.24-13.27
13.32- 13.42
13.49-13.58
13.59-13.63
13.64
14.49 14.61 14.73-14.74 and 15.04-15.05 (including Figure 15.1)

Mediation (your notes)

Mediation (your notes continued)

Mediation (your notes continued)

Chapter 5

Elements of the syllabus which you have now covered for **ADR**

- A cell with heavy outlining means that that area of the syllabus was covered in this Chapter;
- A darkly shaded cell with a tick √ means that the whole of that syllabus element has now been covered;
- A lightly shaded cell means that part of that element of the syllabus has been covered in a previous Chapter; and
- An unshaded cell means that element of the syllabus has not yet been covered.

1.4 √	1.5√	3.3	4.1√	4.2√	5.1√	5.2√	18.1	22.3	

Chapter 6

COSTS [CUR 23]

CASE MANAGEMENT – COSTS MANAGEMENT [CUR 13]

f) Costs and Costs management

THIS CHAPTER CONTAINS THE ITEMS PRINTED IN BOLD IN THE FOLLOWING BOXES

CURRICULUM ("CUR")

First section of the Chapter

Costs
***23.*1 summary and detailed assessment of costs**
23.2 standard and indemnity costs
21.3 is in Chapter 18
23.4 costs orders in civil cases
(Judgments and Orders, Enforcement and Appeals each have their own dedicated Chapters later in this book)

Second section of the Chapter

13.4 Costs management (This is one element of the Case management area of the syllabus)

SYLLABUS

The first section of this Chapter contains

Examinable material will consist of, court discretion as to costs,
[interim costs orders are set out in Chapter 18, in context for interim orders]
standard or indemnity basis of assessment, factors taken into account in deciding amount of costs, procedure for assessing costs, summary assessment of costs, detailed assessment of costs, time for complying with order for costs, and court powers in relation to misconduct and qualified one-way costs shifting; costs in ADR

(Each of the above has its own subheading in this Chapter, flagged by EM:)

- **CPR 44.1**
- **CPR 44.2 (court's discretion as to costs)**
- **CPR 44.3-4**
- **CPR 44.6-7**
- **CPR 44.11**
- **CPR 44.13-16**
- **PD 44 paragraphs 3-6, 8,** [PD 44 paragraph 4 is dealt with in Chapter 18], **9.1-9.2**, **9.5(1), (2) (4) and 9.6**
- **CPR 47.1**
- **CPR 47.2**

- **Commentary is incorporated in context in this Chapter, highlighted in an Activity box between two stars**

- ***The following are the specific leading case authorities with which students should be familiar (and should be able to refer to by name): Sanderson, Bullock***

- **Relevant ADR references to The Jackson ADR Handbook (Second Edition, 2016) are incorporated in context in this Chapter, highlighted in an Activity box between two lightning flashes**

The second section of this Chapter

CPR 3.12-18 and PD 3E paragraphs 1-7

Examinable material from the 'case management, sanctions and striking out' element of the syllabus are also included in this costs Chapter.

These are

- ***costs budgets***
- ***filing and exchanging budgets***
- ***costs management orders***
- ***costs management conferences***
- ***court regard to budgets in making case management decisions.***

Chapter 6 MOCS first section.

- ***Start with loser pays winner's costs***
- ***Court has discretion to adjust and what it considers needs adjusting***
- ***Sanderson order or Bullock order***
- ***QOCS***
- ***Costs regarding each track***
    - ***Small- only 5 possible***
    - ***Fast- trial or hearing less than a day =summary method,***
        - ***standard or indemnity basis***
        - ***unusually, costs budgets***
    - ***Multi- trial or hearing of more than one day = detailed method***
        - ***standard or indemnity basis***
        - ***costs budgets in costs management***
- ***Costs in ADR***

Chapter 6 MOCS second section.

A MOCS summary of Case management so far Chapter 2 MOCS

- ***Court's General Powers of case management***
- ***Court may make orders on its own initiative***
- ***Courts may rectify errors in procedure.***

and in this Chapter 6

- ***Costs budgets***
- ***Costs management orders***

We meet case management again in Chapter 19.

COSTS [CUR 23]

The sessions dealing with this area of the syllabus on my BTC course are	

CUR 23.4 COSTS ORDERS IN CIVIL CASES

General principles

"Costs" is the amount that is due to legal advisers for their services.

The likely amount of costs and who may have to pay them should have an important bearing when deciding whether or not to litigate, BEFORE any litigation is started. That is why, even though costs will not be decided by a judge until after the end of the hearing/trial, this book deals with consideration of likely costs at this very early stage.

At the end of a hearing or trial the court will draw up an order. When an order is silent as to costs no party is entitled to costs; each party therefore pays their own legal advisers' costs. Counsel must therefore ask for an order for costs once judgment has been given.

There now follows an explanation of who pays whose costs and what the court takes into account when exercising its discretion as to costs. After that, the position regarding costs on each track is addressed

CUR 23.3 INTERIM COSTS ORDERS

The court may make an order about costs at any stage in a case. Costs may therefore be ordered both at interim hearings and final trials. The detail of potential costs orders at interim hearings is addressed in Chapter 18 of this book, in context, when dealing with the "what-ifs" interim applications.

CUR 23.4 COSTS ORDERS IN CIVIL CASES (continued)

Who pays whose costs? – the starting point

The starting point is that the **loser pays the costs of the winner, as well as their own** (i.e. **costs follow the event**). There are some types of case for which the costs are fixed by the CPR, although these are not on your syllabus this year.

Who pays whose costs?

General principles

Remember that the starting point is that the **loser** (unsuccessful party) **pays the costs of the winner** (successful party), **as well as their own** (i.e. **costs follow the event**). [Note that this is not the case for Appeals in the Family Division or in probate proceedings]

EM: court discretion as to costs

Then the **court has discretion** and so may make a different order. The court has discretion as to

- whether costs are payable by one party to another;
- the amount of those costs; and
- when they are to be paid.

In using its discretion the court must have **regard to all the circumstances including**

- **how the parties have conducted themselves** pre (including protocol adherence) and per proceedings (and post proceedings where, e.g. there is to be a further detailed assessment of costs – see later in this Chapter) - the reasonableness of the parties' allegations – whether it was reasonable for the parties to pursue the allegations - whether the successful C has exaggerated his claim
- **the level of success of the winner** -whether the parties succeeded in part of their case
- **any admissible offer to settle**; i.e. an offer that was not made 'without prejudice" (detail in Chapter 20 of this book); (but not an offer in relation to offers made under Part 36- see the end of this Chapter and the whole of the following one). So costs for Calderbank offers and non-compliant Part 36 offers (both in the next Chapter) will be approached as in this Chapter 6.

So it may be that the "**loser paying the winner's costs" principle may be adjusted** in the court's discretion, with the loser paying anything in the range between none or all of the winner's costs, as well as paying their own legal advisers' costs as the loser.

The orders which the court may make include an order that a party must pay

- a proportion of another party's costs
- a stated amount in respect of another party's costs
- costs from or until a certain date only
- costs incurred before proceedings have begun
- costs relating to particular steps taken in the proceedings
- costs relating only to a distinct part of the proceedings [Before the court considers making this costs order, it will consider whether it is practicable to make an order for a proportion of another party's costs to be paid or for costs from or until a certain date only to be paid instead].
- interest on costs from or until a certain date, including a date before judgment.

Activity

Remember to make notes on the relevant case law authorities in paragraphs

- **44.2.3 (first, sixth and seventh paragraphs)**
- **44.2.4**
- **44.2.5**
- **44.2.6 (first paragraph)**
- **44.2.7 (first paragraph)**
- **44.2.8 (first paragraph)**
- **44.2.10 (first two paragraphs)**
- **44.2.12 (first two paragraphs)**
- **44.2.13 (first three paragraphs)**
- **44.2.14 (first two paragraphs)**
- **44.2.17 (first two paragraphs)**
- **44.2.18 (first three paragraphs)**
- **44.2.19 (first and fourth paragraphs)**
- **44.2.20**
- **44.2.24**
- **44.2.25 (first and third paragraphs)**
- **44.2.28 (first, second, third, fourth, fifth and sixth paragraphs)**

in the commentary in the White Book.

You may find it useful to add in references to the case law NOW at the appropriate points of this Chapter.

When approaching final revision time, remember to add in the salient findings of the cases at the relevant point in any 'mental crib sheet' into which you have distilled the main points of your learned knowledge.

EM: Note, the following are the specific leading case authorities with which students should be familiar (and should be able to refer to by name): Sanderson, Bullock

In other words,

How the court may exercise its discretion as to costs where there have been multiple Defendants and the Claimant has been successful against some but not all of the Defendants.

When advising your client as to potential costs at the outset of a case you will avert them to the potential costs of a winning or losing outcome, perhaps setting out (as so far in this Chapter)

- General rule of loser pays winner
- Judges can make a different order in their discretion
- They will consider the parties' conduct, whether a party succeeded in part of their case and any admissible non - part 36 offers to settle

  Next, if the case involved multiple Defendants and the Claimant has been successful against some but not all of the Defendants, there will be consideration of whether or not it would be appropriate to make one of the types of the orders which mean that C will not have to pay the costs of the Defendant(s) against whom he was not successful – by a direct costs order known as Sanderson order or by an indemnity to C from those Defendant(s) against whom C was successful, known as a Bullock order.

Imagine you are the Claimant who was injured due to

- being a pedestrian hit due to the negligence of a car(t) driver and a bus driver;
- being a pedestrian hit on a pedestrian crossing because one car braked (late?) to stop to let you cross and one behind did not stop in time, hit the car in front which in turn bumped into you;
- being hit in a car accident where the two occupants of the car each state that the other was the driver;
- the negligence of several different doctors

In these types of cases the Claimant cannot be sure when he begins his case who is the correct D or D's to claim against. At the end of the trial the judge will consider who is to pay whose costs.

Continuing with the examples above, let us simply say that at trial it was found that

- the car(t) driver was found not to be negligent and the bus driver was;
- the first car was found not have braked late and so the accident was fully the fault of the car behind:
- it was found that occupant A of the car was not the driver, but occupant B was;
- it was found that 3 of the doctors were not negligent and 2 of them were negligent.

[In the real world there may well be further complexities such as the car(t) driver having been found negligent in some degree, yet his negligence was totally negated by the bigger amount of negligence on the part of the bus driver, thus rendering the bus driver's negligence equivalent to full liability; or the defendants against whom C was successful were held to have different percentages of liability; or C joining in certain Defendants was or was not reasonable before a case was discontinued against them. For illustrative purposes, we will keep our examples as either no or full liability.]

To reiterate, where a Claimant has succeeded against some but not all of multiple Defendants, the judge when exercising discretion as to costs may choose to order that costs are paid by virtue of **one of two mechanisms/orders**, each of which has as its goal that the Claimant does not have to pay any costs and is not out of pocket for having brought a claim not only against the Defendant(s) against whom he won, but also against those Defendant(s) against whom he lost, when C had **reasonably** joined them in as D's. These two mechanisms thus protect C from an adverse costs award.

The reasoning behind this, is that when bringing the claim, C could not have known that

- it was not the car(t) driver who was at fault but the bus driver
- it was not the first car who was at fault but the second car
- it was not occupant A who was at fault but occupant B
- it was not the fault of 3 of the doctors but of the other 2.

BY VIRTUE OF THIS, IT WAS **REASONABLE** on our simple facts FOR THE CLAIMANT TO BRING CLAIMS AT THE OUTSET AGAINST MULTIPLE DEFENDANTS.

It follows that should the judge find that it was not reasonable for C to join in one or more of the multiple Defendants against whom he was not successful, then C will likely be ordered to pay his own costs for bringing the claim against them – he will not benefit from a direct costs order (Sanderson) nor from an indemnity from those Defendants against whom he was successful (Bullock) for those costs of C.

{Let us pause for a moment to consider how the word reasonable may be interpreted in this context. It may not be reasonable if:-

- C had claimed against too many Defendants (e.g. every vehicle on the road at the time of the accident (!), or every doctor in the hospital (!)) as the cause of action against all of them would not be sustainable;

- C has pursued a second, third, fourth or more defendants in a 'catch-all' approach, just because you are getting close to the end of the Limitation period and you want to try to include the right defendant(s);

- it is obvious that it was plain wrong at the outset to bring proceedings against (a) certain defendant(s).

- the judge finds that proceedings against (a) certain defendant(s) that were discontinued, could have been discontinued earlier; they may only have been reasonable to bring against that D up to a certain point in time. [The details on discontinuance are in Chapter 19 of this book].

It may be reasonable if:-

- C cannot safely omit a D without taking the risk that C would not be compensated at all (for instance if C had pursued only as it turned out, only the wholly innocent party, C would have had to pay that D's costs and would not have been awarded any compensation).

Also the following are frequently examined when judges consider whether there was reasonableness in this context. Although they are not conclusive, they are very relevant and of great importance when judges consider whether or not C acted reasonably in claiming against multiple defendants.

- Did any Defendants try to move the blame onto the others?
- Did the D(s) against whom C was successful cause the D(s) against whom C was unsuccessful to be added to the action?
- Was/were the D(s) against whom D was successful sued in the alternative to those against whom D was unsuccessful?
- Would an early admission by the D(s) against whom C was successful have eliminated the need for C to join in the other D(s)?
- Where C discontinued a claim against the D(s) against whom he was therefore unsuccessful, why was it discontinued and could it have been discontinued earlier?}

So if it the judge finds it *was* **reasonable** for C to have pursued the claim against the multiple defendants against whom he was not successful, it would not be fair, would it, if the injured C then had to pay the costs of these Defendant(s) against whom he was technically the loser, simply by a judge sticking to the starting position of loser pay's winner's costs (r.44.2(2) (a)). Remember also that r.44.2(2) (b) provides for some other order. Thus judges may in their discretion go on to order a Sanderson/Bullock order, as C's success against the bus driver, the second car, occupant B, the other two doctors, ought not to be blighted by having to meet his own costs against the Defendant(s) against whom he was not successful, yet he had reasonably brought them in as Defendants.

On the next page, this is shown in diagram form, where the car(t) driver, the first car, car occupant A and the 3 doctors all won their defence against the losing C and so they have happy, smiley faces; whereas the bus driver, the second car, occupant B and the 2 doctors all have unhappy, upside down smiles, because they were the losers against the winning C.

Please note that rather than continue using either unwieldy wording or referring to multiple Defendants as D1 and D2 etc, I will simply be calling them Smiley or Unhappy. This is to be clear which D(s) we are referring to, because in judgments, some text books and even your course materials D1 will sometimes be the D against whom C was successful and will in other places be the D against whom C was unsuccessful. For the sake of consistency, then, our D's are either Smiley Winners or Unhappy Losers.

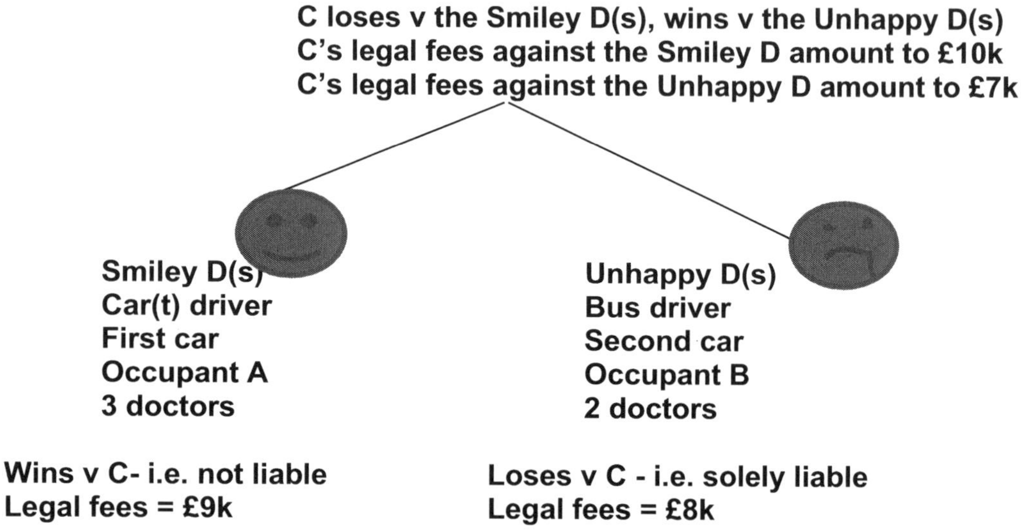

Once the judge has, in his or her discretion, decided that it was **REASONABLE** for C to have included the Smiley Winning Defendants as Defendants in the claim, then that discretion will be used further to decide which of the two orders to make.

Caselaw in 2019 (Fouladi v Daront & Ors) further added that use of one of the two orders is not confined to cases where C did not know which D to sue. Judges will also make one of the two orders when it is **just to do so**, **with regard to all the circumstances of the case**. Perhaps the 'catch-all' close to the end of the Limitation period may, in some cases, on some facts, in some circumstances, be no bar to the award of a Sanderson or Bullock order. Time will tell. {For assessment purposes, I think it wisest to require that Ds were reasonably included in the proceedings, unless your Provider updates you to say this cannot be assumed.}.

Sanderson Order

Shall it be a direct costs **Sanderson** order where the Unhappy Losing Defendants are ordered to pay the costs of the Smiley Winning Defendants as well as those of the winning Claimant?

- The Unhappy Losing D pays Smiley Winning D's costs of defending against C;
- The Unhappy Losing D pays winning C's costs of claiming against the Unhappy Losing D.

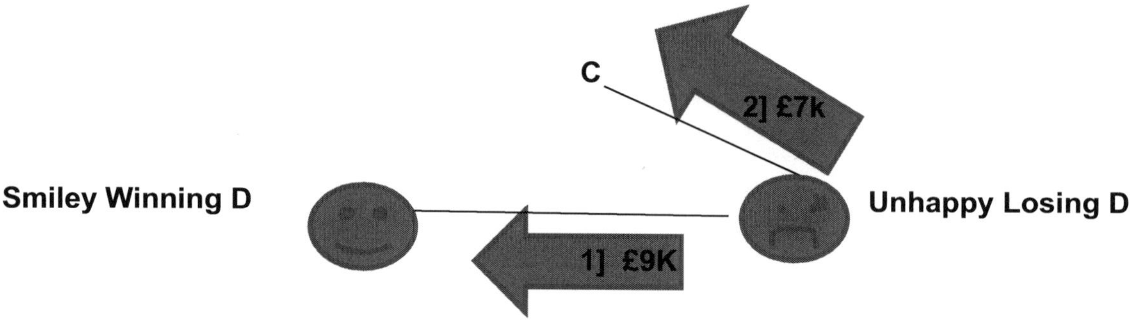

Note that C pays no costs to the Smiley Winning D and that all payments by the Unhappy Losing D are to each of the Smiley Winning D and C in a Sanderson order.

Whilst choosing between a Sanderson and a Bullock order is in the judge's discretion, there are no hard and fast rules as to which order will be made, although a Sanderson order is more likely where circumstances show that C may not be in a position to be able to pay the Smiley Winning D since C is publicly funded or insolvent.

Bullock Order

Or shall it be a **Bullock** order where an **indemnity** is ordered to be paid to C by the Unhappy Losing Ds, **reimbursing C** (as part of C's own costs of the action in pursuing the Unhappy Losing Ds), for the costs he is being ordered to pay to the Smiley Winning Defendants?

A Bullock order is more likely if there is no need to bypass an impecunious C. It is also more likely where the Smiley Winning D needs to be protected by being sure of getting her costs, as Unhappy Losing D has little money.

Thus in a Bullock Order

1] the losing **C pays to the Smiley Winning D** that D's costs of defending against C (i.e. the legal fees).

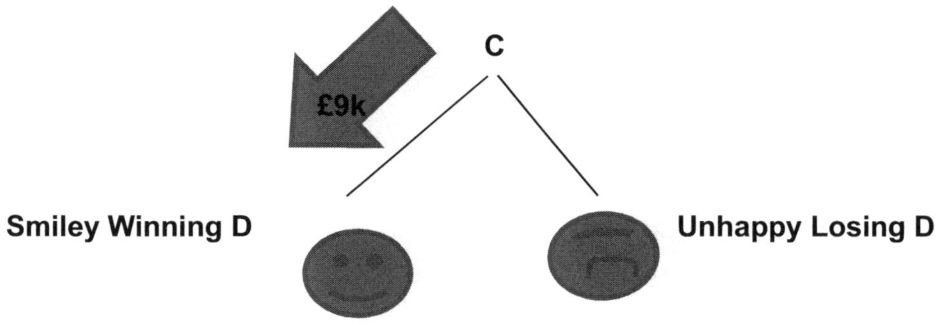

then

2] **C is reimbursed (indemnified)** by the Unhappy Losing D with that same amount of the Smiley Winning D's costs of defending against C.

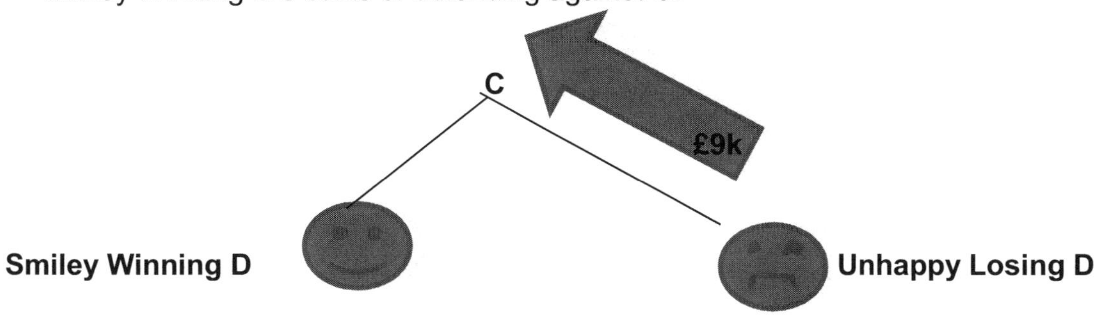

then

3] **the Unhappy Losing D pays the winning C's costs of bringing the claim against the Unhappy Losing D.**

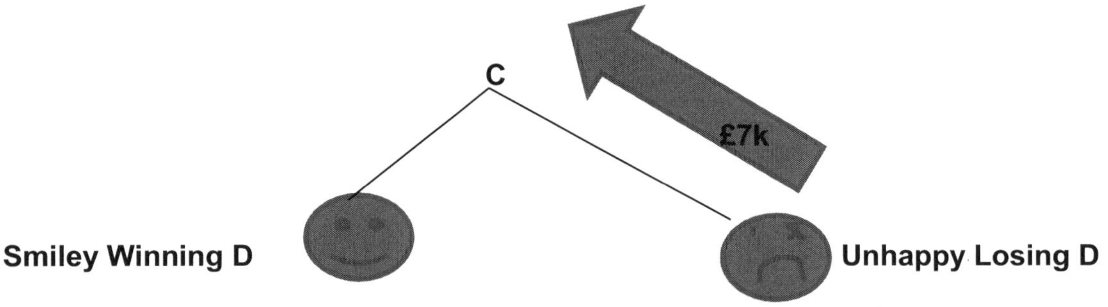

Note that in a Bullock Order, although C pays the costs of the Smiley Winning D, these are reimbursed to C by the Unhappy Losing D, who is in addition ordered to pay the costs of C relating to the claim C has won against the Unhappy Losing D.

An extension to Sanderson and Bullock Orders

In 2017 the case of Jabang v Wadman and in 2018 the case of Woodland v Swimming Teachers' Association and Ors, these orders were extended even further. The Unhappy Losing D(s) were also ordered to pay C's costs of bringing his claim against the Smiley Winning D(s).

These cases therefore bring sharply into focus the risk of costs to Defendants in multiple defendant cases. They need to be advised to carefully consider at the outset whether they really are the ones at fault; if so they should admit liability early, stop blaming others thus causing them to be added to the action, as if those others turn out to be Smiley Winning Defendants, needlessly added by C, the costs for them as Unhappy Losing Defendants could indeed be great, particularly if a judge finds that a 'Jabang' or Woodland' order is appropriate in the circumstances.

Thus a **Sanderson order** could produce the following.

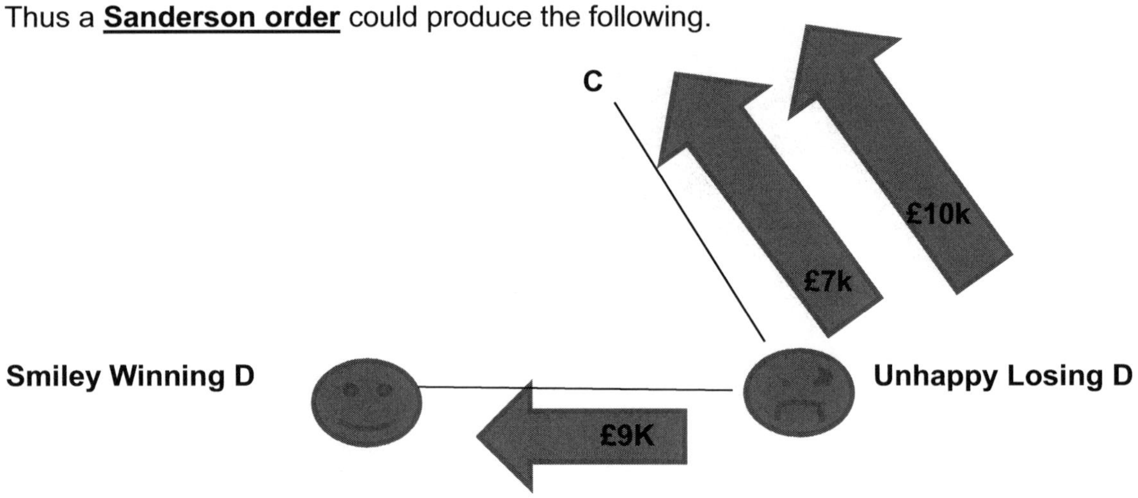

And a **Bullock order** could produce the following

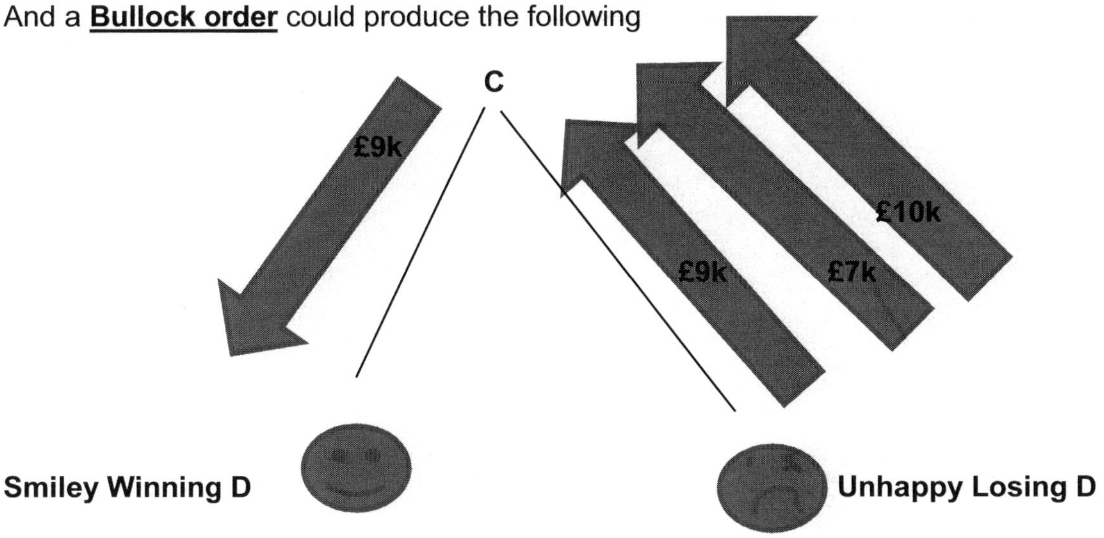

After the judge has ordered one or other of these two orders, they will go on, to consider the BASIS on which these costs should be paid.

The basis on which costs should be paid is relevant to all fast track and multi-track cases and is explained later in this Chapter.

EM: time for complying with order for costs
Costs are to be paid within 14 days of judgment if the amount of costs is stated. If there is a further detailed assessment of costs, the assessment may state the date when payment should be made, or the court may specify when payment should be made.

Qualified one-way costs shifting (QOCS)

This is relevant in proceedings for a claim, counterclaim or additional claim for damages by a **claimant** or by an estate on behalf of which such a claim is brought for **PI / death / fatal accident case where the claimant is the loser.** The Court of Appeal has confirmed that it does apply to a single claim, which as well as personal injury, includes other heads of damage, e.g. claiming for damage caused also to property in the RTA.

Even though the general principle of loser pays winner may be followed, (i.e. by the court making a costs order in favour of the winning D), unless an exception applies, (see below), the winning D can **enforce** payment of the winning D's costs against the losing C *without the permission of the court* **only up to the aggregate amount in money terms that the losing C has been awarded in damages and interest.** This is often referred to as C having QOCS protection.

[Thus a losing C pays no more in costs than the amount they have won in damages and interest on those damages. Since it is likely that the losing C will not have been awarded anything in damages and interest, **D is not able to enforce** against C if C does not pay D's costs].

However, situations where a losing **C will have been awarded something** in damages and interest, **thus giving D an amount enforceable** as to that winning D's costs, are

- where C has had a partial success and has therefore been awarded some damages and interest

– where C wins (and so has been awarded some damages and interest) but has failed to obtain judgment more advantageous than a D's part 36 offer [for explanation and details of this see scenario (iii) in the next Chapter].

This enforcement may only take place after the proceedings have been concluded and the costs have been assessed or agreed. The costs order in favour of the winning D is not treated as an unsatisfied or outstanding judgment against the losing C for the purposes of any court record.

So the costs have been shifted one-way so that enforcement against the losing C is limited/changed/qualified as to the amount they will have to pay of the winning D's costs; limited, that is, to the amount C has won in damages and interest.

Exceptions to qualified one-way costs shifting where no court permission to enforce is required

i.e. situations where QOCS does not apply, so that without needing court permission, a winning **D can still enforce to the full extent** even though the C is a loser in a PI / death / fatal accident case:

– D wins strike out [See later in Chapter 13] on the grounds that
  - C disclosed no reasonable grounds for bringing proceedings; or
  - the proceedings are an abuse of the court's process; or
  - the conduct of C or someone acting on C's behalf with C's knowledge is likely to obstruct the just disposal of the proceedings.

Exceptions to qualified one-way costs shifting where court permission to enforce IS required

i.e. situations where QOCS does not apply, so that a winning D **needs court permission** and once D has it, **can still enforce to the full extent** even though the C is a loser in a PI / death / fatal accident case:

– the claim is found on the balance of probabilities to be fundamentally dishonest
– to the extent that the court considers it just, where
  - the proceedings include a claim which is made for the financial benefit of a person other than the claimant or a dependant within the meaning of section 1(3) of the Fatal Accidents Act 1976 (other than a claim in respect of the gratuitous provision of care, earnings paid by an employer or medical expenses);
    - the court may, (subject to rule 46.2, which is not on your syllabus this year) make an order for costs against a person, other than the claimant, for whose financial benefit the whole or part of the claim was made; or
  - a claim is made for the benefit of the claimant other than a claim to which this Section applies.

Costs regarding each track.

Fuller detail on the matters to which the court will have reference when deciding to which track a case should be allocated are in Chapter 19. Until then you should become conversant with the relevant figures as set out below.

Small claims track and costs

Claims likely to be allocated to the small claims track are those for a total of

- ≤£10k
- PSLA ≤ £1k[7]
- Tenant wanting order for landlord to repair ≤ £1k and any other claim for damages is ≤£1k
- NOT claims by residential tenants re harassment or unlawful eviction by landlord
- A case involving a disputed allegation of dishonesty will not usually be suitable for the small claims track.
- The court may allocate to the small claims track a claim, the value of which is above £10k The court will not normally allow more than one day for the hearing such a claim above £10k.

<u>The **only costs** between the parties are</u>

- court fees, e.g. the court fee payable on issue of a claim form,
- witness travel expenses and loss of earnings up to £95 a day
- disbursements up to £750 per expert
- a litigant in person can claim up to £19 per hour for conducting their own legal work
- an amount the court assesses where any party has behaved unreasonably. Note that legal adviser costs are not normally awarded as an automatic entitlement on this track.

  However, it may be that the court assesses that the costs of the reasonable party are to be paid by the unreasonable party under this head.

---

[7] Part 1 of the Civil Liability Act 2018 which was due to come into force in April 2020 has been delayed, partly because of Covid 19. Unless the BSB states otherwise, you will not be assessed on this. It is something which you will need to add to your knowledge for legal practice.

The small claims limit is projected to increase to £2000 for personal injury claims but where the personal injury claim is RTA related, the Act includes whiplash reforms so that the limit goes up to £5000 in such cases.

Whiplash claims will only be allowed to be settled after a medical report has been obtained.

A portal system is being developed to handle whiplash claims and so litigants in person will use this to bring such a claim after launch.

Children and protected parties are excluded from this new regime increase, new pre-action protocol and new portal system initially.

In addition there is a mechanism proposed for setting a tariff for the amount of damages payable for PSLA in whiplash claims where the injury does not exceed, or is not likely to exceed, two years.

Fast track and costs

Where the court considers that

- the trial is likely to last for no longer than one day (5 hours); and
- oral expert evidence at trial will be limited to
  - one expert per party in relation to any expert field; and
  - expert evidence in two expert fields,

Claims likely to be allocated to the fast track are those for a total of

- >£10k - ≤£25k
- PSLA > £1k

There are further considerations to which the court will have regard when deciding to which track to allocate a claim. These are set out in Chapter 19.

<u>The **costs** between the parties</u>

To repeat:

- The starting point is that **loser pays winner's costs**
- The **court has discretion** and so may make a different order having regard to **all the circumstances including**

  - **how the parties have conducted themselves**
  - **the level of success of the winner**
  - **any admissible offer to settle**;

  So it may be that the **loser pays winner principle may be adjusted**.

CUR 23.1

SUMMARY METHOD OF

ASSESSMENT OF COSTS

EM: procedure for assessing costs

Next, the **METHOD of assessing costs.**

Where the court orders a party to pay costs to another party (other than fixed costs) it may either

- make a **summary assessment** of the costs [simply put, this is for fast track trials or one day long interim hearings – but see further detail in this Chapter] or
- order **detailed assessment** of the costs by a costs officer [simply put, this is for multi-track trials or more than one day long interim hearings – but see further detail in this Chapter] ,

  unless any rule, PD or other enactment provides otherwise.

An order for costs will be treated as an order for the amount of costs to be decided by a detailed assessment unless the order otherwise provides.

EM: court powers in relation to misconduct

Where a party or that party's legal representative, in connection with a summary or detailed assessment, fails to comply with a rule, PD or court order, or it appears to the court that the conduct of a party or that party's legal representative, before or during the proceedings or in the assessment proceedings, was unreasonable or improper, the court may

- disallow all or part of the costs which are being assessed or
- order the party at fault or that party's legal representative to pay costs which that party or legal representative has caused any other party to incur.

Where the court makes such an order against a legally represented party and the party is not present when the order is made, the party's legal representative must notify that party in writing of the order no later than 7 days after the legal representative receives notice of the order.

EM: summary assessment of costs

Summary assessment is where the court determines costs there and then at the end of the hearing or trial, after judgment has been given.

Unless there is good reason not to do so, [for example where the paying party shows substantial grounds for disputing the sum claimed for costs that cannot be dealt with summarily], there will be **summary assessment of costs** (not applicable where litigants are publicly funded) where what is being heard is

- **a fast-track trial or**
- **a one-day long or shorter "any other hearing" i.e. interim application hearing.**

For these two, it is the duty of the parties and their legal representatives to assist the judge in making a summary assessment of costs applies, in accordance with the following:

Each party who intends to claim costs must prepare a **written statement of those costs** showing separately in the form of a schedule –

- the number of hours to be claimed;
- the hourly rate to be claimed;
- the grade of fee earner;
- the amount and nature of any disbursement to be claimed, other than counsel's fee for appearing at the hearing;
- the amount of legal representative's costs to be claimed for attending or appearing at the hearing;
- counsel's fees; and
- any VAT to be claimed on these amounts.

The statement of costs must be **filed** at court and **copies of it must be served on any party** against whom an order for payment of those costs is intended to be sought as soon as possible and in any event

- **for a fast-track trial -** the order will deal with the costs of the whole claim - parties must file the statement of costs **not less than 2 days before the trial**;

- **for a one-day long or shorter "any other hearing" i.e. interim application hearing,** - the order will deal with the costs of the application or matter to which the hearing related, If this hearing disposes of the claim, the order may deal with the costs of the whole claim - **not less than 24 hours before the time fixed for the hearing.**

Failure to do the above, without reasonable excuse, will be taken into account by the court in deciding what order to make about

- the costs of the claim, hearing or application, and
- the costs of any further hearing or detailed assessment hearing that may be necessary as a result of that failure.

That could mean

- adjournment for a short period to allow the losing party to consider a late statement of the winner's costs. In this case the Judge would consider the summary assessment with added leniency towards the losing, paying party; or
- adjournment to a later date for summary assessment before the same judge or for summary assessment in writing; or
- adjournment for further, detailed assessment.

CUR 23.2 ASSESSMENT OF COSTS

COSTS ON THE STANDARD BASIS OR

COSTS ON THE INDEMNITY BASIS

EM: factors taken into account in deciding amount of costs

Note that In particular, the court will give effect to any orders which have already been made.

Note that the court has power to limit the amount that a party may recover with regard to the fees and expenses of an expert. (Expert evidence is addressed in Chapter 22 of this book). One factor which is taken into account is the **BASIS on which costs are assessed.** This will be either on the standard or on the indemnity basis but the court will not in either case allow costs which have been unreasonably incurred or are unreasonable in amount.

Where there is no reference in a costs order to either the standard basis or the indemnity basis, or the court makes an order for costs to be assessed on a basis other than the standard basis or the indemnity basis, the basis of assessment will be the standard basis.

EM: standard basis of assessment

The **standard basis** is the most usual way for the costs for the legal adviser of the receiving winner to be assessed. This is the case when, with regard to all the circumstances the court decides that those costs have been

- **proportionately and reasonably incurred**, or
- are of a **proportionate and reasonable amount**.

Full costs will **not be allowed** if the court considers that

- they have been **unreasonably incurred** or are of an **unreasonable amount**
- they have been disproportionately incurred or are of disproportionate in amount.

Costs which are disproportionate in amount may be disallowed or reduced even if they were reasonably or necessarily incurred and costs incurred are proportionate if they bear a reasonable relationship to

- the sums in issue in the proceedings
- the value of any non-monetary relief in issue in the proceedings
- the complexity of the litigation
- any additional work generated by the conduct of the paying party; and
- any wider factors involved in the proceedings, such as reputation or public importance.

– it has doubts as to whether they were reasonably or proportionately incurred, or whether they are reasonable and proportionate in amount. If there is any doubt about whether or not the winning party's costs are reasonable and proportionate, any **residual doubt will be resolved in favour of the paying loser**, so that at the worst extreme, the costs of the receiving winning party could be disallowed. Here the court will take into account

- the conduct of the parties pre-and per proceedings. Including e.g. how successful C has been, i.e. has there been any reduction in damages for C's contributory negligence?
- efforts made to resolve the case
- any admissible offers to settle
- the value and importance to the parties, the complexity of the case, time spent and work done on the case
- the receiving party's last approved or agreed budget.

EM: indemnity basis of assessment

When, with regard to all the circumstances, the court decides that costs were

- **unreasonably incurred** or
- **unreasonable in amount**

it may award costs on the **indemnity basis,** disallowing unreasonable costs. This is punitive of the poor conduct of a losing opponent. **Any doubt** as to the **reasonableness** of the legal adviser costs of the receiving winner (note that there is no reference to proportionality) will be made **in favour of the winning receiving party** (so indemnifying the winning party for the poor conduct of the losing party).

An example of poor conduct in October 2018, was where C discontinued the case very late - four days into a six week trial. C was ordered to pay D's costs on the indemnity basis.

– Finally, can costs budgets apply to the fast track?

The next section on multi-track and costs includes detail on costs budgets in costs management. It is worthy of note that as CPR 3.1(2)(ll) provides that the court may "order any party to file and exchange a costs budget", it is possible that costs budgets could be ordered on the fast track too. The PD on case management provides that in all cases the court will have regard to the need for litigation to be conducted justly and at proportionate cost in accordance with the overriding objective.

Multi-track and costs

The multi-track is the normal track for any claim for which the small claims track or the fast track is not the normal track. So claims likely to be allocated to the multi-track are

- £>25K
- Claims of real public importance / complex
- Part 8 claims (These are explained in Chapter 10 of this book.)

There are further considerations to which the court will have regard when deciding to which track to allocate a claim. These are set out in Chapter 19.

The **costs** between the parties

As for the fast track, first remember to include that

- The starting point is that **loser pays winner's costs**
- The **court has discretion** and so may make a different order having regard to all circumstances including

  - **how the parties have conducted themselves**
  - **the level of success of the winner**
  - **any admissible offer to settle**;

  So it may be that the **loser pays winner's costs principle may be adjusted**.

CUR 23.1

DETAILED METHOD OF

ASSESSMENT OF COSTS

- Next, the **METHOD of assessing costs.** This will be **detailed assessment.**

  EM: detailed assessment of costs
  The general rule is that the costs of any proceedings or any part of the proceedings are not to be assessed by the detailed procedure until the conclusion of the proceedings, but the court may order them to be assessed immediately. So once there has been an order which entitles a party to costs, a court can expressly order detailed assessment to take place before the conclusion of the proceedings.

  There will be **detailed assessment of costs** where what is being heard is

  - **A multi –track case**

  - **An interim application hearing of more than one day**

  (Where litigants are publicly funded, the provisions for detailed assessment of those cases are in CPR 47.18) which is not on your syllabus this year. For litigants who are not publicly funded, detailed assessment takes place as follows.

In addition, where the amount of costs is not agreed by the parties, the court can order detailed assessment by a costs officer who decides the amount of costs payable by one party to the other. The likely costs order is therefore "final order for costs to be assessed if not agreed"

It must be commenced by the receiving party serving **notice of commencement and the bill of costs** on the paying party within **3 months** of any of the following

- final judgment
- end of the claim by discontinuance [dealt with in Chapter 19 of this book]
- date of an order lifting a stay
- end of the claim by acceptance of a part 36 offer. [You will learn about this way of ending a claim in Chapter 7 of this book].

Points of dispute should be served **within 21 days** of receiving notice of commencement of assessment and the accompanying documents.

Replies to points of dispute (if any) should be served **within 21 days** of receiving the points of dispute.

The court will order the paying party to pay a reasonable sum on account of costs before the detailed assessment so that the winning party's legal advisers get at least some payment straight away, unless there is a good reason not to do so.

Where there is an **appeal**, **detailed assessment is NOT stayed** whilst the appeal is pending unless the court so orders.

EM: fees of counsel

When making an order for costs the court may state an opinion as to whether or not the hearing was fit for the attendance of one or more counsel, and, if it does so, the court conducting a detailed assessment of those costs will have regard to the opinion stated.

The court will generally express an opinion only where

- the paying party asks it to do so
- more than one counsel appeared for a party or
- the court wishes to record its opinion that the case was not fit for the attendance of counsel.

Real property

Where a case was about real property and the court refers any matter (investigating title, reporting on title, preparing documents) to the conveyancing counsel of the court, the fees payable to counsel in respect of the work done or to be done will be assessed by the court in accordance with the matters set out in the section above entitled "court's discretion as to costs".

An appeal from a decision of the court in respect of the fees of such counsel will be dealt with under the general rules as to appeals (please see the final Chapter of this book).

If the appeal is against the decision of an authorised court officer, appeal lies to a costs judge or a district judge of the High Court. The appellant must file an appeal notice within 21 days after the date of the decision against which it is sought to appeal. On receipt of the appeal notice, the court will serve a copy of the notice on the parties to the detailed assessment proceedings and give notice of the appeal hearing to those parties. The court will re-hear the proceedings which gave rise to the decision appealed against and make any order and give any directions as it considers appropriate.

CUR 23.2

COSTS ON THE STANDARD BASIS OR

COSTS ON THE INDEMNITY BASIS

- Next, the **BASIS on which costs are assessed,** again, either standard or indemnity basis as for fast track.

- On the multi-track there is an **addition** to the list for what the court will have regard to when resolving any doubt about the reasonableness of the winning party's costs:

judges will have regard to **the amount agreed in the final costs budget**

EM: costs budgets
EM: filing and exchanging budgets [and budget discussion reports]

Unless the court otherwise orders, all parties except litigants in person must file and exchange budgets

- where the stated value of the claim on the claim form is less than £50,000, with their directions questionnaires; or
- in any other case, not later than 21 days before the first case management conference.

A litigant in person, even though not required to prepare a budget, must nevertheless be provided with a copy of the budget of any other party.

All other parties, not being litigants in person, must file an agreed budget discussion report, using Precedent R, no later than 7 days before the first case management conference (see Chapter 19).

Only Precedent H, the outline of which is annexed to PD 3E and the budget discussion report need to lodged for costs budgeting purposes. These forms are available in Excel format on the Ministry of Justice website so that totals are automatically calculated. They must be in landscape format with an easily legible typeface.

In cases where a party's budgeted costs do not exceed £25,000 or the value of the claim as stated on the claim form is less than £50,000, the parties must only use the first page of Precedent H.

Save in exceptional circumstances the recoverable costs of initially completing Precedent H shall not exceed the higher of £1,000 or 1% of the approved or agreed budget. All other recoverable costs of the budgeting and costs management process shall not exceed 2% of the approved or agreed budget.

The costs budgets must be verified by a statement of truth, the wording for a statement of truth verifying a budget is set out in Practice Direction 22, note 2.2A,

"This budget is a fair and accurate statement of incurred and estimated costs which it would be reasonable and proportionate for my client to incur in this litigation".

If interim applications are made (the "what-ifs" in Chapters 13 – 17 of this book) which, reasonably, were not included in a budget, then the costs of such interim applications shall be treated as additional to the approved budgets.

Failure to file a budget

EM: The following is the specific leading case authority with which students should be familiar (and should be able to refer to by name): Denton.

If a party does not file a budget, or fails to file it within 7 days prior to the date of the first hearing (pressure of work on lawyers being no excuse to this mandatory requirement) the sanction is that he or she is taken to have filed one which deals only with the applicable court fees (CPR 3.14.This will be referred to again in Chapter 7). Courts will not depart from approved/agreed costs budgets when making orders as to costs at the end of the trial unless satisfied there is a good reason to do so. (The Courts do seem to be applying this to the letter, refusing to grant relief from this sanction. (There is one exception to this which you will learn in Chapter 7. It is what I will be referring to as the 50% costs budget point).

The criteria which the court considers should any party apply for relief from this (or any) sanction are set out in CPR 3.9. Full details are in Chapter 19 of this book, where the case of **Denton & Ors v White & Ors [2014] EWCA Civ 906** appears.

If a detailed assessment of the receiving party's costs reveals greater costs claimed than the lower costs budget figure

Where there is a **difference of 20%** or more between the costs claimed by a receiving party on detailed assessment and the lower costs shown in a budget filed by that party

- the receiving party must provide a statement of the **reasons for the difference with the bill of costs.**

  Where it appears to the court that the receiving party has **not provided a satisfactory explanation for that difference**, the court may regard the difference between the costs claimed and the costs shown in the budget as **evidence that the costs claimed are unreasonable or disproportionate.**

- If a **paying party claims to have reasonably relied** on a budget filed by a receiving party **or relies** upon the costs shown in the budget in **order to dispute the reasonableness or proportionality** of the costs claimed, that paying party must **serve a statement setting out the case** in this regard in that party's points of dispute.

  Where it appears to the court that the paying party reasonably relied on the budget, the **court may restrict the recoverable costs** to such sum as is reasonable for the paying party to pay in the light of that reliance, notwithstanding that such sum is less than the amount of costs reasonably and proportionately incurred by the receiving party.

The second section of this Chapter

CUR 13.4 COSTS MANAGEMENT

EM: costs management

Here is the next stage of case management by the Court. Remember that Chapter 2 first introduced case management by the court.

The purpose of costs management following costs budgets (which must be prepared on the multi-track) is that the court should manage both the steps to be taken and the costs to be incurred by the parties to any proceedings, so as to further the overriding objective.

Before looking further at costs management, here is an explanation of when costs management does **not** come into play, even though the claim is on the multi-track.

So **NOT**

- Part 8 claims (see Chapter 10) where the court is to approve a settlement on behalf of a child

- Part 7 claims (see Chapter 10) commenced on or after 22nd April 2014 which are
  - subject to fixed costs;
  - subject to scale costs (these are used in intellectual property claims),
  - >£10million
  - stated to be valued at >£10million, although no full quantification has been given; nor
  - cases where the Claimant has a limited or severely impaired life expectation (5 years or less remaining); nor
  - proceedings commenced on or after 6th April 2016 where a claim is made by or on behalf of a person under the age of 18 (a child) (and on a child reaching majority this exception will continue to apply unless the court otherwise orders); nor
  - those where the court orders otherwise.

  although the PD on costs management provides that the court does nevertheless have discretion to make an order requiring parties to those claims to file cost budgets in the Part 8 and Part 7 situations above.

  So, in these cases, at an early stage in the litigation the parties **should consider** and, where practicable, discuss whether to apply for an order for the provision of costs budgets, with a view to a costs management order being made.

  The PD sets out situations where this may be appropriate, e.g. personal injury and clinical negligence cases where the value of the claim is £10 million or more.

  If all parties consent to an application for an order for provision of costs budgets, the court will (other than in exceptional cases) make such an order.

Thus we can extrapolate that on the **multi track** where costs budgets are always necessary, **apart from those exceptions above, the court may get involved in case management of those budgets in all other multi track cases.**

So case management can happen
- in Part 8 claims which are always multi track claims, not mentioned above
- any Part 8 or other claims or applications involving a substantial dispute of fact and/or likely to require oral evidence and/or extensive disclosure[8]
- in Part 7 claims multi track claims including applications not mentioned above,
- cases where fixed costs are not applied
- cases of between £25k and £10million
- cases of real public importance
- personal injury and clinical negligence cases where the value of the claim is £10 million or more[9]

EM: court regard to budgets in making case management decisions
EM: costs management conferences

In addition to exercising its other powers, the court may manage the costs to be incurred (the budgeted costs) by any party in any proceedings.

Any hearing which is convened solely for the purpose of costs management (for example, to approve a revised budget) is referred to as a 'costs management conference'. Where practicable, costs management conferences should be conducted by telephone or in writing.

EM: costs management orders

Where costs budgets are filed and exchanged, the court will generally make a costs management order.

If a costs management order has been made, the court will thereafter control the parties' budgets in respect of recoverable costs.

When a costs management order will not be made

- An order will not be made if the court is satisfied that the litigation can be conducted justly and at proportionate cost in accordance with the overriding objective without such an order being made.

- The court does not have to get involved by making case management orders. In fact a case management order cannot be made if a court considers a party's costs to be disproportionate, exceeding the value of the claim. In this even the courts will tell the parties to redress that and the costs budgets should then be filed and served again.

Court regard to last filed budget when assessing in costs at the end of trial

Where the parties have filed budgets but the court has not made a costs management order, the winner's recoverable **costs will be assessed by reference to the last approved or agreed budget** and may have regard to any other budget previously filed by that party, or by

[8] Projected from October 2020
[9] Projected to be from October 2020

any other party in the same proceedings. Such other budgets may be taken into account when assessing the reasonableness and proportionality of any costs claimed.

<u>The making of a costs management order</u>

The making of a costs management order concerns the totals allowed for each phase of the budget. It is not the role of the court in the cost management hearing to fix or approve the hourly rates claimed in the budget. The underlying detail in the budget for each phase used by the party to calculate the totals claimed is provided for reference purposes only to assist the court in fixing a budget.

<u>Content of a costs management order</u>

By a costs management order the court

- will record
  - the extent to which the budgeted costs are agreed between the parties
  - the court's approval after making appropriate revisions in respect of the budgeted costs which are not agreed
  - the extent (if any) to which incurred costs are agreed. As part of the costs management process the court may not approve costs incurred before the date of any costs management hearing. The court may, however, record its comments on those costs and will take those costs into account when considering the reasonableness and proportionality of all budgeted costs.

- may set a timetable or give other directions for future reviews of budgets.

If a costs management order has been made, the court will thereafter control the parties' budgets in respect of recoverable costs.

The court's approval of costs budgets will relate only to the total figures for budgeted costs of each phase of the proceedings, although in the course of its review the court may have regard to the constituent elements of each total figure. When reviewing budgeted costs, the court will not undertake a detailed assessment in advance, but rather will consider whether the budgeted costs fall within the range of reasonable and proportionate costs.

Parties can **file amended** budgets as the case proceeds, for **court** consideration and **approval.**

Each party must revise its budget in respect of future costs upwards or downwards, if significant developments in the litigation warrant such revisions. Such amended budgets are to be submitted to the other parties for agreement. In default of agreement, the amended budgets shall be submitted to the court, together with a note of

- the changes made and the reasons for those changes and
- the objections of any other party. The court may approve, vary or disapprove the revisions, having regard to any significant developments which have occurred since the date when the previous budget was approved or agreed.

After its budgeted costs have been approved or agreed, each party has to re-file and re-serve the budget in the form approved or agreed with re-cast figures, annexed to the order approving the budgeted costs or recording the parties' agreement.

Court regard to costs management order when assessing costs at the end of trial

In any case where a costs management order has been made, when assessing costs on the standard basis, the court will have regard to the receiving party's last approved or agreed budget for each phase of the proceedings. The court will not depart from such approved or agreed budget unless satisfied that there is good reason to do so.

Whether or not the court has made a costs management order

When making any case management decision the court will have regard to any available budgets of the parties and will take into account the costs involved in each procedural step, considering whether the budgeted costs fall within the range of **reasonable and proportionate** costs and the steps that parties will be ordered to take to prepare for trial.

Whether or not the court makes a costs management order, it may record on the face of any case management order any comments it has about the incurred costs which are to be taken into account in any subsequent assessment proceedings.

EM: Costs in ADR

Activity

Remember to incorporate the relevant paragraphs from The Jackson ADR Handbook (Second Edition, 2016)

10.01
10.03

You may find it useful to make your notes here, below this box.

Costs in ADR (your notes)

Costs in ADR (your notes continued)

Chapter 6

Elements of the syllabus which you have now covered **in civil litigation and evidence**

- A cell with heavy outlining means that that area of the syllabus was covered in this Chapter;
- A darkly shaded cell with a tick √ means that the whole of that syllabus element has now been covered;
- A lightly shaded cell means that part of that element of the syllabus has been covered in a previous Chapter; and
- An unshaded cell means that element of the syllabus has not yet been covered.

1.1 √	1.2 √	1.3 √	2.1	2.2	3.1	3.2	6.1	6.2	6.3
6.4	7.1	7.2	8.1	8.2	8.3	9.1	9.2	9.3	10.1
10.2	11.1	11.2	12.1	12.2	12.3	13.1	13.2	13.3 √	13.4 √
13.5	13.6	13.7	13.8	14.1	14.2	14.3	14.4	14.5	14.6
15.1	15.2 √	15.3 √	15.4 √	16.1	16.2	17.1	17.2	17.3	17.4
18.2	18.3	18.4 18.5	19.1	19.2	19.3	20.1	20.2	20.3	21.1
21.2	21.3	22.1	22.2	23.1 √	23.2 √	23.3	23.4 √	22.1	

Chapter 7

SETTLEMENT (INCLUDING OFFERS TO SETTLE) [CUR 18]

g) Offers to settle

THIS CHAPTER CONTAINS THE ITEMS PRINTED IN BOLD IN THE FOLLOWING BOXES

CURRICULUM ("CUR)

Settlement (including offers to settle)

18.1 negotiation and joint settlement meetings
18.2 Calderbank offers and offers to settle under Part 36
18.3 consequences of accepting Part 36 offers
18.4 withdrawing, reducing and increasing offers to settle
18.5 consequences of failing to obtain judgment more advantageous than offer to settle

You will recall from Chapter 5 the importance of trying to settle differences without it becoming a litigious matter which proceeds to trial.

There are further refences to settlement in Chapters 1 and 9.

SYLLABUS

Examinable material will consist of negotiation and joint settlement meetings ,Calderbank offers and offers to settle under Part 36, form and content of Part 36 offers, time when a Part 36 offer is made, clarification of a Part 36 offer, withdrawing or changing the terms of a Part 36 offer, acceptance of a Part 36 offer, costs consequences and effects of accepting a Part 36 offer, restrictions on disclosure of a Part 36 offer and costs consequences following judgment.

(Each of the above has its own subheading in this Chapter, flagged by EM:)

- **Relevant ADR references to The Jackson ADR Handbook (Second Edition, 2016) are incorporated in context in this Chapter, highlighted in an Activity box between two lightning flashes.**
- **CPR 36.1**
- **CPR 36.2 (Part 36 Offers to Settle)**
- **CPR 36.13 (costs consequences of acceptance of a Part36 offer) and**
- **CPR 36.17 (costs consequences following judgment).**
- **CPR 36.3-11 and**
- **CPR 36.14-16**
- **The following specific leading case authority (which students should be able to refer to by name): *Calderbank.***
- **Commentary is incorporated in context in this Chapter, highlighted in an Activity box between two stars.**
- In this book Paragraph 8.07 of The Jackson ADR Handbook (Second Edition, 2016) is in Chapter 1

Chapter 7 MOCS

- ***Negotiation and Joint Settlement Meetings***
- ***Calderbank Offers***
- ***Offers to settle under part 36***
  - ***Form and content of a Part 36 Offer***
  - ***Consequences of accepting a Part 36 Offer***
    - ***during the Relevant Period***
    - ***after the Relevant Period***
  - ***Withdrawing a Part 36 offer to settle before or after the Relevant Period***
  - ***Reducing a Part 36 offer to settle before or after the Relevant Period***
  - ***Increasing a Part 36 offer to settle after the Relevant Period***

- **Consequences of failing to beat a reasonable Part 36 Offer that was rejected**

offer	end of RP	offeree 'fails to beat' the offer / trial
	trial loser pays winner's costs to end RP	**offeree PENALISED by having to pay offeror's costs for this part of proceedings Remember that the way these costs are worked out depends on whether offeror was D or C**

The sessions dealing with this area of the syllabus on my BTC course are	

CUR 18.1 NEGOTIATION AND JOINT SETTLEMENT MEETINGS

Negotiation

As you would expect, negotiation may be characterised as a discussion between parties and their lawyers, or between just their lawyers following client instructions (which they must not exceed!). The aim is to achieve a settlement without pursuing the case to litigation, thus avoiding the difficult emotions and the expense that going to court would entail.

Counsel should prepare with the client his or her best and worst alternatives to a negotiated settlement.

Reaching a negotiated settlement may depend on both your and the other side's negotiating styles. Co-operative and collaborative styles may be more conducive to settlement than competitive and positional styles.

Always remember to take a full record of the negotiated settlement before you leave the negotiation! We will meet recording settlements again in Chapter 25.

If a negotiation settles the dispute and the claim is already underway, remember also to inform the court that the case has settled and get it stayed. You met stays in Chapter 5 and will meet them again in Chapters 11 and 19.

Activity

Remember to incorporate the relevant paragraphs from The Jackson ADR Handbook (Second Edition, 2016):-

In this book Paragraph 8.07 is in Chapter 1
12.03-12.04,
12.13-12.14
12.16
12.17

You may find it useful to make your notes here, below this box.

Negotiation and Joint Settlement Meetings (your notes)

Negotiation and Joint Settlement Meetings (your notes continued)

CUR 18.2 CALDERBANK OFFERS AND OFFERS TO SETTLE UNDER PART 36

EM: Calderbank offers and offers to settle under Part 36

CALDERBANK OFFERS	**OFFERS TO SETTLE UNDER PART 36**
An offer set out in a letter; or A non part 36 compliant offer	Part 36 contains a self-contained procedural code about offers to settle made pursuant to the procedure set out in it.
A letter containing a settlement offer which is made on a "without prejudice except as to costs" basis. See below and Chapter 20.	A Part 36 offer is treated as "without prejudice except as to costs". See below and Chapter 20.
This means that where there is a bona fide attempt to settle **the court has no knowledge of the offer** but after the trial may take it into account when exercising its discretion as to costs.	
	Please also see further later in this Chapter on Part 36 restrictions on disclosure to the court..
The court has discretion to decide what weight is given to the offer when using its discretion as to costs. The letter influences but does not govern court discretion.	The court does not have the same amount of discretion to decide what weight is given to the offer. Please refer to the remainder of this Chapter regarding the certainty as to costs that Part 36 can bring.
No more than persuasive re costs consequences of not accepting the offer	Results in clear costs consequences for not accepting an acceptable offer
Use where you want costs to be dealt with in a way different to that imposed by a Part 36 offer	Use where you want costs to have the consequences set out in Part 36. There is more certainty as to how litigation costs will be treated.
More flexible	Strict rules
No restrictions as to the terms of an offer	There are restrictions regarding the form and content of an offer. Please see later in this Chapter.

CALDERBANK OFFERS	OFFERS TO SETTLE UNDER PART 36
Use where D wants to make an offer to settle but feels that she cannot make the payment within 14 days	Unless the parties agree otherwise in writing, payments of an agreed single sum must be made within 14 days of acceptance / or within 14 days of a court order for provisional damages or for periodical payments, unless the court order states otherwise. If not paid by then, C may enter judgment for the unpaid sum. A **defendant's offer** that includes an offer to pay all or part of the sum at a date later than 14 days following the date of acceptance will not be treated as a Part 36 offer unless the claimant offeree accepts the offer Where there is acceptance of a Part 36 offer (or part of a Part 36 offer) which is not payable within the 14 days referred to above and a party alleges that the other party has
	not honoured the terms of the offer, that party may apply to enforce the terms of the offer without the need for a new claim.
Use these where you want to impose a limited time for acceptance of the offer. Once accepted, there is a binding contract between the parties. i.e. you can say what you want in the letter.	Time limited offers are also now possible in Part 36 offers in relation to withdrawal of an offer after the end of the relevant period – see later in this Chapter. Otherwise offers remain open to acceptance unless and until the offer is withdrawn in writing. Please refer further to the section on acceptance later in this Chapter.
Use where Part 36 does not apply – e.g. small claims track and arbitration proceedings.	

General outline and background to Part 36

Dealing with costs can become a very tactical matter.

Part 36 is a formalised system, **outside of the normal rules of contract**, to motivate parties to agree to acceptable offers to settle a claim and so avoid the need and cost of going through proceedings to trial.

We will see later in this Chapter how, in relation to accepting, withdrawing, reducing or increasing an offer, the terminology is simply 'offeror' or 'offeree' as appropriate.

We will see later in the final seven pages of this Chapter how in relation to cost consequences of not accepting a reasonable offer, there are two separate sets of rules within Part 36 to be followed:

- In the first set of rules [the author's terminology], an **offer** may be made **by D** to pay an amount to C to settle (so D is the offeror and C is the offeree) (scenarios (i-iii) in this Chapter);
  - **(scenario (i)** shows when there are **no costs consequences** in refusal by the claimant offeree as the offer was clearly unacceptable since D offered (a lot) less that C won);
  - **(scenario (ii)** shows where there **are cost consequences** in refusal by the claimant offeree, because at trial C failed to beat the defendant's offer, as C's claim was dismissed);
  - **(scenario (iii)** shows where there **are cost consequences** in refusal by the claimant offeree, because C failed to beat the defendant's offer, as C won only the same or less that D's offer) or

- In the second set of rules [the author's terminology], an **offer** may be made **by C** to D where C offers to accept an amount from D to settle the matter, (where C is the offeror and D is the offeree) **(scenario (iv)** in this Chapter).

Refusal by the offeree of a reasonable offer, be it under the author's terminology of the first or second set of rules, will entail costs consequences for the refuser who is likely to have to pay the most expensive part of the costs of the proceedings of the other party, in the court's discretion, as a "penalty" for having taken the matter all the way to trial, when accepting the reasonable offer would have avoided the expense of a trial.

A Part 36 offer may be made in respect of the whole, or part of, or any issue that arises in

- a claim, counterclaim or other additional claim or
- an appeal or cross-appeal from a decision made at a trial.

  In Chapter 12 we will confirm that counterclaims and other additional claims are treated as claims and that references to a C or a D include a party bringing or defending an additional claim.

<u>EM: time when a Part 36 offer is made</u>

A party may make an offer at any time, even before proceedings are started.

The offer is made when it is deemed served on the offeree in accordance with part 6 of the CPR. It is accepted on deemed service of the notice of acceptance (Detail of part 6 is dealt with in Chapter 10 of this book).

Where a Part 36 offer was made in the main proceedings, a new offer needs to be made where a party wants Part 36 protection in relation to an appeal.

Remember that there are cost penalties (i.e. the costs of proceeding onwards to an unnecessary trial) in the form of **cost consequences following judgment**

- for a claimant who does not accept acceptable offers from D, then C fails to obtain judgment for an amount more advantageous at trial than was earlier offered to him; or

- for a defendant who does not accept acceptable offers from C where the judgment against D is at least as advantageous to C as was C's offer.

Remember that

- for acceptance after the Relevant Period
- for scenarios (i-iii), for both the time period to the end RP and the time period from the end of RP, and
- for scenario (iv) to the end of RP the usual basis for assessing costs, unless changed by the court, is the **standard basis**.
- The court could, using its discretion, order that they be paid on the indemnity basis (e.g. if conduct is in issue)

Note, however, that in **scenario (iv)** the costs for post RP are always on the **indemnity basis**.

Remember also that there are times when the court may depart from the costs orders set out in the tables in this Chapter – there are orders that the court must make "unless it is unjust to do so."

- **Do note where these instances occur in the tables in this Chapter.**
- **Do note below the matters which the court takes into consideration**
  - Part 36 sets out what the court must take into consideration when deciding whether it would be unjust not to adjust the costs awards set out in part 36. That is
    - all the circumstances of the case including
      - the terms of the offer
      - how long before trial it was made
      - the information available to the parties at the time when the Part 36 offer was made
      - the conduct of the parties with regard to the giving of or refusal to give information for the purposes of enabling the offer to be made or evaluated
      - whether it was a genuine attempt to settle

      Where it is decided that adjustments are to be made, where that adjustment is as to interest, total interest on the claim must not exceed 10% above base rate.

      Examples of adjustments the court can make in the circumstances include
      - reducing the amount of costs payable
      - changing the basis of costs awarded from the standard basis to the indemnity basis
      - adding further interest to be paid
- **Do note also how the commentary in the starred activity boxes later in this Chapter fits into this consideration of when it is unjust to make the orders set out in the tables in this Chapter,**

<u>EM: form and content of Part 36 offers</u>

<u>Form and content of an offer</u>

It must be
- In writing
- Make clear it is made pursuant to part 36
- State whether the offer relates to the **whole claim** or **part of the claim,** or to **an issue** in the claim and if so to which issue

- State whether it takes into account a counterclaim
- Specify (this is CPR 36.5 (1) (c)) a period of not less than 21 days where if C (the offeree) accepts the offer during this period, thus making C the winner, then the loser (the offeror) D pays the C's winner's costs and the claim is at an end; please see further the activity box below about this, the **relevant period.**

If the offer is invalid for wrong form or content, the court will still include knowledge of it when considering what order to make as to costs.

Activity

Calculation of the relevant period [CPR 36.3(g)]

Refer to CPR 36.3 (g) in the White Book and note it here, to help you understand the definition of the relevant period ("RP")

Activity

Calculation of the relevant period [CPR 36.3(g)] continued

Now see further about the relevant period on acceptance and on withdrawing or changing by reducing or changing by increasing the terms of a Part 36 offer later in this Chapter.

Part 36 offers include interest, so an offer "to pay "£500" or to "accept £500" is [£*x* plus interest = £500 to the end of the RP]; Or, if the offer is made within 21 days of the start of a trial the RP runs to the end of the trial and interest is included until 21 days after the offer was made.

An offer stays open unless and until it is withdrawn, either by written notice or because it is a time limited offer and so interest will continue to accrue.

So, in relation to the example scenarios later in this Chapter, to see whether or not C has obtained a judgment more advantageous at trial than was earlier offered to C, one will need to calculate as appropriate either £*x* + interest to end of RP + accruing interest to date of trial; or £x +interest to 21 days after the offer + any accruing interest should the trail continue for longer than that

EM: clarification of a Part 36 offer

Within 7 days of an offer, the offeree may request clarification.

If the offeror does not give the clarification requested within 7 days of receiving the request, the offeree may, unless the trial has started, make a Part 23 application for an order that the offeror do so.

If such an order is granted, the court must specify the date on which the offer is to be treated as made.

EM: restrictions on disclosure of a Part 36 offer

A Part 36 offer is treated as 'without prejudice except as to costs'. This means that where there is a bona fide attempt to settle in this way, **the court has no knowledge of the offer** but after the trial may take it into account when exercising its discretion as to costs.
Judges are not told about the existence or terms of unaccepted offer until liability and quantum have been finalised at the trial, i.e. until the case has been decided, **unless all parties agree in writing**. If the secrecy is breached the judge can

- continue with trial if s/he is satisfied that there is no prejudice to either side, having regard to the overriding objective; or
- s/he can withdraw from the case.

Where there are split trials, there are circumstances where the court will have some knowledge of the offer(s). A trial is split when a judge, as part of case management decides than any issue in the case could or should be dealt with separately. So a trial can be a trial of all the issues or a trial of liability, quantum, or some other issue in the case.

- Thus the judge may be told about the terms of an unaccepted offer even though the whole case has not been "decided" where any part of, or **issue** in, the case has been **decided and the part 36 offer related only to that**. This means that judges do not find themselves in the position of having to decide whether to make a costs order in respect of preliminary issues following a trial of preliminary issues without knowing whether a part 36 offer has been made.

- Then, where any part of, or issue in, the case has been decided, the judge may be told of **the existence of all part 36 offers in respect of other parts of the case**,
    - but must **not** be told the **terms** of it/them **unless all parties agree in writing**.

CUR 16.3 CONSEQUENCES OF ACCEPTING PART 36 OFFERS

EM: acceptance of a Part 36 offer
EM: costs consequences and effects of accepting a Part 36 offer

- Stay

If a Part 36 offer is accepted, the **claim** will be **stayed.** If the offer relates to the whole claim, the stay will be upon the terms of the offer.

If a Part 36 offer which relates to part only of the claim is accepted, the claim will be stayed as to that part upon the terms of the offer.

- If the approval of the court is required before a settlement can be binding, e.g when C is under a disability, i.e. a child or of mental incapacity, any stay which would otherwise arise on the acceptance of a Part 36 offer will take effect only when that approval has been given.

- Any stay arising under this rule will not affect the power of the court to enforce the terms of a Part 36 offer; or to deal with any question of costs (including interest on costs) relating to the proceedings.

- Acceptance of a Part 36 offer made by one or more, but not all, defendants

If the defendants are sued jointly or in the alternative

C may accept the offer if he discontinues the claim against those defendants who have not made the offer; and those defendants give written consent to the acceptance of the offer.

If C alleges that the defendants have a several liability to him

C may accept the offer; and continue with the claims against the other defendants if entitled to do so.

In all other cases

C must apply to the court for permission to accept the Part 36 offer.

- The remainder of this section on accepting Part 36 offers now continues in table form on the next page.

*****For all diagrams in this Chapter, please read DOWN each column of the table, left hand column first, right hand column second*****

Note, the non-bold text relates to the period between the offer and the end of the RP.

The bold text relates to the time between the end of the RP and the trial/beyond [J denotes judgment].

Italicised wording is applicable to both during RP and after RP.

Accepting a Part 36 offer – continued.

RP 21 days or as agreed	[or RP to end of trial if offer made within 21 days trial - when acceptance here, liability for costs must be determined by the court unless the parties have agreed the costs.]] Trial J
Offer-→	→
Offeree ideally accepts offer within RP, as accepting a reasonable offer avoids cost consequences as set out on the right hand side of this table and. in the scenarios later in this Chapter.	**Offeree can accept it after RP until the end of a time limited offer, or otherwise until a written withdrawal **** **** once a trial is in progress, court permission is required to accept it**

The mechanics of accepting

The offeree

- *~writes to the offeror accepting the offer*
- *~files notice of acceptance at court*
- *~serves notice of the acceptance according to part 6 rules on service*

Offer accepted = offeree wins So loser pays winner. Loser 'or pays ALL these standard basis costs to the date of notice of acceptance being served by winner offeree on loser offeror as per part 6 methods and timeframes. If a part 36 offer is regarding only part of the claim and the rest of the claim is abandoned, then the costs re the part claim offer will also be payable on the standard basis unless the court orders otherwise. C's costs include any costs incurred in dealing with D's counterclaim (see Chapter 12) the Part 36 offer states that it takes that into account.	**Offer accepted after RP but the parties cannot agree the liability for costs = unless unjust, court must order** **~ C's costs to end of RP be paid by D offeror; and** **~ C offeree pays*** (see next page) offeror's cost from end RP to date of notice of acceptance as per part 6 methods and timeframes.** **In whiplash claims where the offer was made before receipt of the offeror's fixed costs medical report, then acceptance by C after the end of RP means acceptance more than 21 days.**
End RP	Trial

*****As regards this payment from end RP, had D failed to put in a costs budget then by CPR 3.14 D's costs should technically be limited only to recovery of her court fees. This would mean no incentive for D to make a part 36 offer as C would not accept it, since if C loses at trial C would only have to pay D's court fees, not any other of D's costs for this period. Therefore part 36 provides that in such circumstances, the cost budget defaulting party's costs will still be 50% of the costs that would otherwise be recoverable.**

Please be aware that I am referring to this * as "the 50% costs budget point" and will refer to it again in this shortened form in scenarios ii), iii) and iv) later in this Chapter.**

Activity

Remember to make notes on the relevant case law authorities in paragraphs 36.2.1, 36.2.4, 36.13.1- 3 in the commentary in the White Book.

You may find it useful to add in references to the case law NOW at the appropriate points of this Chapter.

When approaching final revision time, remember to add in the salient findings of the cases at the relevant point in any 'mental crib sheet' into which you have distilled the main points of your learned knowledge.

CUR 18.4 WITHDRAWING, REDUCING AND INCREASING OFFERS TO SETTLE

EM: withdrawing or changing the terms of a Part 36 offer

Offers may provide for their automatic withdrawal at a date set out in the offer. This is known as a time limited offer. If the offer is not accepted within this time limit, it will not have the part 36 consequences set out in this Chapter once it is withdrawn. This is so that an offeror has the opportunity to protect herself, if she so wishes, from being in the position where the offer is open to acceptance for a long time in the future.

If an offer is time limited it is able to be accepted only until the date set out in the offer which, remember, must be for a period of at least 21 days. Thus an offer can be framed so that it is automatically withdrawn either at the end of the RP or any later date set out in the offer.

If an offer is not time limited, it is able to be accepted in the ways set out on the previous page until it is withdrawn. Once it is withdrawn Part 36 consequences will not apply (now the costs assessments set out in Chapter 6 will apply); although the judge will take account of the withdrawn Part 36 offer – and any rejection of that offer – when ruling as to costs. The rules for withdrawing a part 36 offer are set out in the diagram on the next page. Irrespective of whether or not an offer is time limited, the rules for changing. i.e. reducing or increasing a part 36 offer are also set out in the diagram on the next page.

Please read down each column of the table

Note, the non-bold text relates to the period between the offer and the end of the RP, even where this type appears in the right hand column.

The bold text relates to the time between the end of the RP and the trial.

Italicised wording is applicable to both during RP and after RP

End of RP	Trial
RP 21 days or as agreed Offer →	[Or RP to end of trial if offer made within 21 days trial] →
If there has been no notice of acceptance	
Offeror can serve notice, which takes effect at the end of RP - to withdraw an offer; or - to reduce an offer yet Offeree can still serve acceptance notice before end RP. It has effect unless within 7 days of that notice, offeror applies under Part 23 for court permission to withdraw or reduce it. Court may give permission if satisfied there has been a change of circumstances since the original offer and it is in the interests of justice to give permission.	**Either - Offeror can serve written notice which takes effect when served** **~ to withdraw an offer** **~ to reduce an offer** **~ to increase an offer** ▪ ***Where the change of terms makes them more advantageous to the offeree this is a new part 36 offer whose RP begins on service of the written notice of the more advantageous change, not a withdrawal of the earlier offer.*** ***Thus unless the earlier offer is withdrawn there are now two active offers of settlement on the table.*** **Or - A time limited offer automatically ends in accordance with its terms.** [Where there are fewer than 7 days to trial, offeree can still serve acceptance notice before it starts. It has effect, unless before the first day of the trial, offeror applies under Part 23 for court permission to withdraw/change] [Court may give permission if satisfied there has been a change of circumstances since the original offer and it is in the interests of justice to give permission].

EM: costs consequences following judgment

In scenarios (i-iv), [the beginning of each scenario is circled for ease of reference], the parties' costs are

- C's costs to end RP £18,000
- D's costs to end RP £20,000
- C's costs from end RP £53,000
- D's costs from end RP £58,000

It is these amounts in costs that will be payable by the other side in accordance with the rules in the scenarios below.

C's claim is for £95,000.

Examples of Part 36 scenarios

SCENARIOS (I) TO (III)

OFFERS MADE BY D (includes a respondent on an appeal from a trial decision)

Scenario (i) C (includes an appellant on an appeal from a trial decision – note that a part 36 offer at first instance does NOT carry over into an appeal; a fresh offer is needed to cover the appeal) rejects offer then wins at trial winning more than D offered

e.g. D makes an offer of £70k which C rejects. At trial the judge awards C £90k

i.e. C wins and C DID NOT FAIL to obtain judgment more advantageous

No part 36 cost penalty consequences as the offer was clearly not acceptable, therefore rejected and C wins more at trial than D offered In diagram form

C wins more than D offered so CPR 36.17 (1) (a) does not apply

End of RP

C wins £90k at trial

£70k offer RP 21 days or more as agreed

D £70k Offer

So CPR 36.17 (1) (a) does not apply and neither therefore does CPR 36.17 (3) and D is not entitled to her costs from end of RP

General principles, loser pays winner

So D pays C's costs to end RP

General principles, loser pays winner

So D pays C's costs from end RP to trial

End of RP

Trial

With the result that D pays C's costs from the date of the offer to trial

CUR 18.5 CONSEQUENCES OF FAILING TO OBTAIN JUDGMENT MORE ADVANTAGEOUS THAN OFFER TO SETTLE

Where there ARE part 36 cost penalty consequences at trial following rejected offers

First, the implications of Part 36 at it's simplest.

Note that in scenarios (ii) and (iii) it is the DEFENDANT who is making the offer.

Note that in scenario (iv) it is the CLAIMANT who is making the offer.

Where the Defendant or Claimant offeree 'fails to beat' the offer to settle that was made to them – note that the actual wording of Part 36 is more complex than that – then that Defendant or Claimant is PENALISED because they should have gone to Costsavers- ie. Should have accepted the reasonable offer at the time it was made when instead they chose not to and to go forward to trial instead.

Diagrammatically then:

offeree 'fails to beat' the offer

offer

trial loser pays winner's costs to end RP | **offeree PENALISED by having to pay offeror's costs for this part of proceedings**

end of RP — trial

The following pages go on to put much more meat on the bones of this simple version of Part 36.

Scenario (ii)

– C (includes an appellant on an appeal from a trial decision – remember fresh offer needed) rejects reasonable offer then loses at trial (sometimes phrased as "fails to beat". The CPR phrase is 36.17 (1) (a) "C fails to obtain judgment more advantageous"

e.g. D makes an offer of £70k which C rejects. At trial the judge dismisses the claim so

i.e. C loses - 36.17 (1) (a) C fails to obtain judgment more advantageous than the offer

i.e. Consequences of failing to obtain judgment more advantageous than an offer to settle

i.e. The amount of £nil awarded to C offeree is less than the £70k that D offered

Please see the diagram on the next page for an explanation of how

- a C rejected a part 36 offer and
- that C went on to lose their claim as it was dismissed by the judge
- with the result that C is penalised in costs by having to pay D's costs from the end of the relevant period.

Scenario (ii) continued

In diagram form – remember to give the cost consequences both for costs to the end of RP **AND for costs from end RP to trial**.

C loses as judge dismisses claim i.e. 36.17 (1) (a) C fails to obtain more advantageous.

To end of RP	End of RP → C loses at trial as C's claim dismissed
£70k offer RP 21 days or more as agreed	**C Penalised**
D £70k offer →	→
General principles, loser pays winner,	**36.17 (3) court must order D entitled to her costs, including any recoverable pre-action costs unless unjust, + interest**
So C pays D's costs to end RP	**so C pays D's costs from end RP**
i.e. loser pays winner	**i.e. ("loser pays winner" not re general principles, but re CPR 36.17 (3)**
So C pays D's £20k costs as well as own to end RP	**so C pays D's £58k costs as well as own from end RP**
	****** the 50% costs budget point (please refer back to earlier in this Chapter) So here, if D had defaulted on the costs budget, C would pay half x £58k of D's costs (£29K) as well as his own from end RP; D pays own £29k***
Remember if Personal Injury etc. QOCS means D cannot enforce against C to make C pay D's costs without court permission as C has won £nil	**Remember if PI, QOCS means D cannot enforce against C to make C pay D's costs without court permission as C has won £nil**
End RP	Trial

Where 2 offers are active as a ***result of a second improved offer by D,*** *D can refer back to the first early* ***offer and claim costs from C from that date*** *(the " two* ***offers point")***

Scenario (iii) The CLASSIC Part 36 offer by D and costs consequences for C

– C (includes an appellant on an appeal from a trial decision – remember fresh offer needed) rejects offer then wins at trial but wins the same as or less than D offered

e.g. D makes an offer of £70k which C rejects. At trial the judge awards C £70k or less

i.e. C wins BUT- 36.17 (1) (a) C fails to obtain judgment more advantageous.

i.e. Consequences of failing to obtain judgment more advantageous than an offer to settle

Please see the diagram below, continued on the next page for an explanation of how

- a C rejected a part 36 offer and
- that C went on to win their claim
- either for an amount the same as what D offered
- or for an amount less than D offered
- with the result that C is penalised in costs by having to pay D's costs from the end of the relevant period.

C wins same or less than D's offer i.e. 36.17 (1) (a) C fails to obtain judgment more advantageous.

End of RP

C wins £70k or less at trial

£70k offer RP 21 days or more as agreed

D £70k offer→

C Penalised →

Up to end of RP	From end of RP
General principles, loser pays winner,	**36.17 (3) court must order D entitled to her costs, including any recoverable pre- action costs unless unjust, + interest**
So D pays C's costs to end RP	**So C pays D's costs from end RP**
i.e. loser pays winner on standard basis **D lost at trial so D pays C's costs to end RP**	**i.e. Costs do not follow the event. The idea is that C is penalised in costs for not accepting an offer he should have accepted, paying the costs for the other side for the most expensive bit of the process**
THIS CONTINUES ON THE NEXT PAGE.	**THIS CONTINUES ON THE NEXT PAGE.**

So D pays C's £18k costs as well as own.	**So C pays D's £58k costs as well as own.** **These figures can be set off against one another so that C would pay £40k costs to D. (58 minus 18), in post set-off costs** • **The"2 offers point " referred to in scenario (ii) applies to this scenario for post RP costs to be paid by C** • **The 50% costs budget point as in scenario (ii) = C is to pay £29k of D's costs; then set off the £18k to end RP, so C pays (29-18 = £11k post set-off costs) of D's costs as well as own; and D will have to pay the other £29k of her own costs.** **Remember if PI, that due to QOCS,** **D can enforce the costs of D that C is to pay, (only) up to C's £70k damages award +interest without court permission. In our example D could therefore enforce against C for the £40k (or £11k) post set-off costs.** **Now suppose that C won at trial, but only won £30k in this PI case. D can only enforce against C to pay D's costs up to that £30k. This leaves 10k shortfall that D will have to pay of her own costs;** **If D had neglected to put in a costs budget, D can enforce against C for that £11k (as £11k is less than C's award of £30k), but will have to pay the remainder of her own costs herself. (Here £58k post RP costs minus £11k = £47k for D to pay.)**
	End of RP Trial

SCENARIO IV

OFFER MADE BY C (includes an appellant on an appeal from a trial decision)

Scenario (iv)

The same facts apply as in the three previous scenarios, i.e. the parties' costs are

- C's costs to end RP £18,000
- D's costs to end RP £20,000
- C's costs from end RP £53,000
- D's costs from end RP £58,000.

It is these amounts in costs that will be payable by the other side in accordance with the rules in the diagram on the next page.

C's claim is for £95,000.

You will see that I have made C's offer very close to the full amount of the claim. It could have been for any other sensible amount. Case law has shown that C's offer of a high % of the claim has still been considered a genuine attempt to settle in relation to whether an order in the terms in the scenario (iv) diagram below may be unjust, as claimants with strong claims will make high offers! Some lawyers are concerned about the uncertainty that could arise when considering whether or not there has been a "genuine element of concession." i.e. "genuine attempt to settle".

Please refer to the diagram on the next page.

Scenario (iv)

–C's offer is that he will settle if D pays £94k, which D rejects. C is awarded £95k or more at trial.

CPR 36.17 (1) (b) judgment is against D and the trial award is at least as advantageous to C as was C's offer.

S. 36.17 (1) (b) judgment is against D and the trial award is at least as advantageous to C as was C's offer

	End of RP → C wins £94k or more at trial
£94k offer RP 21 days or more as agreed	**D Penalised**
C "U pay me £94k" →	→
General principles, loser pays winner,	**36.17 (4) court must order C entitled to his costs, including any recoverable pre-action costs on the indemnity basis from end RP unless unjust, + interest + an additional amount (### the meanings of interest and additional amount for this scenario are set out below)**
So D pays C's costs to end RP i.e. loser pays winner on standard basis	**So D pays C's costs from end RP on the indemnity basis** **The idea is that D is penalised in costs for not accepting an offer she should have accepted, paying the costs for the other side for the most expensive bit of the process**
So D pays C's £18k costs as well as own	**So D pays C's £53k costs as well as own.** **The 50% costs budget point as in scenario (ii) also applies in this scenario, so if C's costs would have been limited to court fees, D will pay half of C's costs, C paying the other half of his own costs** **###Interest** **~ Interest on the costs, not exceeding 10% above the Bank of England base rate (interest on C's £53k [or half of £53k] costs in this example)** **~ Up to 10% above base rate interest on the whole or part of the sum awarded (interest based on the £94k award in this example) for some or all of the period from the end of the RP.**

###Additional amount

Provided the case has been decided and there has not been a previous order under 36.17 (4), an additional amount up to £75,000.

For monetary or part-monetary claims it is based on a percentage of the award.

For non-monetary claims it is based on a percentage of the costs.

The percentages are (case law has held that this award is NOT discretionary)

- **if the amount is up to £500,000, then 10% of the amount (so here £9,400)**
- **if the amount is over £500,000, 10% of first £half million as in the previous point + 5% of the rest**

End of RP

Trial

Activity

Remember to make notes on the relevant case law authorities in paragraphs 36.17.1 – 4, 36.17.5 and 36.17.5.1 in the commentary in the White Book.

You may find it useful to add in references to the case law NOW at the appropriate points of this Chapter.

When approaching final revision time, remember to add in the salient findings of the cases at the relevant point in any 'mental crib sheet' into which you have distilled the main points of your learned knowledge.

Chapter 7

Elements of the syllabus which you have now covered

- A cell with heavy outlining means that that area of the syllabus was covered in this Chapter;
- A darkly shaded cell with a tick √ means that the whole of that syllabus element has now been covered;
- A lightly shaded cell means that part of that element of the syllabus has been covered in a previous Chapter; and
- An unshaded cell means that element of the syllabus has not yet been covered.

1.1 √	1.2 √	1.3 √	2.1	2.2	3.1	3.2	4.1	4.2	4.3
4.4	5.1	5.2	6.1	6.2	6.3	7.1	7.2	7.3	8.1
8.2	9.1	9.2	10.1	10.2	10.3	11.1	11.2	11.3 √	11.4 √
11.5	11.6	11.7	11.8	12.1	12.2	12.3	12.4	12.5	12.6
13.1	13.2 √	13.3 √	13.4 √	14.1	14.2	15.1	15.2	15.3	15.4
18.2√	16.3 √	16.4 √	17.1	17.2	17.3	18.1	18.2	18.3	19.1
19.2	19.3	20.1	20.2	21.1 √	21.2 √	21.3	21.4 √	22.1	

Chapter 7

Elements of the syllabus which you have now covered for **ADR**

- A cell with heavy outlining means that that area of the syllabus was covered in this Chapter;
- A darkly shaded cell with a tick √ means that the whole of that syllabus element has now been covered;
- A lightly shaded cell means that part of that element of the syllabus has been covered in a previous Chapter; and
- An unshaded cell means that element of the syllabus has not yet been covered.

1.4 √	1.5√	3.3	4.1√	4.2√	5.1√	5.2√	18.1 √	22.3	

Chapter 8

LIMITATION [CUR 2]

h) Limitation

THIS CHAPTER CONTAINS THE ITEMS PRINTED IN BOLD IN THE FOLLOWING BOXES

CURRICULUM ("CUR")

Limitation, *[pre-action conduct, and commencing proceedings]*

2.1 accrual of causes of action
2.2 limitation periods in cases of tort, latent damage, personal injury, fatal accident, contract, and contribution claims

[Pre - action conduct is in Chapter 9

Commencing proceedings is in Chapter 10]

SYLLABUS

Examinable material will consist of limitation periods for actions in tort, contract, contribution claims, personal injury cases, fatal accident cases, and latent damage cases; extensions of limitation period in case of disability; postponement of limitation periods in cases of fraud, concealment or mistake; and discretionary exclusion of time limits for actions in respect of personal injuries or death.

(Each of the above has its own subheading in this Chapter, flagged by EM:)

- **Limitation Act 1980 sections 2, 5, 10, 11, 12, 14, 14A, 14B, 24, 28, 32, 33 and 38(2), at section 8 of Volume 2 of 'Civil Procedure' (the White Book) 2020.**
- **Commentary is incorporated in context in this Chapter, highlighted in an Activity box between two stars**

CHAPTER 8 MOCS

- ***The Limitation period runs from the date of the cause of action***
- ***In PI it may run from the date of knowledge instead***
- ***In latent damage claims it may run from the date of knowledge***
- ***It runs from other dates where C is under a disability, or where the cause of action is fraud, concealment or mistake.***

- ***Contribution 2 years***
- ***PI/fatal accident 3 years (court can disapply)***
- ***Latent damage 3 or 6 years (15 years)***
- ***Tort 6 years***
- ***Contract 6 years***

The sessions dealing with this area of the syllabus on my BTC course are	

Activity

You may find it useful to copy the definition of Limitation Period from GL here

If C does not deliver the claim form to the court by the last day of the limitation period, he has no right to a remedy. He may still serve the CF, although under the Limitation Act 1980, it is a complete defence for D to plead that C's claim is time barred (also referred to as statute barred). D could then ask for strike out of C's statement of case (i.e. the particulars of claim, which may be included with the CF – see end of Chapter 10) of the statute barred claim asserting that it is an abuse of process or she could apply for summary judgment in her favour in relation to it. More on strike out and summary judgment later in Chapter 13).

How to work out the time from when the limitation period starts to accrue appears next in this Chapter. The length of time of the limitation period starts comes after that.

CUR 2.1 ACCRUAL OF CAUSES OF ACTION

The limitation period accrues (i.e. time starts to run)

Time starts to run from the latest of whichever of the following 4 situations is relevant.

Situation 1

EM: extensions of limitation period in case of disability;

- when C ceases to be under a disability
  - minority is a disability. By **ss 28 and 38(2) LA 1980** when C is a child at the date of the cause of action, time starts to run on their 18th birthday
  - persons lacking capacity to conduct legal proceedings within the meaning of the Mental Capacity Act 2005 are under a disability. Time does not run against persons under such a disability at the time of the cause of action. If this disability were brought on by the cause of action, time starts to run when C is no longer under the disability.

So when calculating when time starts to run for limitation purposes, remember to wait until a person's 18th birthday or until they are declared to have the capacity to conduct legal proceedings, then if it is a PI scenario add the 3 years from then to find the date after which the limitation period will have expired.

Situation 2

EM: postponement of limitation periods in cases of fraud, concealment or mistake;

- when fraud, deliberate concealment or mistake is the main cause of action, time starts to run only when the action is discovered, or could have been discovered with reasonable diligence. **s. 32 LA 1980.**

Situation 3

- from the date of knowledge in latent damage claims and some personal injury (PI)claims (see later in this Chapter for the detail on these).

Situation 4

- otherwise, on the date the cause of action accrued.

The limitation period is calculated as follows.

If a cause of action accrued on Tuesday 17th of November 2020 (e.g. C ceased to be under a disability, a fraud was discovered, it is the date of knowledge in a latent damage case or a relevant PI case, a contract were breached or a negligent act occurred on that date) and there is a party capable of suing and one capable of being sued, then day one of the limitation period was Wednesday 18th November 2020.

As an example, for those causes of action whose limitation period is six years, then the last day that the claim form can be delivered to court for limitation purposes is 19th November 2026.

After the MOCS for this section, there follows detail about the limitation periods for each cause of action on the syllabus.

Time stops running when C delivers the claim form to court, even if it is not issued by the court on that day.

Detail about the limitation periods for each cause of action on the syllabus.

The latest time for delivering a claim form to court to be issued is no later than the last day of the limitation period.

CUR 2.2 LIMITATION PERIODS IN CASES OF TORT, LATENT DAMAGE, PERSONAL INJURY, FATAL ACCIDENT, CONTRACT, AND CONTRIBUTION CLAIMS

EM: Limitation periods for actions in tort, contract, contribution claims, personal injury cases, fatal accident cases, and latent damage cases

Once time has started to run, the claim form must be issued within the following limitation periods.

- ***Tort*** not causing personal injury 6 years: trespass 6 years from the date of the harmful act.

- ***Contract*** 6 years from the date of the breach.

  - Remedies - applicable time limits
    - In any claim for **specific performance** of a contract or for an injunction **or for other equitable relief**, s.36 (1) Limitation Act 1980 states that for actions founded on tort or on simple contract, (and other actions not currently on the BTC syllabus), the time limit under the Act **shall not apply except** insofar as any such time-limit **may be applied by the court by analogy.**
    - The Act goes on to say that the court may nevertheless refuse relief on the ground of acquiescence or otherwise. Case law has shown that acquiescence needs to be for many years, before relief will be refused.

- ***Contribution claims*** 2 years from the relevant date which is
  - the date judgment was given, or in an arbitration when the award was given, or
  - the date a person agreed to the amount she would make in contribution

- ***Personal injury*** 3 years **s.11 LA 1980**
  - **S.14 LA 1980** Time runs from the date the cause of action accrued **or** from the date that C knew (i.e. the date of knowledge) that a cause of action has accrued if that is later than the date of the cause of action itself. Time will start to run from the date C has all the following knowledge
    - that the injury is significant, plus
    - that it is attributable to the act/admission, plus
    - the identity of the defendant, plus
    - the identity of anyone with vicarious liability.

EM: Students should be familiar with the commentary at paragraph 8-37 (time limits for action from date of knowledge) of Volume 2 of the White Book

Activity

Remember to make notes on the commentary at paragraph 8-38 (time limits for action from date of knowledge) of Volume 2 of the White Book.

Note

Students should be familiar with the commentary at paragraph 8-38 (section 14(1) - date of knowledge) and the first two paragraphs of the commentary at paragraph 8-43 (knowledge of claimant in negligence actions) of Volume 2 of 'Civil Procedure' (the White Book) 2018.

You may find it useful to add in references to this NOW at this point on this Chapter.

When approaching final revision time, remember to add in this information at the relevant point in any 'mental crib sheet' into which you have distilled the main points of your learned knowledge.

In the remainder of this Chapter, note in triangles the actual terminology used.

The court always has a **discretion** to **disapply/ exclude** the limitation period **for PI**.

EM: discretionary exclusion of time limits for actions in respect of personal injuries or death.

It is recommended that you note and learn from **s.33 (3) LA 1980** what the court has regard to when deciding whether or not to disapply the time-limit for claims for personal injury or fatal accidents.

Activity

Note and learn from s. 33 (3) Limitation Act 1980 what the court has regard when deciding whether or not to disapply / exclude the time-limit for personal injury or fatal accidents

- ***Fatal accidents*** 3 years **s.12 LA 1980**
  - time runs from
    - the date of death, or
    - the date of knowledge, of the person for whose benefit the proceedings are brought

  - **S.33 LA 1980** As above, remember the court's discretion to disapply the limitation period for fatal accidents

- ***Latent damage*** cases (e.g. in property) caused by negligence where there is no PI **s.14(A) LA 1980**
  - 6 years from accrual i.e. the date of damage as above; or
  - 3 years from the 'starting date' i.e. the earliest date C knew (i.e. the date of knowledge)
    - D's identity; and
    - that the damage is sufficiently serious to justify proceedings; and
      that the damage was caused by an alleged negligence.

  - **S.14(B) LA 1980** provides a maximum of 15 years from the alleged negligent act/admission, after which latent damage cases cannot be brought.

- ***Time limit for actions to enforce judgments.*** (See Chapter 25)
  - 6 years from the date on which the judgment became enforceable
  - Arrears of interest in respect of any judgment debt is not recoverable after 6 years from the date on which the interest became due.

Chapter 8

Elements of the syllabus which you have now covered **in civil litigation and evidence**

- A cell with heavy outlining means that that area of the syllabus was covered in this Chapter;
- A darkly shaded cell with a tick √ means that the whole of that syllabus element has now been covered;
- A lightly shaded cell means that part of that element of the syllabus has been covered in a previous Chapter; and
- An unshaded cell means that element of the syllabus has not yet been covered.

1.1 √	1.2 √	1.3 √	2.1 √	2.2 √	3.1	3.2	6.1	6.2	6.3
6.4	7.1	7.2	8.1	8.2	6.3	9.1	9.2	9.3	10.1
10.2	11.1	11.2	12.1	12.2	12.3	13.1	13.2	13.3 √	13.4 √
13.5	13.6	13.7	13.8	14.1	14.2	14.3	14.4	142.5	14.6
15.1	15.2 √	15.3 √	15.4 √	16.1	16.2	17.1	17.2	17.3	17.4
18.2 √	16.3 √	18.4 √ 18.5	19.1	19.2	19.3	20.1	20.2	20.3	21.1
21.2	21.3	22.1	22.2	23.1 √	23.2 √	23.3	23.4 √	24.1	

Chapter 9

PRE-ACTION CONDUCT [CUR 3]

i) Pre-action conduct

THIS CHAPTER CONTAINS THE ITEMS PRINTED IN BOLD IN THE FOLLOWING BOXES

CURRICULUM ("CUR")

~~Limitation~~ ***pre-action conduct****~~, and commencing proceedings~~*

Limitation was in Chapter 8

3.1 the Practice Direction (Pre-Action Conduct and Protocols)

3.2 consequences of non-compliance

3.3 ADR prior to the issue of proceedings is in Chapter 1 ***and is further referenced in this Chapter 9***

Commencing proceedings is in Chapter 10

SYLLABUS

Examinable material will consist of Practice Direction (Pre-Action Conduct and Protocols), the approach of the courts, principles governing conduct of parties in cases not subject to a pre-action protocol, guidance on pre-action procedure where no pre-action protocol applies, and *(ADR prior to the issue of proceedings is in Chapter 1)*

- **Civil Procedure Rules and/or Practice Directions: Practice Direction (Pre-Action Conduct and Protocols) paragraphs 1-17. •**
- **Commentaries are incorporated in context in this Chapter, highlighted in an Activity box between two stars**
- Relevant ADR references to The Jackson ADR Handbook (Second Edition, 2016) are incorporated in context in Chapter 1, highlighted in Activity boxes between two lightning flashes

The sessions dealing with this area of the syllabus on my BTC course are	

Chapter 9 MOCS

- ***Do not go straight to litigation; try to settle with a form of ADR, a Calderbank offer or a Part 36 offer; if no successful settlement then***
- ***Follow Pre-Action Conduct PD***
- ***Follow any relevant Pre-Action Protocol***
- ***There may be sanctions if you don't***

Pre-action protocols explain the conduct and set out the steps the court would normally expect parties to take before commencing proceedings for particular types of civil claims. The details of these are not on the syllabus this year, and neither is the list, although you may like to be aware generally – and it may be relevant for when, say, you are writing an opinion - that there are currently 15of them. They are for

Resolution of Package Travel Claims
Construction and Engineering
Debt Claims
Media and Communications Claims
Personal Injury
Resolution of Clinical Disputes
Professional Negligence
Judicial Review
Disease and Illness
Housing Conditions Claims (England)
Housing Conditions Cases (Wales)
Possession Claims for Mortgage or Home Purchase Plan Arrears in respect of Residential Property
Possession Claims by Social Landlords

Low Value Personal Injury Road Traffic Accident Claims
Low Value Personal Injury Employers' and Public Liability Claims
Dilapidation of Commercial Property

EM: Principles governing conduct of parties in cases not subject to a pre-action protocol, and guidance on pre-action procedure where no pre-action protocol applies.

If proceedings are started to comply with the statutory time limit (Limitation Period) befothe parties have followed the procedures in the Practice Direction and in any relevant Protocol, e.g. perhaps trying to reach a settlement, the parties should apply to the court for a stay of the proceedings while they so comply.

A **'stay'** imposes a hold on proceedings.

- Parties can **request** a stay (or the court can impose one). For example
  - where ADR/ReDOC is considered and pursued once proceedings have started; or
  - pending consent to medical examination; or
  - whilst awaiting prognosis in a PI case; or
  - where a part 36 offer has been accepted.

  The request must be made in writing at the same time as filing the directions questionnaire [Please see later in Chapter 19 for more on directions questionnaires.]

  If requested by all parties the stay will be for **one month** after which it is lifted**;** the court will notify the parties of this.

  If the request does not come from all parties and the court considers a stay is appropriate, the court will direct that the whole or part of the proceedings are stayed for one month **or for such other period as it considers appropriate.**

  Parties must tell the court if a settlement is reached during the stay. Where settlement has not been reached the court can extend the stay/give such directions as it thinks appropriate.

- As set out when dealing with default judgment in Chapter 11, there is an **automatic** stay imposed by the court **6 months after** the end of the period for filing the defence if
  - D has not admitted / defended / put in a counterclaim; and
  - there has been no application for default judgment or for summary judgment [Summary Judgment will be explained later in Chapter 13].

  Any party can apply for an automatic stay to be **lifted** so that proceedings will continue on their way. This is a Part 23 Application. As this is a relief from a sanction, the court will consider the criteria in CPR 3.9. Full details are in Chapter 19.

CUR 3.1 THE PRACTICE DIRECTION (PRE-ACTION CONDUCT AND PROTOCOLS)

EM: The Practice Direction (Pre-Action Conduct and Protocols)

The White Book sets out this practice direction.

- The idea is that **information is exchanged** so that the parties can
  - understand each other's position;
  - make decisions about how to proceed;
  - try to settle their differences without litigation;
  - consider negotiation or a form of Alternative Dispute Resolution (ADR/ReDOC) to assist with settlement including
    - mediation, a third party facilitating a resolution;
    - arbitration, a third party deciding the dispute;
    - early neutral evaluation, a third party giving an informed opinion on the dispute; and
    - ombudsmen schemes.
  - aid efficient management of proceedings if proceedings do go ahead
  - reduce the costs of resolving the dispute.

  Compliance and costs incurred should be proportionate, parties taking only **reasonable and proportionate** steps to identify, narrow and resolve the legal factual or expert issues. Disproportionate costs will not be recoverable.

  Where there is a relevant pre-action protocol, the parties should comply with that protocol before commencing proceedings. Where there is no relevant pre-action protocol, the parties should exchange correspondence and information to comply with the objectives of exchanging information as set out above. The steps will usually include

  C sending full details in a letter before claim to D, including
  - the basis on which the claim is made
  - a summary of the facts
  - what C wants from D and
  - if money, how the amount is calculated.

  Within a reasonable period D acknowledges the letter (within 14 days), then gives a full written response within up to 3 months, for more complex cases, of receipt of the letter before claim. The reply should include
  - confirmation as to whether the claim is accepted
  - and, if it is not accepted, the reasons why, together with an explanation as to which facts and parts of the claim are disputed and
  - whether the defendant is making a counterclaim, as well as providing details of any counterclaim

The parties should disclose (see Chapter 20) key documents relevant to the issues in dispute.

- Parties should be aware that
  - the **court** must give **permission** before **expert evidence** can be relied upon (see Chapter 22, CPR 35.4(1))
  - the court may limit the fees recoverable
  - many disputes can be resolved without expert advice or evidence. If it is necessary to obtain expert evidence, particularly in low value claims, the parties should consider using a **single expert, jointly instructed** by the parties, with the costs shared equally.

- Parties may negotiate to settle a dispute or may use a form of ADR as set out above.

- If proceedings are issued, the parties may be required by the court to provide evidence that **ADR** has been considered. A party's silence in response to an invitation to participate or a refusal to participate in ADR might be considered unreasonable by the court and could lead to the court ordering that party to pay additional court costs.

  Parties should continue to consider the possibility of reaching a settlement at all times, including after proceedings have been started.

- Where a dispute has not been resolved after the parties have followed [a pre-action protocol] or the Practice Direction (Pre-Action Conduct), they should review their respective positions. They should consider the papers and the evidence to **see if proceedings can be avoided** and at least seek to **narrow the issues** in dispute before the claimant issues proceedings.

EM: The approach of the courts

- The **court expects compliance** and will take into account whether the parties have complied **in substance** and may be more lenient where the non-compliance is minor in relation to an urgent application, eg. for an injunction.

  Examples of non-compliance are where a party
  - did not provide sufficient information
  - did not act within a reasonable period
  - unreasonably refused ADR or did not respond to an invitation to use ADR

  The court will take into account non-compliance when
  - giving directions for the management of proceedings
  - making orders for costs

Activity

Remember to make notes on

- **The Practice Direction for Personal Injury Claims at paragraphs C2-001 to C2-016 of Volume 1 of 'Civil Procedure' (the White Book) 2020**

- **The commentary on the Practice Direction for Personal Injury Claims at paragraphs C2A001 to C2A-005 of Volume 1 of 'Civil Procedure' (the White Book) 2020.**

You may find it useful to add in references to this NOW at this point on this Chapter.

When approaching final revision time, remember to add in this information at the relevant point in any 'mental crib sheet' into which you have distilled the main points of your learned knowledge.

CUR 3.2 THE CONSEQUENCES OF NON-COMPLIANCE

Where there has been non-compliance the court will ask for explanations. The court may order that

- the parties are relieved of the obligation to comply or further comply with the Practice Direction;
- the proceedings are stayed while particular steps are taken to comply with the Practice Direction; or that
- sanctions are to be applied. These may include
  - defaulting party to pay some or all of other's costs
    - possibly on the indemnity basis
    - interest being deprived or added at a higher rate of up to 10% above base rate

Chapter 9

Elements of the syllabus which you have now covered in **civil litigation and evidence**

- A cell with heavy outlining means that that area of the syllabus was covered in this Chapter;
- A darkly shaded cell with a tick √ means that the whole of that syllabus element has now been covered;
- A lightly shaded cell means that part of that element of the syllabus has been covered in a previous Chapter; and
- An unshaded cell means that element of the syllabus has not yet been covered.

1.1 √	1.2 √	1.3 √	2.1 √	2.2 √	3.1 √	3.2 √	6.1	6.2	6.3
6.4	7.1	7.2	8.1	8.2	8.3	9.1	9.2	93	10.1
10.2	11.1	11.2	12.1	12.2	12.3	13.1	13.2	13.3 √	13.4 √
13.5	13.6	13.7	13.8	14.1	14.2	14.3	14.4	14.5	14.6
15.1	15.2 √	15.3 √	15.4 √	16.1	16.2	17.1	17.2	17.3	17.4
18.2. √	18.3 √	18.4 √ 18.5	19.1	19.2	19.3	20.1	20.2	20.3	21.1
21.2	21.3	22.1	22.2	23.1 √	23.2 √	23.3	23.4 √	24.1	

Chapter 10

COMMENCING PROCEEDINGS [CUR 6]

PARTIES [CUR 7]

STATEMENTS OF CASE – CLAIM FORM AND PARTICULARS OF CLAIM [CUR 8]

THIS CHAPTER CONTAINS THE ITEMS PRINTED IN BOLD IN THE FOLLOWING BOXES

i) Claim Form issued and served; Particulars of Claim served

CURRICULUM ("CUR")

- ~~*Limitation*~~ *is in Chapter 8~~,~~*
- ~~*pre-action conduct,*~~ *is in Chapter 9*
- *Commencing Proceedings*
  6.1 the Part 7 procedure
  6.2 validity, extension and service of claim forms
  6.3 service of other court documents within the jurisdiction
  6.4 the Part 8 procedure

- *Parties*
  7.1 partnerships, sole traders, LLPs and companies, trusts and deceased persons
  7.2 children and persons suffering from mental incapacity

- *Statements of Case*
  8.1 claim forms and particulars of claim
  8.2 acknowledgement of service is in Chapter 11,
  8.2 defences, replies, counterclaims is in Chapter 11
  8.3 the effect of not responding to an allegation in a statement of case is in Chapter 11

SYLLABUS

COMMENCING PROCEEDINGS

Examinable material will consist of: where to start proceedings, how to start proceedings, the claim form, title of proceedings, start of proceedings, the right to use one claim form to start two or more claims, particulars of claim, statements of truth, extensions of time for service of a claim form, service of the claim form and other court documents within the jurisdiction, and the alternative procedure for claims under Part 8 CPR.

(Each of the above has its own subheading in this Chapter, flagged by EM:)

COMMENCING PROCEEDINGS (Continued)

- **CPR 6.1-6-9, 6.11, 6.14, 6.15 6.20-6.22 and 6.25-6.27**
- **PD6A paragraphs 1-4, 6 and 8-10**
- **CPR 7.2-7.5**
- **CPR 7.6**
- **PD7A paragraphs 1, 2.1-2.5, 4.1-4.2, 5.1-5.5, 6.1-6.2, 7.1-7.3 and 8.1- 8.2**
- **CPR 8.1-8.2, 8.3-8.4, 8.5-8.6 and 8.8-8.9**
- **PD8A paragraphs 3 and 7**

- **CPR 16.1-16.8, PD 16 paragraphs 1-3, 4.1-4.3, 4.4, 7-15 from CUR 8**

- **Commentary is incorporated in context in this Chapter, highlighted in an Activity box between two stars**

- Paragraphs 4, 4A, 5, 8 and 9 of the High Court and County Courts Jurisdiction Order 1991 (S.I. 1991/724) at section 9B of Volume 2 of 'Civil Procedure' (the White Book) 2020. (This was set out in Chapter 1 regarding which court and value of claims; enforcement is in Chapter Chapter 22).

PARTIES

Examinable material will consist of bringing claims against partnerships, sole traders, LLPs and companies, trusts and deceased persons; and bringing and settling proceedings involving children and protected parties.

STATEMENTS OF CASE

Examinable material will consist of: contents of claim form. *(The remainder of examinable material is in the next Chapter)*

- **CPR 7.2A; PD7A paragraphs 5A and 5C;**
- **CPR 19.7A and 19.8;**
- **CPR 21.1-21.4 and 21.10-21.11; PD 21 paragraphs 5-6;**
- **CPR 39.6.**

- ***Part 7***
    - ***Issue CF within limitation period***
    - ***Serve CF within four months of issue***
    - ***CF always deemed served on second business day after relevant step***
    - ***Serve POC within 14 days deemed serviced of CF***
    - ***POC deemed served re CPR 6.26***
    - ***Rules on how and where to serve the Particulars of Claim, the first statement of case we meet.***
- ***Part 8 when no substantial dispute of fact***

The sessions dealing with this area of the syllabus on my BTC course are	

CUR 7.1 PARTNERSHIPS, SOLE TRADERS, LLPS AND COMPANIES, TRUSTS AND DECEASED PERSONS

Information on the way in which these parties are dealt with are referred to in context in the remainder of this Chapter.

CUR 7.2 CHILDREN AND PERSONS SUFFERING FROM MENTAL INCAPACITY

EM: Proceedings involving children and protected parties.

This is dealt with by CPR Part 21, [although note that Part 21 does not apply to enforcement of specified debts by taking control of goods or related applications (see Chapter 25), where one of the parties to proceedings is a child].

A child

- means someone under 18
- **must have a litigation friend** to conduct proceedings on their behalf **unless** the child applies, on notice to the litigation friend if they already have one (it may be a without

notice application if the child has no litigation friend), to conduct proceedings him or herself and a court orders that the child need not have one.

However, if the court makes such an order and it subsequently appears to the court that it is desirable for a litigation friend to conduct the proceedings on behalf of the child, the **court may appoint** a person to be the child's **litigation friend**.

Where the court has not ordered that the child can conduct proceedings without a litigation friend, so that the child must have one, a person who wishes to do any of the following may not do so (unless they have the court's permission to do so), until the child or protected party has a litigation friend

- make an application against a child or protected party before proceedings have started; or
- take any step in proceedings except
  - issuing and serving a claim form; or
  - applying for the appointment of a litigation friend under rule 21.6 which sets out how a person becomes a litigation friend by court order (not on your syllabus this year).

Any step taken before a child has a litigation friend has no effect unless the court orders otherwise.

<u>For a child, who may be a litigation friend without a court order?</u>

If the court has not appointed a person to be a litigation friend, the following may be a litigation friend without a court order

If nobody has been appointed by the court, a person may act as a litigation friend if he

- can fairly and competently conduct proceedings on behalf of the child
- has no interest adverse to that of the child; and
- where the child is a claimant, undertakes to pay any costs which the child may be ordered to pay in relation to the proceedings, subject to any right he may have to be repaid from the assets of the child.

,

<u>A protected party</u>

- means a party or intended party who lacks capacity to conduct proceedings
- **must have a litigation friend** to conduct proceedings on their behalf

If during proceedings a party lacks capacity to continue to conduct proceedings, no party may take any further step in the proceedings without the permission of the court until the protected party has a litigation friend.

Any step taken before a child or protected party has a litigation friend has no effect unless the court orders otherwise.

<u>For a protected party, who may be a litigation friend without a court order?</u>

If the court has not appointed a person to be a litigation friend, the following may be a litigation friend without a court order

- A deputy appointed by the Court of Protection under the 2005 Act with power to conduct proceedings on the protected party's behalf is entitled to be the litigation friend of the protected party in any proceedings to which his power extends.
- If nobody has been appointed as a deputy a person may act as a litigation friend if he
  - can fairly and competently conduct proceedings on behalf of the protected party;

- has no interest adverse to that of the protected party; and
- where the protected party is a claimant, undertakes to pay any costs which the protected party may be ordered to pay in relation to the proceedings, subject to any right he may have to be repaid from the assets of the protected party.

Where money is recovered or paid into court and accepted by or on behalf of a child or protected party, the court gives directions about how the money will be dealt with. This may be that all or part of it is paid into court and invested or otherwise dealt with.

Further information on the way in which children and protected parties are dealt with are referred to in context in the remainder of this Chapter.

CUR 6.1 THE PART 7 PROCEDURE

EM: Where to start proceedings

The majority of the case studies on your BTC are likely to be under the Part 7 procedure. You should refer back to Chapter 1 of this book to refresh your memory as to which court the type of claim you are dealing with should be started in.

EM: Title of proceedings

The claim form and every other statement of case (others are introduced in Chapters 12 and 13 of this book) must be headed with the title of the proceedings. The title should state:
- the number of proceedings,
- the court or Division in which they are proceeding,
- the full name of each party,
- each party's status in the proceedings (i.e. claimant/defendant).

Where there is more than one claimant and/or more than one defendant, the parties should be described in the title as follows

1. AB
2. CD
3. EF Claimants

and

1. GH
2. IJ
3. KL Defendants

***EM:* How to start proceedings; the claim form; EM: start of proceedings**

Overview of how Part 7 claims are commenced

The claim form ("CF") is one of the documents known as a statement of case. It comes in standard formats and sets out the essence of the claim.

The claimant ("C") completes it and delivers it (with copies for the court and all parties if the court is to serve it) to court[10] and the court issues it. Issue is usually the same day. The date of issue of the CF is the date stamped on the form by the court. This starts the litigation proceedings.

Remember that the CF must be delivered to the court no later than the last day of limitation period. Note that where the CF as issued was received in the court office on a date earlier than the date on which it was issued by the court, the claim is 'brought' for the purposes of the Limitation Act 1980 and any other relevant statute on that earlier date.

CF is then served, usually by the court, on the defendant ("D"). This must be done within 4 months of issue by the court.

Full details of the claim are set out either in the CF itself or in another statement of case called particulars of claim ("POC"). You will learn how to draft the POC on the BTC. The POC can be attached to, filed with and served with the CF on D at the same time.

If the CF is issued and served on D without the POC (the POC may take some time to draft!), then the POC must be served on D within 14 days of the CF being served on her, still within 4 months of the issue of the CF.

EM: The right to use one claim form to start two or more claims. Where there is more than one claim that can conveniently be disposed of in the same proceedings, a single CF may be used.

Detail of commencement of Part 7 claims

How parties are named in statements of case

EM: Bringing proceedings involving children and protected parties.

A **child** is referred to in the heading of a statement of case as, e.g.

Miss AMY BROWN (a child, by Mr JACK BROWN her litigation friend).

---

[10] For when you get into practice, you may like to be aware that some Money Claims may be started online by requesting the issue of a claim form electronically via Her Majesty's Courts and Tribunals Service website.

Claims started using Money Claim Online will be issued in the County Court Business Centre in Northampton and will proceed there unless they are sent to a County Court hearing centre.

A claim may be started using Money Claim Online if it is the only remedy claimed is a specified amount of money of less than £100,000 in sterling (excluding any interest or costs claimed) plus in addition all of the following:-

The part 7 procedure is being used; C must not be a child or protected party or funded by the Legal Services Commission; C's address for service must be within the United Kingdom; the claim must be against a single defendant; or two defendants, if the claim is for a single amount against each of them; D must not be the Crown; or a person known to be a child or protected party; and the defendant's address for service must be within England and Wales.

You should also check what has happened regarding the 2 pilot schemes in footnote 1 in Chapter 1.

A **protected party** is referred to in the heading of a statement of case as, e.g.

Mrs BRENDA GREEN (by Ms JILL SHARP her litigation friend).

An **individual** is referred to in the heading of a statement of case as, e.g. Mr KARL WHITE

EM: claims against sole traders

A sole trader is referred to in the heading of a statement of case as, e.g.

Mr KARL WHITE (trading as White's laundry)

EM: claims against partnerships

A partnership is where two or more people are carrying on a partnership business. It includes those claiming to be entitled as partners and those alleged to be partners. Claims must be brought against the partnership name unless it is inappropriate to do so. That name is the one under which the partnership carried on business at the time of the cause of action accrued.

A partnership is referred to in the heading of a statement of case as, e.g.

BLACK AND WHITE (a firm);

A claim may be brought against a business name as if it were the name of a partnership, where an individual carries on a business within the jurisdiction and the business name is not the individual's own name.

EM: claims against LLPs

HART AND HIND LLP

EM: claims against Companies

Where D is a **Company**, include the correct designation in the heading on the statement of case. E.g. Plc, PLC, Ltd, LTD, LIMITED

A company may be represented at trial by an employee if the employee has been authorised by the company to appear at trial on its behalf. The court's permission is needed.

EM: claims against trusts. For **trusts,** claims will be by or against the trustees. There is no need to join in beneficiaries. Decisions will be binding on the beneficiaries unless the court orders otherwise.

EM: claims against deceased persons. Claims survive the death of **deceased persons.** Personal representatives [(executor (male) or executrix (female) of the will, or the administrator if there is no will] can be ordered to be substituted for the deceased as parties.

Where it is sought to start proceedings against the estate of a deceased defendant where probate or letters of administration have not been granted, the claimant should issue the claim against 'the estate of A.B. deceased'. The claimant should then, before the expiry of the period for service of the claim form, apply to the court for the appointment of a person to represent the estate of the deceased.

CUR 6.2 VALIDITY, EXTENSION AND SERVICE OF CLAIM FORMS

and

CUR 8.1 CLAIM FORMS

EM: contents of claim form

Contents of Part 7 CF

The CF must include

- a concise statement of the **nature of the claim**
- a ***EM: statement of value*** in accordance with rule 16.3 where C is making a claim for money
  - money claim
    - the amount claimed
    - that C expects to recover
      - (i) not more than £10,000
      - (ii) more than £10,000 but not more than £25,000; or
      - (iii) more than £25,000; or
    - that C cannot say how much is likely to be recovered.
  - PI claim
    - the amount C expects to recover as general damages for PSLA is
      - (i) not more than £1,000; or
      - (ii) more than £1,000.
  - If the claim form is to be issued in the High Court it must state that
    - C expects to recover more than £100,000;
    - some other enactment provides that the claim may be commenced only in the High Court and specify that enactment;
    - C expects to recover £50,000 or more if it is a PI claim; or
    - the claim is to be in one of the specialist High Court lists and state which list
  - When calculating how much the claimant expects to recover, the claimant must **disregard** any possibility
    - that the court may make an award of **interest or costs**
    - that the court may make a finding of **contributory negligence**
    - that D may make a counterclaim or that the defence may include a set-off, or
    - that D may be liable to pay an amount of money which the court awards to the claimant to the Secretary of State for Social Security under section 6 of the Social Security (Recovery of Benefits) Act 1997.
    - The statement of value in the claim form does not limit the power of the court to give judgment for the amount which it finds C is entitled to.
- a **statement of the interest** accrued on that sum where C's only claim is for a specified sum
- anything a **PD** specifically requires
- any **representative capacity** of C or D (e.g. a litigation friend; a personal representative of the deceased)
- the **remedy** C wants
  - if not specified, the court may still grant that unspecified remedy if it is a remedy that C is entitled to

- the statement of value in the claim form does not limit the power of the court to give judgment for the amount which it finds C is entitled to

– a statement that the POC, if it is not being served with the CF, will follow
– a statement of truth. ***EM: Statements of Truth,*** This is serious and is what gives the document its legal weight/gravitas as it verifies the factual basis of the case.

  From 1 October 2020 use this wording:-

  '[I believe] [the (claimant or as may be) believes] that the facts stated in this [name document being verified] are true. I understand that proceedings for contempt of court may be brought against anyone who makes, or causes to be made, a false statement in a document verified by a statement of truth without an honest belief in its truth.'

  Proceedings for contempt of court may be brought for making false statements of truth.

In addition, particulars (i.e. details) of the claim may be included in the CF and this will be usually be the case when they are very straight forward.

Where they are not very straight forward and so will take time to prepare, particulars of claim are drafted as a document in their own right, when they **must** be served on D within 14 days of deemed service on D of the CF. (More on this in a few pages time).

EM: Service of the claim form within the jurisdiction

THE RULES GOVERNING **WHO** SERVES IT

The CF is served on the D by the court, unless the court orders or directs otherwise. Service can be done by C if C wishes or if a rule or PD says that C must serve it. A photocopy of it is not sufficient – time only starts to run when the *original* CF is served.

If the court is serving, the court decides on the method to be used. The method is by first class post or any other service which provides for delivery on the next working day.

THE RULES GOVERNING **HOW** IT IS SERVED

Use one of the **required steps** in CPR 7.5

– personal service (this method must be used if an Act, PD or court order says so; it cannot be used to serve on a D's solicitor or the Crown) by
  - leaving it with the individual who is to be served with it (It is sufficient if C tried his hardest to do this and D is being elusive as she knows what it is)
  - leaving it with a person holding a senior position in the company
  - where a partnership is being sued in the name of a firm, by leaving it with
    - a partner; or
    - a person who at time of service has control or management of the partnership business at its principal place of business
– send it by first class post
– send it by DX (document exchange = centres where mail is exchanged using this system)
– use any other method permitted by relevant company or limited liability partnership statutes when D is a company or limited liability partnership
– complete a facsimile (fax) transmission, subject to the requirements set out below when D has given an address for service.
– Send an email, subject to the requirements set out next where D has given an address for service.

Activity

> Please go to PD 6A in the White Book and make notes on the required detail of sending and receiving by these methods within the UK.

<u>THE RULES ON **WHERE** TO SERVE ON D WHERE **D HAS GIVEN AN ADDRESS** FOR SERVICE (CPR 6.8)</u>

- **MUST** serve it at D's solicitor (may leave it there) when
  - D has given the address of a solicitor in writing and
  - D's solicitor has notified C in writing that s/he has instructions from D to accept service at a business address in the jurisdiction.
  - Note that before serving by electronic means, you need the solicitor's indication in writing, that it is ok to serve it on them and by which method/step.

- If not a solicitor's address, at an address D gave, being where D resides or carries on business.
  - Note that before serving by electronic means, you need the receiving party's indication in writing, that it is ok to serve it on them and by which method/step.

<u>THE RULES ON **WHERE** TO SERVE ON D WHERE **D HAS GIVEN NO ADDRESS** FOR SERVICE and so where service at a solicitor's office do not apply (CPR 6.9)</u>

<u>D is an individual</u>

Serve on the individual themselves at their usual or last known address. Reasonable steps must be taken to ascertain D's current address.

<u>EM:claims against sole traders</u>

This is where an individual is sued in the name of a business which s/he operates trading under a name which may not be their personal name. **Serve on** the individual themselves at their usual or last known address. Reasonable steps must be taken to ascertain D's current address.

<u>EM:claims against partnerships and LLPs</u>

Serve on (in no particular order)

- (where partners are being sued in the name of their firm) by leaving it with a partner or a person who, at the time of service, has the control or management of the partnership business at its principal place of business
- (where an individual being sued in the business name of a partnership), at the usual or last known residence of the individual or principal or last known place of business of the partnership
- (where limited liability partnership) the principal office of the partnership or Any place of business of the partnership within the jurisdiction which has a real connection with the claim.

<u>EM: claims against Companies</u>

Serve on (in no particular order)

- the principal office
- the registered office
- a holder of a senior position by personal service by leaving it with that person (at)
- a place with a real connection to the claim

- the last known place of business; you must take reasonable steps to ascertain the current address

Service of CF by a contractually agreed method

If a contract includes a term that the claim form may be served by a specified method or at a specified place, the claim form may be served in that way or at that place. This rule does not apply where the court has made an order allowing a child to conduct proceedings without a litigation friend.

THE RULES ON BY **WHEN** IT MUST BE SERVED **AND WHEN** IT IS **DEEMED** TO HAVE BEEN SERVED ON D

Continuing on from the example dates in Situation 4 of the limitation Chapter, the last day that the claim form can be delivered to court for **limitation purposes is 19th November 2026**. CPR 7.5.

Serve the CF **within** the jurisdiction by midnight on the calendar day **4 months after issue** otherwise the CF is no longer valid.

Let us say that all pre-action conduct matters had led to nothing and that the **claim form** was delivered to court, stamped and therefore **issued on Monday 12th April 2021**, start counting from the next day, 13th April 2021. Thus the required step in CPR 7.5 must be taken by 14th August 2021.

Where service is **outside** the jurisdiction the time limit is extended to **6 months.**

Note that the CF is therefore still valid when sent in time using the required step in CPR 7.5, which is when physical service took place, even though D will be deemed to receive it after the relevant midnight. It is this latter date that will be starting point for calculating by when other steps in the proceedings must take place.

CPR 6.14. D is **deemed** to have received the CF **2 business days** after the required step in CPR 7.5.

Remember that Saturday and Sunday, bank holidays, Good Friday and Christmas Day are not business days; remember not to count the day of the step itself.

A CF sent by the required step to the correct place

- on a Monday, will be deemed received by D (and so served on D) on Wednesday. This is because Tuesday is the first business day after Monday and the second business day is Wednesday;
- on a Friday, will be deemed received by D (and so served on D) on the following Tuesday. This is because Saturday and Sunday are not business days, the first business day after Friday is Monday and the second business day is Tuesday.

This is an **irrebuttable presumption:** even if D received the CF the same day, next day, or if she did not receive it for several weeks, she is deemed to have received it 2 business days after the required step.

EM: Extensions of time for service of a claim form

If it looks like C may be running out of time i.e. the 4 months is shortly due to expire, C can apply to court with evidence, (it will be a 'without notice' application i.e. without notice to the proposed D as D is not yet on the court record) to **extend the time limit for service** under

CPR 7.6(1) and (2). Provided that the application notice is filed at court before 4 months expires, the application can still be issued or heard after the 4 month time limit. Then C can just keep on making applications to extend time further by keeping within the timeframe set out in any previous similar order that C has obtained. In this way C can get more and more time extensions (if the court will allow them). Remember that in making its decision, the court will apply the overriding objective including

- the need to enforce compliance with rules, PDs and orders
- whether there is any prejudice to the other party
- whether the date of a hearing will be affected if an extension is given.

Full details about making without notice applications were set out in Chapter 4. The required evidence for extension of time applications are that the evidence should state

- all the circumstances relied on,
- the date of issue of the claim,
- the expiry date of any rule 7.6 extension, and
- a full explanation as to why the claim has not been served.

If the 4 month limit has already expired, C can still apply to court to extend the time limit under CPR 7.6 (1) and (3) for service but it will be a great hurdle he has to overcome to persuade the court to grant the order. C will need to show that

- he has acted promptly in making this application and either
- the court failed to serve the CF; or
- he has taken all reasonable steps to serve within the 4 month period but has been unable to do so.

If the court refuses the extension of time, provided the limitation period has not run out, then C can simply start afresh with a new CF.

Counsel should always be aware of how close the limitation period is to ending. Once a limitation period has ended, unless the claim is for PI or a fatal accident and the court has disapplied the limitation period, then where a CF was issued, but was not served within the 4 month timeframe, the situation cannot be rectified by simply starting afresh with a new CF if the limitation period has now run out.

Activity

Remember to make notes on the relevant case law authorities in paragraphs 7.6.2 and the first two paragraphs of 7.6.3 in the commentary in the White Book.

You may find it useful to add in references to the case law NOW at the appropriate points of this Chapter.

When approaching final revision time, remember to add in the salient findings of the cases at the relevant point in any 'mental crib sheet' into which you have distilled the main points of your learned knowledge.

Alternative service (by a **step** other than the CPR required step or at a **place** other than the CPR stipulated place)

If a situation arises where C has tried to ascertain D's current address / tried to serve the CF there, yet it is not proving possible to serve using the required step or on the correct the place, C may apply to court under CPR 6.15 for an order allowing **alternative service** of the CF. This will be a Part 23 application, without notice.
Where it appears to the court that there is a good reason to authorise service by a method or at a place not otherwise permitted by this Part, the court may make an order permitting service by an alternative method or at an alternative place.

What is needed for the application:-

- application with
- evidence of good reason for needing the order

What to deal with in your evidence if applying pre-service:-

- the reason why an order is sought;
- what alternative method or place is proposed, and
- why the applicant believes that the document is likely to reach the person to be served by the method or at the place proposed.

What to deal with if applying once service has been tried:-

- the reason why the order is sought;
- what alternative method or alternative place was used;
- when the alternative method or place was used; and
- why the applicant believes that the document is likely to have reached the person to be served by the alternative method or at the alternative place.

- draft order (e.g. ordering that service will be effective if the CF is served on D's usual/last known address, even though it has been shown that D is no longer there). An order under this rule must specify:-
  - the method or place of service;
  - the date on which the claim form is deemed served; and
  - the period for: –
    - filing an acknowledgment of service;
    - filing an admission; or
    - filing a defence.

On an application under this rule, the court may order that steps already taken to bring the claim form to the attention of the defendant by an alternative method or at an alternative place is good service.

CUR 8.1 PARTICULARS OF CLAIM

This is the first statement of case that we meet.

EM: Particulars of Claim ("POC"); EM: Contents of particulars of claim; EM: Matters to be included in particulars of claim

All Particulars of Claim must include

- a concise **statement of the facts** on which C relies;
- an attachment of copies of any obvious relevant documents as set out in PD16.7, such as
  - written contract
  - evidence of oral contract
  - conditions of sale;

    originals of these should be available at the hearing.
- if C is seeking **interest**, a statement to that effect and whether that is
  - under the terms of a contract
  - under an enactment and if so which
  - on some other basis and if so what that basis is
  - if the claim is for a specified amount of money
    - the percentage rate at which interest is claimed (details on the relevant statutes in Chapter 24)
    - the date from which it is claimed
    - the date to which it is calculated, which must not be later than the date on which the claim form is issued
    - the total amount of interest claimed to the date of calculation; and
    - the daily rate at which interest accrues after that date
- a **statement of truth**

<u>EM: matters which must be specifically set out in particulars of claim</u>

- If C is seeking aggravated **damages or exemplary damages**, a statement to that effect and his grounds for claiming them;
- if C is seeking **provisional damages**, a statement to that effect and his grounds for claiming them; and
- anything a PD specifies

A POC for PI claims must also include
- C's date of birth
- brief details of C's personal injuries
- an attached schedule of details of any past and future expenses and losses which he claims
- any report from a medical practitioner that C is using in evidence
  - In a soft tissue injury claim (whiplash), C may not proceed unless the first medical report is a fixed cost medical report from an accredited medical expert selected via the MedCo Portal and any further report from an expert in
    - Consultant Orthopaedic Surgeon
    - Consultant in Accident and Emergency Medicine
    - General Practitioner registered with the General Medical Council
    - Physiotherapist registered with the Health and Care Professions Council

    must also be a fixed cost medical report.

  - The cost of obtaining and using a further report from any other expert need not be a fixed costs report, but must be justified.

A POC in **a provisional damages claim** must also specify that

- this is what C is claiming under either section 32A of the Senior Courts Act 1981 or section 51 of the County Courts Act 1984,

- there is a chance that at some future time the claimant will develop some serious disease or suffer some serious deterioration in his physical or mental condition, and
- the disease or type of deterioration in respect of which an application may be made at a future date.

If C wishes to rely on evidence of a **conviction** of an offence or on a finding of **adultery** or **paternity**, he must include in the POC the type of conviction or the date of the finding and the court where it was made.

Further matters which need to be specifically set out in certain types of claim are listed in PD 16.8.

If ready, the POC should be set out in the CF.

Otherwise the POC must also contain

- the name of the court in which the claim is proceeding
- the claim number allotted to the claim when it was issued (date stamped) by the court
- the title of the proceedings
- C's address for service

CUR 6.3 SERVICE OF OTHER COURT DOCUMENTS WITHIN THE JURISDICTION

EM: Service of other court documents within the jurisdiction

THE RULES ON BY **WHEN** POC MUST BE SERVED **AND WHEN** POC IS **DEEMED** TO HAVE BEEN SERVED ON D

The POC is "a document other than a claim form" for the purposes of the CPR, here CPR 6.26. You will learn how to draft POCs during the BTC. (Remember that in contrast, for Part 8 claims, there is simply a witness statement; no POC is used in Part 8 claims).

The POC must be served on D **within 14 days of deemed service of the CF**, CPR 7.4 [and this must still be within the 4 month midnight deadline for the CF to be valid (unless there has been a disapplication of the time limit in a PI or fatal accidents case)].
If the CF is deemed served 31st March, the latest date for serving the POC on D is on 14th April.

For "documents other than a claim form" there are different timeframes regarding when service of such documents is deemed to have taken place. CPR 6.26.

- when the required step is sending by **first class post, or in the DX,** the document is deemed served on the second day after the requisite step, provided that the day you land on is a business day, otherwise it is the next business day.
  Thus a POC sent separately from the CF, posted or put in the DX on a Thursday is deemed served on [Saturday, but that is not a business day, so the deemed date of service is] Monday.

  Thus a POC sent separately from the CF, posted or put in the DX on a Friday is deemed served on [Sunday, but that is not a business day, so the deemed date of service is] Monday.

- When the required step is **delivering or leaving** a POC sent separately from the CF at the permitted address, or the **transmission of a fax is completed**, or where **email or any other electronic method is sent** or the POC is **served personally** on a business day before 4.30pm, deemed date of service is on that day; if after 4.30pm, deemed date of service is on the next business day after that day.

C must also serve with the POC

- a response pack
  - form of AOS
  - form for defending
  - form for admitting

These forms are in anticipation of D's response to the POC, as set out in full in the next Chapter.

Plus

- if it is a PI claim (PD 16.4) a schedule of past and future losses and also medical reports. For soft tissue injury claims (whiplash) this must be a 'fixed costs medical report'.

CUR 6.4 THE PART 8 PROCEDURE

EM:* *The alternative procedure for claims under Part 8 CPR.

The Part 8 procedure is appropriate when

- the claim is unlikely to involve any substantial dispute of fact; or
- in applying for a Norwich Pharmacal order pre - action; the claim is started as a Part 8 claim where the claim is against the facilitator of the wrong doing; or
- when a PD or a rule allows. They may also allow for the Part 8 procedure to be modified. (Applications for Judicial Review are made by Part 8 procedure modified by CPR Part 54, although this is not on the syllabus this year).

If D contends that the above are not present and so Part 8 should not be used, she must state her reasons and any written evidence when she acknowledges service of the claim form on her. The court will consider these and give directions for how the case is to be managed in future.

If a court officer thinks that Part 8 is the incorrect procedure, s/he may refer the claim to a judge to consider the point.

At any stage the court may order the claim to continue as if C had not used Part 8, the court allocating it to a track and giving directions
A claim under the Part 8 procedure may be made at any County Court hearing centre unless a rule, practice direction or enactment provides otherwise. However, when a claim is given a hearing date, the court may direct that proceedings should be transferred to another hearing centre if it is appropriate to do so.

Contents of a Part 8 CF

- the question C wants the court to decide
- the remedy C seeks and the legal basis for it
- any enactment under which the claim is made
- any representative capacity of C or D (e.g. litigation friend)
- C may rely on the matters in his CF as evidence if it is verified by a statement of truth ***EM: statements of truth.***

Otherwise written evidence, for the BTC, normally in the form of a witness statement, verified by a statement of truth ***EM: statements of truth*** must be filed with the CF.

Part 8 claims must be used for those claims or applications listed in section B, referred to in PD8A paragraph 3; or where an enactment says so.

One instance where Part 8 claims may be used is where there has been a settlement between the parties and a (potential) party to proceedings is 'under a disability', so a child or a protected party – someone who lacks capacity to conduct proceedings, eg. a person suffering from mental incapacity.

Another is consent judgments for provisional damages settled before proceedings started.

Another is for a Norwich Pharmacal order begun before a Part 7 claim has been issued.

EM: Settling proceedings involving children and protected parties.

Where proceedings have not been started before settlement agreed

The Part 8 procedure is used to give the necessary **court approval** of a settlement involving a person under a disability; otherwise the settlement is not valid. Thus these two categories of persons under a disability are prevented from settling claims at too low a value, either due to C's own disability or due to the inexperience of a lawyer.

Remember that under the CPR this means children until their 18th birthday as well as "a protected party", i.e. a person suffering from mental incapacity.

The procedure begins with a Part 8 claim form. This is in standard form which comes with comprehensive guidance on how to fill it in. ***EM: statements of truth*** -The statement of truth in a statement of case, response or application must be signed by

- the party or litigation friend or
- the legal representative on behalf of the party or litigation friend.

A witness statement will be filed with the claim form. This also contains a ***EM: statements of truth*** statement of truth which must be signed by the maker of the statement.

Part 8 claims are usually allocated to the multi-track (explained later in Chapter 19).

Settlement hearings are heard in private, the decisions announced in public.

The court considers whether the proposed settlement is in the interest of the person under the disability (C's prospects of success balanced against the likely level of damages were D to be found fully liable if the case went to trial).

Where part 7 proceedings have been started before settlement agreed

When a settlement involving a party under a disability is reached during any Part 7 proceedings, court approval of the settlement is still needed. The procedure is then to issue an application notice with written evidence.

For both

If the court does not approve the settlement on this occasion it is likely to adjourn the case to allow for further negotiation.

If the court does approve the settlement, it gives directions regarding how the court will administer and invest the money on behalf of the person under a disability. Where the amounts involved are large, directions will be that the money is transferred to the Court of Protection.

Differences between Part 8 and Part 7

Part 8	Part 7
No POC	POC
Written evidence filed **with** claim form* If not, need court permission to rely on it at the hearing.	Written evidence can be filed later
Serve evidence with claim form If not, need court permission to rely on it at the hearing	Can be served separately
D files AOS not later than 14 days after CF served and serve it on C and any other party	See next Chapter – D files AOS not later than 14 days after deemed service of the POC
AOS to state whether the defendant contests the claim; and if the defendant seeks a different remedy from that set out in the claim form, what that remedy is.	
Defendant's written evidence **must** be filed with AOS and served on Claimant. Within 14 days of this, C may file further evidence in reply. Failure to file AOS in required timeframe means D may not take part in the hearing unless the court gives permission	Defendant's written evidence can be later than AOS and separate Failure to file AOS in required timeframe (see next Chapter) allows C to apply for Default Judgment ("DJ") (see next Chapter)
No Defence (see next Chapter)	Defence to be filed and served (see next Chapter)
No requirement to respond	Response Pack
No Default Judgment (see next Chapter)	Can apply for Default Judgment (see next Chapter)
Multi-track	Track allocation procedure

Chapter 10

Elements of the syllabus which you have now covered in **civil litigation and evidence**

- A cell with heavy outlining means that that area of the syllabus was covered in this Chapter;
- A darkly shaded cell with a tick √ means that the whole of that syllabus element has now been covered;
- A lightly shaded cell means that part of that element of the syllabus has been covered in a previous Chapter; and
- An unshaded cell means that element of the syllabus has not yet been covered.

1.1 √	1.2 √	1.3 √	2.1 √	2.2 √	3.1 √	3.2 √	6.1 √	6.2 √	6.3 √
6.4 √	7.1 √	7.2 √	8.1	8.2	8.3	9.1	9.2	9.3	10.1
10.2	11.1	11.2	12.1	12.2	12.3	13.1	13.2	13.3 √	13.4 √
13.5	13.6	13.7	13.8	14.1	14.2	14.3	14.4	14.5	14.6
15.1	15.2 √	15.3 √	15.4 √	16.1	16.2	17.1	17.2	17.3	17.4
18.2. √	18.3 √	18.4 √ 18.5	19.1	19.2	19.3	20.1	20.2	20.3	21.1
21.2	21.3	22.1	22.2 22.3	23.3 √	23.2 √	23.3	23.4 √	24.1	

Elements of the syllabus which you have now covered for **ADR**

- A cell with heavy outlining means that that area of the syllabus was covered in this Chapter;
- A darkly shaded cell with a tick √ means that the whole of that syllabus element has now been covered;
- A lightly shaded cell means that part of that element of the syllabus has been covered in a previous Chapter; and
- An unshaded cell means that element of the syllabus has not yet been covered.

1.4 √	1.5√	3.3 √	4.1√	4.2√	5.1√	5.2√	18.1 √	22.3	

Chapter 11

STATEMENTS OF CASE [continued] [CUR 8]

DEFAULT JUDGMENT [CUR 12]

Either

k) D admits; or acknowledges service of the POC and / or serves her defence

or

l) D defaults by not acknowledging service or serving defence in the correct time frames, so C applies for default judgment against her in the claim

and then

If C is successful, D may want to get the default judgment against her set aside so she gets the chance to properly defend herself in court.

THIS CHAPTER CONTAINS THE ITEMS PRINTED IN BOLD IN THE FOLLOWING BOXES

CURRICULUM ("CUR")

~~(Parties~~ is in Chapter 10)

Statements of Case

8.1 claim forms and particulars of claim is in Chapter 10
8.2 acknowledgement of service, defences, replies, counterclaims
8.3 the effect of not responding to an allegation in a statement of case

Default judgment (~~and summary judgment~~ is in Chapter 13)

12.1 default judgments
12.2 applications to set aside
12.3 summary judgments are in Chapter 13

SYLLABUS

STATEMENTS OF CASE - DEFENCE

Examinable material will consist of: contents of claim form, statements of value, contents of particulars of claim, contents of defence, defence of set-off, reply to defence, court's power to dispense with statements of case, particulars of claim in personal injury, matters to be included in particulars of claim, and matters which must be specifically set out in particulars of claim and the defence; acknowledgement of service, consequence of not filing acknowledgement of service, and period for filing acknowledgement of service; filing a defence, consequence of not filing a defence, period for filing defence, agreement extending of period for filing a defence, service of copy of defence, making a counterclaim, reply to defence, court permission for subsequent statements of case, claimant's notice where defence is that money claimed has been paid, and stay of claim if not defended or admitted.

Notice to admit facts from CUR 19

(Each of the above has its own subheading in this Chapter, flagged by EM:)

- **CPR 10.1-10.3**
- **CPR 15.1-15.11, PD15 paragraphs 1-3**
- CPR 16.1-16.8; and PD 16 paragraphs 1-3, 4.1-4.3, 4.4 and 7-15 was in Chapter 10.
- **CUR 19.3, CPR 32.18**
- Section 35A Senior Courts Act and section 69 County Courts Act, at paragraphs 9A-122 and 9A-554 of Volume 2 of 'Civil Procedure' (the White Book) 2020. (This is dealt with in Chapter 23).

DEFAULT JUDGMENT

Examinable material will consist of: claims in which default judgment may be obtained, conditions to be satisfied for default judgment, procedures for obtaining default judgment, nature of judgment obtained, default judgment in claims against more than one defendant, evidence on requests and applications for default judgment, setting aside or varying default judgment

- **CPR 12.1-12.6, 12.8 and 12.10;**
- **CPR 13.1-13.2,**
- **CPR 13.3 (cases where the court may set aside or vary default judgment)**
- **CPR 13.4**

- **Commentary is incorporated in context in this Chapter, highlighted in an Activity box between two stars.**

CHAPTER 11 MOCS (i)

- ***Time frames for***
  - ***Acknowledgment of Service of Particulars of Claim***
  - ***Defences***
    - ***The effect of not responding to all allegations in the POC***
    - ***The effect of not responding at all to the POC (see next page)***
  - ***Replies***
  - ***Counterclaims***

Chapter 11 MOCS (ii)

Default Judgment *NOT available where there is something else going on.*
When • *Please refer to the timeframes for issue and service of statements of case in the boxes in this Chapter.* • *If there is no response from D within the relevant timeframes*
How • *DJ for Money claims/value of undelivered goods request judgment is entered* • *DJ for Any Other Remedy part 23 application* • *DJ against* — *child/protected party,* } — *spouse or civil partner against the other in tort* } — *D outside England and Wales* } *part 23 applications* — *D is a State* } — *D Is a person with diplomatic immunity* }

<u>*Outcomes*</u> • *DJ **MUST** be set aside if it was wrongly entered* • *DJ **MAY** be set aside if prompt application + RPOS **OR** SOGR. The court will consider the 3 stages of <u>Denton</u> including CPR 3.9.* *Then if the claim is reinstated D gets to defend.*

The sessions dealing with this area of the syllabus on my BTC course are	

<u>CUR 8.1</u> <u>CLAIM FORMS AND PARTICULARS OF CLAIM</u>

The claim form and the particulars of claim are the first two statements of case we have met. (Defences and Counterclaims are introduced later in this Chapter).

For all statements of case a party may
- refer in his or her statement of case to any point of law on which his claim or her defence is based
- give in the statement of case the name of any witness s/he proposes to call, and
- attach to or serve with this statement of case a copy of any document which s/ he considers is necessary to his claim or her defence This includes any expert's report to be filed. Expert reports are dealt with in Chapter 23).

<u>EM: contents of claim form</u>
<u>EM: statements of value</u>

Please refer back to the previous Chapter for the detail of these.

<u>EM: matters to be included in particulars of claim, particulars of claim in personal injury, and matters which must be specifically set out in particulars of claim</u>

Please refer back to the previous Chapter for the detail of these.

<u>EM: Court's power to dispense with statements of case</u>

If a claim form has been issued and served correctly the court may make an order that the claim will continue without any other statement of case.

<u>Reminder of the contents of the previous Chapter</u>

Here, in diagram form is what we covered in the previous Chapter regarding service of the CF and POC (w/i = within)

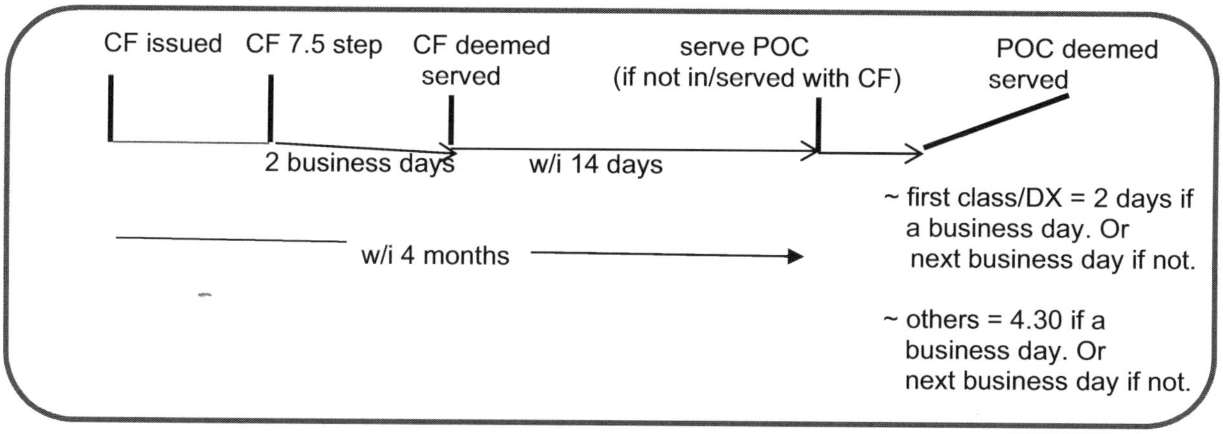

CUR 8.2 ACKNOWLEDGEMENT OF SERVICE, DEFENCES, REPLIES, COUNTERCLAIMS

RESPONDING TO PARTICULARS OF CLAIM

There are five possibilities.

1. D admits everything straightaway; or
2. D acknowledges the service of the POC on her; or
3. D defends, drafting a statement of case called a defence and files that defence at court; or
4. D may also make a claim against C in the form of a counterclaim, usually done in the same document as the defence; or
5. D does nothing - neither acknowledges service on her of the POC nor responds with a defence or defence and counterclaim within the prescribed time limits. (The detail on counterclaims is in the next Chapter).

1. D admits everything

This is the first possibility. If it were a debt claim, D could simply pay what she owes. Otherwise, an unsolicited admission must be made **within 14 days** of deemed service of the CF containing the particulars of the claim (or of POC if CF says POC is to follow). If D does not admit by then and does nothing else either, then C may apply to court for default judgment (see later in this Chapter). If C for some reason does not make such an application then D can admit after the said 14 day period.

CUR 19.3 NOTICES TO ADMIT FACTS

EM: notices to admit facts

A party may solicit an admission by serving notice on another party requiring her to admit the facts, or the part of the case of the serving party, specified in the notice. A notice to admit facts must be served no later than 21 days before the trial.

Where D has **admitted in writing** (e.g. in a notice / a statement of case / a letter), then C makes an interim **application** to court for judgment.

If the claim is simply a money claim D may complete and send to C a court **admission form**. C can then file a **request** at court to obtain judgment.

CUR 8.2 ACKNOWLEDGEMENT OF SERVICE, DEFENCES, REPLIES, COUNTERCLAIMS (continued)

2. D acknowledges service on her of the POC
EM: acknowledgement of service,

This is the second possibility. D sends **AOS** to court **within 14 days** of deemed service of the POC. **EM:** ***period for filing acknowledgement of service.*** By doing this it means she now has 28 days from the deemed date of service of the POC to serve her defence. Remember also that parties can agree between them an extension of up to 28 days on top for D to prepare her defence, in which case D must inform the court of this.

If she felt it appropriate, this is where she would initiate a dispute of the court's jurisdiction.

3. D defends, drafting a statement of case called a defence and files that defence at court
EM: filing a defence, period for filing defence, agreement extending of period for filing a defence.

This is the third possibility. Either

(i) D files Defence at court **14 days** after deemed service of the POC; It is further possible for C and D to agree an extension of up to 28 days and D must notify the court of any such agreement; for example if D felt the need to ask for further information (see Chapter 14) about the contents of the POC which would mean she can draft a proper defence to what C will then have set out in the POC; or

(ii) And repeated from 2. above **- If D filed AOS,** D files Defence at court **28 days** after deemed service of the POC. It is further possible for C and D to agree an extension of up to 28 days and D must notify the court of any such agreement.

In diagram form - time limits for filing the defence

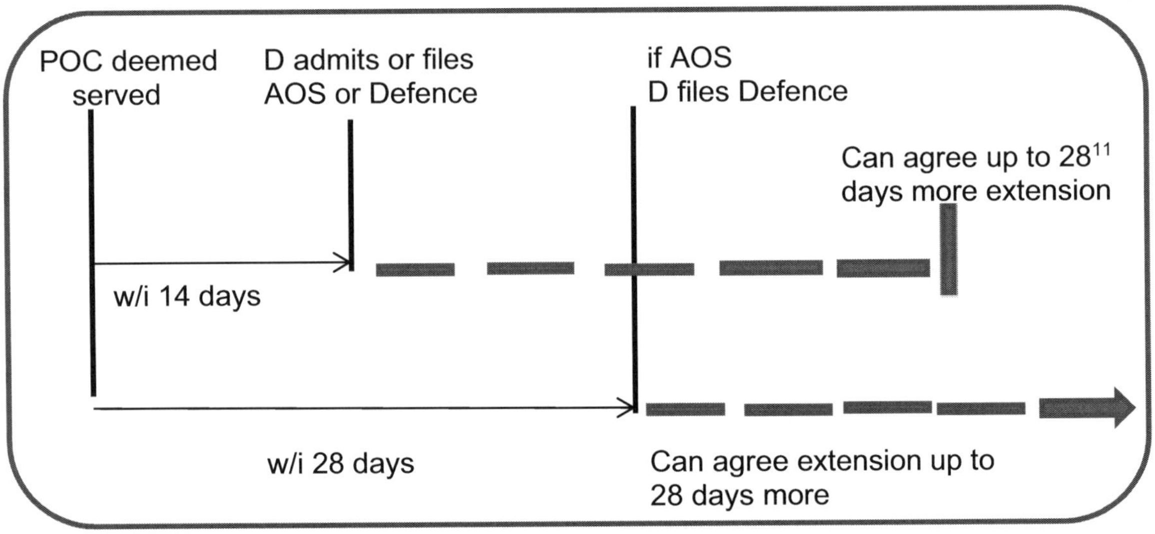

[11] This is to remind you that this 28 day period has its roots in Chapter 2 of this book. **IT IS IMPORTANT THAT YOU ALSO REFER BACK TO THE FOOTNOTES AT THE END OF CHAPTER 2.**

EM: service of copy of defence

A copy of the Defence must be served on every other party.

EM: claimant's notice where defence is that money claimed has been paid

Where the claim is one solely for a specified amount of money (plus interest and costs) and D's defence is that she has already paid C
- the court sends a notice to C asking for a written statement as to whether he wishes to continue with the proceedings
- C responds with a copy response to D
- The claim is stayed if C does not respond within 28 days after service of the court's notice on him
- Any party may apply to lift the stay

No defence needs to be filed if
- the hearing is awaited for an application by D to dispute the court's jurisdiction; or
- if the hearing is awaited for an application by C for summary judgment (see later in Chapter 14 for a full explanation of summary judgment).

EM: contents of defence, matters which must be specifically set out in the defence

You will learn how to draft a defence during the BTC.

In the Defence, one of the following must occur in relation to each statement in C's POC
- D requires C to prove a statement in his POC (require to prove ("**RTP**"))
- D **denies** a statement in C's POC **giving reasons why and giving her own version**
- D **admits** what C has written in his POC

  If D makes none of the 3 above responses to any statement in C's POC, then under CPR 16.5 she is deemed to **admit** that statement. That is **unless** in her defence document she **sets out** the nature of **her case** in relation to the issue to which that allegation is relevant, **or** unless allegations involving **amounts of money** are involved. In these two instances, the effect is that C is now **"RTP"** those statements.

- If D disputes C's statement of value, D must state why and if able, give her own statement of value.
- Statement of the capacity if D is in a representative capacity
- If AOS not filed, D gives an address for service

For PI claims in addition
- Whether in relation to any medical report / PSLA schedule she
  - agrees
  - disputes, giving reasons re the report / alternative figures
  - does neither, but has no knowledge of the matters contained in the report
- attach any medical report of her own

For the limitation defence in addition
- date the limitation period expired

– ***EM: defence of set-off***

In layman's terms, if I owe you £15 and you owe me £20, you should pay me £5. Setting off what I owe you against what you owe me results in you paying me £5.

In legal terminology:- a set-off operates as a defence either to the whole or part of a claim. (i.e. if you bring a claim against me for the £20 I owe you, I will claim set-off the £15 you owe me as a defence to your claim). Therefore, you will learn in the drafting course on the BTC to state the set-off at the end of the Defence when there is a set-off situation. You will also learn that a D claims the amount of the set-off in any counterclaim against C. (D owes C £15 and C brings a claim against D for that £15; at the end of D's defence she states that there is a set-off situation in that C owes her £20; D therefore counterclaims against C, claiming the £5 that he owes her.)

Such mutual debts for liquidated (definite) amounts, (there is no need for the debts to be connected), is one situation where a set-off may occur.

4. **D counterclaims against C**
   EM: *making a counterclaim*

The fourth possibility is where D also makes a claim against C in the form of a counterclaim, usually done in the same document as the defence, to avoid the need for obtaining court permission to bring the counterclaim.

This is an example of an additional claim under Part 20 CPR. Full details are in the next Chapter. So if D now wants to counter with a claim against C she will include a counterclaim, usually in the same document in which she sets out her defence. The name of the statement of case will therefore include DEFENCE and COUNTERCLAIM.

If D made a counterclaim, C will serve a defence to D's counterclaim. It must be filed and served within 14 days of service of the counterclaim.

RESPONDING (replying) TO A DEFENCE [AND COUNTERCLAIM]

EM: reply to defence C does not have to reply to D's defence, but can do so. If he does, the reply must contain a statement of truth.

If C makes no response to a statement in D's defence, then C is **not taken to admit it**.

If C does file a reply but fails to deal with a matter raised in the defence, then C is taken to require D to prove that statement. **"RTP".**

C will therefore file a reply where in relation to D's defence where he wants to
- admit something in the defence; or
- allege facts in answer to D's defence which he had not included in his POC.

The reply, verified by a statement of truth, must be filed at court and served on the other parties with C's directions questionnaire (see Chapter 20) during the next stage of the litigation process.

– Where there is both a counterclaim and a reply, they can be included in the same document. Since the time limits for filing and serving are different, the court may order that the counterclaim and reply be filed together by the time limit as if it were a reply only.

If no such order is made, the counterclaim and reply should be filed separately each within their own time limits.

EM: court permission for subsequent statements of case Court permission is needed if a party wishes to file any statement of case after a reply.

CUR 8.3 THE EFFECT OF NOT RESPONDING TO [AN ALLEGATION IN] A STATEMENT OF CASE

The effects of not responding to particular allegations (i.e. statements) in statements of case are contained on the previous pages of this Chapter.

The effect of not responding at all to a CF/POC is as follows.

CUR 12.1 DEFAULT JUDGMENT

EM: claims in which default judgment may be obtained

The examinable material sets this out as '***claims in which default judgment may be obtained.***' The CPR sets it out as '***claims in which default judgment may NOT be obtained.***'

Where default judgment is not available

(ostensibly where there is something else going on!)

- Claims for delivery of goods under the Consumer Credit Act 1974
- Part 8 claims
- Where a PD says so
- Where D has made an application to get C's case struck out under CPR 3.4 [Please see later in Chapter 13 on strike out] and that hearing is still awaited
- Where there is an application for summary judgment by D which has not been disposed of before DJ was entered for lack of defence [Please see later in Chapter 16 on summary judgment]. It is possible this situation could arise, as D can apply for SJ at any time once proceedings have commenced.
- Where D has paid her debt and any associated costs to C (unless the default judgment was correctly entered, since the deemed date of service of the POC had passed and there had been no response from D within the 14 days of that deemed service, because D had not in fact received the POC (or because of the use of the irrebuttable presumption of 2 business days' deemed date of service of a CF – refer back to Chapter 10). D's remedy would then be to apply to court to get the correctly entered default judgment against her set aside)
- C is seeking judgment on a claim for money; and
- the defendant has filed or served on the claimant an admission under rule 14.4 or 14.7 (admission of liability to pay all of the money claimed) together with a request for time to pay
- Where a "closed material application" under the Justice and Security Act 2013 is pending.

5. **D does nothing**

This is the fifth possibility. D neither admits, nor acknowledges service on her of the POC nor responds with a defence or a defence and counterclaim within the prescribed time limits.

EM: consequence of not filing acknowledgement of service, consequence of not filing a defence.

C applies for default judgment. C applies for judgment in his favour due to D's default in not putting in a defence

EM: conditions to be satisfied for default judgment

If, **by the date the default judgment is entered**, D has not replied to the POC by filing an admission, an AOS or a defence within the timeframes set out in the most recent box diagram above, (or if C does not then reply with a defence to a counterclaim by D within 14 days of deemed service of it (please see Chapter 12 for counterclaims)), "time limits for filing the defence" she is in default of doing so (or he is, if it relates to a D's counterclaim); in default of following the CPR. That entitles C (or D if a counterclaim) to be given judgment without trial, which in these circumstances is known as default judgment. The box diagram shows how to calculate time for entry of default judgment.

EM: stay of claim if not defended or admitted.

C has until 6 months from the end of the period for D to file a defence, to apply for default judgment (or summary judgment, Chapter 14). If no such application is made and if no AOS or defence has been filed by then, there is an automatic stay (suspension) of proceedings.

Further, as you will recall from Chapter 10, an **automatic** stay imposed by the court **6 months after** the end of the period for filing the defence if

- D has not admitted / defended / put in a counterclaim; and
- there has been no application for default judgment or for summary judgment [Summary Judgment will be explained later in Chapter 14].

Any party can apply for an automatic stay to be **lifted** so that proceedings will continue on their way. This is a Part 23 Application. As this is a relief from a sanction, the court will consider the criteria in CPR 3.9. Full details are in Chapter 20.

EM: procedures for obtaining default judgment

There are two procedures for obtaining default judgment and the correct one must be used.

1. Where the claim is for **money/value of undelivered goods** and C has filed a certificate of service of POC at court, C can **request** by filling in the relevant forms that default judgment is **entered** once the time for filing a defence has passed.

   No permission is required for this.

EM: nature of judgment obtained

– The nature of the judgment obtained by filing a request is that the court will enter judgment for the amount plus interest.

Where default judgment is obtained in this way, the request may include the amount of **interest** claimed to the date of judgment **if**

- the POC contains all that it should (please refer back to Chapter 11 in the section on **POC contents**) and
- where statutory interest is claimed, (see Chapter 24) the amount of interest is **no higher than** the rate of **interest payable on judgment debts** (currently 8%) at the date when the CF was issued and
- C's request includes a **calculation** of the amount of interest claimed covering the period from when interest was calculated upto in the CF and the date of the request for judgment, so that the full amount claimed in interest is fully set out.
- If any of these three elements are not met, judgment will be for an amount of interest to be decided by the court.

– Where the claim is for an unspecified amount of money, the court will decide the amount. For those County Court claims where a request for judgment which includes an amount of money to be decided by the court is filed, the claim will be sent to the preferred County Court hearing centre.

EM: default judgment in claims against more than one defendant

C may obtain default judgment against one of two or more Ds and then continue with his claim against the other D or Ds if the claim can be dealt with separately from the claim against the other Ds.

If it cannot, then the court will not enter default judgment against that D and the court must deal with the default judgment application at the same time as it disposes of the claim against the other Ds.

Where default judgment was in relation to possession of **land or delivery of goods** and has been obtained against one of two or more Ds, C can **only enforce** against that D **if**

- he has obtained a **judgment** (by default judgment or otherwise) for possession or delivery **against all the Ds** to the claim **or**
- the **court gives permission.**

2. Where the claim is for **any other remedy** than money/value of undelivered goods and

C has filed a certificate of service of POC at court, C can **apply** to the court under **Part 23** CPR for default judgment to be entered.

Part 23 applications **also** need to be made if

- D is a child/protected party
- The claim is by a spouse or civil partner against the other in tort
- D is outside England and Wales
- D is a State
- D is a person with diplomatic immunity

The outline for how to make a Part 23 application has already been set out in this book in the table towards the end of Chapter 3.

EM: evidence on [requests and] APPLICATIONS for default judgment

Activity

Please refer back to Chapter 3 and refresh your memory/notes on how to make a Part 23 application. You may wish to write it out again here.

When a claim includes a **mix** of a claim for money/value of goods and "any other remedy" then a **Part 23** application must be made for default judgment.

When a claim includes a mix of a claim for money/value of goods and "any other remedy" and the latter claim is abandoned, so that the remaining claim is now only for money/value of goods, then at this point C can simply request to have default judgment entered.

Costs

Remember that costs on default judgment where the claim is for specified sum > £25 = fixed costs as per part 45 Table 1 (Part 45 is not mentioned in the rquired content for the assessment this year). For a claim for an unspecified amount, the costs will be in the court's discretion.

CUR 12.2 APPLICATIONS TO SET ASIDE

EM: setting aside or varying default judgment

D may apply to set-aside a default judgment or to have it varied, **not more than 14 days after** receiving the default judgment, so that if she is successful, the case will continue onwards to trial.

Unless the claim was commenced in a specialist list, (e.g. in the Technology and Construction Court or in the Commercial Court or in the Mercantile Court) then

- where the default judgment was obtained in a court which was not **D's home court**, any application to set it aside or vary it will be moved there (*transferred* from the High Court / *sent* by a County Court officer) where
  - the claim is for a **specified amount of money** and
  - D is an **individual** and
  - the claim has **not already been moved** to the home court of another D

- where the claim was started in the County Court Money Claims Centre in Salford, an application to set aside or vary default judgment will be sent to the **preferred hearing centre** (further correspondence, and any further requests should be sent to / made there) where
  - the claim is for a **specified amount of money** and
  - D is **not an individual** and
  - the claim has not been sent to County Court hearing centre.

There are two sets of circumstances where D will want to make an application to set aside (or vary) a default judgment against her.

The first is where the default judgment against her was wrongly entered.
The court **MUST** set the default judgment aside **if it has been wrongly entered**
- entered in circumstances where DJ is not available (see the paragraph above) or
- administrative mistake, e.g. mistakenly granted before time frame for service of defence had elapsed or
- the whole of the claim was satisfied (e.g. the debtor had paid the creditor) before judgment was entered

The second is where D can show (her application being made **promptly**) **either** that she has a real prospect of successfully defending the claim, **or** there is some other good reason
- why the judgment should be set aside or varied or
- why she should be allowed to defend the claim.

An application to set aside is a **Part 23 application, to include in addition a draft of D's defence, so**
- **Application notice** stating the order sought and why
- **Written evidence,** often a witness statement with exhibits verified by statement of truth
- **Draft defence – OBVIOUSLY!**
- **Draft order**
- In 2014, case law held that setting aside a default judgment is in addition to be dealt with as a relief from the sanction of the default judgment, so that **CPR 3.9** should also be considered using the **three stages** detailed towards the end of Chapter 19 of this book.

This is one of the areas of the examinable material on the BTC syllabus where it is imperative that you know the **exact wording** of the test. It is not acceptable merely to have a vague notion of the elements of the test, or even worse, of only parts of it!

You are therefore **strongly recommended** to complete the following activities.

Activity

Copy out the exact wording of CPR 13.3 here and then learn it.
This sets out where the court MAY set aside default judgment.

Activity

Remember to make notes on the relevant case law authorities in paragraphs 13.3.1-13.3.5 in the commentary in the White Book.

You may find it useful to add in references to the case law NOW at the appropriate points of this Chapter.

When approaching final revision time, remember to add in the salient findings of the cases at the relevant point in any 'mental crib sheet' into which you have distilled the main points of your learned knowledge.

– The likely costs order on an application to set aside is found in PD 44. in the section called "Court's discretion as to costs: rule 44.2" in the table in note 4.2; an order for "costs thrown away". This means that when a judgment is set aside, the party in whose favour the costs order is made is entitled to the costs which have been incurred as a consequence of needing to apply for the relief from the set-aside. This includes the costs of –
- preparing for and attending any hearing at which the judgment or order which has been set aside was made;
- preparing for and attending any hearing to set aside the judgment or order in question;
- preparing for and attending any hearing at which the court orders the proceedings or the part in question to be adjourned;
- any steps taken to enforce a judgment or order which has subsequently been set asid

Chapter 11

Elements of the syllabus which you have now covered for **civil litigation and evidence**

- A cell with heavy outlining means that that area of the syllabus was covered in this Chapter;
- A darkly shaded cell with a tick √ means that the whole of that syllabus element has now been covered;
- A lightly shaded cell means that part of that element of the syllabus has been covered in a previous Chapter; and
- An unshaded cell means that element of the syllabus has not yet been covered.

1.1 √	1.2 √	1.3 √	2.1 √	2.2 √	3.1 √	3.2 √	6.1 √	6.2 √	6.3 √
64 √	7.1 √	7.2 √	8.1 √	8.2 √	8.3 √	9	9.2	9.3	10.1
10.2	11.1	11.2	12.1 √	12.2 √	12.3	13.1	13.2	13.3 √	13.4 √
13.5	13.6	13.7	13.8	14.1	14.2	14.3	14.4	14.5	14.6
15.1	15.2 √	15.3 √	15.4 √	16.1	16.2	17.1	17.2	17.3	17.4
182. √	18.3 √	18.4 √	19.1	19.2	19.3	20.1	20.2	20.3	21.1
21.2	21.3	22.1	22.2 22.3	23.1 √	23.2 √	23.3	23.4 √	22.1	

Chapter 12

MULTIPLE CAUSES OF ACTION [CUR 9]

COUNTERCLAIMS AND OTHER ADDITIONAL CLAIMS [CUR 9]

AMENDMENT [CUR 10]

THIS CHAPTER CONTAINS THE ITEMS PRINTED IN BOLD IN THE FOLLOWING BOXES

n) Multiple Causes of Action, Counterclaims and Other Additional Claims

m) Amending statements of case

CURRICULUM ("CUR")

- ***Multiple causes of action, counterclaims and other additional claims***

9.1 multiple causes of action and multiple parties

9.2 counterclaims against the claimant or an additional party

9.3 contribution notices and claims against third parties and fourth parties

- ***Amendment***

10.1 permission or consent to amend

10.2 costs consequences of amendment

SYLLABUS

MULTIPLE CAUSES OF ACTION, COUNTERCLAIMS AND OTHER ADDITIONAL CLAIMS

Examinable material will consist of: multiple causes of action and multiple parties, changes of parties, provisions where two or more persons are jointly entitled to a remedy, *adding and substituting parties, adding or substituting parties after the end of a relevant limitation period, removal of parties, transfer of interest or liability (included as part of "amendment" below)*
counterclaims against the claimant or an additional party, and claims for contribution or indemnity from another party.

(Each of the above has its own subheading in this Chapter, flagged by EM:)

- **CPR 19.1**
- CPR 19.2 and 19.4 and PD19A paragraphs 1-5 are in the "Amendment" section of this Chapter
- **CPR 19.3**
- CPR 19.5 is in the "Amendment" section of this Chapter
- **CPR 20.1-10 and PD 20 paragraphs 1-7.**

AMENDMENT

Examinable material will consist of
(from above - adding and substituting parties, adding
or substituting parties after the end of a relevant limitation period, removal of parties, transfer of interest or liability)

amendments to statements of case, the power of the court to disallow amendments made without permission, amendments to statements of case with permission of the court and amendments to statements of case after the end of a relevant limitation period.

(Each of the above has its own subheading in this Chapter, flagged by EM:)

- **CUR 9 (continued)**
- **CUR 10**
- **CPR 17.1-17.2; PD17 paragraphs 1-2**
- **The words immediately underneath the heading of PD17, which read as follows: "A party applying for an amendment will usually be responsible for the costs of and arising from the amendment"**
- **CPR 17.3 (amendments to statements of case with permission of the court)**
- **CPR 17.4 (amendments to statements of case after the end of a relevant imitation period)**

- **CPR 19.2, PD 19A paragraphs 1- 5 (from CUR 9)**
- **CPR 19.4 (from CUR 9)**
- **CPR 19.5 (adding or substituting parties after the end of a relevant limitation period) (from CUR 9)**

And returning to CUR 10

.

- **Limitation Act 1980 section 35, at paragraph 8-102 of Volume 2 of 'Civil Procedure' (the White Book) 2020.**
- **Commentary is incorporated in context in this Chapter, highlighted in an Activity box between two stars**

Chapter 12 MOCS (i) – Multiple causes of action

- ***A person can add an additional claim to the main claim***

  a) without court permission if done at or before defence

  b) court permission is needed if done at any other time

  1. as a counterclaim; or

  2. as a claim for a contribution or indemnity against a person who is already a party; or

  3. as a claim for any other additional claim that is not 1. or 2.

  (i) adding a third party (TP) – perhaps for a claim for contribution or indemnity; and there may also follow

  (ii) a third party adding a claim against a fourth party....(and so on).

Chapter 12 MOCS (ii)- Amendment

- ***Statements of case can be amended without court permission before they are served.***

- ***During the limitation period, once they are served :-***

  - ***Where the application is to add, substitute or remove a party, court permission is needed AND the written consent of all parties is a prerequisite to that.***

  - ***Where the application is to make some other amendment, the written consent of all parties is needed although, OR, the court may grant the amendment without all consents.***

- ***After the limitation period it is possible to introduce new causes of action and to add and substitute parties. There are separate requirements for each. (Please refer to the tables in this Chapter).***

The sessions dealing with this area of the syllabus on my BTC course are	

CUR 9.1 MULTIPLE CAUSES OF ACTION AND MULTIPLE PARTIES

The examinable material highlighted in bold above is dealt with in the first part of this Chapter. The non-highlighted material is dealt with under the heading "Amendment" later in this Chapter.

- You will learn from your BTC that it is perfectly usual to bring more than one cause of action at one time, such as setting out a claim in both contract and the tort of negligence in relation to the same set of facts. The section called "Amendments" in this Chapter sets out how to add a cause of action after the relevant statement of case is served.

- You will also learn that it is perfectly usual to join in more than one party, so that there can be multiple claimants and defendants in the same action. Any number of claimants or defendants may be joined as parties to a claim. The section called "Amendments" in this Chapter sets out how to join in parties by adding or substituting them either before or after the relevant statement of case is served.

Where there is a new claim of

- a counterclaim including a set-off
- the addition or substitution of a new cause of action
- the addition or substitution of a new party

time for limitation purposes starts to run from that date on which those proceedings were commenced.

- ***EM: provisions where two or more persons are jointly entitled to a remedy***

  In proceedings other than probate proceedings, where a C claims a remedy to which some other person is jointly entitled with him, so where there should be 2 or more Cs, all persons jointly entitled to the remedy must be parties, i.e. be claimants in the action, unless the court orders otherwise.

  If any person does not agree to be a C he must be made a D, unless the court orders otherwise. How to add that party as a D is set out in the "Amendment" section of this Chapter.

ADDITIONAL CLAIMS

It may be that D wants to add an additional claim of her own to the original main claim that C has brought against her. In so doing she is aiming to pass on some or all liability to someone else.

The contents of an additional claim should be verified by a **statement of truth**.

'[I believe][the (claimant or as may be) believes] that the facts stated in this [name document being verified] are true."

Proceedings for contempt of court may be brought against a person if he makes, or causes to be made, a false statement in a document, here the additional claim, and verifies it by a statement of truth without an honest belief in its truth.

A person on whom an additional claim is served **becomes a party** to the proceedings if he is not a party already.

When an additional claim is served on an existing party for the purpose of requiring the court to decide a question against that party in a further capacity, that party also becomes a party in the further capacity specified in the additional claim.

CUR 9.2 COUNTERCLAIMS AGAINST THE CLAIMANT [or an additional party]

EM: counterclaims against the claimant [or an additional party]

Types of additional claim are set out in CPR 20.2 (1) (a), (b) and (c). For teaching purposes I have renamed these as types 1-3 in the remainder of this Chapter.

Type 1(i) = Counterclaim against the Claimant

CPR 20.2 (1) (a)

Activity

You may find it useful to copy the definition of a counterclaim from GL here

There are two scenarios where a counterclaim can come about.
The first is where

C brings a claim against D, the original claim i.e.

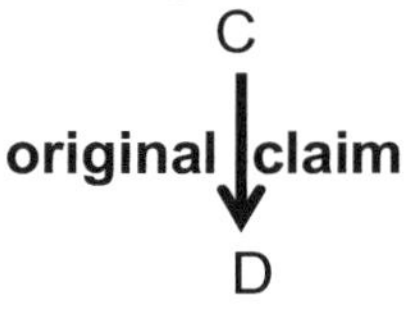

then D wants to counter C with a claim **against C**, i.e.

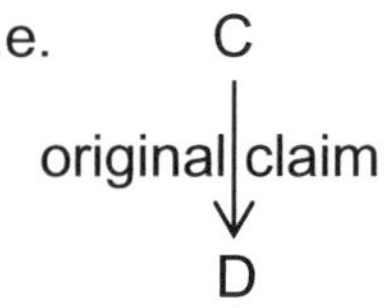

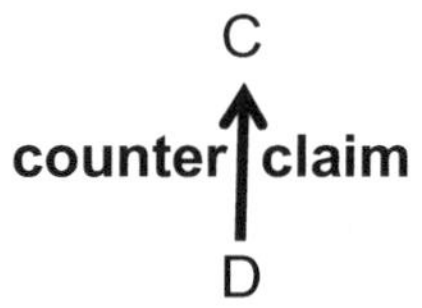

[It may help during the learning process to think in the following way regarding the counterclaim by D against C.

In effect, D is the claimant in the counterclaim and C is the defendant. The parties are NEVER referred to in this way, though. **The original nomenclature is always retained**].

CPR 20.4

When permission is not needed

D does not need court permission for a counterclaim against C **provided** the counterclaim is **filed with her defence.** As you will see in the "Amendments" section of this Chapter, no court permission is needed to amend a statement of case before it has been served.

That is why you will be drafting statements of case called 'Defence and Counterclaim'. The Defence and Counterclaim should normally form one document with the Counterclaim following on from the Defence.

Where permission IS needed

Should D draft a Defence, serve it and then wish to amend it to add in a counterclaim against C, or if D wishes to file the particulars of the counterclaim **at any other time** [than with her Defence]

then **court permission will be needed** to do so. [The reason for the diamond will

become clear in a later Activity box].

Steps to apply for permission to make an additional claim

D should file

- **application notice** {The application may be without serving the notice [except for Type 2 claims – see later] unless the court directs otherwise}.
- **evidence** stating
  - the stage which the proceedings have reached (and where possible, a timetable of the proceedings to date.,
  - the nature of the additional claim to be made or details of the question or issue which needs to be decided
  - a summary of the facts on which the additional claim is based, and
  - the name and address of any proposed additional party.

  If the reason for needing to apply is delay, include an explanation of the delay in the evidence accompanying the application
- **a copy of the proposed additional claim**

What the court will consider

The court will consider the matters set out in CPR 20.9 (2) when deciding whether or not to give permission for it.

Activity

Copy out the contents of CPR 20.9 (2) here.

<u>What happens once the counterclaim has been made and served both (i) when permission was not needed or (ii) when it has been obtained</u>

(i) C <u>may</u> then serve a Reply to D's defence and C <u>does put in a defence</u> to matters raised in D's counterclaim within 14 days of deemed service on C of D's 'Defence and Counterclaim' i.e. statement of case.

Where C is doing both, this should also be in one document containing the Reply to the Defence followed by the Defence to the Counterclaim.

(ii) As C is likely to have replied to D's defence already, if he is going to, then C, similarly to (i) above, <u>does put in a defence</u> to matters raised in D's 'Counterclaim' i.e. statement of case, within 14 days of deemed service on C of D's 'Counterclaim'. C's statement of case this time will simply be called 'Defence to the Counterclaim'.

<u>CUR 9.2</u> <u>COUNTERCLAIMS AGAINST [the claimant or] AN ADDITIONAL PARTY</u>

<u>EM: counterclaims against [the claimant or] an additional party]</u>

<u>Type 1(ii) = Counterclaim against an additional party</u>

<u>The second is where</u>

C brings a claim against D, the original claim i.e.

C

original ↓ **claim**

D

then

D wants to counter C with a claim **<u>against a person other than C as well as against C</u>**, i.e. C   C and a person other than C (called a Third Party (TP)*)

original ↓ claim   **counter ↑ claim**

D   D

*In this example, called the third party. Please refer to PD 20.7 for the explanation as to why)

[Again, it may help to remember that here D is in the position of a claimant and therefore the "person other than C" is in the same position as a second defendant; here, they are the third party to be named in the proceedings, after C and D].

CPR 20.5 sets out that a Defendant who wishes to counterclaim against a person other than the Claimant must apply to the court for an order that that person be added as an additional party.

The procedure for doing so is set out in CPR 20.7 which states that Court permission is not required provided the form is issued **before or at the same time** as D files her defence. Then, pursuant to CPR 20.8 (1) (a) the CF form for the counterclaim must also be **served** on every other party (in this example, on C) **when** a copy of the **defence** to the original claim is **served**.

<u>Where permission IS needed</u>

Should D wish to make an additional claim at **any other time** than before or at the same time as she files her Defence then **court permission will be needed** to do so. [The reason for the diamond will become clear in a later Activity box].

<u>Steps to apply for permission to make an additional claim against a person other than the claimant</u>

- The same steps as for Type 1(i) above
- An application for permission to make an additional claim may be made without notice, unless the court directs otherwise.
- Particulars of an additional claim must be contained in or served with the additional claim.

The court will make directions as to the management of the case.

<u>QOCS in Counterclaims</u>

You will recall from the costs Chapter of this book, the introduction of QOCS. The CPR states in respect of QOCS that 'claimant' means a person bringing a PI / death / fatal accident claim and includes a person making a counterclaim. This means that QOCS applies to the **whole case** after a D has been unsuccessful in her PI counterclaim, as D is the 'claimant' who made a claim in the form of a counterclaim.

In the latest clarification in case law on this point in 2018, a C sued for financial losses arising from an RTA but made no claim for PI; D counterclaimed for PI. C succeeded at trial and the counterclaim was dismissed. This resulted in the conclusion that the wording of the CPR does allow D to avoid payment of costs in the main action. D's Counsel argued that if a claim was totally devoid of merit or was being used as a vehicle in order to give a defendant QOCS protection, "then the part 20 claim would be struck out as being an abuse of a process or disclosing no reasonable grounds".

CUR 10.3 CONTRIBUTION NOTICES

[and claims against third parties and fourth parties]

EM: claims for contribution or indemnity from another party

Type 2 = An additional claim by D for a contribution or indemnity **against a person already a party**

CPR 20.2(1)(b)

Activity

You may find it useful to copy the definition from GL here

Contribution

Activity

You may find it useful to copy the definitions from GL here

Indemnity

C brings a claim, **the original claim**, against two defendants, D1 and D2 i.e.

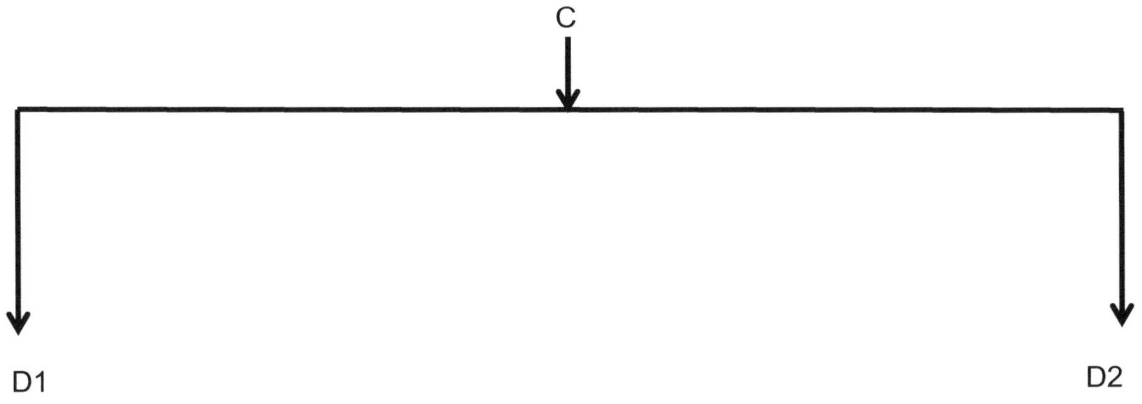

In the example here, the two Ds are already parties as C has joined them both in as Ds.

Then one of the defendants wants to claim contribution or indemnity against the other.

We will say that D1 has filed an AOS or defence to the original claim and wants to make an additional claim for contribution or indemnity against D2. (It could be the other way around).

A contribution is fault based and relates to D1's right to recover from D2 all or part of the amount that D1 is liable to pay to C.

An indemnity is D1's right to recover from D2 the whole amount which D1 is liable to pay; under contract (e.g. insurance), or by statute, or in by virtue of an agent/principal relationship.

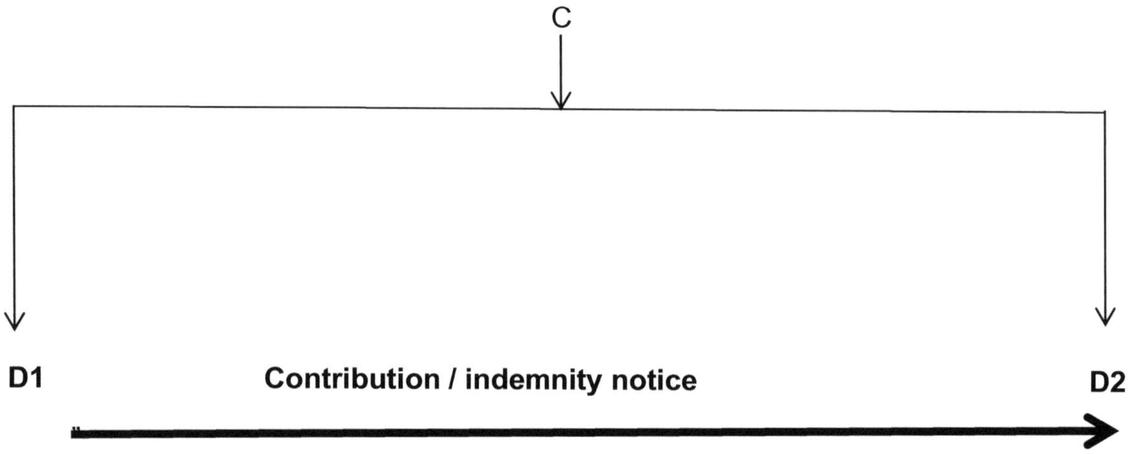

CPR 20.6

A D who has filed an acknowledgment of service or a defence may make an additional claim for contribution or indemnity against a person who is already a party to the proceedings by

- filing a notice containing a statement of the nature and grounds of his additional claim; and
- serving the notice on that party.

When permission is not needed

CPR 20.6 (2) (a) (i). **D1 does not need court permission** for an additional claim for contribution against the other D

- **provided** she files and serves it **with her defence** to the original claim. This can be achieved in the same statement of case; or
- if her additional claim for contribution or indemnity is against a party added to the claim later, within 28 days after that party files her defence.

When permission IS needed

CPR 20 .6 (2) (b) where the notice is filed ***and served*** at **any other time** than as set out in the previous sub heading, the **court's permission will be needed**.

What the court will consider

(i.e. matters relevant to question of whether an additional claim should be separate from the claim)

The court will consider the matters set out in CPR 20.9 (2) when deciding whether or not to give permission for this type of additional claim to be brought.

<u>If needed, once permission is granted the procedure for applying for this type of additional claim is</u>

- A (D1 or D2) files a notice containing a statement of the nature and grounds of her additional claim; and
- serves the notice on the other party (D1 or D2).

Please be aware that contribution/ indemnity can also be claimed in the next section of this Chapter, where appropriate.

<u>QOCS in claims for contribution and indemnity?</u>

You will recall from the costs Chapter of this book, the introduction of QOCS. The CPR states in respect of QOCS that 'claimant' means a person bringing a PI / death / fatal accident claim and includes a person making a counterclaim or an additional claim. This means that QOCS applies to the whole case after a D has been unsuccessful in her PI counterclaim/additional claim, as D is the 'claimant' who made a claim in the form of a counterclaim or additional claim.

QOCS has hitherto been considered not relevant where D also claims for indemnity or contribution against a third party, as that is a dispute between commercial parties about which of them is liable to pay damages to C. Whether or not this will still be argued to be the case, remains to be seen, since such claims are also Part 20 claims, although not mentioned by name in r44.13(2); plus the reference to 'proceedings' in CPR 44(1) has by some been given the broad meaning in case law of including Part 20 claims.

<u>CUR 9.3</u> **<u>[...] AND CLAIMS AGAINST THIRD PARTIES AND FOURTH PARTIES]</u>**

<u>Type 3 = An additional claim by D for **any other additional claim** against any person **not already a party.**</u>

<u>Type 3 (i)</u>

<u>CPR 20.2 (1) (b)</u>

C brings a claim against D, the original claim i.e.

C

original ↓ **claim**

D

then

the additional claim is where D wants to bring an additional claim [not one of those set out above in this Chapter] of her own - perhaps for contribution or indemnity - against someone else who is **not already a party**, called a third party (TP).

C

original ↓ claim

D

↓ **An additional claim by D against a third party (perhaps for a contribution or indemnity) against whom C had not brought a claim in the original claim (and so the TP is added to claim later)**

TP

This has **advantages or benefits** in that it

- saves the expense of having two trials
- safeguards against different courts providing different results on the same facts
- ensures that the TP claim (or fourth party's claim, who will be referred to by name in the Type 3(ii) scenario) is decided at or around the same time as the other claims
- ensures that TP / named fourth party is bound by the decision regarding C and D in the original claim.
- Note that if C accepts an offer from D to settle after D has brought the additional claim against TP, that the additional claim between D and TP still exists and will continue!

<u>When permission is not needed</u>

CPR 20.7 (3) (a). **D does not need court permission** for an additional claim of this type **provided** she issues the CF against TP **before or at the same time as filing her defence** to the original claim.

<u>When permission IS needed</u>

CPR 20.7 (3) (b) If D wishes make the additional claim at **any other time** than before or with her defence, the **court's permission will be needed**.

<u>Steps to apply for permission to make an additional claim</u>

As set out in Type 1 above.

<u>What the court will consider</u>

The court will consider the

matters set out in CPR 20.9 (2) when deciding whether or not to give permission.

<u>Next steps in making additional claims against third parties</u>

- CPR 20.7 (2). D issues the "Part 20" CF for the additional claim against TP.
- CPR 20.8 (1). Within 14 days after the date of issue of the CF,
- CPR 20.7 (4). D serves CF and POC together **at the same time** on TP.
- CPR 20.7 refers to CPR 15.4. So within 14 days deemed service of the {CF with POC with Response pack} on TP, TP can do one of
  - Admit
  - File AOS
  - File Defence

- As here, where D to an additional claim files a Defence, other than to a counterclaim, the court will arrange a hearing to consider case management of the additional claim. This will normally be at the same time as a case management hearing for the original claim and any other additional claims.
- The court will give notice of the hearing to each party likely to be affected by any order made at the hearing
- Where D's additional claim for contribution or indemnity is against a party added to the claim later (TP), court permission is not needed for that additional claim provided that D brings it within 28 days after that party (TP) files her defence

- At the hearing the court may:
  - treat the hearing as a summary judgment hearing,
  - order that the additional claim be dismissed,
  - give directions about the way any claim, question or issue set out in or arising from the additional claim should be dealt with,
  - (4) give directions as to the part, if any, the additional defendant will take at the trial of the claim,
  - give directions about the extent to which the additional defendant is to be bound by any judgment or decision to be made in the claim.

  The court may make any of these 5 orders either before or after any judgment in the claim has been entered by C against D.

Activity

It would be useful if you gathered together here, the references to when court permission is needed to make an additional claim. These are highlighted above by being placed in diamonds.

Type 3 (ii) = Where an additional claim has been made against a person who is not already a party, any additional claim made by that person against any other person (whether or not already a party).

CPR 20.2 (1) (c)

We will start with the diagram from the section above, reproduced here.

C

original ↓ claim

D

↓ An additional claim by D against a third party against whom C had not brought a claim in the original claim

TP

The next additional claim is where TP wants to bring a claim of his/her own against someone else who is not already a party, called by the BSB a fourth party. This latter will be **called by their name** rather than being known as a fourth party in statements of case.

Once the additional claim has been issued by TP against the fourth Party, then the fourth party will be a party.

Once that fourth party is a party, he/she may want to bring a claim of his/her own against someone else who is not already a party, a fifth party.

Once the additional claim has been issued by the fourth party against the fifth party, then the fifth party, who will be called by name rather than as a fifth party in statements of case, will be a party.

And so on.

It is likely, though, that by this point, the claims should instead be made in their own right as original claims, rather than being additional to the original claim, being so far removed from it.

This is in diagram form on the next page.

C

original ↓ claim

D

↓ An additional claim by D against a third party against whom C had not brought a claim in the original claim.

TP

↓ **An additional claim by TP against a fourth party against whom C had not brought a claim in the original claim and D had not brought a claim against in the previous additional claim.**

Eliza Doolittle (who will be referred to by name, which may be suitable abbreviated if appropriate, not as the fourth party, in the statements of case)

CPR 20.7, 20.8, 20.11 and 20.12

The procedure/steps each time is as previously set out under Type 3 (i).

QOCS in additional claims

You will recall from the costs Chapter of this book, the introduction of QOCS. The CPR states in respect of QOCS that 'claimant' means a person bringing a PI / death / fatal accident claim and includes a person making a counterclaim **or an additional claim.** This means that QOCS applies to the **whole case** after a D has been unsuccessful in her PI counterclaim/additional claim, as D is the 'claimant' who made a claim in the form of a counterclaim **or additional claim.**

Amendment

CUR 10.1 PERMISSION OR CONSENT TO AMEND

The statements of case so far introduced in this book are the claim form ("CF"), the particulars of claim, ("POC") and the defence (and counterclaim). In addition we have met Reply to Defence and Defence to Counterclaim earlier in this Chapter.

EM: amendments to statements of case

Statements of case can be amended at any time before they are served (and no permission is needed to do this!)

EM: the power of the court to disallow amendments made without permission

A party can apply to the court for an order that any frivolous/vexatious amendments made before the statement of case is served be disallowed. The application must be made within 14 days from when the statement of case was deemed served on the applicant.

EM: amendments to statements of case with permission of the court

Once the (CF) has been served

Amendment refers to a party wishing to amend a statement of case so as to
1. add or substitute or remove a party; or
2. do something other than add or substitute or remove a party, so e.g.
   - amend the cause(s) of action
   - add in issues

Do note the different requirements for court permission for each of 1. and 2. These differing requirements are set out below.

AMENDING STATEMENTS OF CASE *BEFORE* THE END OF THE RELEVANT LIMITATION PERIOD

1. Where the amendment is to add / substitute / remove a party (remember that there can be any number of Cs or Ds).

An existing party who wishes to add or substitute a party [or a person who wishes to be **added, substituted or removed** as a party] once the statement of case has been served must

- First obtain the written consent of all other parties then
- Apply for court permission

Adding and substituting parties

Adding a party - How to apply for court permission

The applicant needs (Part 23 application)
- **application notice**
- the **written consent** of all the other parties, including that of the party to be added and to file that consent at court with the application notice for court permission to add a party
- The accompanying **evidence** should set out the proposed new party's interest in or connection with the claim
- **the proposed amended** claim form and particulars of claim

Remember that the application **may be dealt with without a hearing** where all the existing parties and the proposed new party are in agreement:

EM: applications dealt with without a hearing

The court may deal with an application without a hearing if
- The parties agree to this and to the terms of the order sought or
- The court does not consider that a hearing would be appropriate.

Likelihood of obtaining court permission

The court is likely to grant an order to add a party if
- it is desirable to add the additional party so that the court can resolve the case; or
- there is an issue involving the new party (Y) and the existing party (X) connected to the case and the addition of the new party is desirable so that the court can resolve the case

Steps to give effect to the order to add a new claimant

Where the court has made an order adding **new claimant**, the court may direct
- a copy of the order to be served on every party to the proceedings and any other person affected by the order, unless the court orders otherwise
- copies of the amended statements of case and of documents referred to in any statement of case to be served on the new party, unless the court orders otherwise
- the party who made the application to file within 14 days (or as ordered) an amended claim form and particulars of claim.

If the signed, written consent of the new claimant has not been filed, the order and the addition of the new party as claimant will **not** take effect **until** the signed, written consent of the new claimant is filed.

Steps to give effect to the order to add a defendant

Where the court has made an order adding a **defendant** whether on its own initiative or on an application, the court may direct
- the claimant to file with the court within 14 days (or as ordered) an amended claim form and particulars of claim for the court file
- a copy of the order to be served on all parties to the proceedings and any other person affected by it
- the amended claim form and particulars of claim, forms for admitting, defending and acknowledging the claim and copies of the statements of case and any other documents referred to in any statement of case to be served on the new defendant. A new defendant does **not** become a party to the proceedings **until** the amended claim form has been served on her
- unless the court orders otherwise, the amended claim form and particulars of claim to be served on any other defendants.
- The court may give consequential directions regarding amendments to be made to any other statement of case; filing and serving documents, including service of any amended statement of caseand regarding the management of the case.

Substituting a party - How to apply for court permission

An existing party or a person who wishes to be substituted as a party may make the application. It is done in the same was an application to add a party with the following addition
- to evidence the stage the proceedings have reached and to evidence what change has occurred to cause the transfer of interest or liability

Likelihood of obtaining court permission

The court is likely to grant the order if

- ***EM: transfer of interest or liability*** the substitution is because the existing party's interest or liability has passed to Y because either X has died and Y is his executor, or because X is bankrupt and Y is his trustee in bankruptcy; **and**
- it is desirable to substitute Y for X so that the court can resolve the case.

Steps to give effect to the order to substitute a claimant or a defendant

These are the same as for adding a party.

Amending statements of case - General

- The amended statement of case and the court copy of it should be endorsed as follows:

    - Where the court's permission was required

      "Amended [Particulars of Claim or as may be] by Order of [Master ....][District Judge...... or as may be] [Legal Adviser] dated..............."

    - Where the court's permission was not required

      "Amended [Particulars of Claim or as may be] under CPR [rule 17.1(1) or (2)(a)] dated.................."

- The statement of case in its amended form need not show the original text. Where, however, the court thinks it desirable for both the original text and the amendments to be shown, the court may direct that the amendments should be shown either
    - by coloured amendments, either manuscript or computer generated, or
    - by use of a numerical code in a monochrome computer- generated document.

- Where colour is used, the text to be deleted should be struck through in colour and any text replacing it should be inserted or underlined in the same colour.

- The order of colours to be used for successive amendments is

    - (1) red,
    - (2) green,
    - (3) violet and
    - (4) yellow.

EM: removal of parties

The court can order that a party be removed if it considers it is not desirable that they are a party.

C must file with the court an amended claim form and particulars of claim, and a copy of the order must be served on every party to the proceedings and on any other person affected by the order.

The court may give consequential directions regarding amendments to be made to any other statement of case; filing and serving documents, including service of any amended statement of case and regarding the management of the case.

2. Where the amendment is for **something other** than to add / substitute / remove a party; e.g. to
    - change the cause(s) of action,
    - change a mistake in a name or
    - abandon one of several remedies claimed (for this latter see 'discontinuance' at the end of Chapter 19)
    - add in issues; or
    - respond to a statement of case where a response was omitted in error.

The applicant needs

- the **written consent** of the other parties and to file the consent at court **or**
- court **permission,** so if all the parties do not consent in writing the court may nevertheless grant permission.

If the substance of the statement of case is changed by reason of the amendment, the statement of case should be re-verified by a statement of truth.

Steps to give effect to the order to amend **something other** in a statement of case

These are the same as for adding a party, where court permission is required.

Amending statements of case – General

This is the same as above.

This is summarised in table form on the next page.

Please read down the columns.

AMENDMENT OF STATEMENTS OF CASE DURING THE LIMITATION PERIOD

TO AMEND SOMETHING OTHER THAN PARTIES	TO ADD OR SUBSTITUTE OR REMOVE A PARTY
• Cause of action • Change mistake in a name • Add an issue • Respond to statement of case where response omitted in error	
Can do this before the document has been served	Can do this before the document has been served
To do it **after** document served need • Either written **consent** of all others • **OR if cannot get it** make a Part 23 application for court permission likely to succeed if desirable so the court can resolve the case.	To do it **after** document served need • Both written **consent** of all others • **AND** make a Part 23 application for court permission
	(see tables below)

TO ADD A PARTY	TO SUBSTITUTE A PARTY
Likely to succeed if desirable so the court can resolve the case	Likely to succeed if • desirable so the court can resolve the case **AND** • is due to a transfer of interest or liability

Steps to give effect to add new C	Steps to give effect to add new D		
Takes effect when signed consent of new C is filed	Takes effect when amended CF served on D		

same	same
same	same

REMOVAL OF PARTIES

IN SOME CIRCUMSTANCES STATEMENTS OF CASE MAY BE AMENDED *AFTER* THE END OF THE RELEVANT LIMITATION PERIOD

EM: amendments to statements of case after the end of a relevant limitation period.

This is still possible in the following three circumstances and could occur, for example, where the cause of action in contract accrued over 6 years ago and the claim form was issued in time, but it has taken a long time to progress through the litigation process and the six-year limitation period has now passed, or where the CF was issued very close to the end of the limitation period.

Circumstance 1. Introducing new causes of action

Where, for example, a claimant wishes to amend the statement of case, to add negligence to or substitute negligence for the contract claim, or to add in a counterclaim or a set-off, when **making a part 23 application** for **court permission** he must show that the new claim arises out of **(substantially) the same facts** for which he has already claimed a remedy. In exercising its discretion the court will consider the **promptness** of the application and the **prospects of success** of the new claim.

Circumstance 2. Correcting a mistake in a name.

For example changing Catherine to Kathryn.

The mistake must be
- as to the name and not one that would cause reasonable doubt as to the identity (e.g. the right description, the wrong name)
- genuine
- such that no-one was misled.

Circumstance 3. Adding or substituting parties

EM: adding or substituting parties after the end of a relevant limitation period

Proceedings must have started during the limitation period and adding/substituting must be **necessary for the determination of the original action** in order to progress the case to its conclusion.

- a) Y was the intended party and X was there in mistake for Y; i.e. the wrong entity was used, e.g. another company with a similar name, another John Smith and so the mistake can only be cured by this substitution, not John and Jane Smith but just Jane Smith.

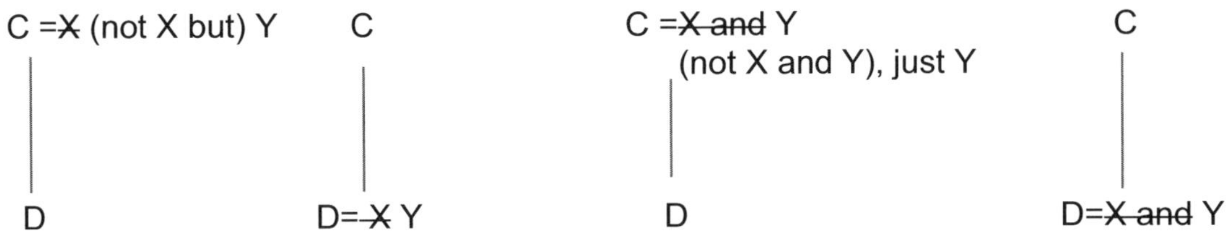

– b) The new Y needs to be substituted or added for the claim to be properly carried on by or against the original X.

C = ~~X~~ Y; or
X+Y

D

C

D = ~~X~~ Y; or
X+ Y

– c) X dies so X's executor needs to be substituted; X is bankrupt so X's trustee in bankruptcy needs to be substituted.

In addition, in a PI/fatal accident claim, where the court directs that the special time limit relating to date of knowledge shall not apply to the claim by or against a new party, or where the issue of whether or not it applies is to be determined at court, the court may add or substitute a party.

Activity

Remember to make notes on the relevant case law authorities in paragraphs 17.3.5-17.3.9 and 17.4.2; + 19.5.1, 19.5.2 19.5.4-5 in the commentary in the White Book.

You may find it useful to add in references to the case law NOW at the appropriate points of this Chapter.

When approaching final revision time, remember to .... Etc!

CUR 10.2 COSTS CONSEQUENCES OF AMENDMENT

This year it is specifically set out in your syllabus that "students should be familiar with the words in italics immediately underneath the heading of PD17, which read as follows: "A party applying for an amendment will usually be responsible for the costs of and arising from the amendment".

A party applying for an amendment will usually be responsible for the costs of and arising from the amendment.

This also occurs in the following PD which appears in your syllabus under Costs -

The likely costs consequence of amending statements of case is found in PD 44. in the section called "Court's discretion as to costs: rule 44.2" in the table in note 4.2 The order is likely to be for "costs of and caused by" the amendment. The **amending party** is usually ordered to **pay the costs of the other** party, **unless**, for example the other party unreasonably refused to consent to the amendments, thereby increasing costs.
The party in whose favour the costs order is made is entitled to the **costs of preparing for and attending the application** and the **costs of any consequential amendments to his or her own statement of case.**

<table>
<tr><th colspan="2">AMENDMENT OF STATEMENTS OF CASE <u>AFTER</u> THE LIMITATION PERIOD</th></tr>
<tr><td>TO AMEND SOMETHING OTHER THAN PARTIES<ul><li>Cause of action</li><li>Change mistake in a name. mistake must be<ul><li>as to the name and not be one that would cause reasonable doubt as to the identity</li><li>genuine</li><li>such that no one was misled</li></ul></li><li>Add an issue</li><li>Respond to statement of case where response omitted in error</li></ul></td><td>TO ADD OR SUBSTITUTE (OR REMOVE) A PARTY</td></tr>
<tr><td><ul><li>make a Part 23 application for court permission,<ul><li>show is on substantially the same facts</li><li>court considers prompt application and prospects of success</li></ul></li></ul></td><td><ul><li>Proceedings must have started during LP</li><li>Plus one of<ul><li>Must be necessary to determine the original action because it had the wrong entity OR</li><li>Needed for the claim to be properly carried on OR</li><li>Need to add a party's executor or trustee in bankruptcy</li></ul></li></ul></td></tr>
<tr><td colspan="2">COST CONSEQUENCES</td></tr>
</table>

Chapter 12

Elements of the syllabus which you have now covered **in civil litigation and evidence**

- A cell with heavy outlining means that that area of the syllabus was covered in this Chapter;
- A darkly shaded cell with a tick √ means that the whole of that syllabus element has now been covered;
- A lightly shaded cell means that part of that element of the syllabus has been covered in a previous Chapter; and
- An unshaded cell means that element of the syllabus has not yet been covered.

1.1 √	1.2 √	1.3 √	2.1 √	2.2 √	3.1 √	3.2 √	61 √	6.2 √	6.3 √
7.4 √	7.1 √	7.2 √	8.1 √	8.2 √	8.3 √	9.1 √	9.2 √	9.3 √	10.1 √
10.2 √	11.1	11.2	12.1 √	12.2 √	12.3	13.1	13.2	13.3 √	13.4 √
13.5	13.6	13.7	13.8	14.1	14.2	14.3	14.4	14.5	14.6
15.1	15.2 √	15.3 √	15.4 √	16.1	16.2	17.1	17.2	17.3	17.4
18.2. √	18.3 √	18.4 18.5	19.1	19.2	19.3	20.1	20.2	20.3	21.1
21.2	21.3	22.1	22.2 22.3	23.1 √	23.2 √	23.3	23.4 √	24.1	

Chapter 13

STRIKING OUT [CUR 13] and/or SUMMARY JUDGMENT [CUR 12]

"What if" (i)

What if D thinks that there are no reasonable grounds for the Claimant ("C") bringing the claim, or that C's claim is an abuse of court process, or that C has failed to comply with a rule, PD or court order?

THIS CHAPTER CONTAINS THE ITEMS PRINTED IN BOLD IN THE FOLLOWING BOXES

CURRICULUM ("CUR")

~~Case management (Chapters 2, 6 and 19), sanctions (Chapter 19)~~ and

Striking Out *(continued in Chapter 19)*

13.7 **striking out a claim**

~~Default judgment (Chapter 11)~~ and

Summary Judgment

12.3 summary judgments

SYLLABUS

Striking out

Examinable material will consist of power to strike out statements of case.
(Please refer to the box above for where to find the remainder of the examinable material in this book).

- **CPR 3.4 (power to strike out a statement of case)**

Summary Judgment

Examinable material will consist of: grounds for summary judgment, proceedings in which summary judgment is available, procedure for obtaining summary judgment, evidence at a summary judgment hearing, the court's powers on a summary judgment application and setting aside orders for summary judgment.

(Each of the above has its own subheading in this Chapter, flagged by EM:)

- From CUR 12:-
- CPR 24.1
- CPR 24.2 (grounds for summary judgment).
- and 24.3-5
- 24.6 (court's powers when it determines a summary judgment application).
- PD 24 paragraphs 1-6 and 8-10.
- Commentary is incorporated in context in this Chapter, highlighted in an Activity box between two stars

Chapter 13 MOCS (i) - Power to strike out a statement of case

❖ ***Strike out all or part of a statement of case at the outset*** ***NOT in developing law*** ***NOT if possible the claim will succeed.***	***Strike out for failing to comply with rule/PD/court order*** ***This will be completed in Chapter 19.***
When ***Once D served AOS/Defence***	***When***
How ***Part 23 application showing*** • ***no reasonable grounds for bringing or defending*** • ***abuse of process***	***How***
Outcome ***Either strike out judgment entered Or the case continues and consequential orders are made about this***	***Outcome***
And/or	
❖ ***Apply for summary judgment*** ***If the other party has NRPOS AND NOCR*** ***Continued on the next page.***	

Chapter 13 MOCS (ii) – Summary Judgment

Summary Judgment

NOT available for C against D to

- ***possess D's home,***
- ***seize D's vessel, nor***
- ***where set off is claimed in D's counterclaim – yet remember the availability of the cheque rule***

When

- ***by court at any time on its own initiative***
- ***by D once proceedings commenced***
- ***by C once D has filed AOS if C has complied with Pre-action Conduct or Protocols; or***
- ***by C once D has filed Defence***

How

Part 23 application with the 14 – 7 – 3 days timeframes showing

- ***D's belief that C has NRPOS in his claim AND there is NOCR for case/issue to go to trial***
- ***C's belief that D has NRPOS in her defence AND there is NOCR for case/issue to go to trial***

Outcome

Summary Judgment	***if R failed to attend the hearing, R can apply for it to be set aside or it can be done on the court's own initiative.***
Whole claim dismissed	***A can appeal***
SJ application dismissed	***case goes to trial. A can appeal against this outcome.***
Conditional order	***court thinks the case may succeed, tho' improbable.***

STRIKING OUT (i) at the outset

The sessions dealing with this area of the syllabus on my BTC course are	

But first -

In this book you have already been introduced to "with notice" applications under part 23 CPR, Here they are listed in table form as a reminder.

"With notice" interim applications made under Part 23 CPR, met so far in this book	
Application for	**Chapter of this book**
• Pre action disclosure made by prospective C before a claim is begun. • Norwich Pharmacal Order where secrecy is not important and a Part 7 claim form has already been issued	3
• Setting aside or varying orders made without notice by R, e.g. where prospective C obtained an urgent prohibitory injunction without notice to the prospective D (now R).	4
Applications made after a claim has begun i.e. made after the issuing of a CF	
• Default Judgment o for any remedy other than purely money/value of undelivered goods o when a claim includes a mix of money/value of undelivered goods and "any other remedy" o when D is ▪ a child/protected party ▪ outside England and Wales ▪ is a State ▪ a person with diplomatic immunity o when the claim is by a spouse or civil partner against the other in tort when D has not replied to POC within the required timeframes	11 11

• Setting aside Default Judgment D applies not more than 14 days after receiving DJ.	11
• Court permission to amend a statement of case to add/substitute/remove a party once written consent of all other parties has been obtained	12
• Court permission to amend a statement of case where the amendment is for **something other** than to add/substitute/remove a party. Note that consent of all other parties is not necessary	12

[The use of **strike out as a sanction for not following court directions and the use of CPR 3.9** is dealt with at the end of Chapter 19 of this book.]

<u>EM:- Power to strike out statements of case</u>

Applications for "strike out or in the alternative summary judgment" are dealt with in this Chapter. They are further examples of interim applications under **Part 23 CPR.** They are often referred to as interim applications because they are made in the interim stages of the litigation process, either before proceedings are issued or between proceedings commencing and trial, or even following a judgment.

If a claim were procedurally straightforward, then once a defence has been filed the next stage of the process would be the court giving notice to the parties of the proposed track allocation.

The completion and filing of parties' directions questionnaires follows this. Where a party wishes to apply for interim remedies their **intention to do so should be included with their directions questionnaires** when they are filed at court. (See Chapter 19). Ideally, though the remedy of "early stage" strike out should be applied for before track allocation.

Before continuing on in this book to look at track allocation and beyond, we are now first going to pause to consider the interim applications that parties may seek on the way to trial - those that may arise at the defence stage and afterwards. This section of the book is therefore called the "what if" section- "What if one of the following circumstances arises at or after the defence stage?"

WHAT IF D THINKS THAT THERE ARE NO REASONABLE GROUNDS FOR C BRINGING THE CLAIM OR THAT C'S CLAIM IS AN ABUSE OF COURT PROCESS?

[THIS CHAPTER].

(OR THAT C HAS FAILED TO COMPLY WITH A RULE, PD OR COURT ORDER?

[CHAPTER 19])

CUR 13 STRIKING OUT A CLAIM [or a Defence, or in the alternative asking for summary judgment]

Where strike out may not be appropriate

Strike out may be refused in developing areas of the law.
It will be refused if the application involves detailed examination of documents

Where, however, there is any possibility that a claim or defence or issue may succeed, but it is improbable that it will do so, strike out is not appropriate as this would deny the relevant party a fair hearing.

Only where there is a real prospect of establishing the case as amended, may a court allow amendment instead of striking-out.

Strike out or summary judgment?

In reality the applicant applies for either remedy according to the court's discretion, the application for a claim (or defence as the case may be) "to be struck out or in the alternative for summary judgment".

- Once D has served her AOS/Defence, D could choose to apply for the remedy of **strike out** of a claim or part of a claim; **or in the alternative**
- At any time once proceedings have been commenced, D can apply for summary judgment against C.
- **summary judgment**, where the grounds for summary judgment can be made out (see later in this Chapter).

Note

that although dealt with here in the context of D applying to strike out C's claim, this CPR rule can be used in relation to any statement of case and is framed so that for example **C could ask for D's defence to be struck out.**

Activity

Note here the actual text of CPR 3.4 (2)

The requirements set out below deal first with an application for strike out of C's claim by D and [then in square brackets, the wording for application for strike out of D's Defence by C].

<u>What the applicant needs to show for a successful **strike out** of a claim **at the outset**</u>

- If C's statement of case, i.e. C's claim [or D's statement of case, i.e. D's Defence] shows **no reasonable grounds** for bringing the claim [or for defending the claim]. E.g. if
  - there are no facts to show what the claim is about [no facts to show what the defence is, or if there is simply a bare denial], or
  - the claim [the defence] is incoherent and makes no sense, or
  - [the defence does not make it clear how much of the claim is admitted and how much is denied], or
  - it is simply wrong in law, [it is simply wrong in law, not amounting to a defence in law] or
- If the claim would be an **abuse of court process**
  - likely to obstruct the just disposal of proceedings (because it is vexatious, scurrilous or obviously ill founded) [same for C's application to strike out the defence]
  - issued after the end of the limitation period
  - judicial review would be the correct process
  - Res judicata translates as 'the thing has already been adjudicated'.
  - If C seeks to reopen old litigation/renew an issue, i.e. with the same parties, facts and cause of action which has already been finally adjudicated, the court may strike out this attempt at proceedings as an abuse of process, where either the court's findings or a compromise in the previous action estop C from bringing fresh proceedings.
  - Settlement of earlier proceedings may include terms preventing further claims, or

then as the claim is bound to fail as the result of one of the above two reasons, the court will order written material to be deleted from a statement of case so that it may not be relied upon and the court may then make any consequential order.

If there has been a **failure to comply** with a rule, PD or court order [same for C's application to strike out the defence], there are different pre-requisites for this iteration of strikeout. (Please see Chapter 19).

<u>Orders that the court may make on striking out for no reasonable grounds / abuse of process</u>

- On striking-out the court may
  - enter such judgment as the successful party appears entitled to
  - make any consequential orders it considers appropriate
  - include allocation and case management if the case will now continue.

<u>After the strike out</u>

- Where
  - the court has struck out C's statement of case and
  - C has been ordered to pay costs to the defendant; and
  - before C pays those costs, C starts another claim against the same defendant, arising out of facts which are the same or substantially the same as those relating to the claim in which the statement of case was struck out, the court may, on D's application, stay that other claim until the costs of the first claim have been paid.

- If the court strikes out C's statement of case and it considers that the claim is totally without merit

- the court's order must record that fact; and
- the court must at the same time consider whether it is appropriate to make a civil restraint order.

Activity

Remember to make notes on the relevant case law authorities in paragraphs
3.4.1,
3.4.2,
3.4.3,
the first three paragraphs of 3.4.3.2,
the first paragraph of 3.4.3.3
3.4.5
in the commentary in the White Book.

(3.9 commentary is in Chapter 19)

You may find it useful to add in references to the case law NOW at the appropriate points of this Chapter.

When approaching final revision time, remember to add in the salient findings of the cases at the relevant point in any 'mental crib sheet' into which you have distilled the main points of your learned knowledge.

<u>CUR 12.3</u> <u>SUMMARY JUDGMENT</u>

Summary judgment is the second way of obtaining **judgment without trial.** (Remember that we have also seen default judgment, that is obtaining judgment against D in default of D filing AOS/defence as set out in Chapter 11.

<u>EM: grounds for summary judgment</u>

<u>The test to be applied – the grounds for summary judgment</u>

A party may apply for summary judgment where that party (the applicant) considers that the other (the respondent), in respect of the claim or on a particular issue has

No real (i.e. not fanciful, imaginary or false) **prospect of succeeding in the claim/successfully defending the claim AND** there is
No other compelling reason (no witnesses or experts needed to enhance a party's case) **for** the case/issue to be disposed of at **trial.**

Activity

The grounds for summary judgment is one of the tests in the CPR where it is advisable to know the exact wording of CPR 24.2 for assessment.
You may find it useful to copy it in to here.

The application for summary judgment may be based on
- a point of law (including a question of construction of a document)
- the evidence which can reasonably be expected to be available at trial or the lack of it, or
- a combination of these.

Activity

Remember to make notes on the relevant case law authorities in paragraphs 24.2.3-24.2.7 in the commentary in the White Book.

You may find it useful to add in references to the case law NOW at the appropriate points of this Chapter.

When approaching final revision time, remember to add in the salient findings of the cases at the relevant point in any 'mental crib sheet' into which you have distilled the main points of your learned knowledge.

<u>EM: proceedings in which summary judgment is available</u>

- The court may give summary judgment **for D against C in any type** of proceedings;
- The court may give summary judgment **for C against a D in any type of proceedings;**

- **Except**

  - in relation to possession of a D's **home** (i.e. unpaid mortgage, or a tenant or person holding over after the end of her tenancy whose occupancy is protected within the meaning of the Rent Act 1977 or Housing Act 1988);

  - in an **Admiralty** claims *in rem* e.g. seizing a vessel;

  - in a counterclaim **if there is a set-off situation as below**

    Set-offs

    In layman's terms, if I owe you £15 and you owe me £20, you should pay me £5. Setting off what I owe you against what you owe me results in you paying me £5.

    In legal terminology, a set-off operates as a defence. You will learn in the drafting course on the BTC to state the set-off at the end of a defence when there is a set-off situation. You will also learn that a D claims the amount of the set-off in her counterclaim against C. (D owes C £15 and C brings a claim against D for that £15; at the end of D's defence she states that there is a set-off situation in that C owes her £20; D therefore counterclaims against C, claiming the £5 that he owes her.)

    Such mutual debts for liquidated (definite) amounts, (there is no need for the debts to be connected), is one situation where a set-off may occur.

    Further situations where set-offs may occur (and so summary judgment cannot be claimed) are where

    - C claims the unpaid price on a contract for the **sale of goods**; D can set off against this her counterclaim for C's **breach of statutory duty** – perhaps D's defence is that the goods were not of satisfactory quality, which is why D has not paid any or all of the price
    - C is a workman claiming payment for **services**; D can set off against this her counterclaim that the standard of workmanship was **poor**
    - C is a landlord claiming for **rent arrears**; D can set off against this her counterclaim that the landlord is in **breach of covenants in the lease arise**
    - An equitable set-off is claimed – where if none of the above situations arise, it would nevertheless be inequitable not to set off D's defence and counterclaim against C's claim.

      Thus if a counterclaim amounts to a set-off where the amount set off in D's defence (£20) is equal to or greater than the value of the claim (£15), there is a real prospect of successfully defending the claim and C cannot apply successfully for summary judgement.

      Whereas on a counterclaim amounting to a set-off where the amount set-off (say £7000) is **less** than the claim (say £15,000), **C can claim summary judgement** for the undisputed £8,000 balance as there is a real prospect of succeeding in the claim.

    Set-off is not available in an action on a dishonoured cheque. Note the beneficial use of the cheque rule in the following example. There is no defence to a dishonoured cheque. Summary judgement is thus available.

The cheque rule

.Where there is an underlying contract to buy goods and a collateral contract to pay for them by cheque, C should sue on the collateral cheque contract, not on the contract for the sale of goods.

Let's say that C sells a car to D and that D pays £15,000 for it by cheque.
D then has to spend £7,000 on the car in repairs, and so stops the £15,000 cheque.

If C claims on the contract for the sale of the car, D can raise the repairs as a defence and set-off the £7,000 she paid for the repairs. C could claim summary judgment for the undisputed £8,000.

Whereas, if C claims on the collateral cheque contract, D can only raise defences relating to the cheque itself. With no defence to a dishonoured cheque and set-off not available to D, C can claim summary judgment for the full £15,000.

EM: procedure for obtaining summary judgment

Who may apply (and when)

As usual, under CPR 3.3 **the court** could exercise its powers to make an order, (here for summary judgment) **of its own initiative**, rather than on an application.

D can apply for summary judgment at any time once proceedings have been commenced, where she believes C does not have a case.

C can apply after D has filed AOS/Defence, where he believes D has no defence;

C can apply before that if the court gives permission or if a PD so provides; if C applies before the defence is filed, D need not file a defence before the summary judgment hearing.

Where C has failed to comply with Practice Direction (Pre-Action Conduct) [or any relevant pre-action protocol], an action for summary judgment will not normally be entertained before the defence has been filed or, alternatively, the time for doing so has expired.

Where the proceedings are "against the Crown" as defined in s23(2) of the Crown Proceedings Act 1947, C needs to wait for the end of the period for filing of the defence before applying for summary judgment.

Any party who is in the position of a C or a D may apply for summary judgment. Remember that in a counterclaim where D is counterclaiming against C, D is still called D in the statements of case, although she is in the position of a C with respect to the counterclaim. C is still called C in the statements of case, although he is in the position of a D with respect to the counterclaim.

Awarding summary judgment is not in contravention of Article 6 ECHR, the right to a fair trial.

The procedure

This is a Part 23 application with some slight differences from the way we have met it before.

Whereas the rule for other interim applications is to serve the application notice at least 3 clear days before the court is to deal with the application at the interim application hearing.....

….. for Summary Judgment, once the applicant has the hearing date set by the court

- R must be given **at least** (14) clear **days' notice** of the date fixed for the hearing and of the issues it is proposed that the court will decide [a PD may provide for a different period of notice to be given; e.g. remember that where C is the applicant applying for summary judgment in respect of a contract relating to real property, he may do so once the CF is served. The application notice evidence and draft order must be served on D not less than *4 days before* the hearing of the application.]

- ***EM: evidence at a summary judgment hearing***

  At least (7) clear **days** before the hearing R files, then serves on A written Evidence in Response and the application notice should draw R's attention to this. (Likewise if the hearing is fixed by the court of its own initiative, for any party wishing to rely on written evidence, where unless the court orders otherwise, copies must be served on every other party)
- At least (3) clear **days** A files then serves on R written Evidence in Reply before the hearing (likewise if the hearing is fixed by the court of its own initiative, for any party wishing to rely on written evidence, where unless the court orders otherwise, copies must be served on every other party)

Both parties file & serve a statement of costs 24 hours before hearing.

Written evidence need not be filed again if it was previously filed with the original claim.

Activity

Please note carefully these three timeframes for notice and evidence in reply in summary judgment applications.

You should now turn back to the table a couple of pages from the end of in Chapter 3 of this book and fill in the box that said you would.

Note that you still end up on the 3 days clear that already appears in that table; it's simply that there are the extra additions of 14 and 7 working down to that for summary judgment applications.

EM: the court's powers on a summary judgment application

Possible outcomes

- As C/A wins**, Judgment for A** so that SJ is granted. The new form number 44 will be used for judgment for the claimant. Form number 44A for judgment for the defendant.

- As D/A wins, the whole **claim is struck out**/ dismissed

- As A loses, **Dismissal of the SJ application** so that the case continues to full trial. Form number 44B will be used. The court can make directions as to the filing and service of a defence or give further directions about the management of the case when determining the SJ application. If it does not, then directions will be given after the filing of directions questionnaires, or at a directions hearing or case management conference (see Chapter 19).

- **Conditional order.** The new form number 44C will be used. Where it appears to the court that it is possible that a claim, defence or issue **may succeed, although improbable**, the court may make a conditional order. This means that the case carries on with certain conditions. The respondent party with the improbable case has to pay a sum of money into court and/or take a specified step i.e. the respondent has to "put their money where their mouth is" or e.g. file a defence that is fully compliant with the requirements in the CPR. If (s)he doesn't comply then the claim will be dismissed or her/his statement of case struck out.

Activity

Remember to make notes on the relevant case law authorities in paragraphs 24.6.6 in the commentary in the White Book.

You may find it useful to add in references to the case law NOW at the appropriate points of this Chapter.

When approaching final revision time, remember to add in the salient findings of the cases at the relevant point in any 'mental crib sheet' into which you have distilled the main points of your learned knowledge.

<u>After the judgment</u>

Fixed costs as per Part 45 CPR Tables 1 and 4 may be applied - (not on your syllabus this year).

Where dismissed, the court gives directions regarding proceeding to full trial as above, if not done when the SJ application was determined

Where an application for summary judgment is unsuccessful, it is open to the applicant to appeal that decision. [A Chapter on appeals appears later in this book].

<u>EM: setting aside orders for summary judgment</u>

If an order for summary judgment is made against a respondent who fails to attend the hearing of the application, the respondent may apply for the order to be set aside or varied or the court can do this of its own volition. The summary judgment application may then be re-listed.

At the hearing of such an application the court may make such order as it thinks just.

<u>Chapter 13</u>

Elements of the syllabus which you have now covered									

<u>Elements of the syllabus which you have now covered</u>

- A cell with heavy outlining means that that area of the syllabus was covered in this Chapter;
- A darkly shaded cell with a tick √ means that the whole of that syllabus element has now been covered;
- A lightly shaded cell means that part of that element of the syllabus has been covered in a previous Chapter; and
- An unshaded cell means that element of the syllabus has not yet been covered.

1.1 √	1.2 √	1.3 √	2.1 √	2.2 √	3.1 √	3.2 √	6.1 √	6.2 √	4.3 √
6.4 √	7.1 √	7.2 √	8.1 √	8.2 √	8.3 √	9.1 √	9.2 √	9.3 √	10.1 √
10.2 √	11.1	11.2	12.1 √	12.2 √	12.3 √	13.1	13.2	13.3 √	13.4 √
13.5	13.6	13.7	13.8	14.1	14.2	14.3	14.4	14.5	14.6
15.1	15.2 √	15.3 √	15.4 √	16.1	16.2	17.1	17.2	17.3	17.4
18.2. √	18.3 √	18.4 √ 18.5 √	19.1	19.2	19.3	20.1	20.2	20.3	21.1
221.2	21.3	22.1	22.2	23.1 √	23.2 √	23.3	23.4 √	24.1	

Chapter 14

FURTHER INFORMATION [CUR 11]

"What if" (ii)

What if D or any party needs more clarification or information about a matter in dispute, whether or not the matter is contained or referred to in a statement of case, so, e.g. when she sees the Claim Form and the Particulars of Claim or other papers provided by C)?

THIS CHAPTER CONTAINS THE ITEMS PRINTED IN BOLD IN THE FOLLOWING BOXES

CURRICULUM ("CUR")

~~*Amendment and (see the second half of Chapter 12)*~~
Further information
11.1 requests for further information
11.2 responding to a request for further information

SYLLABUS

Examinable material will consist of obtaining further information, requests for further information, responding to requests for further information and restriction on the use of further information.

(Each of the above has its own subheading in this Chapter, flagged by EM:)

- **CPR 18.1-18.2;**
- **PD 18 paragraphs 1-5**
- **Commentary is incorporated in context in this Chapter, highlighted in an Activity box between two stars**

Chapter 14 MOCS

Parties can request further information from each other.

The request is made to the other party in writing including a statement of truth; if no information is received in response, apply to court.

The sessions dealing with this area of the syllabus on my BTC course are	

CUR 10.1 REQUESTS FOR FURTHER INFORMATION

EM: obtaining further information

Remember again that CPR 3.3 states that the court has the power to make an order of its own initiative. Thus it may at any time order clarification / a party to give additional information.

Subject to any rule of law to the contrary, D as the first party would **request further information** from C, the second party, where matters are not clear / precise.

This allows D to be better able to prepare her own case or understand the case she has to meet.

Therefore, if Counsel is doing this on behalf of a client D, do pay attention to times frames. For example, if a POC is unclear and the time limit for AOS/Defence is fast approaching – remember from Chapter 11 that you have 14 days from the date of deemed service of the POC – then it may be prudent to ask C to agree to an extension of the time for filing the Defence and for you then to inform the court of that. In this way you can meet the 14 day time limit for filing an AOS and have extra time to draft a full defence to a fuller POC once you have been given the further information that, say, you did not receive until close to (or after) the 14 day time limit.

EM: requests for further information

Such requests are not usually used on the small claims track, although they can be.

- The first party sends a written request for further information to the second party in a single comprehensive document containing only the request. keeping it **concise**, limiting it to what is **reasonably necessary** for preparing the case/understanding the other side's case, keeping it **proportionate**
- Whether made by letter or in a separate document) a Request must
  - be headed with the name of the court and the title and number of the claim,
  - in its heading state that it is a Request made under Part 18, identify the first party and the second party and state the date on which it is made,
  - set out in a separate numbered paragraph each request for information or clarification,
  - where a Request relates to a document, identify that document and (if relevant) the paragraph or words to which it relates,
  - state the date by which the first party expects a response to the Request.
  - be by email if possible
- A Request which is not in the form of a letter may, if convenient, be prepared in such a way that the response may be given on the same document.
- To do this the numbered paragraphs of the Request should appear on the left hand half of each sheet so that the paragraphs of the response may then appear on the right.
- Where a Request is prepared in this form an extra copy should be served for the use of the second party.

CUR 10.2 RESPONDING TO A REQUEST FOR FURTHER INFORMATION

EM: responding to requests for further information

The response must be in writing, dated and signed by the second party or his legal representative. If the response is in the form of a letter, it should identify itself as the response to the request and deal only with the response, in the same numbered paragraphs as the request.

File at court the written response, verified by a statement of truth and serve it on the other parties.

If the second party cannot or will not respond, e.g. where they are claiming that the information is privileged (privilege is dealt with in Chapter 20 of this book), or that the cost of procuring the information would be disproportionate in the circumstances, then that second party must promptly inform the other in writing of the reasons for the lack of response.

If there is no response, the first party applies under Part 23 for a court order that further information be provided; so

- **application notice** (there is no need to serve this on the non-responsive second party; it must be served on any other second party who did respond and on all other parties)
- **written evidence** re the above, including details of any response
- **draft order** remembering to include costs.

The court can deal with the request without a hearing if 14 days have passed since the reasonable time for response stated in the first party's written request.

EM: obtaining further information

Where a court makes an order for clarification or additional information the party against whom it is made must file his response verified by a statement of truth and serve it on the other parties within the time specified by the court.

Activity

Remember to make notes on the relevant case law authorities in paragraph 18.1.10 in the commentary in the White Book.

You may find it useful to add in references to the case law NOW at the appropriate points of this Chapter.

When approaching final revision time, remember to add in the salient findings of the cases at the relevant point in any 'mental crib sheet' into which you have distilled the main points of your learned knowledge.

EM: restriction on the use of further information

The court may direct that information provided, whether given voluntarily or following a court order for further information, must not be used for any purpose except for that of the proceedings in which it is given.

Chapter 14

Elements of the syllabus which you have now covered

- A cell with heavy outlining means that that area of the syllabus was covered in this Chapter;
- A darkly shaded cell with a tick √ means that the whole of that syllabus element has now been covered;
- A lightly shaded cell means that part of that element of the syllabus has been covered in a previous Chapter; and
- An unshaded cell means that element of the syllabus has not yet been covered.

1.1 √	1.2 √	1.3 √	2.1 √	2.2 √	3.1 √	3.2 √	6.1 √	6.2 √	6.3 √
6.4 √	7.1 √	7.2 √	8.1 √	8.2 √	8.3 √	9.1 √	9.2 √	9.3 √	10.1 √
10.2 √	11.1 √	11.2 √	11.1 √	11.2 √	12.3 √	13.1	13.2	13.3 √	13.4 √
13.5	13.6	13.7	13.8	14.1	14.2	14.3	14.4	14.5	14.6
151	15.2 √	15.3 √	15.4 √	16.1	16.2	17.1	17.2	17.3	17.4
18.2. √	18.3 √	18.4 √ 18.5 √	19.1	19.2	19.3	20.1	20.2	20.3	21.1
21.2	21.3	22.1	22.2	23.1 √	23.2 √	23.3	23.4 √	24.1	

Chapter 15

SECURITY FOR COSTS [CUR 16]

"What if" (iii)

What if D has concerns that C will not be able to afford to pay D's costs when/if D wins?

THIS CHAPTER CONTAINS THE ITEMS PRINTED IN BOLD IN THE FOLLOWING BOXES

CURRICULUM ("CUR")

~~Interim applications~~ (Chapters 3 and 4 and between Chapters 16 and 17),
~~interim payments,~~(Chapter 16)
16.2 Security for Costs
~~and interim injunctions~~ (Chapters 4 and 17)

SYLLABUS

***Examinable material will consist of** the procedure for applying for interim payments, conditions to be satisfied and matters to be taken into account, evidence on interim payment applications, powers of the court where it has made an order for interim payment, restrictions on disclosure of interim payments,*
applying for security for costs, and the conditions to be satisfied on an application for security for costs.

***This Chapter deals with the examinable material in bold;** the next Chapter deals with the other material.*

- CPR 25.6-9 is in the next Chapter
- **CPR 25.12**
- **CPR 25.13**
- PD 25B paragraph 2. Is in the next Chapter
- **Commentary is incorporated in context in this Chapter, highlighted in an Activity box between two stars**

- ***For a party in the position of a Defendant***
  - ***D may make a Part 23 application for security for costs.***
    - ***Order made if***
      in all circumstances, to do so is

      just and

      C resides in the extended world beyond Europe; or

      C is an impecunious company; or

      another CPR 25.13 (2) condition exists.

The sessions dealing with this area of the syllabus on my BTC course are	

CUR 16.2 SECURITY FOR COSTS

What if D has concerns that C will not be able to afford to pay D's costs when/if D wins?

The same question arises when there is **a party in the position of a D.** We have met before the C who is in the position of a D when D has counterclaimed against C. There are other such situations, shown in diagram form below.

Meaning of "Party in the position of a Defendant".

'Party 1' is the way we will refer to a party in the position of a Defendant who thinks the other side, 'Party 2' will lose. Where Party 1 is worried that Party 2 will not be able to afford to pay Party 1's costs, then Party 1 can apply for Security for Costs.

a) C = Party 2. (Party 1 wants a security for costs order against Party 2.)

↓

D = Party 1 (who thinks that Party 2 will lose and be unable to pay Party 1's costs.)

Then building on this, D could counterclaim against C:-

b) C — **C = Party 1** (who thinks that Party 2 will lose the counterclaim and be unable to pay Party 1's costs).

then — D counterclaims against C

D — D = Party 2. (Party 1 wants a security for costs order against Party 2.)

Another example could be where D loses at trial then appeals, so now she is appellant "A", making C the respondent "R":-

c) D/A = Party 2. (Party 1 wants a security for costs order against Party 2.)

C/R= Party 1 (who thinks that Party 2 will lose and be unable to pay Party 1's costs.)

A further example could be where C loses the appeal and the criteria for a second appeal are fulfilled, so he is now appellant "A", making D the respondent "R":-

d) C ~~R~~ A = Party 2 (Party 1 wants a security for costs order against Party 2.)

D ~~A~~ R = Party 1 (who thinks that Party 2 will lose and be unable to pay Party 1's costs.)

The question posed for this Chapter is **What if D has concerns that C will not be able to afford to pay D's costs when/if D wins?**

The answer is

The party in the position of a D makes an application for an order for security for costs; an order whereby D obtains some comfort that C is good for the payment of costs, shown by C giving some security for it.

So the court may order security for costs of an appeal against

- an appellant – c) above [even if A is a limited company and there is reason to believe it will be unable to pay the costs of the other parties to the appeal should its appeal be unsuccessful].
- a respondent who also appeals – d) above [even if RA is a limited company and there is reason to believe it will be unable to pay the costs of the other parties to the appeal should its appeal be unsuccessful].
-

on the same grounds as it may order security for costs against Party 2 as set out in this Chapter.

Party 2 may be ordered to give this security by paying some money into court or by obtaining and giving a guarantee for the costs or by providing some other security. The conditions arising out of the order will be that proceedings will be stayed until that condition has been fulfilled. If Party 2 does not provide the security, Party 1 can apply to have the claim struck out. (Please refer to Chapter 19 for more on strike out).

EM: applying for security for costs

Party 1 **after serving her/his AOS/defence**. can make the Part 23 application It may be made at any stage of the proceedings after that, but should be made **promptly as soon as the facts justifying the order are known.**

EM: the conditions to be satisfied on an application for security for costs

Test/Grounds

Please note that the CPR refers to what we have been calling Party 1, as "C"; and what we have been calling Party 2 as "D".

The court may in its discretion make such an order **if** in all the circumstances (remember the overriding objective and the need for things to be just and proportionate)
- it is **JUST** to do so, having regard to all the circumstances of the case (balancing the possible prejudice to the parties)
- **AND**
  - An Enactment allows the court to require security for costs or
  - **ONE** or more of the six CPR 25.13 (2) conditions exists
    a) **C is resident outside the jurisdiction** - for when C is resident **in the extended world beyond Europe.** The CPR phrasing is "not resident in a Brussels Contracting State, a State bound by the Lugano Convention or a Regulation State, as defined in section 1(3) of the Civil Jurisdiction and Judgments Act 1982" So if e.g. C is in France, security for costs will not be awarded under this head.
    b) There is no longer a b).

c) C is an impecunious **company or other body** (whether incorporated inside or outside Great Britain). C is a company in or outside of the jurisdiction, and there is reason to believe that C **will be unable to pay D's costs**. The court in exercising its discretion may include in its considerations of all the circumstances e.g. whether
  - C's claim is bona fide
  - C has reasonable prospects of success
  - D has admitted anything
  - The proposed payment into court or any open offer is substantial
  - D's application is to stifle a genuine claim
  - C's want of means was caused by D's conduct or breach
  - D's application is late in the proceedings

(d) C has changed his address since the claim was commenced with a view to evading the consequences of the litigation

(e) C failed to give his address in the claim form, or gave an incorrect address in that form

(f) C is acting as a nominal claimant, other than as a representative claimant under Part 19 (parties and litigation), and there is reason to believe that he will be unable to pay D's costs if ordered to do so

(g) C has taken steps in relation to his assets that would make it difficult to enforce an order for costs against him.

(Rule 3.4 allows the court to strike out a statement of case and Part 24 for it to give summary judgment).

[Notice that CPR 25.13 (2) concludes with the reminder about rule 3.4 and Part 24. This is a good example of how the rules need to be applied, several parts of the CPR interlinking at a time.

Therefore this would be a good SBA type question, where you have to decide, on the facts of the scenario, whether the BEST way forward is – just strike out? Just summary judgement? Both? All are possible, but which is the best on the given facts?

- **Are the tests for all fulfilled and if not, does that limit your client's choices?**
- **At what point in the litigation process does the scenario take place, and when is the first time in the process that each of the possible ways forward are available? – (the earlier it is in this book, then that is the first time that some actions are possible!)**
- **Are the likely costs of the possible actions too high for your client – does the scenario tell you that the client is a millionaire, or a pauper?**
- **How long do you have to carry out any of the proposed actions? Is your client in a rush, or do they have all the time in the world?**
- **Are there issues around the limitation period?**
- **Does your client need a litigation friend?**

Thus I repeat again, please do not learn 'topics' from the syllabus in isolation. You need to get a feel for how it all can link together in any one scenario.]

<u>When an order for security of costs has been made</u>

Where the court makes an order for security for costs in favour of D against C, it will determine the amount of security C must pay and direct the manner in which and the time within which the security must be given.

Activity

Remember to make notes on the relevant case law authorities in paragraphs 25.13.1, 25.13.12, 25.13.13, 25.13.14 and 25.13.18 in the commentary in the White Book.

You may find it useful to add in references to the case law NOW at the appropriate points of this Chapter.

When approaching final revision time, remember to add in the salient findings of the cases at the relevant point in any 'mental crib sheet' into which you have distilled the main points of your learned knowledge.

Chapter 15

Elements of the syllabus which you have now covered

- A cell with heavy outlining means that that area of the syllabus was covered in this Chapter;
- A darkly shaded cell with a tick √ means that the whole of that syllabus element has now been covered;
- A lightly shaded cell means that part of that element of the syllabus has been covered in a previous Chapter; and
- An unshaded cell means that element of the syllabus has not yet been covered.

1.1 √	1.2 √	1.3 √	2.1 √	2.2 √	3.1 √	3.2 √	6.1 √	6.2 √	6.3 √
4.4 √	71 √	7.2 √	8.1 √	8.2 √	8.3 √	9.1 √	9.2 √	9.3 √	10.1 √
10.2 √	11.1 √	11.2 √	12.1 √	12.2 √	12.3 √	13.1	13.2	13.3 √	13.4 √
13.5	13.6	13.7	13.8	14.1	14.2	14.3	14.4	14.5	14.6
15.1	15.2 √	15.3 √	15.4 √	16.1	16.2 √	17.1	17.2	17.3	17.4
18.2. √	18.3 √	18.4 √ 18.5 √	19.1	19.2	19.3	20.1	20.2	20.3	21.1
21.2	21.3	22.1	22.2	23.1 √	23.2 √	23.3	23.4 √	24.1	

Chapter 16

INTERIM PAYMENTS [CUR 16]

"What if" (iv)

What if C wants to claim an advance payment of what he believes he will win in damages?

THIS CHAPTER CONTAINS THE ITEMS PRINTED IN BOLD IN THE FOLLOWING BOXES

CURRICULUM ("CUR")

~~*Interim applications*~~ *(Chapters 3 and 4 and between Chapters 16 and 17),*
16.1 interim payments,
~~*security for costs*~~ *(Chapter 15)*
~~*and interim injunctions*~~ *(Chapters 4 and 17)*

SYLLABUS

Examinable material will consist of the procedure for applying for interim payments, conditions to be satisfied and matters to be taken into account, evidence on interim payment applications, powers of the court where it has made an order for interim payment, restrictions on disclosure of interim payments, *applying for security for costs, and the conditions to be satisfied on an application for security for costs.*

- **CPR 25.6-9; PD 25B paragraph 2.**
- CPR 25.12 and 25.13 are in the previous Chapter
- **Commentary is incorporated in context in this Chapter, highlighted in an Activity box between two stars**

Chapter 16 MOCS

- ***For a Claimant wishing to claim advanced payment of what he believes he will win in damages***

Once the period for filing AOS is over, C can apply for an interim payment if one of the grounds is satisfied.

The court can adjust interim orders after they have been made

Final judgment will award interest on overpayments at interim stage where final judgment is for less than that payment

The sessions dealing with this area of the syllabus on my BTC course are	

CUR 16.1 INTERIM PAYMENTS

What if C wants to claim an advance payment of what he believes he will win in damages?

C applies for an interim payment; a payment to C from D on account of damages.

EM: conditions to be satisfied and matters to be taken into account

When

C can apply after the end of the period for D filing an AOS and may make more than one application for an interim payment.

The court may make an order where any of the following are satisfied

- D has admitted liability to pay
- C already has judgment, with damages yet to be assessed or with a sum of money other than costs to be assessed
- The court is satisfied that if the claim went to trial, C **would** obtain judgment against D (i.e. D would be found liable) for a **substantial amount** ("amount" is known as quantum) against that D, whether or not that D is the only D or one of a number of D's
- C wants an order for possession of land and the court is satisfied that if the case went to trial, D would be liable to pay a sum of money for her occupation and use of the land whilst this claim was pending (even if the claim for possession against her fails)
- Where there are 2 or more Ds and an order for interim payment is sought against one or more of them **and**
  - the court is satisfied that if the matter proceeds to trial, C would obtain judgment for a substantial amount of money against at least one of the Ds (but the court cannot determine which) **and**
  - all the defendants are either
    - insured; or
    - the motor insurance bureau will meet the liability; or
    - the defendant is a public body.

EM: restrictions on disclosure of interim payments

Unless D agrees, an interim payment is not disclosed to the trial judge until all questions of liability and quantum have been decided.

EM: the procedure for applying for interim payments

How

This is a Part 23 application but with the same slight differences (as for summary judgment) that we mentioned before.

Activity

You may wish to refer back to Chapter 13 and the procedure on summary judgment and copy out those timeframes again here.

Activity

Please note carefully these three timeframes for notice and evidence in reply in summary judgment applications.

THE SAME 14 – 7 – 3 DAYS TIMEFRAMES APPLY TO APPLICATIONS FOR INTERIM PAYMENTS

You should now turn back to the table in Chapter 3 of this book and fill in the box that said you would.

Note that you still end up on the 3 days clear that already appears in that table; it's simply that there are the extra additions of 14 and 7 working down to that for interim payment applications.

EM: evidence on interim payment applications

The evidence to support an application for an interim payment of damages is set out in 25BPD.2.

- the amount sought
- the items regarding which it is sought
- the likely amounts on final judgment
- the reasons for believing that one of the grounds for applying is satisfied
- any other relevant matters
- if PI, details of special damages and past and future loss
- if a fatal accident, details of the person on whose behalf the claim is made and the nature of the claim; and
- exhibit any documents in support including medical reports.

The order for interim payment

The court **must not** order an interim payment of more than a reasonable proportion of the likely amount of the final judgment.

The court **must** take into account when ordering the amount of any interim payment, any contributory negligence by C and any relevant set-off or counterclaim by D.

The court may order an interim payment in one sum or in instalments.

EM: powers of the court where it has made an order for interim payment

Order to adjust

This may be done without an application by any party if the court makes the order when it disposes of the claim or any part of it.

Where D has been ordered to make an interim payment, or she has in fact made one (whether voluntarily or under an order), the court may make an order to adjust the interim payment.

The court may in particular

- order all or part of the interim payment to be **repaid**
- **vary or discharge** the order for the interim payment
- **order D to reimburse**, either wholly or partly, another defendant who has made an interim payment. The defendant to be reimbursed must have made the interim payment in relation to a claim in respect of which she has made a claim against D for a contribution, indemnity or other remedy. The claim or part to which the interim payment relates must not have been discontinued or disposed of, and the ***conditions to be satisfied and matters to be taken into account*** *as* set out at the beginning of this Chapter, must be satisfied in the claim to which the interim payment relates.

In a final judgment

If the interim payment by D was more than the total amount awarded by the judge under the final judgment the court may award her interest on the overpaid amount from the date when she made the interim payment.

Chapter 16

Elements of the syllabus which you have now covered **in civil litigation and evidence**

- A cell with heavy outlining means that that area of the syllabus was covered in this Chapter;
- A darkly shaded cell with a tick √ means that the whole of that syllabus element has now been covered;
- A lightly shaded cell means that part of that element of the syllabus has been covered in a previous Chapter; and
- An unshaded cell means that element of the syllabus has not yet been covered.

1.1 √	1.2 √	1.3 √	2.1 √	2.2 √	3.1 √	3.2 √	6.1 √	6.2 √	6.3 √
6.4 √	7.1 √	7.2 √	8.1 √	8.2 √	8.3 √	9.1 √	9.2 √	9.3 √	10.1 √
10.2 √	11.1 √	11.2 √	12.1 √	12.2 √	12.3 √	13.1	13.2	13.3 √	13.4 √
11.5	11.6	11.7	11.8	12.1	14.2	14.3	14.4	14.5	14.6
15.1	15.2 √	15.3 √	15.4 √	16.1 √	16.2 √	17.1	17.2	17.3	17.4
18.2. √	18.3 √	18.4 √ 18.5 √	19.1	19.2	19.3	20.1	20.2	20.3	21.1
21.2	21.3	22.1	22.2	23.1 √	23.2 √	23.3	23.4 √	24.1	

Norwich Pharmacal order during proceedings

"What if" (v)

What if, during proceedings, C becomes aware of the need to find out the identity of another potential D?

THIS SECTION CONTAINS

MORE ON APPLYING FOR A *NORWICH PHARMACAL* ORDER FROM CUR 14

You have met Norwich Pharmacal orders before, in Chapter 3

The sessions dealing with this area of the syllabus on my BTC course are	

Examinable material will consist of: disclosure and inspection, right of inspection of disclosed documents, the meaning of document, standard disclosure, duty of search, disclosure of documents in party's control, disclosure of copies, procedure for standard disclosure, disclosure lists, disclosure statements, withholding disclosure or inspection, specific disclosure or inspection, disclosure in stages, documents referred to in statements of case, inspection and copying of documents, pre-action disclosure, disclosure against non-parties, and ***other powers of the court to order disclosure.***

EM*: The following specific leading case authority (which students should be able to refer to by name): *Norwich Pharmacal

The unemboldened examinable material above was covered in Chapter 3 in relation to interim applications before proceedings are issued. In relation to disclosure and inspection as part of the process once proceedings have been issued, this will be dealt with in Chapter 20.

Also in Chapter 3 you have already met how to apply for a Norwich Pharmacal Order **before** proceedings are issued, as a Part 8 claim. Part 8 claims are dealt with in Chapter 10.

Now in addition you just need to know that if, **during proceedings**, i.e. once proceedings have started, i.e. once a claim form has been issued, i.e. where a part 7 claim has already been originated in the court, C becomes aware of the need to find out the identity of another potential D, then this will be a **Part 23 application**, applied for in the same way as with notice applications which were explained in the second half of Chapter 3. In brief, as a reminder:

(i) Application notice (An application is known as a **with notice** application if this notice and the documents in (ii) and (iii) are served on the other side, thus giving them notice of the application). You will remember that one requirement in an application notice is that C "states the order sought and state why it is sought". For a Norwich Pharmacal application this could be something like

"This is an application for a Norwich Pharmacal Order. The order is sought because the Applicant needs to know the identity of the driver of the car which did not stop after the accident. The car was clearly marked as from "Hirecar". "Hirecar" is the facilitator of the wrong-doing. The Applicant is seeking an order to compel "Hirecar" either to tell the Applicant who it hired the car to on that day, and / or to provide him with documents or other relevant information to enable the Applicant to discover the identity of the Defendant".

(ii) Evidence (unless the court orders otherwise)
(iii) A draft of the requested order

A review of applications made so far with notice and without notice

Revisiting "with notice" applications

Back at the beginning of Chapter 13 we set out a table of those Part 23 applications made **with notice** to the other side that we had already met.

That table is reproduced here and then continued, to update it with the interim Part 23 **with notice** applications we have met since then.

"With notice" applications made under Part 23 CPR, met so far in this book	
Application for	**Chapter of this book**
• Pre-action disclosure made by prospective C before a claim is begun • Norwich Pharmacal Order where secrecy is not important and a Part 7 claim form has already been issued	3 Immediately after Chapter 16
• Setting aside or varying orders made without notice by R, e.g. where prospective C obtained an urgent prohibitory injunction without notice to the prospective D (now R).	4
Applications made after a claim has begun i.e. made after the issuing of a CF; i.e. during proceedings	
• Default Judgment o for any remedy other than purely money/value of undelivered goods o when a claim includes a mix of money/value of undelivered goods and "any other remedy" o when D is ▪ a child/protected party ▪ outside England and Wales ▪ is a State ▪ a person with diplomatic immunity o when the claim is by a spouse or civil partner against the other in tort when D has not replied to POC within the required timeframe	11

• Setting aside Default Judgment D applies not more than 14 days after receiving DJ.	In addition, include a draft of D's defence 11
• Court permission to amend a statement of case to add/substitute/remove a party once written consent of all other parties has been obtained	12
• Court permission to amend a statement of case where the amendment is for **something other** than to add/substitute/remove a party. Note that consent of all other parties is not necessary	12
• Strike out or in the alternative summary judgment Strike out by D when she has served her AOS/Defence Summary judgment by D against C at any time once proceedings have commenced; i.e. after service of CF. Summary Judgment by C against D once D has filed her AOS/Defence (or before if court permission or PD provides, in which case D need not file Defence before the SJ hearing).	13 Remember the additional timescales for the amount of notice to be given.
• Where R failed to attend the SJ hearing. Application by R for the SJ made against R to be set aside or varied	13
• Where no response to a request for further information, first party applies for a court order that it be given	14
• Security of costs by D After D has served her AOS/Defence	15
• Interim payment by C After the end of the period for D filing AOS	16 Remember the additional timescales for the amount of notice to be given

Revisiting "without notice" applications

There now follows in the table below a review of the **without notice** interim applications that we have met so far in this book. You will recall from Chapter 4 that there also exist interim applications that can be made before proceedings have started **without notice** to the other side. This is where you were first introduced to interim injunctions, in the form of urgent prohibitory injunctions.

Here is a summary of **without notice** applications you have met so far in this book. You may wish to look back to the table at the end of Chapter 4 to remind yourself how to apply for them.

"Without notice" applications made under Part 23 CPR, met so far in this book	
Application for	**Chapter of this book**
• Urgent prohibitory injunction Made by prospective C before a claim is begun.	4
• Extension of time for service of a CF • Alternative Service	10
• Court order for further information By the first party following no response from the second party to the first party's written request for further information.	14

Elements of the syllabus which you have now covered

- A cell with heavy outlining means that that area of the syllabus was covered in this Chapter;
- A darkly shaded cell with a tick √ means that the whole of that syllabus element has now been covered;
- A lightly shaded cell means that part of that element of the syllabus has been covered in a previous Chapter; and
- An unshaded cell means that element of the syllabus has not yet been covered.

1.1 √	1.2 √	1.3 √	2.1 √	2.2 √	3.1 √	3.2 √	6.1 √	6.2 √	6.3 √
6.4 √	7.1	7.2 √	8.1 √	8.2 √	8.3 √	9.1 √	9.2 √	9.3 √	10.1 √
10.2 √	11.1 √	11.2 √	12.1 √	12.2 √	12.3 √	13.1	13.2	13.3 √	13.4 √
13.5	13.6	13.7	13.8	14.1 √	14.2	14.3	14.4	14.5	14.6
15.1	15.2 √	15.3 √	15.4 √	16.1 √	16.2 √	17.1	17.2	17.3	17.4
18.2. √	18.3 √	18.4 √ 18.5 √	19.1	19.2	19.3	20.1	20.2	20.3	21.1
21.2	21.3	22.1	22.2 22.3	23.1 √	23.2 √	23.3	23.4 √	24.1	

Chapter 17

INTERIM INJUNCTIONS ("two") [CUR 17.2 and 17.3]

At the hearing, whether the application for this interim remedy was made

before or during proceedings:

the contents of your advocacy

"What if" (vi)

What if, during proceedings, C wants an injunction to stop D doing something or to require D to do something?

CURRICULUM

~~*Interim applications*~~ *(Chapters 3 and 4 and between Chapters 16 and 17),* ~~*interim payments*~~ *(Chapter 16)* ~~*security for costs*~~ *(Chapter 15)* ***Interim Injunctions*** *- (See also Chapter 4)* **17.1 interim injunctions** **17.2 American Cyanamid principles** **17.3 exceptions and variations to American Cyanamid** **17.4 usual undertakings and cross-undertakings**

SYLLABUS

Examinable material will consist of applying for interim injunctions; principles and guidelines to be applied (American Cyanamid case); guidelines - adequacy of damages as a remedy and the balance of convenience; particular guidelines; interlocutory ruling in effect disposing of action finally; cases excepted from guidelines; mandatory injunctions; and cross-undertaking as to damages.

(Each of the above has its own subheading in this chapter, flagged by EM:)

- **CPR 25.1, 25.2 and 25.3 are in Chapter 4**
- **The following specific leading case authority (which students should be able to refer to by name): American Cyanamid.**
- **Commentary is incorporated in context in this Chapter, highlighted in an Activity box between two stars**

Chapter 17 MOCS

❖ ***It is possible to make a part 23 application with notice for an interim injunction when a claim for a substantive cause of action has already been issued.*** ❖ ***Advocacy will need to work through the American Cyanamid principles for both pre-action and during the action*** ***unless*** ***the action falls within one of the six exceptions set out in this Chapter*** ***or unless*** ***the application is for a mandatory interim injunction when the principles are varied***

The sessions dealing with this area of the syllabus on my BTC course are	

You will recall form Chapter 4 that an interim injunction may be granted even before proceedings have been issued, during proceedings or after judgment – "at any time".

In addition, where proceedings have been issued and when the need for an interim injunction arises, they can also be applied for, **with notice** to the other side, to take effect pending a final decision by the court at trial; e.g. when C has already issued a claim for a substantive cause of action (say for breach of covenant) and also wants an interim prohibitory injunction against D to stop the breach occurring until trial date is reached.

The procedure is broadly the same, whether proceedings have been issued or not. you should apply to the court for the required injunction exactly the same way as set out in Chapter 4, except for the obvious changes of:

EM: where to make an application

For interim applications being made after proceedings have started, the general rule is that the application must be made to the County Court hearing centre where the claim was started with the issue of the CF.

Since CPR 25.2 (2) states that an order for an interim remedy, is subject to any rule, practice direction or other enactment which provides otherwise, where it is D who wishes to apply for an interim injunction, then unless the court orders otherwise, D needs to have filed either an AOS or a defence before she can do so.

Note the obviously needed omission from the modification list in Chapter 4, *"The A will undertake to issue - and pay the fee for - the claim form for the substantive cause of action"* as when proceedings - that is the CF - have been issued before an urgent prohibitory injunction is needed, there is obviously no need to undertake to issue them!

<u>Preparing the advocacy for an application for an [urgent, without notice,] interim [prohibitory or mandatory] injunction.</u>

- State whom you represent and that the application is for e,g an urgent prohibitory injunction and so without notice; or for e.g. a mandatory injunction
- Check that the judge has the relevant bundles, whether (s)he has had the opportunity to read them, whether (s)he would like a summary of the background to the case
- Signpost to the judge what the structure of your submissions is going to be
- [The requirements below are taken from Chapter 4]
  - Set out the urgency or why it is desirable in the interests of justice for an injunction to be granted
  - Set out the substantive cause of action
  - Set out how you will demonstrate to the court that it will be just and convenient to grant this equitable remedy (by use and application of the American Cyanamid case law guidelines referred to below [as well as by taking into account where appropriate e.g for mandatory injunctions] variations and exceptions; these are set out later in this Chapter])
  - Show that the correct documentation is available or that there are the relevant undertakings
    - Set out which are the relevant matters in this case allowing for an application notice not to have been served on R if such is the case
    - Refer to the evidence / undertakings for it
    - Refer to the draft order
  - Flesh out your skeleton argument (you will be taught how to prepare these during your BTC) to persuade the court to grant the injunction. Be sure to take the court to specific parts of your evidence (witness statement) to bolster your arguments. Where the application is for an urgent prohibitory injunction which would not effectively finally dispose of the case, or for any other injunction on your syllabus not subject to the exceptions and variation of the guidelines, you will take the court through the guidelines set out in the case of ***<u>American Cyanamid Co v Ethicon Ltd [1975] AC 396.</u>***
  - Summarise your arguments and finish in a strong persuasive way.

<u>CUR 17.1</u> <u>INTERIM INJUNCTIONS</u>

<u>EM: applying for interim injunctions</u>

Although final injunctions may be granted at the trial for the substantive cause of action, in this Chapter we are talking about **interim** injunctions. These are injunctions applied for "in the interim," at a hearing somewhere along the way to the trial. The party applying for the interim injunction is called the applicant, the other party, the respondent.

<u>CUR 17.2</u> *<u>AMERICAN CYANAMID</u>* <u>PRINCIPLES</u>

<u>EM:</u>* *<u>principles and guidelines to be applied (American Cyanamid case)</u>

<u>American Cyanamid principles (American Cyanamid Co v Ethicon Ltd BSB[1975] AC 396)</u>

This authority provides guidelines/principles for a court to consider and for an advocate to follow when trying to persuade the court to exercise its **discretion** as to whether or not to grant an interim injunction, so that it is not necessary to consider all the evidence regarding the merits of the case at the interim application stage, (unless the grant of the interim injunction would effectively fully dispose of the case without the need for a trial and so the merits of the case would be considered. [other variations and exceptions to the way these principles are to be used appear later in this Chapter]).

The principles that Counsel should argue to persuade a court to grant an interim injunction, are, **<u>IN THIS ORDER:</u>**

- That there is a **serious issue to be tried.** If yes, continue on to argue the next point. The court will refuse the injunction if there is not a serious issue to be tried.

- ***<u>EM:</u>* *<u>guidelines - adequacy of damages as a remedy</u>***

  Would damages be an adequate remedy for A (i.e. would money suffice rather than an injunction)? If so, the court will refuse the injunction as an injunction would therefore not be needed. Damages would not be an adequate remedy in the following circumstances; where

  - R is unlikely to be able to pay the sum of damages likely to be awarded against her at trial; or
  - the damage is irreparable; or
  - the damage is not translatable into money terms e.g. a libel / nuisance claim; or
  - there is no available market elsewhere to buy items that would be the subject of the injunction ; or
  - damages are difficult to assess; or
  - there is a provision in a contract for liquidated damages for a sum lower than A could be awarded on a successful claim for breach of the contract.

  Once Counsel has established that damages would not be an adequate remedy for A, continue on to argue the next point.

- **Would A's undertaking in damages provide adequate protection for R?** (This particular principle of *American Cyanamid* can be dispensed with where the claimant/applicant is publicly funded).

  The court considers how it would be if A undertook to pay compensation to R if the interim injunction is granted against R and if it ultimately turns out that the interim injunction was wrongly granted; would R be adequately protected by being awarded compensation from A in these circumstances? Once Counsel has advocated in order to persuade the court that R would thus be adequately compensated for any loss caused by the interim injunction, then Counsel should go on to argue the next point.

- ***EM: guidelines - the balance of convenience***

  Where does the balance of convenience lie? This principle suggests that if it lies in favour of neither one party nor the other, then the "status quo" should prevail and no interim injunction should be granted where positions are "evenly balanced."

  "Status quo" is either
  - the position as it was immediately before the issue of the claim form claiming the permanent injunction; or,
  - if there has been unreasonable delay between the issue of the claim form and the application for the interim injunction, the position as it was immediately before this interim application.

- Counsel can also ask the court to consider any **special factors**.

- Counsel will only argue and the court will only consider the **merits of the case** as a **last resort** if the strength of one party's case is disproportionate to that of the other. (Unless the interim injunction will finally dispose of the case – see exceptions and variations below.)

As you would expect, the principles that Counsel should argue to persuade a court NOT to grant an interim [prohibitory] injunction against their respondent lay client are the converse of the above, as well as showing the existence any of the usual bars to equitable remedies such as delay or no clean hands.

CUR 17.4 CROSS-UNDERTAKINGS AS TO DAMAGES

EM: cross-undertakings in interim injunction cases.

Undertakings

An undertaking is a solemn binding legal promise. We have already seen the undertaking that A will give in the American Cyanamid principles, where A undertakes to pay damages to R if it turns out that the interim injunction was wrongly granted; and that this undertaking must be adequate protection for R should that turn out to be the case.

We have also seen undertakings by A to do what he has not already done in urgent interim injunctions and how a penal notice is included in an order for an urgent interim injunction so that breach of the undertaking included in the order amounts to contempt of court.

Cross undertakings

R may choose not to contest an application for an interim injunction. In this case R gives undertakings to A akin to what A wanted in the injunction. R will be in contempt if she breaches these undertakings.

Where this situation arises A must give a cross undertaking in damages to protect R so that she will receive compensation from A in the event that at trial A is not granted a final injunction.

CUR 17.3 CASES EXCEPTED FROM GUIDELINES; MANDATORY INJUNCTIONS

EM: cases excepted from guidelines; mandatory interim injunctions

There follow some exceptions and variations to the use of the American Cyanamid principles.

Exception One

– Cases where there is no arguable defence

Where this is the case, the court will not consider the balance of convenience. An interim injunction will be granted subject to the usual equitable considerations.

Remember that where the requirements for a successful application for summary judgment are met, it is possible to apply for summary judgment including a final order for an injunction rather than just applying for an interim injunction.

Exception Two

– ***EM: interlocutory ruling in effect disposing of action finally***

A successful interim application will be a final disposal of the case at the interim stage where Counsel persuades the court that overwhelmingly on the merits of the case, if the interim injunction is granted there is no realistic possibility either

- of R insisting on continuing on to trial; or
- of the claim proceeding to trial.

Exception Three

– Restraint of trade cases

It may be that a contract of employment contains express restraint of trade clauses to protect the employer. For example, it may provide that after an employee leaves the employ of that employer, the employee may not, for a period of, say, six months, work for a competitor, or may not work in the same line of business in the same town.

Where trial cannot be arranged before a valid express restrictive (negative) covenant comes to an end, (i.e. say the court date is 8 months hence and the restrictive covenants were for 6 months), an interim injunction will protect the contractual rights of the employer.

Courts **will** "as of course" grant an interim injunction in favour of the employer if

- all the facts are before the court; and
- the covenants in restraint of trade are prima facie valid (reasonable in time, place and activity that they restrain).

Exception Four

– Defamation claims

The overriding public interest is in the right to free speech.

Where an applicant is bringing a claim for slander or libel, there will be **no injunction** to stop the respondent from saying or writing what the applicant considers defamatory where the respondent is pleading the defence that the imputation conveyed by the statement complained of is **substantially true** and the alleged defamation is not obviously untruthful.

– Cases involving freedom of expression

Subject to a restriction for the protection of the reputation and rights of others [Art 10 (2) ECHR], everyone has the right to freedom of expression [Art 10 (1) ECHR].

So where the applicant wishes to obtain an in interim injunction to stop the respondent publishing something [s.12 (3) HRA 1998], Counsel will have to satisfy the court that at trial the applicant is likely to establish, on the balance of probabilities, that his Art 10 (2) reputation and rights justify being protected.

Exception Five

– Cases involving privacy

Where the applicant wishes to obtain an interim injunction to stop, say, a newspaper or magazine publishing an article or photographs of him or his family, he is claiming his Article 8 (1) ECHR right to protection of private and family life.

The court will balance that right against the rights of the respondent to her Article 10 (1) ECHR freedom of expression.

The court is likely to grant the interim injunction where it is satisfied that on the balance of probabilities the applicant is likely to establish a breach of his privacy as there has been a breach of confidence. In such cases, restricting the respondent's Article 10 right to freedom of expression is justified.

Where there has been no breach of confidence the court will consider whether there is any public interest served by not granting an interim injunction, thus allowing the information about the applicant's private or family life to be disclosed.

What if the claimant wants an injunction to require the defendant do something?

EM: applying for interim injunctions

When C wants to require D to do something, C applies for a mandatory injunction.

– Mandatory interim injunction [CPR volume 2 section 15]

This is where the applicant is asking the court to make an order that the respondent do something, e.g. effect repairs. In such interim applications there is a variation to the way that the American Cyanamid principles are applied. At the balance of convenience stage Counsel needs to persuade the court that it can have **a high degree of assurance** that at the trial it would appear that the mandatory injunction was rightly granted at the interim stage, given the merits of the claimant's cause of action.

The overriding consideration is to **keep the risk of injustice as low as possible**, either

- in case it turns out at trial that the applicant wins and so a mandatory interim injunction should have been granted where it was not; or
- in case it turns out that a mandatory interim injunction should not have been granted as the applicant continues on to fail at trial. Granting a mandatory interim injunction gives a greater risk of injustice and to persuade the court to grant one, Counsel will have to show that there is more risk of injustice if it is not granted than if it is.

  This is because a mandatory injunction is often more likely to cause irremediable prejudice than in cases in which D is merely prevented from taking or continuing with some course of action.

Activity

Remember to make notes on the relevant case law authorities in paragraphs

25.1.9-25.1.11
25.1.14.1
25.1.14.2
25.1.15
in the commentary in Volume 1 of the White Book.

Remember <u>also</u> to consider the material in Volume 2 of the White Book in paragraphs

15-7 to 15-18
15-20 to 15-22
15-24 to 15-27
15-29 to 15-30

You may find it useful to add in references to the case law and Volume 2 material NOW at the appropriate points of this Chapter.

When approaching final revision time, remember to add in the salient findings of the cases at the relevant point in any 'mental crib sheet' into which you have distilled the main points of your learned knowledge.

<u>After the hearing for an application for an interim injunction.</u>

- Remember that after the hearing, where an urgent pre-action interim injunction is ordered, A must fulfil all his undertakings, serving as much as possible on R at the same time as serving the order for the urgent interim prohibitory injunction, especially the claim form.

- Where the application for an interim injunctions is not successful and the injunction not granted,, a copy of the application notice and any evidence in support must, unless the court orders otherwise, be served on the person(s) against whom the order was sought

Chapter 17

Elements of the syllabus which you have now covered

- A cell with heavy outlining means that that area of the syllabus was covered in this Chapter;
- A darkly shaded cell with a tick √ means that the whole of that syllabus element has now been covered;
- A lightly shaded cell means that part of that element of the syllabus has been covered in a previous Chapter; and
- An unshaded cell means that element of the syllabus has not yet been covered.

1.1 √	1.2 √	1.3 √	2.1 √	2.2 √	3.1 √	3.2 √	6.1 √	6.2 √	63 √
6.4 √	7.1 √	7.2 √	8.1 √	8.2 √	8.3 √	9.1 √	9.2 √	9.3 √	10.1 √
10.2 √	11.1 √	11.2 √	12.1 √	12.2 √	12.3 √	13.1	13.2	13.3 √	13.4 √
13.5	13.6	13.7	13.8	14.1 √	14.2	14.3	14.4	14.5	14.6
15.1 √	15.2 √	15.3 √	15.4 √	16.1 √	16.2 √	17.1 √	17.2 √	17.3 √	17.4 √
18.2. √	18.3 √	18.4 √ 18.5 √	19.1	19.2	19.3	20.1	20.2	20.3	21.1
21.2	21.3	21.1	22.2	22.1 √	22.2 √	22.3	22.4 √	25.1	

Chapter 18

This Chapter contains INTERIM COSTS ORDERS [CUR 23.3]

CURRICULUM

~~Judgments, Orders, Enforcement,~~ ***Costs*** *~~and Appeals Assessment~~*

23.3 interim costs orders

(Judgments and Orders,
Enforcement and
Appeals each have their own dedicated Chapters later in this book)

SYLLABUS

Examinable material will consist of, court discretion as to costs *(etc below)*

Please see Chapter 6 for the rest of the costs syllabus:-
Costs management,
standard or indemnity basis of assessment, factors taken into account in deciding amount of costs, procedure for assessing costs, summary assessment of costs, detailed assessment of costs, time for complying with order for costs, and court powers in relation to misconduct and qualified one-way costs shifting.

- **PD 44 paragraph 4**

Chapter 18 MOCS

- ***There is a table setting out possible interim cost orders in PD 44 in the section called***

"Court's discretion as to costs: rule 44.2"

The sessions dealing with this area of the syllabus on my BTC course are	

CUR 23.3 INTERIM COSTS ORDERS

EM: interim costs orders

You will recall from the Chapter on costs that costs orders following any interim application will be subject to a summary assessment by the judge at the end of the interim hearing.

A short statement of costs must be served by the parties 24 hours before the hearing.

Activity

Please refer back to the Chapter on costs for what happens if this statement is not served. You may wish to copy it out again here.

Interim costs are payable within 14 days of them becoming due.

Possible interim cost orders are set out in the table at PD 44 in the section called "Court's discretion as to costs: rule 44.2" in the table in note 4.2

- **Costs in any event**

This means that in any event, no matter what the outcome of the final trial, the loser of the interim hearing pays the costs of the winner of the interim hearing.

Remember the effect of QOCS where the claimant in a PI / fatal accidents case is the loser both at the interim hearing and at the final trial:

Because CPR rule 44.14 (2) says that QOCS can only be enforced 'after proceedings are concluded and costs have been assessed or agreed', then if the court does not award any damages or interest to C at the final trial because he is the loser there too, if C has not paid D's interim costs, D will be unable to enforce against C for payment of her interim costs.

- **Costs in the case**

This means that parties will 'wait-and-see' what the cost order is in the case at the end, then the loser in the final trial pays the other's costs of both the interim hearing and the final trial.

- **Costs reserved**

This means that the matter of costs will be deferred until the final trial. Should there be no costs order made at final trial, then the position will be costs in the case.

- **Claimant's/Defendant's costs in the case**

  - Claimant's costs in the case

1. C wins at interim hearing
2. C wins at final trial and is awarded costs
3. D pays C's costs of the interim hearing (and the rest of C's costs too).

Or

1. C wins at interim hearing
2. D wins at final trial and is awarded costs
3. D is not liable for C's interim costs, so C pays his own interim costs (and the rest of D's costs too)

  - Defendant's costs in the case

1. D wins at interim hearing
2. D wins at final trial and is awarded costs
3. C should pay D's costs of the interim hearing (and the rest of D's costs too) (subject to QOCS where relevant)

Or

1. D wins at interim hearing
2. C wins at final trial and is awarded costs
3. C is not liable for D's interim costs, so D pays her own interim costs (and the rest of C's costs too)

- **Costs thrown away**

The detail of this type of costs order was set out towards the end of Chapter 11.

Activity

You may find it useful to copy it out again here.

– **Costs of and caused by**

The detail of this type of costs order was set out at the end of Chapter 12.

Activity

You may find it useful to copy this costs order out again here.

– **Costs here and below**

This is an order available to the Court of Appeal relating to costs both in that court and in the court from which the appeal was made.

– **No order as to costs**

Either where Counsel does not ask for an order as to costs or where the court chooses not to make one, each party bears their own costs of the interim application whatever costs order the court makes in relation to the final trial.

Chapter 18

Elements of the syllabus which you have now covered

- A cell with heavy outlining means that that area of the syllabus was covered in this Chapter;
- A darkly shaded cell with a tick √ means that the whole of that syllabus element has now been covered;
- A lightly shaded cell means that part of that element of the syllabus has been covered in a previous Chapter; and
- An unshaded cell means that element of the syllabus has not yet been covered.

1.1 √	1.2 √	1.3 √	2.1 √	2.2 √	3.1 √	3.2 √	6.1 √	6.2 √	63 √
6.4 √	7.1 √	7.2 √	8.1 √	8.2 √	8.3 √	9.1 √	9.2 √	9.3 √	10.1 √
10.2 √	11.1 √	11.2 √	12.1 √	12.2 √	12.3 √	13.1	13.2	13.3 √	13.4 √
13.5	13.6	13.7	13.8	14.1 √	14.2	14.3	14.4	14.5	14.6
15.1 √	15.2 √	15.3 √	15.4 √	16.1 √	16.2 √	17.1 √	17.2 √	17.3 √	17.4 √
18.2. √	18.3 √	18.4 √ 18.5 √	19.1	19.2	19.3	20.1	20.2	20.3	21.1
21.2	21.3	21.1	22.2 22.	22.1 √	22.2 √	22.3 √	22.4 √	25.1	

Chapter 19

CASE MANAGEMENT,

SANCTIONS AND STRIKING OUT [CUR 13]

o) Track Allocation, Court management of cases, Sanctions and relief from sanctions

THIS CHAPTER CONTAINS THE ITEMS PRINTED IN BOLD IN THE FOLLOWING BOXES

CURRICULUM ("CUR")

Case management, sanctions and striking out

13.1 the small claims track, fast track and multi-track

13.2 allocation

13.3 case management conferences

13.4 costs management is in Chapter 6

13.5 directions

13.6 relief from sanctions

13.7 striking out a claim

13.8 discontinuance

SYLLABUS

Examinable material will consist of *the court's case management powers, court's power to make orders of its own initiative*, ***power to strike out statements of case, sanctions, relief from sanctions****, power of court to rectify where there have been errors of procedure, costs management,* ***case management, directions questionnaires, stays to allow for settlement, referrals to mediation, scope of the small claims track, fast track and multi-track, allocation, directions in fast track cases and case management in multi-track cases.***

(Each of the above has its own subheading in this chapter, flagged by EM:)

- CPR 2.8 appears in context in Chapter 3 under CUR 15.3 Periods of notice in interim applications and in Chapter 10 under CUR 6.3 Service of other court documents within the jurisdiction.
- CPR 2.11 is in Chapter 2
- CPR 3.1, 3.1A, 3.3, 3.10 is in Chapter 2
- CPR 3.4 is dealt with in Chapter 13 on striking out
- **CPR 3.5**
- **CPR 3.9**
- CPR 3.12-3.18; PD 3E paragraphs 1-7 are dealt with in Chapter 6 on costs
- **CPR 26.1 and 26.3-26.10; PD 26 paragraphs 7, 9 and 11**
- **CPR 28.3-4**
- **CPR 29.1-29.9; PD 29 paragraphs 3-10**

SANCTIONS

- ***CPR 3.8 (1)***
- ***CPR 3.8 (2)***
- ***CPR 3.9***
- **The following specific leading case authority (which students should be able to refer to by name): *Denton*,** (is also in Chapter 13)
- **Commentary is incorporated in context** in Chapter 13 **and further in this chapter 19, highlighted in an Activity box between two stars**

DISCONTINUANCE

- **CPR 38.1-7**

Before beginning this Chapter, remind yourself of the **MOCS** on case management so far:-

From Chapter 2

Court's General Powers of case management

Court may make orders on its own initiative

Courts may rectify errors in procedure.

and from Chapter 6

Costs budgets

Costs management orders

From this Chapter 19

❖ ***Case Management***

- ***D files defence***
- ***Proposed track allocation by a court officer then within 14 days deemed service of this for small track or 28 days for the other tracks***
- ***Directions Questionnaires filed, C replies to D's defence with this, request 1 month stay if all agree, court will decide if parties do not agree.***
- ***Procedural Judge allocates track***
- ***Case management on each of the tracks.***

This concludes case management on this course.

❖ ***STRIKE OUT***

- ***Failure to comply with a rule, PD or court order can lead to***
- ***an "unless" order which can lead to***
- ***a request for judgment without trial after striking out, then***
- ***automatic strike out if a wholly "money" claim or***
- ***if not wholly money, then a Part 23 application for strike out.***

The left hand column of the following table you have met before in Chapter 13. The right hand column is now added.

<u>Strike out at the outset</u> ***NOT in developing law*** ***NOT if possible the claim will succeed.***	***<u>Strike out for failing to comply with rule/PD/court order</u>***
<u>When</u> ***Once D served AOS/Defence***	***<u>When</u>*** ***As this is a sanction of last resort*** ***1. Once have warned the other side that you intend to apply for an unless order.*** ***If still no compliance then 2.***
<u>How</u> ***<u>Part 23 application showing</u>*** • ***no reasonable grounds*** • ***abuse of process***	***<u>How</u>*** ***2. Apply for an unless order. If no extension agreed between parties or if extension[12] ended and still not complied then 3.*** ***3a). If re £££, where it is C wanting strike out, C can request that judgment is entered which leads to an automatic strike out; or 3b) if 3a) is not applicable.*** ***3b). Part 23 application***
<u>Outcome</u> ***Either strike out judgment entered*** ***Or the case continues and consequential orders are made about this***	***<u>Outcome</u>*** ***Either struck out and judgment entered*** ***And 3a) no further order is required; or*** ***3b) if the application is successful, no further order is required; or*** ***3b) the application is unsuccessful and the case continues and consequential orders are made about this***

[12] This is to remind you that you have met this 28 day extension point before, both in Chapter 2 and in Chapter 11. **IT IS IMPORTANT THAT YOU ALSO REFER BACK TO THE FOOTNOTES AT THE END OF CHAPTER 2 regarding the change to 56 days (possibly temporary but possibly not) in relation to the Coronavirus pandemic.**

❖ ***RELIEF FROM SANCTIONS***

- ***Appeal the order for costs if that was the sanction or***

- ***For other sanctions apply for relief from the sanction. The court will consider the 3 stage test set out in Denton:-***

  - ***Serious or significant non compliance?***
  - ***Was the reason for the non compliance a good one?***
  - ***All the circumstances with particular weight to CPR 3.9***
    - ***Litigation efficiently and at proportionate cost?***
    - ***Do facts show a need to enforce compliance?***

      Plus

      - ***Promptness of application for relief from sanction***
      - ***History of past breaches***

❖ ***DISCONTINUANCE OF ALL OR PART OF A CLAIM***

- ***Procedure***
- ***When it takes effect***
- ***Set-aside discontinuance***
- ***Liability for costs***
- ***Subsequent proceedings***

The sessions dealing with this area of the syllabus on my BTC course are	

You will recall that the court has general case management powers as set out in Chapter 2. You will further recall that you have also met case management in relation to costs management on the multi-track in Chapter 6.

Now, having considered the "what-ifs" in the previous six Chapters, we pick up again from the end of Chapter 12. In this current Chapter we start from the point where the defence has been filed.

The next stage of the process is the court, under it is case management powers, giving notice to parties of which track it proposes to allocate the case to – the small claims track, the fast track or the multi-track, of which further detail later in this Chapter.

CUR 13.2 ALLOCATION

EM: allocation

The allocation of business between the small claims track, the fast track and the multi-track

This section entails

1. Notice of the proposed track allocation
2. When directions questionnaires are to be filed and served by the parties
3. Formal allocation to track by a procedural judge by notice of allocation

1. Notice of the proposed track allocation

After D has filed her defence / where there are 2 or more Ds, the sooner of when
– all have filed their defences or
– one of them has filed a defence and the time for filing the last defence has expired,
a court officer completes forms which are served on all parties giving notice of the proposed track allocation.

Contents of the notice of proposed track allocation.

- A date by which the parties must file and serve the completed directions questionnaire
- A reminder that parties should consult one another and cooperate in the completion of the directions questionnaire
- A reminder that parties should try to agree the court management directions they will invite the court to make. In so doing the parties must have regard to those matters which are relevant to the procedural judge when (s)he makes the formal, final decision as to track allocation. These are set out in CPR 26.8 and include the amount of the claim, the remedy sought, the complexity of the facts/law, the number of parties. Note that at this stage, consideration is not given to any amounts which are not in dispute, nor to interest, nor to costs, nor to whether there is a claim for contributory negligence. The court will approve the agreed court management directions that the parties invite the court to make if it finds them suitable.
- Remember that where the proposed allocation is to the multi-track, the notice of proposed track allocation may specify the date for the filing of costs budgets. If it does not the latest date for doing so is 7 days before the first case management conference.

2. When ***EM: directions questionnaires*** are to be filed and served by the parties

- If proposed allocation is to the small claims track, at least 14 days after deemed service of notice of proposed allocation
- If proposed allocation is to the fast track or to the multi-track, at least 28 days after deemed service of notice of proposed allocation
- If any interim remedies are to be pursued, they must be notified to the court at this point
- If C has replied to D's defence, he must
  - file the reply with a directions questionnaire and
  - serve the reply on the other parties at the same time as it is filed. (see Chapter 11);
- ***EM: stays to allow for settlement*** If a party or parties wish to request a stay a written request can be made to the court at this point. The stay will be for one month if all parties make the request. If the request does not come from all parties, the court, if it considers a stay appropriate, will direct that the whole or part of the proceedings are stayed for one month or such other period as it considers appropriate.

Sanctions for not filing directions questionnaires

- For **money only claims** the court serves a notice requiring it to be filed within an additional 7 days. Further non-compliance will lead to an automatic strike out.
- For **other types of claim** the court makes such order as it thinks appropriate. This could be the court
  - giving further directions; or
  - striking out the claim; or
  - striking out the defence and entering judgment; or
  - listing the matter for a case management conference.

3. Formal allocation to track by a procedural judge by notice of allocation

CUR 13.1 THE SMALL CLAIMS TRACK, FAST TRACK AND MULTI-TRACK

EM: scope of the small claims track, fast track and multi-track

Once all parties have filed their directions questionnaires, or at the end of a period of a stay, the procedural judge allocates a claim to a track.

Before allocating proceedings, the court may order a party to provide further information about their case.

The procedural judge can allocate a claim to a lower track regardless of the wishes of the parties, e.g. if the claim is a straightforward one.

Where the court is to decide whether to allocate to the fast track or the multi-track a claim for which the normal track is the fast track, it will allocate the claim to the fast track unless it believes that it cannot be dealt with justly on that track.

So it may be that the CPR 26.8 relevant matters lead the procedural judge to allocate what initially looks like a case for the fast track, 'up' to the multi- track.

Those relevant matters include

- **the financial value, if any, of the claim**
  - It is for the court to assess the financial value of a claim. Where the court believes that the amount C is seeking exceeds what he may reasonably be expected to recover it may make an order directing him to justify the amount.
  - When assessing the financial value of a claim the court will *disregard*
    - *(i) any amount not in dispute*
      - any sum in respect of an item forming part of the claim for which judgment has been entered (for example a summary judgment) is not in dispute
      - any specific sum claimed as a distinct item and which D admits she is liable to pay is not in dispute
      - any sum offered by D which has been accepted by C in satisfaction of any item which forms a distinct part of the claim is not in dispute.

    Any amount for which D does not admit liability is in dispute [if D makes an admission before allocation that reduces the amount in dispute to a figure below £10,000, the normal track for the claim will be the small claims track. C can then, before allocation, apply for judgment with costs on the amount of the claim that has been admitted]

    - *(ii) any claim for interest;*
    - *(iii) costs; and*
    - *(iv) any contributory negligence.*

- **the nature of the remedy sought;**
- **the likely complexity of the facts, law or evidence;**
- **the number of parties or likely parties;**
- **the value of any counterclaim or other Part 20 claim and the complexity of any matters relating to it;**
  - Where the case involves more than one money claim (for example where there is a Part 20 claim or there is more than one claimant each making separate claims) the court will not generally aggregate the claims. Instead it will generally regard the largest of them as determining the financial value of the claims.
  - Where the case involves a counterclaim or other Part 20 claim that will be tried with the claim and as a result the trial will last more than a day, the court may not allocate it to the fast track.
- **the amount of oral evidence which may be required;**
- **the importance of the claim to persons who are not parties to the proceedings;**
- **the views expressed by the parties** This is one of "all the circumstances " that the court will consider when making its decision.
- **the circumstances of the parties.**

The directions given in the notice of allocation may include fixing a pre - trial review date.

When it has allocated a claim to a track, the court will serve notice of allocation on every party.

Activity

Have a look at the costs Chapter again and copy out here the monetary value of those claims likely to be allocated to

Small claims track

~
~
~

Fast track

~
~
~

Multi track

~
~
~

Re-allocation of claims and the variation of directions

Where a party is dissatisfied with an order made allocating the claim to a track he may

- appeal if the order was made at a hearing at which he was present or represented, or of which he was given due notice; or
- apply to the court to re-allocate the claim.

Where there has been a change in the circumstances since an order was made allocating the claim to a track the court may re-allocate the claim. It may do so on application or on its own initiative.

SMALL CLAIMS TRACK

- ***EM: referrals to mediation***

  Where a claim would normally be allocated to the small claims track [**and** the claim is **not an RTA** claim, **PI** claim or **housing disrepair** claim], where all parties indicate on their directions questionnaire that they agree to mediation, the claim will be referred to the Small Claims Mediation Service operated by Her Majesty's Courts and Tribunals Service.

  If mediation brings about settlement the proceedings will automatically be stayed with permission to apply for
  - judgment for the unpaid balance of the outstanding sum of the settlement agreement; or
  - the claim to be restored for hearing of the full amount claimed,

unless the parties have agreed that the claim is to be discontinued or dismissed.

If the court has not been notified in writing that a settlement has been agreed, the claim will be allocated to a track no later than four weeks from the date on which the last directions questionnaire is filed.

- Small Claims are heard before a district judge in chambers. The atmosphere is informal. There are no strict rules of evidence. Parties can advocate for themselves. Evidence need not be on oath, the court may limit cross-examination.

- Some CPRs do not apply. There are no interim remedies, no part 36 offers. Only the court, not the parties can require further information to be provided.

- <u>Typical directions in the small claims track</u>

  These are referred to in the notice of allocation. Where the district judge specifies no other directions, standard directions are set out in Appendix B of PD27. They are that the parties must

  - disclose documents on which they rely. (Disclosure is dealt with fully in the next Chapter). Copies of these documents must be served (this will include the letter before claim and any reply, together with any expert reports) no later than 14 days before the hearing;

  - bring all <u>original</u> documents to the hearing

  - contact each other to try to settle

  - remember that they need to apply for the court's permission if they want to use an expert's report. On the small claims track, if it appears to the court that expert evidence is necessary, permission will be given for one expert jointly instructed by the parties. Appendix C of PD27 includes draft special directions for this.

<u>FAST TRACK</u>

- The trial is no longer than one day (5 hours).
- A claim may be allocated to the fast track or ordered to remain on that track although there is to be a split trial (see the next Chapter).
- In the notice of allocation the court either approves the case management directions agreed by the parties in the directions questionnaire or amends and then approves them.

<u>CUR 13.5 DIRECTIONS (FAST TRACK)</u>

<u>EM: directions in fast track cases</u>

When it allocates a case to the fast track, the court will give directions for the management of the case and set a timetable for the steps to be taken between the giving of the directions and the trial.

The court may also give directions at the listing stage and if necessary at other times.

In either case directions can be given with or without a hearing. The trial judge may, at or before the trial, give directions for its conduct.

The directions impose a 30 week timetable to trial and include directions regarding

- Parties giving standard disclosure (this is explained in the next Chapter)

  If the court decides not to direct standard disclosure, it may direct that no disclosure take place; or specify the documents or the classes of documents which the parties must disclose.

- Service of witness statements

- Expert evidence
  - Giving permission for the use of experts
  - Directing that there be a single joint expert, unless there is a good reason not to do so, if both sides want an expert in the same field
  - Using the expert's written report at trial; experts are directed to attend only if the court considers that it is in the interests of justice that they do so.
  - Limiting oral expert evidence at trial to one expert each and to two fields (therefore 2 experts)
  - Limiting the amount of fees recoverable from another party in respect of experts' fees

- You will remember from Chapter 2 of this book that CPR 28.4 (variation of case management timetable – fast track) that
  - A party must apply to the court if he wishes to vary the date which the court has fixed for
    ~ the return of a pre-trial check list under rule 28.5
    ~ the trial or
    ~ the trial period.

The next stage of case management, where the court can give further directions, will be when the pre-trial check lists are filed.

MULTI-TRACK
(from here to the case management MOC later in the Chapter)

Case management will generally be dealt with by:

- a Master in cases proceeding in the Royal Courts of Justice,
- a district judge in cases proceeding in a District Registry of the High Court, and
- a district judge or a Circuit Judge in cases proceeding in a county court.

A Master or a district judge may consult and seek the directions of a judge of a higher level about any aspect of case management.

A member of the court staff who is dealing with the listing of a hearing may seek the directions of any judge about any aspect of that listing.

You will recall from Chapter 2 that **both the parties and the court must**, when drafting case management directions in the multi-track and fast track, take as their starting point any relevant standard directions which can be found online at www.justice.gov.uk/courts/procedure-rules/civil and adapt them as appropriate to the circumstances of the case.

CUR 13.5 DIRECTIONS (MULTI-TRACK)

When it allocates a case to the multi-track, the court

- **will** give directions for the management of the case and set a timetable for the steps to be taken between the giving of directions and the trial; or
- **may** fix
  - a case management conference; or
  - a pre-trial review
  - or both

  and give such other directions relating to the management of the case as it sees fit.

In particular it will have regard to the extent to which Practice Direction (Pre-Action Conduct) [or any pre-action protocol – not on your syllabus this year] has or (as the case may be) has not been complied with.

At this stage the court's first concern will be to ensure that the **issues** between the parties are **identified** and that the necessary **evidence is prepared and disclosed.**

The court may have regard to any document filed by a party with his directions questionnaire containing further information, provided that the document states either that its contents has been agreed with every other party or that it has been served on every other party, and when it was served.

The court will hold a hearing to give directions whenever it appears necessary or desirable to do so, and where this happens because of the default of a party or his legal representative it will usually impose a sanction.

When the court fixes a hearing to give directions it will give the parties at least 3 days' notice of the hearing unless it is to be a pre-trial review (see below), when 7 days' notice is to be given.

Trial date or period fixed

The court will fix the trial date or the period in which the trial is to take place as soon as practicable. It will give notice to the parties of the date or period and specify the date by which the parties must file a pre-trial check list.

Case management conference and pre-trial review

On the allocation of a claim to the multi-track the court will consider whether it is desirable or necessary to hold a case management conference straight away, or whether it is appropriate instead to give directions on its own initiative.

The court may fix a case management conference or a pre-trial review, at any time after the claim has been allocated.

If a party has a legal representative, i.e. a representative familiar with the case and with sufficient authority to deal with any issues that are likely to arise, that legal representative must attend case management conferences and pre-trial reviews.

CUR 13.3 CASE MANAGEMENT CONFERENCES

Steps taken by the parties

The parties must endeavour to agree appropriate directions for the management of the proceedings and **submit agreed directions**, or their respective proposals to the court **at least seven days before any case management conference ("CMC").**

To obtain the court's approval the agreed directions must

- set out a timetable by reference to calendar dates for the taking of steps for the preparation of the case,
- include a date or a period (the trial period) when it is proposed that the trial will take place,
- include provision about **disclosure of documents** (see next Chapter in the section on multi-track). The provision may
  - limit disclosure to standard disclosure or less than that, and/or
  - direct that disclosure will take place by the supply of copy documents without a list, but it must in that case say either that the parties must serve a disclosure statement with the copies or that they have agreed to disclose in that way without such a statement
  - 29PD4 sets out further matters, to which you should make reference when you have completed the course in readiness for the assessment, when you will understand what they are each referring to
- include provision about both factual and **expert evidence.** This could be simply that none is required.

Where the court approves agreed directions, or issues its own directions, the parties will be so notified by the court and the slot for the case management conference will be vacated as it is not needed. Where these are not vacated and so held, a CMC includes

- ensuring the identification of the real **issues** between the parties
- identifying what **documents/evidence/experts** are necessary and any amendments needed, what disclosure is necessary, what arrangements should be made about the giving of clarification or further information and the putting of questions to experts
- viewing the **cost budgets** (remember that the latest time for filing these is the date specified in the notice of allocation or if none, 7 days before first case management conference).
- recording reasonable agreements in relation to what is at issue between the parties .
- laying down **directions**,
- considering whether it will be just and will save costs to order a split trial or the trial of one or more preliminary issues.
- possibly fixing the date of a pre - trial review.

Further case management conferences may be directed at any time up to the listing stage. These will

- assess the progress of the case
- assess whether initial directions have been complied with
- review the steps taken by parties so far
- review costs budgets

- record any further agreements between the parties
- lay down further directions

[There is a section at the end of this Chapter which deals with sanctions (e.g. for when a party fails to comply with directions – further detail on this is in PD29.7) and then how a party can obtain relief from those sanctions].

Where a party has a legal representative, s/he must attend a CMC, s/he must be familiar with the case, have sufficient ability and have the authority to agree outcomes on the client's behalf. If the legal representative is inadequate, not up to speed on all matters or without the authority to agree, there will be a wasted costs order against the party represented by that Counsel.

Variation of directions

Where a party is dissatisfied with a direction given by the court, where the parties have agreed about changes they wish made to the directions given, or where a party wishes to apply to vary a direction, they can appeal or apply to the court to reconsider.

The **procedure** is as follows. It must be carried out **as soon as possible.** If not started within 14 days of service of the order containing the directions, the court will assume that parties are content that the directions were correct in the circumstances then existing.

Where there has been a change in the circumstances since the order was made, the court may set aside or vary a direction it has given. It may do so on application or on its own initiative

Otherwise,

- **appeal** is appropriate where the party was present at the hearing **or** had reasonable notice of it;
- **application** for reconsideration is appropriate if they weren't or hadn't.

Where the parties agree about the change they wish to make to directions

- if the CPR allows for variation by written agreement between the parties, the written agreement need not be filed at court.
- In any other case the parties must apply for an order by consent.
    - The parties must file a draft of the order sought and an agreed statement of the reasons why the variation is sought.
    - The court may make an order in the agreed terms or in other terms without a hearing, but it may direct that a hearing is to be listed.

An application will usually be heard by the judge who gave the directions or another judge of the same level, the court will give all parties at least 3 days' notice of the hearing, and the court may confirm its directions or make a different order.

Variation of case management timetable

You will remember from Chapter 2 of this book that a party must **apply to the court** if he wishes **to vary the date** which the court has fixed for

- a case management conference
- a pre-trial review;

- the return of a pre-trial check list (explained below)
- the trial; or
- the trial period.

Any date set by the court or the CPR for doing any act may not be varied by the parties if the variation would make it necessary to vary any of these 5 dates.

Pre-trial check list (listing questionnaire)

Unless it considers that the claim can proceed to trial without the need for a pre-trial check list, the court will, at least 14 days before it is due to be returned, send to the parties a pre-trial check list (listing questionnaire) for completion and return. The date for return was specified at track allocation stage, and will be not later than 8 weeks before the trial date or the start of the trial period.

Parties are encouraged to exchange copies of the check lists before they are filed at court.

Each party must file the completed pre-trial check list by the date specified by the court.

If no party files the completed pre-trial checklist by the date specified, the court will generally order that unless a completed pre-trial checklist is filed within 7 days from service of that order, the claim, defence and any counterclaim will be struck out without further order of the court.

Or the court may give such directions as it thinks appropriate where
- a party files a completed pre-trial checklist but another party does not, the court will generally fix a hearing as early as possible and the parties will be given at least 3 days' notice of the date. Whether or not the defaulting party attends the hearing, the court will normally fix or confirm the trial date and make other orders about the steps to be taken to prepare the case for trial.
- a party has failed to give all the information requested by the pre-trial checklist; or
- the court considers that a hearing is necessary to enable it to decide what directions to give in order to complete preparation of the case for trial

Pre-trial review

If, on receipt of the parties' pre-trial check lists, the court decides to hold a pre-trial review or to cancel a pre-trial review which has already been fixed, it will serve notice of its decision at least 7 days before the date fixed for the hearing or, as the case may be, the cancelled hearing.

Where a party has a legal representative, s/he must attend any pre-trial review, s/he must be familiar with the case, have sufficient ability and have the authority to agree outcomes on the client's behalf. If the legal representative is inadequate, not up to speed on all matters or without the authority to agree, there will be a wasted costs order against the party represented by that Counsel.

Setting a trial timetable and confirming the trial date or week

As soon as practicable after
- each party has filed a completed pre-trial check list
- the court has held a listing hearing; or
- the court has held a pre-trial review

the court will

- unless a timetable has already been fixed, or the court considers that it would be inappropriate to do so, **set a timetable** for the trial; for example setting time limits for opening speeches, XIC, XX, closing speeches, and for the consideration of the judgment.
- confirm the **date for trial** or the week within which the trial is to begin; and
- **notify the parties** of the trial timetable (where one is fixed) and the date or trial period
- fix the **place of trial**
- give a **time estimate**

Other directions as to listing

- The parties should seek to agree directions and may file an agreed order. The court may make an order in those terms or it may make a different order.
- Agreed directions should include provision about:
  - evidence especially expert evidence. It determines which expert evidence will be given solely on papers, or where oral expert evidence may be given.
  - a trial timetable and time estimate,
  - the preparation of a trial bundle, and
  - any other matter needed to prepare the case for trial.

The court will include such of these provisions as are appropriate in any order that it may make, whether or not the parties have filed agreed directions.

Unless a direction doing so has been given before, a direction giving permission to use expert evidence will say whether it gives permission to use oral evidence or reports or both and will name the experts concerned.

The principles about variation of directions earlier in this Chapter apply equally to directions given at this stage.

Conduct of trial

Unless the trial judge otherwise directs, the trial will be conducted in accordance with any order previously made.

CUR 13.7 STRIKING OUT A CLAIM

Now we return to Strike Out.

You will recall from Chapter 13 that early strike out is possible if the other side shows no reasonable grounds for bringing or defending the claim or if the claim is an abuse of process.

In this, Chapter 19, we are looking at strike out for failure to comply with a rule, PD or court order

STRIKING OUT

- **CPR 3.8 (3 and 4)**
- **CPR 3.5**

EM: power to strike out statements of case

EM: judgment without trial after striking out

Enforcement of a direction in the first instance is likely to be by way of the sanction of an **"unless order,"** which may lead to the sanction of strike out as set out below.

Although it is possible to apply for the court to strike out the case, **strike out is a sanction of last resort.**

Application for an "unless" order, followed by the sanction of strike out if it is not fulfilled.

A must **warn** the other side of his intention to apply for an "unless order" before **apply**ing to the court for one under Part 23.

The court may **order that unless** the party **complies** with the direction within a certain timeframe, it **will strike out that party's case** and enter judgment for the other party.

[Where a rule, PD or court order requires a party to do something within a specified time and specifies the consequences of a failure to comply, (e.g. "unless you comply with directions within 14 days of the this order, then your case will be struck out and judgment entered for the other party"), CPR 3.8 (4) states that the **time** for doing the act in question **may be extended by prior written agreement of the parties for up to a maximum of 28 days** without an application to the court provided that any such extension does not put at risk any hearing date. That is, unless the court orders otherwise]. [13]

In cases where there has been no extension for compliance, as in the above paragraph, where a rule, PD or order states that the whole of a statement of case 'shall be struck out or dismissed' or 'will be struck out or dismissed' this means that

(i) Where **C** is the party wishing to obtain judgment and D has not complied with an unless order, C as the Applicant can file a **request for judgment without trial after striking out, with costs.** The request must state that the right to enter judgment has arisen because the

[13] This is to remind you that you have met this 28 day extension point before, both in Chapter 2 and in Chapter 11. **IT IS IMPORTANT THAT YOU ALSO REFER BACK TO THE FOOTNOTES AT THE END OF CHAPTER 2 regarding the change to 56 days (possibly temporary but possibly not) in relation to the Coronavirus pandemic.**

court's unless order has not been complied with. The claim will then be **struck out automatically** and judgment given for C **IF** it is for any of the following

- a specified sum of money
- an amount of money to be decided by the court
- delivery of goods where the claim form gives D the alternative of paying their value (it will be judgment requiring D to deliver goods, or (if she does not do so) to pay the value of the goods as decided by the court (less any payments made); or
- any combination of these remedies

and no further order of the court is required; or

(ii) If the application is not by C for one of the above mentioned claims (specified sum of money etc), or where the application is for strike out of only part of a claim, the way to apply for judgment without trial after striking out is with a Part 23 application.

(iii) QOCS

Remember from Chapter 6 that in a PI/fatal accident case where the strike out has been due to C's conduct there is no QOCS protection for C. Costs against C would therefore be enforceable to the full extent.

SANCTIONS

EM: sanctions

Sanctions can be imposed for

- Non-compliance with the relevant Pre-Action procedure
- Non-compliance with the CPR
- Non-compliance with Directions

EM: sanctions have effect unless defaulting party obtains relief.

Where a party has failed to comply with a rule, PD or court order, sanctions have effect unless the defaulting party obtains relief from the sanction.

So D can apply not more than 14 days after receiving the judgment against her for relief from e.g the sanction of strike out of her defence. The court will consider CPR 3.9 when considering whether to grant relief from a sanction. (Please see below).

CUR 13.6 RELIEF FROM SANCTIONS

EM: relief from sanctions

CPR on relief from sanctions

Where the sanction is the payment of costs, the party who is in default of paying the costs may only obtain relief from the sanction of having to pay the other side's costs by appealing against the order for costs.

For relief from other sanctions, Rule 3.9 sets out the circumstances which the court will consider on an application to grant relief from a sanction. You have already met references to rule 3.9 in Chapters 6, 9 and 11 of this book.

Relief from sanctions

When a court considers granting relief from sanctions, in addition to considering the overriding objective, it considers the criteria in

- **CPR 3.9 (1) ....all the circumstances of the case so as to enable it to deal justly with the application including the need**
  - **(a) for litigation to be conducted efficiently and at proportionate cost; and**
  - **(b) to enforce compliance with rules, PDs and orders.**

  Please note when referring back to Chapter 11 on setting aside default judgment, that 2014 case law has held that these set-aside applications are applications for relief from the sanction of default judgment. This means that after applying the principles on applications to set aside as set out in Chapter 11, then, as for relief from other sanctions (apart from those for payment of costs), the court should consider CPR 3.9 as incorporated in the three-stage test set out in the case of Denton.

EM: The following specific leading case authority (which students should be able to refer to by name): Denton

The 3 stages set out in Denton show how the courts will consider any applications for relief from sanctions.

Denton & Ors v White & Ors [2014] EWCA Civ 906

The court set out three stages which a court should follow when applying CPR 3.9.

1. Identify and assess the seriousness or significance of the failure to comply
2. Consider why the failure or default occurred. Is there a good reason for the breach? Even if there is not, the court will go on to
3. Consider all the circumstances of the case

1. How **serious or significant** has any non - compliance with rules, PDs or orders been?
   - Failure to pay court fees and disruption of hearing dates are always serious acts of non-compliance and so no relief from the sanction is likely to be given
   - Less serious acts of non - compliance may not necessarily be a bar to obtaining relief from the sanction.

2. How **good** was the **reason** for the non-compliance?
   - If the reason for non-compliance is considered a bad one, relief from the sanction is less likely to be given, although lack of any good reason for the breach does not render the other considerations void.
   - Good reasons are likely to be
     - those beyond the party's control
     - the breach was trivial; or
     - the original compliance period was unreasonably short

     and as such may not necessarily be a bar to obtaining relief from the sanction.

3. The court considers next **all the circumstances**
   - It is of particular importance that **CPR 3.9(a) and (b)** are considered in every case and they should be given particular weight
     - (a) apply the facts, considering how far or how little litigation has been conducted efficiently and at proportionate cost

- (b) the extent to which the facts show a need to enforce compliance with rules, PDs and orders.
- All the circumstances should **also include**
  - how promptly the application for relief from the sanction was made and
  - any history of past breaches of other orders.

Activity

Remember to make notes on the relevant case law authorities in paragraphs 3.9.1 and 3.9.2-3.9.8 in the commentary in Volume 1 of the White Book.

You may find it useful to add in references to the case law NOW at the appropriate points of this Chapter.

When approaching final revision time, remember to add in the salient findings of the cases at the relevant point in any 'mental crib sheet' into which you have distilled the main points of your learned knowle

CUR 13.8 DISCONTINUANCE

You will recall that the procedure on amendment of statements of case in Chapter 12 is that to use where a C claims more than one remedy then wishes to abandon a claim for a particular remedy but wishes to continue with his claim for the other remedies.

Where a claimant wishes to discontinue **all or part of a claim**

C may discontinue a claim subject to the following.

- C will need court permission where
  - The court has granted an interim injunction; or
  - any party has given an undertaking to the court

  Whereas

- where C has received an interim payment in relation to a claim (whether voluntarily or pursuant to an order under Part 25), he may discontinue that claim only if
  - the D who made the interim payment consents in writing; or
  - the court gives permission

  Whereas

- where the C who wishes to discontinue is one of several Cs, either
  - every other claimant consents in writing; or
  - the court gives permission

Where there are several Ds, C may discontinue all or part of a claim against all or any of the defendants.

Procedure for discontinuing

C must
- file a notice of discontinuance, (specifying against which Ds the claim is discontinued if there are several Ds); and
- serve a copy of it on every other party to the proceedings, stating in the notice that he has done so
- attach to the notice a copy of any consent needed from any other party

When discontinuance takes effect on D(s) where permission of the court is not needed

Discontinuance takes effect on the date when notice of discontinuance is served on her and the proceedings are brought to an end as against her on that date if there is no application to set aside. The end of proceedings against D does not, however, affect proceedings to deal with any question of costs.

Right to apply to have notice of discontinuance set aside

D may apply to have the notice of discontinuance set aside. This must be done within 28 days of the date that the notice of discontinuance was served on her.

Liability for costs

[This rule does not apply to claims allocated to the small claims track].

Unless the court orders otherwise the discontinuing C pays the costs of her against whom he has discontinued; this is the costs D has incurred on or before the date on which notice of discontinuance was served on her.

If proceedings are only partly discontinued C is liable for costs relating only to the part of the proceedings which he is discontinuing. Unless the court orders otherwise, the costs which the claimant is liable to pay must not be assessed until the conclusion of the rest of the proceedings.

The costs order will be deemed to have been made on the standard basis.

Discontinuance and subsequent proceedings

A claimant who discontinues a claim needs the permission of the court to make another claim against the same defendant if

- he discontinued the claim after D filed a defence; **and**
- the other claim arises out of facts which are the same or substantially the same as those relating to the discontinued claim.

Chapter 19

Elements of the syllabus which you have now covered

- A cell with heavy outlining means that that area of the syllabus was covered in this Chapter;
- A darkly shaded cell with a tick √ means that the whole of that syllabus element has now been covered;
- A lightly shaded cell means that part of that element of the syllabus has been covered in a previous Chapter; and
- An unshaded cell means that element of the syllabus has not yet been covered.

1.1 √	1.2 √	1.3 √	2.1 √	2.2 √	3.1 √	3.2 √	6.1 √	6.2 √	63 √
6.4 √	7.1 √	7.2 √	8.1 √	8.2 √	8.3 √	9.1 √	9.2 √	9.3 √	10.1 √
10.2 √	11.1 √	11.2 √	12.1 √	12.2 √	12.3 √	13.1 √	13.2 √	13.3 √	13.4 √
13.5 √	13.6 √	13.7 √	13.8 √	14.1 √	14.2	14.3	14.4	14.5	144.6
15.1 √	15.2 √	15.3 √	15.4 √	16.1 √	16.2 √	17.1 √	17.2 √	17.3 √	17.4 √
18.2. √	18.3 √	18.4 √ 18.5 √	19.1	19.2	19.3	20.1	20.2	20.3	21.1
21.2	21.3	22.1	20.2	23.1 √	23.2 √	23.3 √	23.4 √	24.1	

Chapter 20

DISCLOSURE AND INSPECTION OF DOCUMENTS [CUR 14]

p) Disclosure and Inspection of Documents (and Privilege) during proceedings

THIS CHAPTER CONTAINS THE ITEMS PRINTED IN BOLD IN THE FOLLOWING BOXES

CURRICULUM ("CUR")

Disclosure and inspection of documents

14.1 disclosure and inspection of documents
14.2 specific disclosure
14.3 collateral use of disclosed documents
14.4 pre-action disclosure is in Chapter 3
14.5 disclosure against non-parties *(see also Norwich Pharmacal in Chapter 3 and between Chapters 16 and 17)*
14.6 legal professional privilege and without prejudice communications in civil cases

SYLLABUS

Examinable material will consist of: disclosure and inspection, right of inspection of disclosed documents, the meaning of document, standard disclosure, duty of search, disclosure of documents in party's control, disclosure of copies, procedure for standard disclosure, disclosure lists, disclosure statements, withholding disclosure or inspection, specific disclosure or inspection, documents referred to in statements of case, inspection and copying of documents, *pre-action disclosure,* ***disclosure against non-parties, and*** *other powers of the court to order disclosure,* ***privacy, legal professional privilege and*** *confidentiality in ADR* (is in Chapter 1) ***the 'without prejudice' principle.***
notices to prove documents from CUR 19
(Each of the above has its own subheading in this chapter, flagged by EM:)

- **CPR 31.1-31.2; PD 31A paragraphs 1-2, 2A and 3-8.**
- **CPR 31.3 (right of inspection of a disclosed document)**
- **CPR, 31.4-31.5**
- **CPR 31.6 (standard disclosure – what documents are to be disclosed)**
- **CPR 31.7-31.11**
- **CPR 31.12 (specific disclosure or inspection)**
- **CPR 31.14-31.15**
- CPR 31.16 is in Chapter 3
- **CPR 31.17 (Orders for disclosure against a person not a party)**
- **CPR 31.18 (Rules not to limit other powers of the court to order disclosure)**
- **CPR 31.19-31.23**
- **CUR 19.3, CPR 32.19**

- Senior Courts Act 1981 section 34, County Courts Act 1984 section 53 at section 9A of Volume 2 of 'Civil Procedure' (the White Book) 2019 was dealt with in Chapter 3 of this book.
- The following specific leading case authority (which students should be able to refer to by name): Norwich Pharmacal is in Chapter 3 and also between Chapters 16 and 17
- **Commentary is incorporated in context in this Chapter, highlighted in an Activity box between two stars** (except for 31.6.3 -5 which is in Chapter 2)

Chapter 20 MOCS

- ***Disclosure of documents***
  - ***Menu option disclosure for non-PI multi-track***
  - ***CPR 31.6 standard disclosure for everything else, unless the court directs otherwise.***
  - ***Collateral use of disclosed documents***
- ***Inspection of documents***
  - ***Inspection of documents not possible where***
    - ***Disclosure statement states that to do so would be disproportionate;***
    - ***Privilege is claimed;***
      - ***Legal professional privilege***
      - ***Litigation privilege***

      or
    - ***Documents no longer exist***
- ***Specific disclosure or inspection***
- ***Disclosure against non-parties once proceedings have started if the criteria are met.***

The sessions dealing with this area of the syllabus on my BTC course are	

CUR 14.4 PRE - ACTION DISCLOSURE

Remember that this book is ordered to reflect the earliest possible time at which matters take place. Please, therefore, refer back to Chapter 3 of this book to refresh your knowledge on pre-action disclosure, before continuing on with this Chapter 20.

CUR 14.1 DISCLOSURE AND INSPECTION OF DOCUMENTS

You will have learned in the previous Chapter that the court gives directions on each of the three tracks, which involve directions in the court's discretion about the timing, nature and scope of the disclosure of documents.

Nevertheless, parties ought to engage in considering disclosure at an early stage of proceedings, or, preferably, before proceedings have begun.

First, some explanations.

EM: the meaning of document

A **document, or copy of a document** is anything that is recorded. It therefore includes texts, e-mails, CCTV, DVDs, USB sticks and the like.

EM: disclosure of copies,

Disclose means setting out on a form for the other party that **documents exist or did exist** in relation to the claim.

Only one copy of a document need be disclosed. Yet where a document contains a modification, it is to be treated as a separate document

- where a party intends to rely on that copy, yet modified, document or
- where the document adversely affects his own case or another party's case or supports another party's case.

A party's disclosure obligations will often continue throughout the claim such that documents or modified copy documents created by a party during the course of the claim may be disclosable.

EM: disclosure of documents in party's control,

Exist or did exist means that the document is or has been in the parties' physical control, or that the parties have the right to it, or have the right to inspect or take copies of it.

EM: right of inspection of disclosed documents

A party to whom a document has been disclosed has a right to inspect that document except when it doesn't! These exceptions are

circled in context throughout this Chapter.

EM: documents referred to in statements of case,

A party may inspect a document mentioned in
- a statement of case;
- a witness statement;
- a witness summary; or
- an affidavit

Please see later in this Chapter in the section on legal privilege regarding applications for an order for inspection of any document mentioned in an expert's report which has not already been disclosed in the proceedings.

CUR 19.3 NOTICES TO PROVE DOCUMENTS

EM: notices to prove documents

A party shall be deemed to admit the authenticity of a document disclosed to him under Part 31 unless he serves notice that he wishes the document to be proved at trial.

A notice to prove a document must be served
- by the latest date for serving witness statements or
- within 7 days of disclosure of the document, whichever is later.

CUR 14.1 DISCLOSURE AND INSPECTION OF DOCUMENTS (continued)

You will have learned in the previous Chapter that the court gives directions on

EM: withholding disclosure or inspection (Privacy)

The CPR states that the rules below on withholding disclosure or inspection do not affect any rule of law which permits or requires a document to be withheld from disclosure or inspection on the ground that its disclosure or inspection would damage the public interest.

Withholding disclosure

On the ground that disclosure would damage the public interest, a person may apply, supported by evidence, without notice, for an order permitting him to **withhold disclosure** of a document or part of a document. If granted, the resulting order must not be served on any other person and must not be open to inspection by any person unless the court orders otherwise.

Withholding inspection

Where a person wishes to claim the right to w**ithhold inspection** the written application to do so must state
- that A has such a right or duty
- the grounds on which s/he claims that right or duty.

The statement must be made in the list in which the document is disclosed; or if there is no list, to the person wishing to inspect the document. A party may apply to the court to decide whether such a claim should be upheld. The application must be supported by evidence.

Both

When considering its decision on whether to uphold an application to withhold disclosure or inspection, the court may require the person seeking to withhold disclosure or inspection of a document to produce that document to the court and invite any person, whether or not a party, to make representations.

HOW DISCLOSURE WORKS ON EACH OF THE TRACKS.

Small claims track

Parties are only obliged to disclose documents on which they rely.

The other tracks

The courts are encouraged to use their case management powers to ensure that the costs of litigation are proportionate to the sums in dispute. This will include the costs of the disclosure exercise, which is one of the most expensive aspects of any litigation.

We will deal with

1. Disclosure for non-PI multi-track claims; then
2. Standard disclosure, which is used
   - where the disclosure order has been for standard disclosure in a non-PI multi-track claim
   - for PI multi-track claims; and
   - for all fast track claims

1. Non-PI multi-track claims

The **menu option disclosure** process is managed in three stages

- Stage I: disclosure report 14 days before the case management conference
- Stage II: discussion to agree the disclosure proposal
- Stage III: a case management conference disclosure order will be made

Stage I

Not less than 14 days before the first CMC, each party must file and serve a report verified by a statement of truth which

- describes briefly what documents exist which are or may be relevant to the matters in issue and where and with whom these are located or how (in the case of electronically stored documents) they are stored
- estimates the broad range of costs which would be incurred if giving standard disclosure (dealt with later in this Chapter)
- states which type of disclosure order is to be sought.

Stage II

Not less than 7 days before the first CMC, the parties must, at a meeting or by telephone, discuss and seek to agree a proposal in relation to disclosure that meets the overriding objective.

If the parties agree a proposal and when it is filed at court, the court considers the proposal to be 'appropriate in all the circumstances' the court may approve the approach without the need for a hearing.

Stage III

At the first CMC, the court will decide on a disclosure order from the following "**menu**" of **options**

i. Dispensing with disclosure altogether
ii. Disclosing only documents on which a party relies, and for the parties to request any specific disclosure required from the other parties
iii. Disclosing documents on an issue-by-issue basis
iv. Disclosing any documents which it is reasonable to suppose may contain information which enables that party to advance its own case or to damage that of any other party, or which leads to an enquiry which has either of those consequences
v. Giving standard disclosure (dealt with in the next section of this Chapter)
vi. Any other order which it thinks appropriate

At any time

The court may **at any time** give directions as to how disclosure is to be given and in particular in relation to

- searches – where, for what, by whom and in respect of what time periods
- the need for lists of documents
- the form or need for a disclosure statement
- the format of documents disclosed
- documents which no longer exist
- disclosure in stages.

2. PI multi- track claims and all fast track claims

EM: standard disclosure

Unless the court orders otherwise, the usual direction is an order for standard disclosure.

The court may dispense with or limit standard disclosure and the parties may agree in writing to dispense with disclosure or to limit standard disclosure.

Standard Disclosure is set out in CPR 31.6. Parties who have documents in their control as set out a couple of pages back, must disclose

- Documents on which they rely and which
  - adversely affect their own case or another party's case or
  - support another party's case; plus
- Documents which a PD says must be disclosed

Activity

Remember to make notes on the relevant case law authorities in paragraphs 31.6.2-31.6.4 and 31.6.8 in the commentary in the White Book.

You may find it useful to add in references to the case law NOW at the appropriate points of this Chapter…. Etc!

EM: duty of search

Parties have a duty to do a reasonable search; that is a search which is reasonable given
- the number of documents
- the nature and complexity of the proceedings
- how easy it will be to retrieve the documents; and given
- the significance of document.

Where a party has not searched on the grounds of unreasonableness, he must state this in his disclosure statement (see below), identifying the category or class of document.

Once a party has seen the form completed by the other party disclosing the documents, it is likely the other party will wish to inspect some or all of the disclosed documents.

We will consider the form that the disclosure list takes before looking at how a party indicates their wish to inspect and before looking at instances where they may not inspect some documents.

EM: procedure for standard disclosure. EM: disclosure lists EM: disclosure statements

How the disclosure list is set out

After the headings, it begins with a **disclosure statement**
- confirming the extent to which documents have been searched for
- certifying that the disclosing party understands the duty to disclose
- certifying that that duty has been carried out during the search
- stating, where relevant, that inspection of one or more documents is not being permitted,

  as to do so would be disproportionate to the issues in the case; and stating why.
- If made by e.g. a company, identifying the person making the statement, explaining why s/he is the appropriate person to make it

The parties may agree in writing to disclose documents without making a list and to dispense with a disclosure statement.

A non-party can make the statement if a PD permits.

An application for contempt of court may be made against a person who makes or causes to be made a false disclosure statement without an honest belief in its truth.

Then

Section 1 of the form/document giving disclosure of documents in the case

Here a party discloses documents that exist, that they possess and that they do not object to the other party inspecting, as the disclosing party does not claim that the documents are privileged. (Privilege is explained in Section 2 below).

EM: inspection and copying of documents

The party to whom they have been disclosed will give written notice of their wish to inspect these documents. They must be permitted to inspect them within 7 days of the notice of the wish to inspect. Inspection will either be of the originals at the offices of either party, or copies will be sent, the party requesting disclosure undertaking to pay reasonable copying charges.

CUR 14.3 COLLATERAL USE OF DISCLOSED DOCUMENTS

Disclosed documents may only be used for the purposes of the proceedings in which they are disclosed unless

- they are read or referred to in open court (are in the public domain) (the court may nevertheless make an order restricting or prohibiting the use of such a document following an application by a party or by any person to whom the document belongs); or
- the disclosing party and the person to whom the document belongs agree to their collateral use; or
- the court gives permission for their collateral use.

Section 2 of the document giving disclosure

Here a party discloses documents that exist, that they possess but that they **do object** to the other party inspecting, as the disclosing party claims that the documents are privileged.

When a party claims that a document is privileged, that party is asserting

a right or duty to withhold it from inspection.

CUR 14.6 LEGAL PROFESSIONAL PRIVILEGE AND WITHOUT PREJUDICE COMMUNICATIONS IN CIVIL CASES (Privacy)

There are three types of privilege on the syllabus this year; legal professional privilege, without prejudice communications and the privilege against self-incrimination.

- **Legal Professional Privilege**. There are two types.
  - **legal advice privilege,** relating to **any legal advice between** lawyer/client
  - **litigation privilege,** covering documents between lawyer/client/third-party (witness) where the document was
    - **for use in** pending contemplated or existing **litigation**
    - where the **dominant purpose** at the time the document was **created** is for use in **these proceedings**.

Be aware that when **expert**s are instructed (Chapter 22 of this book), one of the elements that their report must state is the substance of all material **instructions**, whether written or oral, on the basis of which the report was written.

A party may apply for an order for inspection of any document mentioned in an expert's report which has not already been disclosed in the proceedings.The CPR expressly states, note, that these instructions shall **not** be **privileged** against disclosure **but** the court will not, in relation to those instructions

- order disclosure of any specific document; or
- permit any questioning in court, other than by the party who instructed the expert,

unless it is satisfied that there are reasonable grounds to consider the statement of instructions to be inaccurate or incomplete.

Waiver of privilege The party to whom Legal Professional Privilege relates can waive the privilege if they wish.

– **Without prejudice communications.**

Communications may only be claimed to be without prejudice if at the time they were made proceedings were in contemplation or had already been started.

Genuine attempts at settlement may be withheld from inspection. Parties can claim privilege for oral statements or written documents containing any genuine attempt at settlement. It is not necessary to state the words "without prejudice" for a statement or document to be such a communication. Similarly, merely stating that a statement or document is "without prejudice" does not make it such a statement or document if it is not a genuine attempt to settle!

Waiver of privilege Both parties have the privilege; either party to statements or correspondence protected by without prejudice privilege can assert it, so both consents to waiver are needed if the privilege is to be waived.

Activity

Remember to make notes on the relevant case law authorities in paragraphs

31.3.4-31.3.6,
31.3.8-9,
31.3.11
31.3.24
31.3.39;
in the commentary in the White Book.

You may find it useful to add in references to the case law NOW at the appropriate points of this Chapter.

When approaching final revision time, remember to add in the salient findings of the cases at the relevant point in any 'mental crib sheet' into which you have distilled the main points of your learned knowledge.

Privilege against self-incrimination A party may refrain from incriminating him or herself OR their spouse, although the privilege is not available for Intellectual Property or passing off cases, theft, fraud, or care of children cases. The party to whom the privilege belongs may waive it if they wish.

Use of secondary facts

If a document for which privilege is being claimed is accidentally nevertheless provided for inspection, **court permission** is needed for the party to whom it was disclosed and who inspected it, to use it at trial.

The disclosing party can try for an injunction to stop the other side using it, if there is no equitable reason for a court not to grant one e.g. delay/misconduct on the disclosing party's part. Such an injunction may be granted where
- the other party got the document by fraud or
- there was an obvious mistake in revealing the document to them.

Section 3 of the document giving disclosure

Here a party discloses documents that did exist – they no longer have them,

stating what happened to them; for example they have already been sent the other side or they have been lost or destroyed.

After this first disclosure, remember that the **duty to disclose is ongoing until the proceedings are concluded** so parties may need to do additional lists later. If documents to which the duty extends come to a party's notice at any time during the proceedings, s/he must immediately notify every party.

Where a party failed to disclose documents or permit inspection, that party may not rely on those documents unless the court gives permission.

CUR 14.2 SPECIFIC DISCLOSURE

EM: specific disclosure or inspection

Where a party is aware that the other party has a document that does not appear on the disclosure list, that party can apply for an order for specific disclosure of that specific document. The Part 23 application may be for
- documents or classes of documents to be disclosed
- a search to be carried out (the required extent of the search will be stated in the order)
- any documents located as a result of the search to be disclosed

Similarly an order for specific inspection allowing a party to inspect one of the above documents can be made.

In exercising its discretion the court considers
- all the circumstances of the case
- the overriding objective
- the relevance of the documents sought, by looking at the statements of case
- whether the documents are or have been in the parties' control, by looking at the statements of case.

Activity

Remember to make notes on the relevant case law authorities in paragraphs

31.12.1.1
31.12.2
in the commentary in the White Book.

You may find it useful to add in references to the case law NOW at the appropriate points of this Chapter.

When approaching final revision time, remember to add in the salient findings of the cases at the relevant point in any 'mental crib sheet' into which you have distilled the main points of your learned knowledge.

CUR.14.5 DISCLOSURE AGAINST NON-PARTIES

EM: disclosure against non-parties

Proceedings must have started; so once they have, a party can apply, supporting the application with evidence, to the court for an order that a witness produce documents in advance of the trial. Such an order will only be made if

- the documents are likely to support A's case / adversely affect one of the other parties
- **AND** it is necessary to dispose of the case fairly or save costs.

The order must specify the documents to be disclosed by R. It must also specify that in making the disclosure R must specify any which are no longer in his control or in respect of which he claims a right or duty to withhold inspection.

The order may require R to say what has happened to any documents no longer in his control and it may specify the time and place for disclosure and inspection.

The witness can be brought to the trial with the original document by means of a witness summons. These are dealt with in the next Chapter.

Activity

Remember to make notes on the relevant case law authorities in paragraphs

31.17.1
31.17.2.1
31.17.3
31.17.4.

EM: other powers of the court to order disclosure

In proceedings for **personal injury or death** the court has power to order against a **non-party** the disclosure of documents, and the inspection, photographing, preservation, custody and detention of property, where the documents or property are the subject-matter of the proceedings or in relation to which any question arises in the proceedings, and the taking of samples of any such property and the carrying out of any experiment on or with any such property.

The court will not make such an order if it is likely to be injurious to the public interest.

Unless the court otherwise directs, the costs of obtaining the order are usually payable by the party requesting it.

The Crown is bound by this type of order, although it is not bound when the Crown is in the capacity of Her Majesty in Her private capacity or to Her Majesty in right of Her Duchy of Lancaster or to the Duke of Cornwall.

The court's power to order disclosure against non-parties as set out above does not limit any other power it may have to do so.

Activity

Remember to make notes on the relevant case law authorities in paragraphs 13.18.2-7 in the commentary in the White Book.... Etc!

Chapter 20

Elements of the syllabus which you have now covered

- A cell with heavy outlining means that that area of the syllabus was covered in this Chapter;
- A darkly shaded cell with a tick √ means that the whole of that syllabus element has now been covered;
- A lightly shaded cell means that part of that element of the syllabus has been covered in a previous Chapter; and
- An unshaded cell means that element of the syllabus has not yet been covered.

1.1 √	1.2 √	1.3 √	2.1 √	2.2 √	3.1 √	3.2 √	6.1 √	6.2 √	6.3 √
6.4 √	7.1 √	7.2 √	8.1 √	8.2 √	8.3 √	9.1 √	9.2 √	9.3 √	10.1 √
10.2 √	11.1 √	11.2 √	12.1 √	12.2 √	12.3 √	13.1 √	13.2 √	13.3 √	13.4 √
13.5 √	13.6 √	13.7 √	13.8 √	14.1 √	14.2 √	14.3 √	14.4 √	14.5 √	14.6 √
15.1 √	15.2 √	15.3 √	15.4 √	16.1 √	16.2 √	17.1 √	15.2 √	17.3 √	17.4 √
18.2. √	18.3 √	18.4 √ 18.5 √	19.1	19.2	19.3 √	20.1	20.2	20.3	21.1
21.2	21.3	22.1	22.2	23.1√	23.2 √	23.3 √	23.4 √	24.1	

Chapter 21

EVIDENCE "one" – EVIDENCE OF FACT [CUR 19]

Q (I) Witness Statements, Witness Summaries, Witness Summonses, Depositions

THIS CHAPTER CONTAINS THE ITEMS PRINTED IN BOLD IN THE FOLLOWING BOXES

CURRICULUM ("CUR")

Evidence of fact *(and expert evidence is in Chapter 22)*

- ***19.1 evidence of fact in civil proceedings***
- ***19.2 witness statements and witness summonses***
- *19.3 notices to admit facts is in Chapter 11 and notices to prove documents is in Chapter 20*

SYLLABUS

Examinable material will consist of the power of the court to control evidence, evidence of witnesses, service and use of witness statements at trial and other hearings, witness summaries, use of witness statements for other purposes, false statements in witness statements, *notices to admit facts, notices to prove documents,* ***issuing and serving witness summonses, and evidence by deposition.***

- ***CPR 32.1-4***
- ***CPR 32.5 (Use at trial of witness statements which have been served).***
- ***CPR 32.6-16***
- ***CPR 32.18-19*** *notices to admit facts, notices to prove documents are dealt with in Chapters 11 and 20 respectively*
- ***CPR 34.1-12***
- **Commentary is incorporated in context in this Chapter, highlighted in an Activity box between two stars**

CHAPTER 21 MOCS

Witness statements served on other parties, for use at trial, standing as XIC

Witness summonses

Witness summaries

Depositions

The sessions dealing with this area of the syllabus on my BTC course are	

CUR 19.1 EVIDENCE OF FACT IN CIVIL PROCEEDINGS

EM: service and use of witness statements at hearings

We have already seen that where facts need to be proved by witness evidence at hearings **other than trials**, such as Part 23 interim applications, the evidence is provided **in writing** with the application, (unless the CPR or a court order says otherwise).

At hearings other than the trial, a party may rely on the matters set out in his statement of case or his application notice, if the statement of case or application notice is verified by a statement of truth.

At hearings other than the trial, where evidence is given in writing, any party may apply to the court for permission to cross-examine the person giving the evidence. If the court gives permission but the person in question does not attend as required by the order, his evidence may not be used unless the court gives permission.

Affidavit evidence

Evidence must be given by affidavit instead of or in addition to a witness statement if this is required by the court, a provision contained in any other rule, a practice direction or any other enactment.

Otherwise, at hearings other than the trial, a witness can give evidence by affidavit if he chooses to do so, but he may not recover the additional cost of making it from any other party unless the court orders otherwise.

– Format of affidavits

Activity

Please refer to 32PD.6.1 and make notes here on the format of Affidavits.

EM: the power of the court to control evidence
EM: evidence of witnesses

Where facts need to be proved by witness evidence at **trials**, the evidence is provided by the witness ("W") **orally in public** (unless a court orders otherwise).

This is subject to any provision to the contrary contained in the CPR or elsewhere, or to any order of the court.

Courts may allow evidence at trials to be given by video link[14] or other means, e.g. by using plans, models or photographs.

Any evidence that W would be allowed to give orally in court will most commonly be set out in the form of a witness statement. The court will have included in its directions how witness

[14] The Coronavirus Act 2020 received Royal Assent on 25th March 2020 and is initially in force for 2 years, whilst incorporating powers to alter that expiry date. Practice Direction 51Y came into effect on 21st July 2020 and stays in effect until the Act ceases to have effect. The 2020 Act inserted s.85A into the Courts Act 2003 the provision that as before, if the court directs that proceedings are to be conducted wholly as video proceedings or wholly as audio proceedings, the court may direct that the proceedings are to be broadcast (in the manner specified in the direction) for the purpose of enabling members of the public to see and hear the proceedings; and further that the court may direct that a recording of the proceedings is to be made (in the manner specified in the direction) for the purpose of enabling the court to keep an audio-visual record of the proceedings.

Whilst this PD is in force, where the court directs that proceedings are to be conducted wholly as video or audio proceedings and it is not practicable for the hearing to be broadcast in a court building, the court may direct that the hearing must take place in private where it is necessary to do so to secure the proper administration of justice, unless it is the case that a media representative is able to access proceedings remotely while they are taking place, they will be public proceedings. Any hearing held in private must be recorded, where that is practicable, in a manner directed by the court. The court may direct the hearing to be video recorded, otherwise the hearing must be audio recorded. On the application of any person, any recording so made is to be accessed in a court building, with the consent of the court.

statements are to be dealt with in the case. Most commonly, a witness will be questioned on the basis of their witness statement. In the civil courts, **the witness statement stands as XIC unless the court orders otherwise.** So if nothing has changed since the witness statement was served, that witness will not be questioned by their own Counsel at the beginning of the case.

A witness statement which stands as XIC is open to inspection during the course of the trial unless the court otherwise directs. Any person may ask for a direction that a witness statement is not open to inspection. The court will not make this direction unless it is satisfied that a witness statement should not be open to inspection because of

- the interests of justice
- the public interest
- the nature of any expert medical evidence in the statement
- the nature of any confidential information (including information relating to personal financial matters) in the statement or
- the need to protect the interests of any child or protected party.

The court may exclude from inspection words or passages in the statement.

At trial, if new matters have arisen since the witness statement was served on the other parties, Counsel should ask the court's **permission to amplify** the witness statement and give evidence in relation to new matters which have arisen since the witness statement was served on the other parties. The court is likely to grant this if it considers there is a good reason to do so. Counsel will then conduct XIC so that W can give evidence in relation to these matters and get them before the court).

The court may control the evidence by giving directions as to

- the issues on which it requires evidence, identifying or limiting the issues to which factual evidence may be directed. The court may exclude evidence that would otherwise be admissible
- the nature of the evidence which it requires to decide those issues
- the way in which the evidence is to be placed before the court. The court may limit cross-examination.

CUR 19.2 WITNESS STATEMENTS AND WITNESS SUMMONSES

Witness statements

- A **witness statement** is a signed statement of witness evidence that W would be allowed to give orally in court. It must contain a **statement of truth** and be **signed by W**.

  'I believe that the facts stated in this witness statement are true. I understand that proceedings for contempt of court may be brought against anyone who makes, or causes to be made, a false statement in a document verified by a statement of truth without an honest belief in its truth.'

  Therefore a lot of weight is given to witness statements.

- Format of witness statements

Activity

You should refer to case studies given to you by your Provider for examples of well- drafted witness statements.

Please refer to 32PD.17-20 and make notes here on the format of witness statements.

***EM: service and use of witness statements at trial*.**

- The court will order a party to serve on the other parties any witness statement of the oral evidence which the party serving the statement intends to rely on in relation to any issues of fact to be decided at the trial.

- When the court gives directions it may set out
  - whether or not witness statements are to be filed. They are filed in the court where the CF was issued / where proceedings are now proceeding if that is different
  - the witnesses who may be called or whose evidence may be read
  - the issues to which factual evidence may be directed
  - the length or format of witness statements
  - the order in which witness statements are to be served
  - by when witness statements are to be served if parties intend to rely on them at trial
  - [If not served within the time specified by the court, court permission is needed to call W to give oral evidence]

- If a party has served a witness statement and he wishes to rely at trial on the evidence of the witness who made the statement, he must call the witness to give oral evidence unless the court orders otherwise or he puts the statement in as hearsay evidence.

  If a party who has served a witness statement does not use it either as oral evidence at trial or as hearsay evidence, any other party may put the witness statement in as hearsay evidence. (Hearsay evidence is detailed in Chapter 23 of this book)

Activity

Remember to make notes on the relevant case law authorities in paragraphs 32.5.1-32.5.3.1 in the commentary in the White Book.

You may find it useful to add in references to the case law NOW at the appropriate points of this Chapter.

When approaching final revision time, remember to add in the salient findings of the cases at the relevant point in any 'mental crib sheet' into which you have distilled the main points of your learned knowledge

- Where a witness is called to give evidence at trial, he may be cross-examined on his witness statement whether or not the statement or any part of it was referred to during the witness's evidence in chief.

<u>EM: false statements in witness statements</u>

Remember that proceedings for contempt of court may be brought against a person if he makes, or causes to be made, a false statement in a document verified by a statement of truth without an honest belief in its truth.[15]

<u>Affidavit evidence</u>

Evidence must be given by affidavit instead of or in addition to a witness statement if this is required by the court, a provision contained in any other rule, a practice direction or any other enactment.

<u>EM: use of witness statements for other purposes</u>

This is possible only if
- the witness gives consent in writing to some other use of it
- the court gives permission for some other use or
- the witness statement has been put in evidence at a hearing held in public.

Otherwise a witness statement may be used only for the purpose of the proceedings in which it is served.

<u>EM: witness summaries</u>

Where the court has directed a party to serve a witness statement for use at trial, but that party has been unable to obtain one from the relevant witness, the party may **apply** without notice **for permission** to serve a **witness summary** instead.

---

[15] an amendment to the Pre-Action Conduct and Protocols PD makes it clear that contempt sanctions may apply in relation to a false statement made before the commencement of proceedings where the statement is made in a pre-action protocol letter **or other document prepared in anticipation of proceedings**.

A witness summary is a summary of

- the evidence, if known, which would otherwise be included in a witness statement or
- if the party does not know what the relevant witness would say in evidence, the party serving the witness summary states the matters about which they propose to question the witness.

It follows that there is no statement of truth in a witness summary. It thus carries less weight than a witness statement.

Unless the court orders otherwise, a witness summary must include the name and address of the intended witness

Unless the court orders otherwise, a witness summary must be served within the period in which a witness statement would have had to be served.

Where a party serves a witness summary, so far as practicable, the rules regarding

- the requirement to serve witness statements for use at trial
- amplifying witness statements and
- form of witness statement

shall apply to the summary.

If not served within the time specified by the court, court permission is needed to call W to give oral evidence.

Witness summonses

EM: issuing and serving witness summonses.

Use

A witness summons is used

- to compel W to attend at court to give evidence or
- in relation to a document that person could be required to produce at the hearing/trial, to produce a document in their possession at court, either on the date fixed for a hearing/trial or on such date as the court may direct.

There must be a separate witness summons for each witness. A witness summons must be in the relevant practice form.

Issue

The issue date of the witness summons is the date entered on the summons by the court. Court **permission** is needed to issue one where a party wishes to

- have a summons issued **less than 7 days before** the date of the **trial**
- have a summons issued for a witness to attend court to give evidence or to produce documents **on any date except the trial date** or
- have a summons issued for a witness to attend court to give evidence or to produce documents **at any hearing except the trial**.

A witness summons must be issued by the court where the case is proceeding or the court where the hearing in question will be held. The court may set aside or vary a witness summons it has issued.

Where a court or tribunal does not have power to issue a witness summons in relation to proceedings before it, a court superior to it with such power may issue a witness summons in aid of that inferior court or tribunal. The court which issued the witness summons may set it aside.

<u>Service</u>

A witness summons is binding until the conclusion of the hearing at which the attendance of the witness is required if served at least 7 days before attendance at court is required. It may be served later than this with court permission.

The court serves witness summonses. It is also possible for the summons to be served by personal service, if the party on whose behalf it is issued indicates in writing when he asks the court to issue the summons, that he wishes to serve it himself.

W has a right to reasonable expenses for
- travel to and from home or work to court and
- based on the sums payable to witnesses attending the Crown Court as fixed by statute, for loss of earnings or benefit which must be offered or paid at the time of service of the summons.

Where the court is to serve the witness summons, the party on whose behalf it is issued must deposit, in the court office, the money to be paid or offered to the witness.

Where the party issuing the witness summons wishes to serve it himself, he must notify the court in writing that he wishes to do so, and at the time of service offer the witness the sums mentioned in above.

<u>Failure to attend</u>

Failure to attend court following a witness summons is contempt of court, punishable by a fine/prison.

Deposition

<u>EM: evidence by deposition</u>

Say, for example that a key witness is ill or unable to travel, or abroad, the solution is a **deposition**. (If W is outside the jurisdiction a letter of request must be sent to the judicial authorities of the country they are in).

- A **applies for an order** that the witness – **the deponent** – be examined before the hearing. (See further Chapter 23 called 'Evidence "three" -civil trial and evidence' later in this book). W will be on oath before a judge/court examiner/court appointed person. The deponent gets expenses for making the deposition.

  The order
  - may require the production of any document which the court considers is necessary for the purposes of the examination

- must state the date, time and place of the examination

– The deponent has a right to **reasonable expenses** for
  - travel to and from home or work to court and
  - based on on the sums payable to witnesses attending the Crown Court as fixed by statute, for loss of time - earnings or benefit which must be offered or paid at the time of service of the summons.

– Where the court makes an order for a deposition to be taken, it may also order the party who obtained the order to serve a witness statement or witness summary in relation to the evidence to be given by the person to be examined.

– Subject to any directions contained in the order for examination, the examination must be **conducted in the same way as** if the witness were giving evidence at a **trial**.

  The examiner
  - **may**, if all the parties are present, conduct the examination of a person not named in the order for examination if all the parties and the person to be examined consent.
  - **may** conduct the examination in private if he considers it appropriate to do so
  - **must** ensure that the evidence given by the witness is recorded in full
  - **must** send a copy of the deposition to the person who obtained the order for the examination of the witness and to the court where the case is proceeding.

  The party who obtained the order must send each of the other parties a copy of the deposition which he receives from the examiner

– If a person served with an order to attend before an examiner **fails to attend or refuses to be sworn** for the purpose of the examination or to answer any lawful question or produce any document at the examination, the examiner will certify this and the certificate will be filed by A.
  A may then apply without notice to the court for an order requiring that person to attend or to be sworn or to answer any question or produce any document.

  The court may order the person against whom an order is made under this rule to pay any costs resulting from his failure or refusal.

– The deposition may then be given in evidence at a hearing unless the court orders otherwise.

  Notice of intention to use the deposition must be served on every other party at least 21 days before the hearing/trial. [The court may require a deponent to attend the hearing and give evidence orally].The deposition is then treated as a witness statement at trial regarding inspection during the course of the trial unless the court otherwise directs. Any person may ask for a direction that the deposition is not open to inspection. The court will not make this direction unless it is satisfied that a deposition should not be open to inspection because of

  - the interests of justice
  - the public interest
  - the nature of any expert medical evidence in the statement
  - the nature of any confidential information (including information relating to personal financial matters) in the statement or
  - the need to protect the interests of any child or protected party.

The court may exclude from inspection words or passages in the deposition.

– Where the court orders a party to be examined about his or any other assets for the purpose of any hearing except the trial, the deposition may be used only for the purpose of the proceedings in which the order was made.

However, it may be used for some other purpose
- by the party who was examined
- if the party who was examined agrees or
- if the court gives permission.

Chapter 21

Elements of the syllabus which you have now covered

- A cell with heavy outlining means that that area of the syllabus was covered in this Chapter;
- A darkly shaded cell with a tick √ means that the whole of that syllabus element has now been covered;
- A lightly shaded cell means that part of that element of the syllabus has been covered in a previous Chapter; and
- An unshaded cell means that element of the syllabus has not yet been covered.

1.1 √	1.2 √	1.3 √	2.1 √	2.2 √	3.1 √	3.2 √	6.1 √	6.2 √	4.3 √
6.4 √	7.1 √	7.2 √	8.1 √	8.2 √	8.3 √	9.1 √	9.2 √	9.3 √	10.1 √
10.2 √	11.1 √	11.2 √	11.1 √	12.2 √	12.3 √	13.1 √	13.2 √	13.3 √	13.4 √
13.5 √	13.6 √	13.7 √	13.8 √	14.1 √	14.2 √	14.3 √	14.4 √	14.5 √	14.6 √
15.1 √	15.2 √	15.3 √	15.4 √	16.1 √	16.2 √	17.1 √	17.2 √	17.3 √	17.4 √
18.2. √	18.3 √	18.4 √ 18.5 √	19.1 √	19.2 √	19.3 √	20.1	20.2	20.3	21.1
21.2	21.3	22.1	22.2	23.1 √	23.2 √	23.3 √	23.4 √	24.1	

Chapter 22

EVIDENCE "two"- EXPERT EVIDENCE [CUR 20]

Q (II)) Expert Evidence

THIS CHAPTER CONTAINS THE ITEMS PRINTED IN BOLD IN THE FOLLOWING BOXES

CURRICULUM ("CUR")

~~Evidence of fact and~~ (Chapter 21)

Expert Evidence

20.1 the general exclusionary rule in relation to evidence of opinion
20.2 the main exceptions to the rule
20.3 expert opinion evidence in civil proceedings

SYLLABUS

Examinable material will consist of the general exclusionary rule in relation to evidence of opinion and main exceptions to the rule, the use of expert opinion evidence in civil proceedings, expert evidence at trial, the court's duty and power to restrict expert evidence, duties and responsibilities of experts, expert reports, written questions to experts, single joint experts, discussions between experts, consequences of failing to disclose an expert's report, and obtaining further expert evidence.

(Each of the above has its own subheading in this chapter, flagged by EM:)

- **CPR 35.1 (court's duty to restrict expert evidence)**
- **CPR 35.2**
- **CPR 35.3 (expert's overriding duty to the court)**
- **CPR 35.4-6**
- **CPR 35.7 (court's power to direct that evidence is to be given by a single joint expert).**
- **CPR 35.10; PD35 paragraphs 1-9.**
- **CPR 35.11 (use by one party of expert's report disclosed by another)**
- **CPR 35.12-14**
- **Section 3 of the Civil Evidence Act 1972, at paragraph 9B-1060 of Volume 2 of 'Civil Procedure' (the White Book) 2020.**
- **Commentary is incorporated in context in this Chapter, highlighted in an Activity box between two stars**

Chapter 22 MOCS

- ***Personal opinion is not admissible unless***
  - ***of an expert; or unless***
  - ***it is what a non-expert personally perceived***
- ***Expert opinion is admissible with court permission although the court can restrict it***
- ***Discussions between experts if useful or at court's direction***
- ***Expert duties***
- ***Expert reports***
- ***Written questions to experts***
- ***Obtaining further expert evidence***

The sessions dealing with this area of the syllabus on my BTC course are	

CUR 20.1 and 20.2 **THE GENERAL EXCLUSIONARY RULE IN RELATION TO EVIDENCE OF OPINION and THE MAIN EXCEPTIONS TO THE RULE**

Evidence which is the **personal opinion** of the witness is **not admissible.** That is **unless**

- W is an expert witness opining on something within their expertise as set out in the remainder of this Chapter or unless
- The personal opinion of a non-expert is the only way that the relevant matter (which includes an issue in the proceedings in question) which they personally perceived can be expressed. e.g. W giving his/her opinion in an RTA related claim that a vehicle was travelling far too fast. It is then admissible as evidence of what that non-expert perceived.

CUR 20.3 EXPERT OPINION EVIDENCE IN CIVIL PROCEEDINGS

EM: the use of expert opinion evidence in civil proceedings
EM: expert evidence at trial

Section 3 of the Civil Evidence Act 1972 states that, "where a person is called as a witness in any civil proceedings, his opinion on any relevant matter on which he is qualified to give **expert evidence** shall be **admissible** in evidence".

Experts should be **kept informed** about deadlines for all matters concerning them. Those instructing experts should send them promptly copies of all court orders and directions that may affect the preparation of their reports or any other matters concerning their obligations.

Experts should be aware that they will be required to **provide estimates** for the court and that the **court may limit the amount** to be paid as part of any order for **budgeted costs.**

EM: the court's duty and power to restrict expert evidence

Many disputes can be resolved without expert advice or evidence. It is important that full consideration is given to **whether** expert witness evidence is **reasonably required** to resolve the proceedings.

The CPR provides that court permission is needed before expert evidence can be relied upon or before an expert can be called to give oral evidence.

Permission

Applications for **court permission to call an expert** or put in an expert's report must be made. The application needs to identify

- the **field** in which expert evidence is required (reasonably required, that is, to enable proceedings to be finalised, being relevant to a matter in dispute between the parties)
- where practicable the **name** of the expert (with details of qualifications/experience)
- the amount of costs with a **costs estimate.** The court may limit the amount of a party's expert's fees and expenses that may be recovered from any other party.

If permission is granted it shall be in relation only to the expert named or the field identified. The order granting permission may specify the issues which the expert evidence should address.

In a soft tissue injury claim, permission may normally only be given for one expert medical report. Permission may not be given initially unless the medical report is a fixed cost medical report. The report must be a fixed cost medical report where C seeks permission to obtain a further medical report, if the report is from a

- Consultant Orthopaedic Surgeon
- Consultant in Accident and Emergency Medicine;General Practitioner registered with the General Medical Council or
- Physiotherapist registered with the Health and Care Professions Council

'Soft tissue injury claim' means a claim brought by an occupant of a motor vehicle where the significant physical injury caused is a soft tissue injury (for instance, whiplash claims) and includes claims where there is a minor psychological injury secondary in significance to the physical injury.

'Fixed cost medical report' means a report in a soft tissue injury claim which is from a medical expert who, save in exceptional circumstances

- has not provided treatment to the claimant;
- is not associated with any person who has provided treatment; and
- does not propose or recommend treatment that they or an associate then provide.

EM: single joint experts

'Single joint expert' means an expert instructed to prepare a report for the court on behalf of two or more of the parties (including the claimant) to the proceedings.
If it is necessary to obtain expert evidence, particularly in low value claims, the parties should consider using a **single expert, jointly instructed** by the parties, with the costs shared equally. Wherever possible a joint report should be obtained. Single joint experts are the norm in cases allocated to the small claims track and the fast track. It keeps costs down when working to narrow the issues.

The parties should try to agree joint instructions to single joint experts, but in default of agreement, each party may give instructions. In particular, all parties should try to agree what documents should be included with instructions and what assumptions single joint experts should make.

Some of the circumstances the court will consider when deciding whether expert evidence should be given by a single joint expert are whether

- it is proportionate to have separate experts for each party on a particular issue with reference to

  - the amount in dispute
  - the importance to the parties and
  - the complexity of the issue

- the instruction of a single joint expert is likely to assist the parties and the court to resolve the issue more speedily and in a more cost-effective way than separately instructed experts
- expert evidence is to be given on the issue of liability, causation or quantum
- the expert evidence falls within a substantially established area of knowledge which is unlikely to be in dispute or there is likely to be a range of expert opinion
- a party has already instructed an expert on the issue in question and whether or not that was done in compliance with any practice direction or relevant pre-action protocol
- written questions about an expert's report (see later in this Chapter) are likely to remove the need for the other party to instruct an expert if one party has already instructed an expert
- questions put to a single joint expert may not conclusively deal with all issues that may require testing prior to trial
- a conference may be required with the legal representatives, experts and other witnesses which may make instruction of a single joint expert impractical and
- a claim to privilege (See Chapter 20) makes the instruction of any expert as a single joint expert inappropriate.

Permission on the small claims and the fast track will be given for one expert on one issue.

Single joint experts provide a **single report and** should **serve** copies of it **simultaneously** on all instructing parties.

Permission on the multi-track

If both sides want an expert in the same field, unless there is a good reason not to, the court can direct that there is a single joint expert. Oral expert evidence at trial is limited to one expert each and two fields (therefore 2 experts)

EM: discussions between experts

Where a court did not direct a single joint expert or all parties cannot agree on a single one, the court may, at any stage, direct that

- expert reports are exchanged. (Failure to exchange means that unless the court gives permission, the report may not be used at trial / the expert may not be called to give evidence at trial).
- the experts meet to identify the expert issues and agree an opinion were possible
- the experts prepare a statement for the court setting out where they agree or disagree and why.

The court may specify the issues which the experts must discuss.

Unless directed by the court discussions between experts are not mandatory. Parties must consider, with their experts, at an early stage, whether there is likely to be any useful purpose in holding an experts' discussion and if so when.

The purpose of discussions between experts is not for experts to settle cases but to agree and narrow issues and in particular to identify

- the extent of the agreement between them
- the points of and short reasons for any disagreement
- action, if any, which may be taken to resolve any outstanding points of disagreement and
- any further material issues not raised and the extent to which these issues are agreed.

At the end of the discussion, a statement must be prepared by the experts dealing with these 4 points. Experts must give their own opinions to assist the court and do not require the authority of the parties to sign a joint statement. If an expert significantly alters an opinion, the joint statement must include a note or addendum by that expert explaining the change of opinion. Individual copies of the statements must be signed by the experts at the conclusion of the discussion, or as soon thereafter as practicable, and in any event within 7 days. Copies of the statements must be provided to the parties no later than 14 days after signing.

Where the experts are to meet, the parties must discuss and if possible agree whether an agenda is necessary, and if so attempt to agree one that helps the experts to focus on the issues which need to be discussed. The agenda must not be in the form of leading questions or hostile in tone.

Unless ordered by the court, or agreed by all parties, and the experts, neither the parties nor their legal representatives may attend experts' discussions.

If the legal representatives do attend they should not normally intervene in the discussion, except to answer questions put to them by the experts or to advise on the law and the experts may if they so wish hold part of their discussions in the absence of the legal representatives.

The content of the discussion between the experts shall not be referred to at the trial unless the parties agree.

Where experts reach agreement on an issue during their discussions, the agreement shall not bind the parties unless the parties expressly agree to be bound by the agreement.

Experts **may request directions** from the court where discussions with relevant persons have been unfruitful.

EM: duties and responsibilities of experts

National Justice Compania Naviera SA v Prudential Life Assurance Co[1993]

'The Ikarian Reefer'

In this case, Cresswell J summarised what should be included in the duties of an expert in civil proceedings which are often cited. Where they occur in the next two sections of this Chapter, they appear in ***bold italics***.

An expert

- does not need to be formally qualified. They may be an expert due to skills acquired through experience. It must be established that they have appropriate expertise.
- opines on matters material to the dispute ***in their area of expertise***, giving ***objective, unbiased opinions*** restricted to what is reasonably required to resolve the proceedings
- has the following duties and obligations with which they must be made familiar
  - a primary duty to the court, an overriding duty to help the court on matters within their expertise This duty overrides any obligation to the person from whom experts have received instructions or by whom they are paid
  - to work with reference to the overriding objective that courts deal with cases
    - justly,
    - keeping the work and costs in proportion to the value and importance of the case to the parties
    - expeditiously and
    - fairly
  - ***to state the facts or assumptions upon which their opinion is based.***
  - ***to not omit to consider material facts which could detract from their concluded opinion***
  - ***to make it clear when a particular question or issue falls outside their expertise***
  - ***to state if their opinion is not properly researched because the expert considers that insufficient data is available, and to indicate that the opinion is no more than a provisional one***
  - to provide opinions that ***are and are seen to be the independent product of the expert uninfluenced by the exigencies of litigation,*** so that they would express the same opinion if given the same instructions by another party
  - to provide answers to questions properly put (see later in this Chapter)
  - to be aware of the sanctions that any failure to comply with the rules or court orders may bring. (See later in this Chapter).
  - to be aware that any excessive delay for which they are responsible, may result in the parties who instructed them being penalised in costs, or debarred from relying upon the expert evidence
  - ***An expert witness in the High Court should never assume the role of an advocate***.

Activity

Remember to make notes on the relevant case law authorities in paragraphs
35.0.1 (first three paragraphs)
35.0.2
35.0.3
35.0.4
35.1.1
35.1.2 (first, second and eleventh paragraphs only),
35.3.3
35.4.2 (first, second, third, fourth, fifth and sixth paragraphs)
35.7.4
35.11.1 in the commentary in the White Book.

You may find it useful to add in references to the case law NOW at the appropriate points of this Chapter. Etc!

EM: expert reports

Expert evidence is to be given in a written report unless the court directs otherwise.

If a claim is on the small claims track or the fast track, the court will not direct an expert to attend a hearing unless it is necessary to do so in the interests of justice.

Expert reports need to
- be addressed to the court and not to the party from whom the expert has received instructions
- set out the expert's qualifications or experience
- give details of literature relied on in making the report
- set out the substance of all the facts and instructions, whether written or oral, material to the opinions in the report. You will recall from Chapter 20 that these instructions are not privileged, although courts will not order disclosure of any specific document, nor permit any questioning in court, other than by the party who instructed the expert, unless it has reasonable grounds to consider the statement of instructions to be inaccurate or incomplete
- show which facts are in the expert's own knowledge
- identify, giving their qualifications, anyone who may have for example carried out tests, the results of which are contained in the report, and whether the expert supervised the tests
- set out the range of the expert's opinion, summarising the range and giving reasons for the expert's own opinion
- draw attention to anything the expert wishes to qualify in the report and to any further information required
- summarise the conclusions reached
- confirm that the expert understands his/her duties to the court
- confirm that the expert has complied with that duty
- contain a **statement of truth.** In cases where an expert witness, who has prepared a report, could not assert that the report contained the truth, the whole truth and nothing but the truth without some qualification, that qualification should be stated in the report.

Activity

Copy out here 35PD.3 note 3.3, the prescribed form of the **statement of truth** for expert reports.

Where expert evidence refers to photographs, plans, calculations, analyses, measurements, survey reports or other similar documents, these must be provided to the opposite party at the same time as the exchange of reports

If, after exchange of reports, an expert witness changes his view on a material matter having read the other side's expert's report or for any other reason, such change of view should be communicated (through legal representatives) to the other side without delay and when appropriate to the court.

Where a party has disclosed an expert's report, any party may use that expert's report as evidence at the trial.

EM: consequences of failing to disclose an expert's report

Where our own expert provides a report unfavourable to our client, this must be disclosed, although we can withhold inspection of it as it is privileged, being in contemplation of litigation.

Where a subsequent new expert report is commissioned, the court usually orders the initial unfavourable report to be disclosed as a condition for giving permission to rely on a new expert's report

A party who fails to disclose an expert's report may not use the report at the trial or call the expert to give evidence orally unless the court gives permission.

EM: written questions to experts

Where experts are to give oral evidence, all parties may ask questions. In general, written questions should be put to single joint experts or to an expert instructed by another party before requests are made for them to attend court for the purpose of cross-examination.

Within 28 days of service of the expert report, in order **to clarify** the report, the other side may put proportionate written questions to the expert **only once.** These requirements in bold must be adhered to unless the court gives permission or the other party agrees. Where a party sends a written question or questions direct to an expert, a copy of the questions must, at the same time, be sent to the other party or parties.

Experts have a duty to provide answers to questions properly put.

The responses become part of the report. Experts should copy their answers to those instructing them.

The party or parties instructing the expert must pay any fees charged by that expert for answering these questions This does not affect any decision of the court as to the party who is ultimately to bear the expert's fees.

Sanctions that the court may impose against the other party who instructed the expert, for the expert's failure to reply to the clarification questions, are that the party instructing the expert may not rely on the expert evidence and/or may not recover from the other party the fees and expenses of that expert.

EM: obtaining further expert evidence

Where one party has **access to information that is not readily available to the other party,** the court may direct the party who has access to the information to prepare, file and copy to the other party a document recording the information.

If experts require such information which has not been disclosed, they should discuss the position with those instructing them without delay, so that a request for the information can be made, and, if not forthcoming, an application can be made to the court. Any request for further information from the other party made by an expert should be in a letter to the expert's instructing party and should state why the information is necessary and the significance in relation to the expert issues in the case.

Chapter 22

Elements of the syllabus which you have now covered

- A cell with heavy outlining means that that area of the syllabus was covered in this Chapter;
- A darkly shaded cell with a tick √ means that the whole of that syllabus element has now been covered;
- A lightly shaded cell means that part of that element of the syllabus has been covered in a previous Chapter; and
- An unshaded cell means that element of the syllabus has not yet been covered.

1.1 √	1.2 √	1.3 √	2.1 √	2.2 √	3.1 √	3.2 √	6.1 √	6.2 √	6.3 √
6.4 √	7.1 √	7.2 √	8.1 √	8.2 √	8.3 √	9.1 √	9.2 √	9.3 √	10.1 √
10.2 √	11.1 √	11.2 √	12.1 √	12.2 √	12.3 √	13.1 √	13.2 √	13.3 √	13.4 √
13.5 √	13.6 √	13.7 √	13.8 √	14.1 √	14.2 √	14.3 √	14.4 √	14.5 √	14.6 √
15.1 √	15.2 √	15.3 √	15.4 √	16.1 √	16.2 √	17.1 √	17.2 √	17.3 √	17.4 √
18.1 √	18.2. √ 16.3 √	16.4 √ 18.5 √	19.1 √	19.2 √	19.3 √	20.1 √	20.2 √	20.3 √	21.1
21.2	21.3	22.1	22.2	23.1 √	23.2 √	23.3 √	21.4 √	24.1	

Chapter 23

EVIDENCE "three" CIVIL TRIAL AND EVIDENCE [CUR 21]

Q (III) Evidence at trial, Hearsay

THIS CHAPTER CONTAINS THE ITEMS PRINTED IN BOLD IN THE FOLLOWING BOXES

CURRICULUM ("CUR")

Civil Trial and Evidence
21.1 the trial of civil cases
21.1 hearsay evidence in civil proceedings
21.3 convictions as evidence in civil proceedings

SYLLABUS

Examinable material will consist of the power of the court to control evidence, evidence of witnesses, evidence by video link, use of witness statements at trial, the use of hearsay evidence at trial, the use of plans, models and photographs as evidence, convictions as evidence in civil proceedings, and the trial of civil cases, including trial timetables, order of speeches, calling and examining witnesses, judgment, submissions on orders for costs and permission to appeal.

- **CPR 32.1-3**
- CPR 32.5 (Use at trial of witness statements which have been served) is in Chapter 21 along with associated commentary
- **CPR 33.1-33.6;**
- **PD 28 paragraph 8; and**
- **PD 29 paragraph 10.**
- **Section 11 Civil Evidence Act 1968, at paragraph 9B-1032 of Volume 2 of 'Civil Procedure' (the White Book) 2020**
- Sections 1-4 Civil Evidence Act 1995, at paragraphs 9B-1071 to 9B-1074 of Volume 2 of 'Civil Procedure' (the White Book) 2020
- **Section 35A Senior Courts Act and section 69 County Courts Act, at paragraphs 9A-122 and 9A-554 of Volume 2 of 'Civil Procedure' (the White Book) 2020**

Chapter 23 MOst Concise Summary (MOCS)

- **Burden of proof[16]**
  - **It is for the party making the assertion to prove it.**

- **Standard of Proof[17]**
  - **On the balance of probabilities**

- **The trial of civil cases**

- **Hearsay evidence is admissible**
  - **The correct procedure must be followed**

- **Convictions as evidence in civil proceedings**
  - **Admissible if unspent, subsisting.**

The sessions dealing with this area of the syllabus on my BTC course ar	

BURDEN AND STANDARD OF PROOF[18]

Standard of Proof

The standard of proof in civil cases is "**on the balance of probabilities**". That means that if the judge can say "I think it is more probable than not" then the standard is met and the case proven; but if the probabilities are equal, the standard is not met.

Burden of Proof

Matters must be proved by the person who asserts those matters: **It is for the party making the assertion to prove it**. So

- C in the main claim
- D when alleging C's contributory negligence
- D when alleging C's failure to mitigate
- D when counterclaiming against C
- D when the claim is under s.2 (1) Misrepresentation Act 1967, must show that "D had reasonable grounds to believe and did believe up to the time of the contract that the facts represented were true".

[16] This is not referred to in the syllabus for 2020 onwards; the author considers it important enough that you should be aware of it.
[17] Ditto
[18] Ditto

CUR 21.1 THE TRIAL OF CIVIL CASES

EM: power of the court to control evidence
EM: evidence of witnesses and evidence by video link [19]
EM: use of witness statements at trial

The examinable material on the above three points and the CPR references and White Book commentary on them are exact repeats of the same points set out in the syllabus required content on Evidence of Fact in Chapter 21 of this book.

EM: the trial of civil cases

You should recall also, from the Chapter on Evidence of Fact, that the court has power to control evidence and to restrict cross-examination and that witness statements stand as examination in chief.

Fast track

On the fast track the trial will normally take place at the court where the case is being managed, but it may be at another court if it is appropriate having regard to the needs of the parties and the availability of court resources.

The judge will generally have read the papers in the trial bundle and may dispense with an opening address.

EM: trial timetables Fast track Timetable

In consultation with the parties, as soon as practicable after

- the date specified for filing the pre-trial checklist

the court will
- fix the date for the trial;
- give directions it considers appropriate, including the trial timetable; and
- specify any further steps that need to be taken before trial.

The court will give at least 3 weeks' notice of the trial date, although shorter notice can be given in exceptional circumstances.

At trial, the judge may confirm or vary any timetable given previously or, if none has been given, set his or her own.

Where, at the date of the trial, the claim is allocated to the fast track, at the conclusion of the trial the judge will normally summarily assess the costs of the claim in accordance with Section VI of Part 45 on fast track trial costs. [Note that there is no specific reference to Part 45 in the required content for the assessment this year].

Where a trial is not finished on the day for which it is listed the judge will normally sit on the next court day to complete it.

---

[19] Please refer also to the footnote in Chapter 21

EM: permission to appeal.

Please see Chapter 26 for the detail about the need to apply for permission to appeal and how to do it.

Multi-track

On the multi-track the trial will normally take place at a **Civil Trial Centre** but it may be at another court if it is appropriate having regard to the needs of the parties and the availability of court resources.

The judge will generally have read the papers in the trial bundle and may dispense with an opening address.

EM: trial timetables Multi-track timetable

In consultation with the parties, as soon as practicable after

- each party has filed the completed pre-trial checklist; or
- the court has held a listing hearing; or
- the court has held the pre-trial review following receipt of the parties' pre-trial check lists

the court will

- set the timetable to trial unless it considers it inappropriate to do so;
- set the trial date / the week for trial to begin; and
- notify parties of the trial timetable and the date or period for it.

Trial bundle

Unless the court orders otherwise, **C** files it not more than 7 and not less than 3 clear days before the start of the trial.

39APD.3 provides a list of what they should contain (not on your syllabus this year). Otherwise a court order will set this out.

At trial, the judge may confirm or vary any timetable given previously or, if none has been given, set his own.

Procedure

Trial hearings are in public unless they involve e.g. national security, or it is necessary to protect the interests of a child or a protected party. In such cases they may be in private.

EM: order of speeches

C opening speech

C's case

XIC of C. (Remember that the witness statement stands as XIC. Remember that there may be XIC on new matters if C's counsel obtains court permission to amplify.

XX of C. This may include ***EM: calling and examining witnesses.*** Please refer to the earlier Chapters with "EVIDENCE" in their title.

Re-examination

D may submit no case to answer,

D's case

XIC of D. (Remember that the witness statement stands as XIC. Remember that there may be XIC on new matters if C's counsel obtains court permission to amplify. This amplification may include ***EM: calling and examining witnesses.*** Please refer to the earlier Chapters with "EVIDENCE" in their title.

XX of D. This may include **calling and examining witnesses.** Please refer to the earlier Chapters with "EVIDENCE" in their title.

Re-examination

D closing speech

C closing speech

Judgment (either now or deferred/reserved until later)

Submissions on costs

Order as to costs

Application for permission to appeal can be made orally at this point. (See the later Chapter on appeals).

EM: Submissions on orders for costs

Remember that if an order makes no mention of costs then each party will bear their own costs. So Counsel must include submissions as to costs to persuade the court to exercise its discretion in the client's favour where appropriate.

Thus the Particulars of Claim ("POC") will include **the following statutory provisions which may also be assessed: section 35A Senior Courts Act and section 69 County Courts Act, at section 9A of Volume 2 of 'Civil Procedure' (the White Book) 2019.**

- the authority for the Court's power to award interest claimed on debts and damages.for claiming the interest (either s.69 County Courts Act 1984 or s.35A Senior Courts Act 1981 if you are in the High Court)
  - both s 69(5) and s35A (1) provide that the court may calculate different interest at different rates regarding different periods of time
  - s35A (2) provides that where the award for PI or death is greater than £200, unless the court is satisfied that there are special reasons to the contrary, the amount of interest includes simple interest as the court thinks fit, on all or part of the claim.

- the period covered by the interest (the date when a successful C should have been paid until the date he is paid; therefore from the date of loss to the date of judgment).

  Where the claim is for a specific sum of money, the Particulars of Claim will show the daily rate of interest at 1/365th (even in a leap year) and will provide that interest continues to accrue at this daily rate until it is paid in full.

- the rate of interest (usually pitched at the 8% taken from the Judgments Act 1838 – see below).

Worked example of interest on a debt claim

Suppose that C is claiming for a debt of £5,600 and that 140 days have passed since the debt became due. The POC is being drafted now.

C will claim £5,600 + interest at 8% per annum.

1% per annum would be £5600/100 = £56; so 8% per annum = £56 x 8 = £448

If the debt were repaid exactly a year later, interest on it would be £448; so we need to calculate what that equates to per day. £448/365 = £1.227p per day.

The daily rate is £1.227.

At the date of drafting the POC, C is owed £1.227p x 140 days = £171.78 in interest.

So the POC will claim "interest pursuant to section 69 of the County Courts Act 1984 on the sum of £5,600.00 from 10th June [year] at the rate of 8% per annum, amounting to £171.78 at 29th October [year] and continuing at the daily rate of £1.23 until judgment or sooner payment."

Before making submissions as to costs in court, Counsel should update this information to the figures for the current date.

EM: permission to appeal.

Please see Chapter 26 for the detail about the need to apply for permission to appeal and how to do it.

CUR 21.2 HEARSAY EVIDENCE IN CIVIL PROCEEDINGS

EM: the use of hearsay evidence at trial, the use of plans, models and photographs as evidence

ss1-4 Civil Evidence Act 1995.

Hearsay evidence is **admissible**:

Hearsay is "a statement made otherwise than by a person while giving oral evidence in the proceedings which is tendered as evidence of the matters stated"

If a witness giving oral evidence intends to rely on hearsay evidence at trial, or if a witness (or some kind of document!) is not giving oral evidence at court, the witness statement and exhibits, (or the documents, such as letters, emails, texts, maps, **plans** books, **models** anything with writing on it, **photos** which are being brought as evidence but which are not part of exhibits to witness statements), could alternatively be put in as hearsay evidence.

If the evidence includes business records, they must be certified by an officer of the business, to be admissible.

You will recall from Chapter 21 of this book that if a party who has served a witness statement does not use it either as oral evidence at trial or as hearsay evidence, any other party may put the witness statement in as hearsay evidence.

Where a party intends to rely on hearsay evidence at trial and either that evidence

- is to be given by a witness giving oral evidence or
- is contained in a witness statement of a person who is not being called to give oral evidence, the procedure is as follows.

- Procedure

  - **Serve** the **witness statement** and exhibits (or just the other documents/evidence of them if they are not exhibited to a witness statement) on the other parties within the timeframe directed by the court, no later than the latest date for serving witness statements, **together with notice** that the witness statement (or documents) will be put in as **hearsay** evidence and

    on request, such **particulars** of or relating to the evidence, as is reasonable and practicable in the circumstances for the purpose of enabling him or them to deal with any matters arising from its being hearsay.

    Where a party intends to use e.g. plans, photographs or models *as evidence of any fact,* he must give notice at least 21 days before the hearing at which he proposes to put in the evidence, if there are not to be witness statements or he intends to put in the evidence solely in order to disprove an allegation made in a witness statement).

    Where the evidence is e.g. plans, photographs or models and forms *part of expert evidence,* he must give notice when the expert's report is served on the other party.

    Where the evidence is e.g. plans, photographs or models and is being produced to the court *for any reason other* than as part of factual or expert evidence, he must give notice at least 21 days before the hearing at which he proposes to put in the evidence.

    Where a party has given notice that he intends to put e.g. plans, photographs or models in evidence, he must give every other party an opportunity to inspect it and to agree to its admission without further proof.

    The contents of the notice for all types of hearsay are that it
    - identifies the hearsay evidence;
    - states that the party serving the notice proposes to rely on the hearsay evidence at trial; and
    - gives the reason why the witness will not be called.

    The service of the notice may be excluded by agreement of the parties; or waived by the person to whom notice is required to be given:

  - Where the evidence is contained in a witness statement of a person who is not being called to give oral evidence, in addition, when serving the witness statement, the party intending to rely on hearsay evidence must inform the other parties that the witness is not being called to give oral evidence and state why W is not being called to give oral evidence.

  - Where the hearsay evidence is to be in a document, the party proposing to rely on the hearsay evidence must supply a copy to any party who requests him to do so.

  - If the notice is not served in circumstances where it should have been, hearsay evidence is still admissible, although it may affect the weight attached to it and any costs order.

Note that there is no duty to give a notice
- o for evidence at hearings other than trials
- o where an affidavit or witness statement to be used at trial does not contain hearsay evidence
- o where a party to a probate action wishes to put a statement in evidence and the statement is alleged to have been made by the person whose estate is the subject of the proceedings
- o where a PD excludes the duty

- Not more than 14 days after service of the hearsay notice, **any other party** to the proceedings may, with the leave of the court, call the person not called as a witness as their evidence was put in as hearsay, and XX him on the statement as if he had been called in the first place as if the hearsay statement were his evidence in chief.

- In the same timeframe another party can give **notice** to the party proposing to give the hearsay statement in evidence of their **intention** to call evidence **to attack the credibility** of the person whose evidence is to be presented as hearsay.

– Weight given to hearsay evidence

- The court has regard to any circumstances from which an **inference** can be reasonably drawn **as to the reliability** or otherwise **of the evidence**. Such circumstances are
  - o The ease with which the person who made the statement could have been brought to court. It should be easy to produce a person living round the corner, harder or impossible if the person is abroad or dead. Less weight will be given to the hearsay evidence of a person living round the corner;
  - o How close in time the hearsay evidence was created to the actual event being evidenced. More weight is given to a note of a car registration number taken at the scene of the accident than to a note made of it from memory several hours later;
  - o The greater the number of hearsay evidences in a case, the less weight they will lend to the case;
  - o Does any person involved have a motive to conceal/misrepresent matters
  - o Was the original statement an edited account or was it made in collaboration with another or for a particular purpose;
  - o Do circumstances suggest an attempt to prevent the proper evaluation of the weight of the hearsay evidence.
  - o Whether due notice of the hearsay was given

CUR 21.3 CONVICTIONS AS EVIDENCE IN CIVIL PROCEEDINGS

EM: convictions as evidence in civil proceedings

CEA 1968, s. 11 = convictions as evidence in civil proceedings.

Unspent, subsisting convictions are **admissible** in evidence for the purpose of proving that a person committed that offence. A convicted person is taken to have committed that offence unless the contrary is proved.

Reference may be made to

- the contents of any document which is admissible as evidence of the conviction, and the contents of the information, complaint, indictment or charge-sheet on which the person in question was convicted
- any other admissible evidence for the purpose of identifying the facts on which the conviction was based.

  Court certified or authenticated Copies of the whole or part of the relevant document, or such documents certified or authenticated by an authority having custody of it may be used. They are taken to be a true copy of that document or part unless the contrary is shown.

Chapter 23

Elements of the syllabus which you have now covered

- A cell with heavy outlining means that that area of the syllabus was covered in this Chapter;
- A darkly shaded cell with a tick √ means that the whole of that syllabus element has now been covered;
- A lightly shaded cell means that part of that element of the syllabus has been covered in a previous Chapter; and
- An unshaded cell means that element of the syllabus has not yet been covered.

1.1 √	1.2 √	1.3 √	2.1 √	2.2 √	3.1 √	3.2 √	6.1 √	6.2 √	6.3 √
6.4 √	7.1 √	7.2 √	8.1 √	8.2 √	8.3 √	9.1 √	9.2 √	9.3 √	10.1 √
10.2 √	11.1 √	11.2 √	12.1 √	12.2 √	12.3 √	13.1 √	13.2 √	13.3 √	13.4 √
13.5 √	13.6 √	13.7 √	13.8 √	14.1 √	14.2 √	14.3 √	14.4 √	14.5 √	14.6 √
15.1 √	15.2 √	15.3 √	15.4 √	16.1 √	16.2 √	17.1 √	17.2 √	17.3 √	17.4 √
18.1 √	18.2. √ 16.3 √	16.4 √ 18.5 √	19.1 √	19.2 √	19.3 √	20.1 √	20.2 √	20.3 √	21.1 √
21.2 √	21.3 √	22.1	22.2	23.1 √	23.2 √	23.3 √	21.4 √	24.1	

Chapter 24

JUDGMENTS, ORDERS [CUR 22]

r) Judgments and orders

THIS CHAPTER CONTAINS THE ITEMS PRINTED IN BOLD IN THE FOLLOWING BOXES

CURRICULUM ("CUR")

Judgments, Orders

22.1 judgment and orders, including Tomlin orders
22.2 enforcing money judgments is in chapter 25
22.3 recording *(and enforcement of settlements is in the next Chapter)* ***following ADR***

SYLLABUS

Examinable material will consist of drawing up and filing judgments and orders, service of judgments and orders, when judgments and orders take effect, consent judgments and orders, Tomlin orders, applying to set aside or vary judgments and orders, time for complying with judgments and orders, correction of errors in judgments and orders, judgments on both claim and counterclaim, *[methods of enforcing judgments and orders, and transfer of proceedings for enforcement are in the next Chapter],* ***recording*** *[and enforcement]* ***of settlements following ADR.***

- **CPR 40.3-4,**
- **CPR 40.6**
- **CPR40.7-9,**
- **CPR 40.11-13**
- **PD 40B paragraphs 4 and 8**
- CPR 70.1-2A, 70.3, 70.4 and 70.6; CPR 71.1-2, 71.6 and 71.8; CPR 72.1-3; CPR 73.3; CPR 83.2; CPR 84.3; CPR 89.3-4 are in the next Chapter
- PD 70 paragraphs 1A.1 and 1.1; PD 71 paragraphs 1, 2, 4 and 5; PD 72 paragraph 1; and PD 73 paragraph 1 are in the next Chapter
- The editorial introductions to CPR Parts 71-73, 83-84 and 89 at paragraphs 71.0.1, 72.0.1, 72.2.15, 73.0.1, 73.0.4 (1) and (2), 83.0.2-3, the second paragraph of 83.0.17, 84.0.2-3 and 89.0.1 of Volume 1 of 'Civil Procedure' (the White Book) 2020 are in an activity box in the next Chapter
- Section 6(1)-(5) of the Attachment of Earnings Act 1971 at paragraph 9B-965 of Volume 2 of 'Civil Procedure' (the White Book) 2020 is in the next Chapter
- **Commentary is incorporated in context in this chapter, highlighted in an Activity box between two stars**
- **Relevant ADR references to The Jackson ADR Handbook (Second Edition, 2016) are incorporated in context in this Chapter, highlighted in an Activity box between two lightning flashes**

Chapter 24 MOCS

- ***Rules as to who draws up the judgment or order***
- ***When they take effect***
- ***Payment of money within 14 days unless judgment or order specifies differently***
- ***Consent orders***
- ***Tomlin orders***
- ***Recording of settlements following ADR***

The sessions dealing with this area of the syllabus on my BTC course are	

CUR 22.1 JUDGMENT AND ORDERS, INCLUDING TOMLIN ORDERS

EM: drawing up and filing judgments and orders

QBD and Administrative Court

Unless the court orders otherwise, judgments or orders
- made in QBD are drawn up by the parties
- made in the Administrative Court are drawn up by the court

Other courts

Unless a PD orders otherwise, every other judgment or order will be drawn up by the court, although
- the court may order a party to draw it up
- a party, with the permission of the court may agree to draw it up
- the court may dispense with the need to draw it up

The court may direct that
- a judgment or an order drawn up by a party must be checked by the court before it is sealed or
- before a judgment or an order is drawn up by the court, the parties must file an agreed statement of its terms.

- A party doing the drawing up must file the judgment / order at court within 7 days of the date when it was ordered or permitted to be drawn up so that it can be sealed by the court.

If he fails to file it within that period, any other party may draw it up and file it.

- Consent orders (see later in this Chapter) also follow all the above.

EM: service of judgments and orders

A **party** to proceedings **serves a document prepared by them** except where
- a rule or practice direction provides that the court will serve the document or
- the court orders otherwise.

The **court serves a document prepared by it** except where
- a rule or practice direction provides that a party must serve the document
- the party on whose behalf the document is to be served notifies the court that the party wishes to serve it or
- the court orders otherwise.

Where a judgment or an order has been drawn up by a party and is to be served by the court, the party who drew it up must file a copy to be retained at court and sufficient copies for service on him and on the other parties and, once it has been sealed, the court must serve a copy of it on each party to the proceedings.

Where the court is to serve a document, it is for the court to decide which method of service is to be used.

Unless the court directs otherwise, any order made otherwise than at trial must be served on
- the applicant and the respondent and
- any other person on whom the court orders it to be served.

EM: when judgments and orders take effect

A judgment or order takes effect from the day when it is given or made, or such later date as the court may specify.

Interest begins to run from the date that judgment is given unless a rule in another Part or a practice direction makes different provision or the court orders otherwise.

The court may order that interest shall begin to run from a date before the date that judgment is given.

EM: applying to set aside or vary judgments and orders

A person who is not a party but who is directly affected by a judgment or order may apply to have the judgment or order set aside or varied.

EM: time for complying with judgments and orders

Payment of an amount of money

A party must comply with a judgment or order for the **payment of an amount of money** (including costs) within 14 days of the date of the judgment or order - if unpaid after this date C is entitled to enter judgment for the unpaid sum - unless
- it specifies a different date (including specifying payment by instalments)
- a CPR rule specifies a different date; or
- the court has stayed the proceedings or judgment.
- An order which requires an act to be done

An order which requires an act to be done (other than a judgment or order for the payment of an amount of money) must specify the time within which the act should be done.

The consequences of failure to do an act within the time specified may be set out in the order. In this case the wording of the following examples set out in the PD, suitably adapted must be used

(1) Unless the [claimant][defendant] serves his list of documents by 4.00 p.m. on Friday, January 22, 1999 his [claim][defence] will be struck out and judgment entered for the [defendant][claimant], or

(2) Unless the [claimant][defendant] serves his list of documents within 14 days of service of this order his [claim][defence] will be struck out and judgment entered for the [defendant][claimant].

Example (1) should be used wherever possible.

EM: correction of errors in judgments and orders

The court may at any time correct an accidental slip or omission in a judgment or order.

Where a judgment or order contains an accidental slip or omission a party may apply for it to be corrected

The application notice (which may be an informal document such as a letter) should describe the error and set out the correction required. An application may be dealt with without a hearing where the applicant so requests, with the consent of the parties, or where the court does not consider that a hearing would be appropriate.

The judge may deal with the application without notice if the slip or omission is obvious or may direct notice of the application to be given to the other party or parties.

If the application is opposed it should, if practicable, be listed for hearing before the judge who gave the judgment or made the order.

The court has an inherent power to vary its own orders to make the meaning and intention of the court clear.

EM: judgments on both claim and counterclaim

Where the court gives judgment for specified amounts both for the claimant on his claim and against the claimant on a counterclaim, if there is a balance in favour of one of the parties, it may order the party whose judgment is for the lesser amount to pay the balance.

So for instance

C wins £500 on the claim

D wins £800 on the counterclaim (i.e. the judge finds against the claimant on the counterclaim made by D)

Balance of £300 in favour of D.

C got judgment for the lesser amount and so C pays the balance of £300 to D.

The court may make a separate order as to costs against each party.

EM: consent judgments and orders

Where all the parties agree the terms in which a judgment should be given or an order should be made, a court officer may enter and seal that agreed judgment or order if
- the judgment / order is listed in CPR 40.6(3);
- none of the parties is a litigant in person; and
- the approval of the court is not required.

Such consent judgments and orders must be
- drawn up in the terms agreed
- expressed as being "By Consent"
- signed by the legal representative for each of the parties to whom the order relates
- signed by the party if he has applied for the judgment/order as a litigant in person

Where all parties do not agree the terms, any party may apply for a judgment or order in the terms agreed and the court may deal with the application without a hearing.

Activity

Remember to make notes on the relevant case law authorities in paragraphs 40.6.2 in the commentary in the White Book.

You may find it useful to add in references to the case law NOW at the appropriate points of this Chapter.

When approaching final revision time, remember to add in the salient findings of the cases at the relevant point in any 'mental crib sheets into sheets into which you have distilled the main points of your learned knowledge.

EM: Tomlin orders

They are used for confidential or complex matters.

Details of the agreement are not shown on the face of the order, only in the confidential schedule. Costs are shown on the face of the order. When a Tomlin order is made, proceedings are stayed with "liberty to apply". This simply means that the party has liberty to apply to court to get the stay lifted so that the terms in the schedule can be carried into effect. When enforcing a Tomlin order, this is the first stage. The second stage of the enforcement of the order is by using one of the usual methods of enforcement. These are set out in the next Chapter on enforcement of judgments and orders.

EM: Recording of settlements following ADR

Activity

Remember to incorporate the relevant paragraphs from The Jackson ADR Handbook (Second Edition, 2016):-

18.03,
18.06-18.09,
19.02,
19.10-19.13

You may find it useful to add in references to the case law NOW at the appropriate points of this chapter.

When approaching final revision time, remember to add in the salient findings of the cases at the relevant point in any 'mental crib sheet' into which

Chapter 24

Elements of the syllabus which you have now covered in **civil litigation and evidence**

- A cell with heavy outlining means that that area of the syllabus was covered in this Chapter;
- A darkly shaded cell with a tick √ means that the whole of that syllabus element has now been covered;
- A lightly shaded cell means that part of that element of the syllabus has been covered in a previous Chapter; and
- An unshaded cell means that element of the syllabus has not yet been covered.

1.1 √	1.2 √	1.3 √	2.1 √	2.2 √	3.1 √	3.2 √	6.1 √	6.2 √	6.3 √
6.4 √	7.1 √	7.2 √	8.1 √	8.2 √	8.3 √	9.1 √	9.2 √	9.3 √	10.1 √
10.2 √	11.1 √	11.2 √	12.1 √	12.2 √	12.3 √	13.1 √	13.2 √	13.3 √	13.4 √
13.5 √	13.6 √	13.7 √	13.8 √	14.1 √	14.2 √	14.3 √	14.4 √	14.5 √	14.6 √
15.1 √	15.2 √	15.3 √	15.4 √	16.1 √	16.2 √	17.1 √	17.2 √	17.3 √	17.4 √
18.1 √	18.2. √ 16.3 √	16.4 √ 18.5 √	19.1 √	19.2 √	19.3 √	20.1 √	20.2 √	20.3 √	21.1 √
21.2 √	21.3 √	22.1 √	22.2	23.1 √	23.2 √	23.3 √	21.4 √	24.1	

Elements of the syllabus which you have now covered for **ADR**

- A cell with heavy outlining means that that area of the syllabus was covered in this Chapter;
- A darkly shaded cell with a tick √ means that the whole of that syllabus element has now been covered;
- A lightly shaded cell means that part of that element of the syllabus has been covered in a previous Chapter; and
- An unshaded cell means that element of the syllabus has not yet been covered.

1.4 √	1.5√	3.3 √	4.1√	4.2√	5.1√	5.2√	18.1 √	22.3 V record	22.3 enforce

Chapter 25

ENFORCEMENT [CUR 22]

rr) Enforcement of judgments

THIS CHAPTER CONTAINS THE ITEMS PRINTED IN BOLD IN THE FOLLOWING BOXES

CURRICULUM ("CUR")

Enforcement
22.1 judgment and orders, including Tomlin orders (see previous Chapter)
22.2 enforcing money judgments
22.3 recording and **enforcement of settlements following ADR**

SYLLABUS

Examinable material will consist of drawing up and filing judgments and orders, service of judgments and orders, when judgments and orders take effect, consent judgments and orders, Tomlin orders, applying to set aside or vary judgments and orders, time for complying with judgments and orders, correction of errors in judgments and orders, judgments on both claim and counterclaim, ***methods of enforcing judgments and orders, and transfer of proceedings for enforcement are in the next Chapter,*** *[recording – previous Chapter]* ***and enforcement of settlements following ADR.***

- CPR 40.3-4, (please see previous Chapter)
- CPR 40.6 (please see previous Chapter)
- CPR40.7-9, (please see previous Chapter)
- CPR 40.11-13 (please see previous Chapter)
- PD 40B paragraphs 4 and 8 (please see previous Chapter)
- **CPR 70.1-2A (transfer of proceedings for enforcement), 70.3, 70.4 and 70.6; CPR 71.1-2, 71.6 and 71.8; CPR 72.1-3; CPR 73.3; CPR 83.2; CPR 84.3; CPR 89.3-4**
- **PD 70 paragraphs 1A.1 and 1.1; PD 71 paragraphs 1, 2, 4 and 5; PD 72 paragraph 1; and PD 73 paragraph 1**
- **The editorial introductions to CPR Parts 71-73, 83-84 and 89 at paragraphs 71.0.1, 72.0.1, 72.2.15, 73.0.1, 73.0.4 (1) and (2), 83.0.2-3, the second paragraph of 83.0.17, 84.0.2-3 and 89.0.1 of Volume 1 of 'Civil Procedure' (the White Book) 2020**
- **Section 6(1)-(5) of the Attachment of Earnings Act 1971 at paragraph 9B-965 of Volume 2 of 'Civil Procedure' (the White Book) 2020**
- **Commentary is incorporated in context in this chapter, highlighted in an Activity box between two stars**
- **Relevant ADR references to The Jackson ADR Handbook (Second Edition, 2016) are incorporated in context in this Chapter, highlighted in an Activity box between two lightning flashes**

Chapter 25 MOCS

- ***How to apply for an order that a judgment debtor attend court to give information about her assets.***
- ***For money judgments, the method or combination of methods of enforcement***

  CARTSS

  will depend on the circumstances of both the judgment debtor and the judgment creditor
- ***Enforcement of settlements following ADR***

The sessions dealing with this area of the syllabus on my BTC course are	

CUR 22.1 ENFORCING MONEY JUDGMENTS

You will recall from the end of Chapter 8 that the

Time limit for actions to enforce judgments.

- 6 years from the date on which the judgment became enforceable
- Arrears of interest in respect of any judgment debt is not recoverable after 6 years from the date on which the interest became due.

EM: methods of enforcing judgments and orders,

Methods of enforcing

In the context of enforcing money judgments, a 'judgment or order' includes an award which the court has registered for enforcement, ordered to be enforced, or given permission to enforce as if it were a judgment or order of the court, and in relation to such an award, 'the court which made the judgment or order' means the court which registered the award or made such an order.

A 'judgment or order for the payment of money' includes a judgment or order for the payment of costs, but does not include a judgment or order for the payment of money into court.

When the losing party. i.e. the judgment debtor, the person against whom a judgment or order was given or made does not comply with the judgment or order, there are ways to enforce it through the courts.

Orders to obtain information from judgment debtors – Part 71

Activity

Remember in addition to make notes on the editorial Introduction to CPR Part 71 at paragraph 71.0.1 in the White Book as the syllabus says "Note. Students should be familiar with this editorial introduction."

Where a judgment creditor, i.e. a person who has obtained or is entitled to enforce a judgment or order does not know what assets the judgment debtor owns, he may apply without notice to the County Court hearing centre which made the judgment or order which it is sought to enforce, (or to the court where the proceedings have been transferred to, [or if it is to enforce a judgment made in the County Court Money Claims Centre, the application be issued in accordance with section 2 of Practice Direction 70 (not on your syllabus this year)].

The application will be for a **court order** to require a judgment debtor or an officer of a judgment debtor company **to attend court to provide information**, for the purpose of enabling a judgment creditor to enforce a judgment or order against her or it.

Form and content of the application notice to get the debtor to attend court to answer questions

The application notice must be in Practice Form N316 if the application is to question an individual judgment debtor, or N316A if the application is to question an officer of a company or other corporation

It must

- state the name and address of the judgment debtor
- identify the judgment or order which the judgment creditor is seeking to enforce
- if the application is to enforce a judgment or order for the payment of money, state the amount presently owed by the judgment debtor under the judgment or order
- if the judgment debtor is a company or other corporation, state
    - the name and address of the officer of that body whom the judgment creditor wishes to be ordered to attend court and
    - his position in the company
- if the judgment creditor wishes the questioning to be conducted before a judge, state this and give his reasons
- if the judgment creditor wishes the judgment debtor (or other person to be questioned) to be ordered to produce specific documents at court, identify those documents and
- if the application is to enforce a judgment or order which is not for the payment of money, identify the matters about which the judgment creditor wishes the judgment debtor (or officer of the judgment debtor) to be questioned.

The court officer considering the application notice may, in any appropriate case, refer it to a judge (rule 3.2) and will refer it to a judge for consideration, if the judgment creditor requests the judgment debtor (or officer of the judgment debtor) to be questioned before a judge.

Or the application may be dealt with without a hearing.

If the application notice complies with the requirements for form and content set out above, an order to attend court will be issued in the following terms

The court order to attend

The order will provide for the judgment debtor (or other person to be questioned) to attend the County Court hearing centre, serving the address where the judgment debtor resides or carries on business, unless a judge decides otherwise.

The order will provide for questioning to take place before a judge only if the judge considering the request decides that there are compelling reasons to make such an order.

- A person served with an order issued under this rule must
  - attend court at the time and place specified in the order
  - when she does so, produce at court documents in her control which are described in the order and
  - answer on oath such questions as the court may require

  It will contain a notice to the effect that
  - "If you the within-named [ ] do not comply with this order you may be held to be in contempt of court and imprisoned or fined, or your assets may be seized."

Conduct of the hearing

- The person ordered to attend court will be questioned on oath
  - The court officer will ask a standard series of questions, as set out in the forms in Appendixes A and B to PD71. The form in Appendix A will be used if the person being questioned is the judgment debtor, and the form in Appendix B will be used if the person is an officer of a company or other corporation.
- The questioning will be carried out **by a court officer** unless the court has ordered that the hearing shall be before a judge, Normal procedure is before a court officer.
  - The judgment creditor or his representative **may attend** and ask questions himself where the questioning takes place before a court officer or request the court officer to ask additional questions, by attaching a list of proposed additional questions to his application notice
  - The court officer will
    - make a written record of the evidence given, unless the proceedings are tape recorded
    - at the end of the questioning, read the record of evidence to the person being questioned and ask him to sign it and
    - if the person refuses to sign it, note that refusal on the record of evidence.
- Where the order is to attend **before a judge**
  - The judgment creditor or his representative **must attend** and conduct the questioning if the hearing is before a judge. The questioning will be conducted by the judgment creditor or his representative, and the standard questions in the forms in Appendixes A and B will not be used. The proceedings will be tape recorded and the court will not make a written record of the evidence.

Failure to comply with order

- If a person against whom such an order has been made
  - fails to attend court
  - refuses at the hearing to take the oath or to answer any question or
  - otherwise fails to comply with the order

  the court will refer the matter to a High Court judge or Circuit Judge.

- That judge may make a committal order against the person [if the judgment creditor has complied with rules 71.4 and 71.5 (not on your syllabus this year)].

- If a committal order is made, the judge will direct that
  - the order shall be suspended provided that the person
    - attends court at a time and place specified in the order and
    - complies with all the terms of that order and the original order and
  - if the person fails to comply with any term on which the committal order is suspended, she shall be brought before a judge to consider whether the committal order should be discharged.

A judgment creditor may, except where an enactment, rule or PD provides otherwise, use **ANY METHOD** of enforcement which is **AVAILABLE** and use **MORE THAN ONE METHOD** of enforcement, **EITHER AT THE SAME TIME OR ONE AFTER ANOTHER.**

Factors affecting the choice of method or methods of execution will depend on what assets the judgment debtor has and also how quickly the judgment creditor wishes or needs to get hold of the money.

Stay of execution

A judgment debtor can ask the court for a stay of execution to give her time to pay.

Enforcement of judgment or order by or against non-party

If a judgment or order is given or made in favour of or against a person who is not a party to proceedings, it may be enforced by or against that person by the same methods as if she were a party.

The court may order an act to be done at expense of the disobedient party

Where a party has not complied with a mandatory order, an injunction or a judgment or order for the specific performance of a contract, then that means they are the disobedient party.

The court may direct that the act required to be done may, so far as practicable, be done by another person, being

- the party by whom the order or judgment was obtained; or
- some other person appointed by the court.

The costs to another person of doing the act will be borne by the disobedient party. Upon the act being done the expenses incurred may be ascertained in such manner as the court directs and execution may issue against the disobedient party for the amount so ascertained and for costs.

This is without prejudice to

- the court's powers under section 39 of the Senior Courts Act 1981, i.e. execution of an instrument by a person nominated by the High Court,
  - where the High Court has given or made a judgment or order directing a person to execute any conveyance, contract or other document, or to indorse any negotiable instrument, then, if that person
    - neglects or refuses to comply with the judgment or order; or
    - cannot after reasonable inquiry be found,

    the High Court may, on such terms and conditions, if any, as may be just, order the conveyance, contract or other document to be executed, or the negotiable instrument to be indorsed, by such person as the court may nominate for that purpose.
  - A conveyance, contract, document or instrument executed or indorsed in pursuance of an section 39 order operates, and is for all purposes available, as if it had been executed or indorsed by the person originally directed to execute or indorse it

and also without prejudice to the court's powers to punish the disobedient party for contempt.

The mechanics of how enforcement of money judgments works

The available methods of enforcing may be remembered using the acronym **CARTSS**.

I will first set out the methods and where transfer of proceedings for enforcement is necessary. Secondly, I will give more detail on each of the methods of enforcement of judges and orders.

EM: transfer of proceedings for enforcement

When transfer of court is necessary

- **C**ontrol – Warrant of Control in the County Court, Writ of Control in the High Court for taking control of goods

  *Where the judgment or order was for **less than £600** in the High Court, for enforcement by this method, MUST TRANSFER to County Court*

  *Where the judgment or order was for **over £5k** in the County Court, for enforcement by this method, MUST TRANSFER to High Court The creditor makes a request in writing to the court for a certificate of judgment for the purpose of enforcing the judgment or order in the High Court, stating that it is intended to enforce the judgment or order by taking control of goods. The grant of a certificate by the court – the certificate may be signed by a court officer - will take effect as an order to transfer the proceedings to the High Court and the transfer will have effect on the grant of that certificate. The County Court will give notice to the debtor that the proceedings have been transferred and make an entry of the fact of transfer in the court records.*

  The request for the certificate will not be dealt with whilst any of the following proceedings are pending
  - *an application for a variation in the date or rate of payment of money due under a judgment or order*
  - *an application for a judgment or order to be set aside, where a party does not attend court and the court gives judgment or makes an order against her*

- *an application to set aside or vary a default judgment*
- *a request for an administration order or*
- *an application for a stay of execution under section 88 of the County Courts Act 1984.*

– **A**ttachment of earnings order

Where the judgment or order was made in the High Court, for enforcement by this method, MUST TRANSFER to County Court as attachment of earnings orders can only be granted in the County Court Money Claims Centre.

– **R**eceiver to be appointed. Not necessary to transfer.

– **T**hird Party Debt order. Not necessary to transfer.

– **S**um of less than £5k in respect of which a Charging Order was made.

Where the judgment or order was made in the High Court, for enforcement by this method, MUST TRANSFER to County Court Money Claims Centre

– **S**ale of real property as a result of a Charging Order where the sum owed is greater than £350k

Where the judgment or order was made in the County Court, for enforcement by this method, MUST TRANSFER to High Court The creditor makes a request in writing to the court for a certificate of judgment for the purpose of enforcing the judgment or order in the High Court, confirming that an application has been made for an order under section 42 of the County Courts Act 1984 [6](transfer to High Court by order of the County Court) and attaching a copy of the application to the request for a certificate.
The grant of a certificate by the court – the certificate may be signed by a court officer - will take effect as an order to transfer the proceedings to the High Court and the transfer will have effect on the grant of that certificate. The County Court will give notice to the debtor that the proceedings have been transferred and make an entry of the fact of transfer in the court records.

The request for the certificate will not be dealt with whilst any of the following proceedings are pending

- *an application for a variation in the date or rate of payment of money due under a judgment or order*
- *an application for a judgment or order to be set aside, where a party does not attend court and the court gives judgment or makes an order against her*
- *an application to set aside or vary a default judgment*
- *a request for an administration order or*
- *an application for a stay of execution under section 88 of the County Courts Act 1984.*

Activity

Remember to make notes on the relevant case law authorities in paragraphs 70.3.2 in the commentary in the White Book.

You may find it useful to add in references to the case law NOW at the appropriate points of this Chapter. Etc!

Further steps for enforcement after any necessary transfer of court has taken place

Taking **C**ontrol of goods - Where and how to make applications

Activity

Remember in addition to make notes on the editorial introduction to CPR Part 84, paragraph 84.0.2-3 in the White Book as the syllabus says "Note. Students should be familiar with this editorial introduction."

Apply to the correct court in accordance with the procedure in Part 23 as modified by Part 84, as follows.

- If there has been a transfer then apply to the High Court or the County Court hearing centre to which the claim has been transferred or sent, unless there is good reason to make the application to a different court.
- Where there are no pre-existing proceedings, an application to take control of goods must be made to the County Court

The result of a successful application is that the **enforcement agent (County Court)** or **enforcement officer (High Court)** removes / secures goods to the value of the debt owed in order to sell them; or enters into a controlled goods agreement with the judgment debtor. Any removal, securing or agreement does not include domestic appliances or 'tools of the trade' of which they may not take control.
They can use only reasonably necessary force at the home/place of business of the judgment debtor and entry must be via a door or normal place of entry.

Do take special note of the names of the methods of enforcement:

Warrant of control in **County** Court; or
Writ of control in **High** Court.

Both are valid for 12 months.

After, where, necessary, transferring to the correct court for enforcement (*see the section in italics on previous pages of this Chapter*), the judgment creditor then makes a request to court with a draft warrant of control (if in County Court) or a draft writ of control (if in High Court) and pays the fee, provided none of the situations requiring court permission issue a warrant or writ (set out below) are not present.

Where permission is needed to issue the warrant or writ

A writ or warrant must not be issued without the **permission of the court** where
- six years or more have elapsed since the date of the judgment or order
- any change has taken place, whether by death or otherwise, in the parties
  - entitled to enforce the judgment or order or
  - liable to have it enforced against them
- the judgment or order is against the assets of a deceased person coming into the hands of that person's executors or administrators after the date of the judgment or order, and it is sought to issue execution against such assets;

- any goods to be seized under the writ or warrant are in the hands of a receiver appointed by a court or sequestrator
- under the judgment or order, any person is entitled to a remedy subject to the fulfilment of any condition, and it is alleged that the condition has been fulfilled (other than where non-compliance with the terms of suspension of enforcement of the judgment or order is the failure to pay money) or
- the permission sought is for a writ of control and that writ is to be in aid of another writ of control
  - This last is without prejudice to section 2 of the Reserve and Auxiliary Forces (Protection of Civil Interests) Act 1951 and any enactment, rule or direction by virtue of which a person is required to obtain the permission of the court for the issue of a warrant or to proceed to execution or otherwise to the enforcement of a judgment or order.

An **application for permission** may be made in accordance with Part 23 and must
- identify the judgment or order to which the application relates
- if the judgment or order is for the payment of money, state the amount originally due and, if different, the amount due at the date the application notice is filed
- where six years or more have elapsed since the date of the judgment or order, state the reasons for the delay in enforcing the judgment or order
- where any change has taken place, state the change which has taken place in the parties entitled or liable to execution since the date of the judgment or order
  - If because of one event an applicant seeks permission to enforce more than one judgment or order, the applicant need only make one application for permission.
  - a schedule must be attached to the application for permission, specifying all the judgments or orders in respect of which the application for permission is made and
  - if the application notice is directed to be served on any person, it need set out only such part of the application as affects that person.
- where the assets are now in the hands of executors, administrators, or court appointed receivers or sequestrators, state that a demand to satisfy the judgment or order was made on the person liable to satisfy it and that that person has refused or failed to do so
- give such other information as is necessary to satisfy the court that the applicant is entitled to proceed to execution on the judgment or order, and that the person against whom it is sought to issue execution is liable to execution on it.

An application for permission **may be made without notice** being served on any other party unless the court directs otherwise.

Where the court grants permission for the issue of a writ of control or a writ of execution and the writ is not issued within one year after the date of the permission order, the permission order will cease to have effect. In this case, the court may grant a fresh permission order.

Activity

Remember in addition to make notes on the editorial introduction to CPR Part 83, paragraph 83.0.2-3 and the second paragraph of 83.0.17 in the White Book as the syllabus says "Note. Students should be familiar with this editorial introduction."

Once a warrant or writ is granted, at least 7 clear days' notice in prescribed form is given by the enforcement agent/officer to the debtor at her home or business address.

If this prompts payment, the property is returned. If this does not prompt the judgment debtor to pay, she is given 7 clear days' notice of the sale by auction of the controlled goods, following valuation.

Attachment of earnings order - Where to make applications

Activity

Remember in addition to make notes on the editorial introduction to CPR Part 89, paragraph 89.0.1 in the White Book as the syllabus says "Note. Students should be familiar with this editorial introduction."

An application to the County Court for an attachment of earnings order must be made to the **County Court Money Claims Centre.** Responses to the application will be dealt with there, but where the judgment debtor does not respond the process will be sent to a local County Court hearing centre.

An application for an attachment of earnings order must include a certificate of the amount of money remaining due under the judgment or order and that the whole or part of any instalment due remains unpaid.

Where an attachment of earnings order is sought to enforce an order of a magistrates' court, the applicant must also file with the application

- a certified copy of the order; and
- a witness statement verifying the amount due under the order or, if payments under the order are required to be made to the designated officer for the magistrates' court, a certificate by that designated officer to the same effect.

EM*: *Section 6(1)-(5) of the Attachment of Earnings Act 1971 at paragraph 9B-965 of Volume 2 of 'Civil Procedure' (the White Book) 2020

CONSEQUENCES OF ATTACHMENT ORDER

Effect and contents of an attachment of earnings order.

The order is directed to a person who appears to the court / fines officer to have the debtor in his **employment**; i.e.one of them as a principal and not as a servant or agent, pays to the other any sums defined as earnings by section 24 of the Act.

The order shall contain prescribed particulars enabling the debtor to be identified by the employer.

The order specifies the whole amount payable under the relevant adjudication (or so much of that amount as remains unpaid), including any relevant costs.

The order directs the employer to (a) make periodical deductions - e.g. weekly or monthly - from the debtor's earnings and (b) to pay the amounts deducted at such times as the order may require, to the collecting officer of the court, as specified in the order.

- These "attachable earnings", in relation to a pay-day, are the earnings which remain payable to the debtor on that day after deduction by the employer of income tax and other statutory deductions.
- The order will also set out
  - the amount to be deducted from the judgment debtor's earnings on a pay-day
  - the level of protected earnings, below which the judgment debtor's available earnings should not be reduced
    - ❖ In the case of an attachment of earnings order made to secure the payment of a judgment debt or payments under an administration order, the employer shall on any pay-day
      - if the attachable earnings exceed the protected earnings, deduct from the attachable earnings the amount of the excess or the normal deduction, whichever is the less
      - make no deduction if the attachable earnings are equal to, or less than, the protected earnings
    - ❖ Where it is not a case of an attachment of earnings order made to secure the payment of a judgment debt or payments under an administration order, if on a pay-day the attachable earnings exceed the sum of
      - the protected earnings; and
      - so much of any amount by which the attachable earnings on any previous pay-day fell short of the protected earnings as has not been made good by virtue of this sub-paragraph on another previous pay-day,

      then, in so far as the excess allows, the employer shall deduct from the attachable earnings the amount as follows

      - ➢ the normal deduction; and
      - ➢ so much of the normal deduction on any previous pay-day as was not deducted on that day and has not been paid by virtue of this sub-paragraph on any other previous pay-day.

      - No deduction shall be made on any pay-day when the attachable earnings are equal to, or less than, the protected earnings.
      - In the case of an attachment of earnings order made under Schedule 5 to the Courts Act 2003, the employer shall make deductions from the debtor's earnings in accordance with fines collection regulations made under that Schedule.
  - the dates to be taken as the start and end dates of the attachment of earnings order.

<u>The meaning of "earnings"</u>

Earnings include

- fees, wages, bonus and commission, salary, overtime pay or other emoluments payable in addition to wages or salary or payable under a contract of service
- pension (including an annuity in respect of past services, whether or not rendered to the person paying the annuity, and including periodical payments by way of compensation for the loss, abolition or relinquishment, or diminution in the emoluments, of any office or employment
- statutory sick pay.

Earnings do **NOT** include

- sums payable by any public department of the Government of Northern Ireland or of a territory outside the United Kingdom
- pay or allowances payable to the debtor as a member of Her Majesty's forces [other than pay or allowances payable by his employer to him as a special member of a reserve force (within the meaning of the Reserve Forces Act 1996)];
- a tax credit (within the meaning of the Tax Credits Act 2002);**]**
- pension, allowances or benefit payable under any [enactment relating to social security;]
- pension or allowances payable in respect of disablement or disability;
- [except in relation to a maintenance order] wages payable to a person as a seaman - "seaman" includes every person (except masters and pilots) employed or engaged in any capacity on board any ship - ; and
- other than wages – including emoluments - payable to him as a seaman of a fishing boat - "fishing boat" means a vessel of whatever size, and in whatever way propelled, which is for the time being employed in sea fishing or in the sea-fishing service;
- guaranteed minimum pension within the meaning of the [Pension Schemes Act 1993].]

Where the judgment debtor is employed and has missed one instalment following the judgment and there are no other available assets the judgment creditor can

- make a request to the court.
- The court sends to the judgment debtor a questionnaire in advance of a hearing
- The judgment debtor completes the questionnaire which is considered in the absence of the parties by a court administration officer
- If an order is made it is served on the parties
- If the court officer does not make an order or if there are any objections the matter will go before the District Judge

Receiver to be appointed.

Where a company borrows money from a bank it will normally sign a loan document called a debenture with a fixed charge over real property and a floating charge over other assets. This offers the bank security over the assets of the company.

If the terms of the agreement are breached or the company does not conform to the bank's wishes, the bank as charge holder may appoint a receiver to administer and receive the company's assets. The receiver's duty is to collect the debt to the bank.

Third Party Debt order

Activity

Remember in addition to make notes on the editorial introduction to CPR Part 72, paragraphs 72.0.1 and 72.2.15 in the White Book as the syllabus says "Note. Students should be familiar with this editorial introduction."

This is an order obtained from the court on application by the judgment creditor, ordering a third party to pay directly to the judgment creditor the amount owed by the judgment debtor.

The third party could be for example the debtor's bank, or her tenant or client, because

- When the account is in credit, her bank owes the money in her account to her
  - the account must be in her sole name if a third party debt order is applied for
  - 'bank or building society' includes any person carrying on a business in the course of which he lawfully accepts deposits in the United Kingdom
- tenants may owe money to her as a landlord
- people to whom she has provided services may yet be to pay her

Obtaining a third party debt order is a two stage process.

- **The first stage** is an **interim order**.
  - Apply to court, filing an application notice in Practice Form N349. **It** must contain the following information
    - the name and address of the judgment debtor
    - details of the judgment or order sought to be enforced
    - the amount of money remaining due under the judgment or order
    - if the judgment debt is payable by instalments, the amount of any instalments which have fallen due and remain unpaid
    - the name and address of the third party
    - if the third party is a bank or building society
      - its name and the address of the branch at which the judgment debtor's account is believed to be held and
      - the account number
      - or, if the judgment creditor does not know all or part of this information, that fact
    - confirmation that to the best of the judgment creditor's knowledge or belief the third party
      - is within the jurisdiction; and
      - owes money to or holds money to the credit of the judgment debtor
    - if the judgment creditor knows or believes that any person other than the judgment debtor has any claim to the money owed by the third party
      - his name and (if known) his address and
      - such information as is known to the judgment creditor about his claim
    - details of any other applications for third party debt orders issued by the judgment creditor in respect of the same judgment debt and
    - the sources or grounds of the judgment creditor's knowledge or belief of the matters referred to in these final three white circles

    It must be verified by a statement of truth.

    The court will not grant speculative applications for third party debt orders, and will only make an interim third party debt order against a bank or building society if the judgment creditor's application notice contains evidence to substantiate his belief that the judgment debtor has an account with the bank or building society in question.

  - The application may be without notice and is considered without a hearing
  - It must be issued in the court which made the judgment or order which it is sought to enforce
  - If the interim order is made the judge fixes a date for the second stage hearing, directing that the third party cannot make any payment which would reduce the amount s/he owes to the judgment debtor to less than the amount specified in the order

- The interim order is served on the third party not less than 21 days before the second stage hearing. The third party must now freeze anything s/he owes to the judgment debtor
- The interim order is served on the judgment debtor not less than 7 days after the copy order was served on the third party and not less than 7 days before the second stage hearing. A certificate of service is needed if the interim order is served by the judgment creditor and not by the court.
- Any written objections to a final third party debt order are to be filed not less than 3 days before the second stage hearing

– **The second stage** is the **hearing** to consider whether a final order should be made. This will be not less than 28 days after the interim order was made. The court may
  - discharge the interim order
  - decide/direct a trial on any issues
  - make a final third party debt order, ordering the third party to pay
    - the amount of any debt due or accruing due to the judgment debtor the judgment creditor or
    - so much of that debt as is sufficient to satisfy the judgment debt and the judgment creditor's costs of the application

      Any requirement on the account that a receipt for money deposited in the account must be produced before any money is withdrawn will be disregarded when considering whether or not to grant a third party debt order.

      The equivalent amount paid to the judgment creditor is thus expunged from the third party's debt to the judgment debtor.

<u>S. S.</u> – <u>Application for a Charging Order</u>

This is an order obtained from the court to put a charge on an asset. This acts as security for the money judgment. You may remember charges and mortgages on the charges register of registered properties from your pre – BTC studies. This charge would be put on there and so may not be a first charge if there is a pre-existing mortgage or charge on the property. A judgment creditor may be running the risk of there being insufficient funds to pay his second or later charge once the first or previous charges on the property have been settled if he chooses this method of enforcement against real property.

Charges may also be obtained against stock or unit trust securities.

Obtaining a charging order is a two stage process.

An application for a charging order may be made without notice.

– **The first stage** is an **interim order**.
  - Apply to court
    - There is now centralised handling of the majority of applications for charging in orders in the County Court. Applications will be processed at the County Court Money Claims Centre and will be paper based for the most part. The address is

      County Court Money Claims Centre
      PO Box 527
      M5 0BY

    - An application to the County Court for a charging order over an interest in a fund in court must be made to the County Court hearing centre where the order or judgment was made.
    - Subject to the previous two paragraphs, a judgment creditor may apply for a single charging order in respect of more than one judgment or order against the same judgment debtor.
- How
    - An application for a charging order must be made by filing an application notice in Practice Form, one for if the application relates to land, another if the application relates to securities.
- The application must contain the following information
    - the name and address of the judgment debtor
    - details of the judgment or order sought to be enforced
    - the amount of money remaining due under the judgment or order
    - if the judgment debt is payable by instalments
    - whether the order was made on or after 1 October 2012 and
    - the amount of any instalments which have fallen due and remain unpaid
- if the judgment creditor knows of the existence of any other creditors of the judgment debtor, their names and (if known) their addresses;
- identification of the asset or assets which it is intended to charge including, where applicable, the title number under which any land upon which it is sought to impose a charge is registered;
- details of the judgment debtor's interest in the asset; and
- the names and addresses of the persons on whom an interim charging order must be served
    - the judgment debtor
    - any other creditors that the court directs such as a mortgagee
    - any co-owners
- The application must be verified by a statement of truth.

A judgment creditor may apply in a single application notice for charging orders over more than one asset, but if the court makes interim charging orders over more than one asset, it will draw up a separate order relating to each asset.

- The application may be considered without a hearing; A court officer at CCMCC may make the interim order providing certain conditions (not on your syllabus this year) are met in respect of a charge over land. If the interim order is made a date is fixed for the second stage hearing
- Once an interim order is made at the CCMCC and served on the judgment debtor, on any other creditors as the court directs such as a mortgagee and on any co-owners, the parties will have a period of 28 days between service on them of the interim order and referral to a judge to object to the making of the final charging order. If an objection is received the matter will be sent to a local County Court hearing centre. A certificate of service is needed if the interim order is served by the judgment creditor and not by the court.
- any written objections to a final charging order are to be filed not less than 7 days before the second stage hearing
- remember to register the interim order on the charges register of registered property (or at the central land charges registry should the property still be unregistered title)

- <u>**The second stage**</u> is the **hearing** to consider whether a final order should be made. The court may
    - discharge the interim order
    - decide/direct a trial on any issues

- make a final charging order. If made, remember to register the final order on the charges register of a registered property (or at the central land charges registry should the property still be unregistered title).

There will be no payment of the debt until the property is sold; or if money is needed now the judgment creditor can bring a Part 8 claim to claim an order for sale if the judgment debtor is sole owner. If the property is co-owned an order for sale would be pursuant to the Trusts of Land and Appointment of Trustees Act 2002.

Activity

Remember in addition to make notes on the editorial introduction to CPR Part 73, paragraph 73.0.1 and 73.0.4 (1) and (2) in the White Book as the syllabus says "Note. Students should be familiar with this editorial introduction."

Effect of setting aside judgment or order

If a judgment or order is set aside, any enforcement of the judgment or order shall cease to have effect unless the court otherwise orders.

EM: Enforcement of settlements following ADR

Activity

Remember to incorporate the relevant paragraphs from The Jackson ADR Handbook (Second Edition, 2016):-

20.02, and 20.09 (including Table 1)

You may find it useful to add in references to the case law NOW at the appropriate points of this chapter.

When approaching final revision time, remember to add in the salient findings of the cases at the relevant point in any 'mental crib sheet' into which you have distilled the main points of your learned knowledge.

Chapter 25

Elements of the syllabus which you have now covered

- A cell with heavy outlining means that that area of the syllabus was covered in this Chapter;
- A darkly shaded cell with a tick √ means that the whole of that syllabus element has now been covered;
- A lightly shaded cell means that part of that element of the syllabus has been covered in a previous Chapter; and
- An unshaded cell means that element of the syllabus has not yet been covered.

1.1 √	1.2 √	1.3 √	2.1 √	2.2 √	3.1 √	3.2 √	6.1 √	6.2 √	6.3 √
6.4 √	7.1 √	7.2 √	8.1 √	8.2 √	8.3 √	9.1 √	9.2 √	9.3 √	10.1 √
10.2 √	11.1 √	11.2 √	12.1 √	12.2 √	12.3 √	13.1 √	13.2 √	13.3 √	13.4 √
13.5 √	13.6 √	13.7 √	13.8 √	14.1 √	14.2 √	14.3 √	14.4 √	14.5 √	14.6 √
15.1 √	15.2 √	15.3 √	15.4 √	16.1 √	16.2 √	17.1 √	17.2 √	17.3 √	17.4 √
18.1 √	18.2. √ 16.3 √	16.4 √ 18.5 √	19.1 √	19.2 √	19.3 √	20.1 √	20.2 √	20.3 √	21.1 √
21.2 √	21.3 √	22.1 √	22.2 √	23.1 √	23.2 √	23.3 √	23.4 √	24.1	

Elements of the syllabus which you have now covered for **ADR**

- A cell with heavy outlining means that that area of the syllabus was covered in this Chapter;
- A darkly shaded cell with a tick √ means that the whole of that syllabus element has now been covered;
- A lightly shaded cell means that part of that element of the syllabus has been covered in a previous Chapter; and
- An unshaded cell means that element of the syllabus has not yet been covered.

1.4 √	1.5√	3.3 √	4.1√	4.2√	5.1√	5.2√	18.1 √	22.3 √ record	22.3 √ enforce

Chapter 26

APPEALS [CUR 24]

s) Appeals

THIS CHAPTER CONTAINS THE ITEMS PRINTED IN BOLD IN THE FOLLOWING BOXES

CURRICULUM ("CUR")

Appeals
24.1 Civil appeals in England and Wales (excluding appeals to the Supreme Court)

SYLLABUS

> ***Examinable material will consist of permission to appeal, routes of appeal, time for appealing, appellant's notice, grounds on which appeals may succeed, appeal court powers, hearing of appeals, fresh evidence in appeals, respondent's notice, and skeleton arguments***
>
> ***(Each of the above has its own subheading in this chapter, flagged by EM:)***
>
> - **CPR 52.1**
> - **CPR 52.3-7**
> - **CPR 52.12-16**
> - **CPR 52.20;**
> - **CPR 52.21 (hearing of appeals)**
> - **PD52A Section 3 (destinations of appeal), Section 4 (obtaining permission to appeal and allocation of appeals) and Section 5 (skeleton arguments)**
> - **Commentary is incorporated in context in this chapter, highlighted in an Activity box between two stars**

CHAPTER 26 MOCS

The broad outline in ascending order of Courts is

- **FIRST APPEALS WITHIN THE COUNTY COURT**

  FROM DISTRICT JUDGE TO CIRCUIT JUDGE

  Appeal regarding **any** decision except for

  - Non-insolvency proceedings brought THROUGH the COMPANIES ACTS
  - Individual insolvency
  - Corporate insolvency
  - Family

- **FIRST APPEALS FROM THE COUNTY COURT TO THE HIGH COURT**

  a) Mostly FROM DISTRICT JUDGE IN COUNTY COURT TO HIGH COURT JUDGE, unless stated differently here

  Appeal regarding

  - **Non-insolvency** proceedings brought **through** the **Companies Acts**
  - **Individual insolvency** [unless it is an appeal from an ICC Judge. These appeals must be filed in the RCJ and heard by a Registrar in Bankruptcy.]
  - **Corporate insolvency** [unless it is an appeal from an ICC Judge. These appeals must be filed in the RCJ and heard by a Registrar in Bankruptcy**; {**except where the appeal is from a District Judge in District Registry, Supervisors in Business and Property Courts may then allow it to be heard by Circuit Judge acting as a judge of the High Court.}**]**
  - Family

  b) FROM CIRCUIT JUDGE OR RECORDER IN COUNTY COURT TO HIGH COURT JUDGE

  Appeal regarding any decision

- **FIRST APPEALS FROM THE HIGH COURT TO THE HIGH COURT**

  APPEALS FROM MASTERS, REGISTRARS AND DISTRICT JUDGES IN THE HIGH COURT TO HIGH COURT JUDGE

- **FIRST APPEALS FROM THE HIGH COURT TO THE COURT OF APPEAL**

The sessions dealing with this area of the syllabus on my BTC course are	

CUR 24.1 CIVIL APPEALS IN ENGLAND AND WALES (EXCLUDING APPEALS TO THE SUPREME COURT)

EM: appeal court powers

A decision made in a lower court can be appealed to a higher, appellate court.

Subject to any rule, enactment or PD which sets out special provisions with regard to any particular category of appeal, in relation to an appeal the appeal court **has all the powers of the lower court.** It may exercise its powers in relation to the whole or part of an order of the lower court.

Appeal courts can
- affirm / set aside / vary any order or judgment made or given by the lower court
- refer any claim or issue for determination by the lower court
- order a new trial or hearing [In an appeal from a claim tried with a jury (e.g. some defamation claims) the Court of Appeal may, instead of ordering a new trial make an order for damages or vary an award of damages made by the jury.
- make orders for the payment of interest
- make a costs order. (Where a Part 36 offer was made in the main proceedings, a new offer needs to be made where a party wants Part 36 protection in relation to the appeal).

If the appeal court strikes out an appellant's notice, dismisses an appeal or refuses an application for permission to appeal and it considers that the application, the appellant's notice or the appeal is totally **without merit,** the court's order **must record** the fact that it considers the application, the appellant's notice or the appeal to be totally without merit and must at the same time consider whether it is appropriate to make a civil restraint order.

You will recall from Chapter 15 on **security for costs,** from boxes c) and d) at the beginning of that Chapter that

- the court may order security for costs of an appeal against an appellant or against a respondent who also appeals, on the same grounds as set out in that Chapter; and

- the court may also make such an order where the appellant, or the respondent who also appeals, is a limited company and there is reason to believe it will be unable to pay the costs of the other parties to the appeal should its appeal be unsuccessful.

Further, it goes without saying that by the time an appeal is reached, the AOS/Defence were filed long ago at the beginning of the claim.

Unless LC or AC orders otherwise, or the appeal is from the Immigration and Asylum Chamber of the Upper Tribunal, bringing an appeal does not stay the decision of the lower court and the decision can be enforced. Therefore **A should apply for a stay of the proceedings in the lower court when applying for permission to appeal.**

EM: grounds on which appeals may succeed

The test is RPOS or SOCR.

PERMISSION TO APPEAL

EM: permission to appeal

In a few pages' time there is a group of tables consolidating the tables relevant to the assessment in the White Book, showing routes of first appeals, permission to appeal and allocation of appeals and other detail of first appeals.

The detail of the second columns regarding permission is set out here in this permission to appeal section.

Need permission

[**Unless** the appeal is against

- a commital order (i.e. a person in contempt of court wants to appeal an immediate or suspended prison sentence)
- refusal to grant habeas corpus
- a Children Act secure accommodation order

so then A simply notifies R that he is appealing against one of those.]

Permission from either the lower court orally at the end of the hearing in the lower court after costs have been awarded - the test is RPOS or SOCR; the lower court may adjourn the hearing to give a party an opportunity to apply for permission to appeal,

or where the lower court refuses permission to appeal or where no application is made to the lower court, by applying to the **appellate court** in an appeal notice.

APPEALS WITHIN THE COUNTY COURT

The Designated Civil Judge in consultation with the appropriate Presiding or Supervising Judge has responsibility for allocating appeals from decisions of District Judges in the County Court to Circuit Judges and/or Recorders. Such an appeal may only be allocated to a Recorder in exceptional circumstances.

PERMISSION TO APPEAL FROM THE COUNTY COURT TO THE HIGH COURT

First, some definitions

'Group C Judge' - a person authorised to act as a judge of the High Court, being the Senior President of Tribunals or a Circuit Judge

'Group A Judge' - a person authorised to act as a judge of the High Court, being a judge of the Court of Appeal, a person who has been one, or a person who has been a puisne judge of the High Court

Proceedings brought **pursuant to the Companies Acts**

Where the appeal is from a District Judge in proceedings brought **pursuant to the Companies Acts**, permission to appeal to the High Court will be dealt with as follows.

- Applications for permission to appeal must be heard in accordance with the following provisions
  - if the appeal centre is the RCJ, by a salaried Registrar in Bankruptcy; or
  - in any other appeal centre, by
    - a Group C Judge or
    - a Group A Judge who is
      - a judge allocated to the Insolvency and Companies List of the Business and Property Courts or is
      - authorised by the Chancellor of the High Court to **hear the appeal** in any other appeal centre

Proceedings **NOT** brought pursuant to the Companies Acts

Where the appeal is from a District Judge in proceedings which are **NOT** brought **pursuant to the Companies Acts**, applications for permission to appeal must be heard by a Group A Judge.

PERMISSION FOR APPEALS FROM MASTERS, REGISTRARS AND DISTRICT JUDGES OF THE HIGH COURT

From Masters in the High Court

Applications for permission to appeal must be heard by a Group A Judge

From Registrars in the High Court

Applications for permission to appeal must be heard by a Group A Judge.

From District Judges in the High Court

Applications for permission to appeal must be heard by a Group A Judge.

PERMISSION TO APPEAL IN RELATION TO CASE MANAGEMENT DECISION

Where the application is for permission to **appeal from a case management decision,** the court dealing with the application may take into account whether
- the issue is of sufficient significance to justify the costs of an appeal
- the procedural consequences of an appeal (e.g. loss of trial date) outweigh the significance of the case management decision
- it would be more convenient to determine the issue at or after trial.

Case management decisions include decisions made under rule 3.1(2) – the court's general powers of management - and decisions about disclosure, filing of witness statements or experts' reports, directions about the timetable of the claim, adding a party to a claim and security for costs.

EM: appellant's notice

Where the appellant seeks permission from the appeal court, it must be requested in the appellant's notice.

Permission to appeal is sought in an appeal notice, (form N161 or N164 (small claims track)).

Contents of the **Appellant's Appeal Notice** applying for permission to appeal

The notice is on form **N161**, to set out
- why the LC was wrong; whether the appeal is on an error of fact/law; A needs to show that no reasonable judge using discretion could have reached the same decision
- may include an application to vary the time limit for appealing (i.e. if out of time for this)
- may include application for interim remedies

EM: time for appealing

The appellant must file the appellant's notice at the appeal court within such period as may be directed by the lower court (which may be longer or shorter than 21 days).

Where the court makes no such direction, [and subject to matters not on your syllabus this year], 21 days after the date of the decision of the lower court which the appellant wishes to appeal.

Unless the appeal court orders otherwise, an appellant's notice must be served on each respondent as soon as practicable and in any event not later than 7 days after it is filed.

Variation of time

An application to vary the time limit for filing an appeal notice must be made to the appeal court.

The parties may not agree to extend any date or time set by

- the CPR, or
- Practice Direction 52A (and others not on your syllabus this year) (those on your syllabus are Section 3 destinations of appeal, Section 4 obtaining permission to appeal and Section 5 skeleton arguments; these are all included in this Chapter); or
- an order of the appeal court or the lower court.

(Rule 3.1(2)(a) provides that the court may extend or shorten the time for compliance with any rule, practice direction or court order (even if an application for extension is made after the time for compliance has expired).

(Rule 3.1(2)(b) provides that the court may adjourn or bring forward a hearing.)

More on permission to appeal

Where an appellant seeks permission to appeal against a decision to refuse to grant an interim injunction under section 41 of the Policing and Crime Act 2009 the appellant is not required to serve the appellant's notice on the respondent.

A needs AC permission if A subsequently wishes to amend the AN.

Where a party attempts to file an AN in a court which does not have jurisdiction to issue the notice, a court officer may notify that party in writing that the appeal court does not have jurisdiction in respect of the notice.

Before doing so the court officer must confer with a judge of the appeal court or where the Court of Appeal is the appeal court, with a court officer who exercises the jurisdiction of that Court under rule 52.24. (Rule 52.24 is not on your syllabus this year)

A judge hearing an application for permission to appeal may, in what is known as a "rolled-up" hearing, hear the application for permission to appeal and the appeal at the same time, if possible and appropriate.

Pursuant to the court's general powers of management, an order giving permission to appeal, where it is needed and granted may

- limit the issues to be heard
- be made subject to conditions.
- order security for costs
-

ALLOCATION OF APPEALS

In a few pages' time there is a group of tables consolidating the tables relevant to the assessment in the White Book, showing routes of first appeals, permission to appeal and allocation of appeals and other detail of first appeals.

The detail of the fourth columns regarding allocation of appeals is set out here in this allocation of appeals section.

APPEALS WITHIN THE COUNTY COURT

The Designated Civil Judge in consultation with the appropriate Presiding or Supervising Judge has responsibility for allocating appeals from decisions of District Judges in the County Court to Circuit Judges and/or Recorders. Such an appeal may only be allocated to a Recorder in exceptional circumstances.

APPEALS FROM THE COUNTY COURT TO THE HIGH COURT

First, two more definitions.

'Group D Judge' - a person authorised to act as a judge of the High Court, being a

- recorder or
- person who is
    - a Chamber President, or a Deputy Chamber President, of a chamber of the Upper Tribunal or of a chamber of the First-tier Tribunal,
    - a judge of the Upper Tribunal
    - a transferred-in judge of the Upper Tribunal
    - a deputy judge of the Upper Tribunal or
    - the President of Employment Tribunals

‘Group B Judge’ - any person who is authorised to act as a judge of the High Court, being a

- puisne judge of the High Court
- circuit judge
- recorder or
- person who is
  - a Chamber President, or a Deputy Chamber President, of a chamber of the Upper Tribunal or of a chamber of the First-tier Tribunal,
  - a judge of the Upper Tribunal
  - a transferred-in judge of the Upper Tribunal
  - a deputy judge of the Upper Tribunal or
  - the President of Employment Tribunals

Proceedings brought **pursuant to the Companies Acts**

Where the appeal is from a District Judge in proceedings brought **pursuant to the Companies Acts,** appeal to the High Court will be dealt with as follows.

If permission to appeal was needed and is given, or if it was not needed

- for appeals in which the appeal centre is the RCJ: appeals must be heard by a Registrar

- for appeals in any other appeal centre, appeals may be heard by a Group A Judge or a Group B Judge, provided that
  - the Group A Judge is a judge allocated to the Insolvency and Companies List of the Business and Property Courts or is authorised by the Chancellor of the High Court to hear the appeal;
  - if the Group B judge is a Group D Judge, they have been authorised by the Supervising Judge of the Business and Property Courts to hear the appeal;
  - if the Group B Judge is a Group C Judge, they have appropriate authorisation.

(Note: the Practice Direction Insolvency Proceedings makes provision for obtaining permission to appeal and allocation of appeals in insolvency proceedings.) This is included in the consolidating Table in a few pages’ time.

Proceedings which are **NOT** brought pursuant to the Companies Acts

Where the appeal is from a District Judge in proceedings which are **NOT** brought **pursuant to the Companies Acts**, appeal to the High Court will be dealt with as follows.

If permission to appeal was needed and is given, or if it was not needed

- where the appeal is from a Recorder, the appeal may be heard by either
  - a Group A Judge or,
  - in exceptional circumstances, a Group C Judge authorised to hear the appeal by the Appropriate Presiding or Supervising Judge

- in all other cases, the appeal may be heard by either
  - a Group A Judge or,
  - in exceptional circumstances, a Group D Judge authorised to hear the appeal by the Appropriate Presiding or Supervising Judge.

APPEALS FROM MASTERS, REGISTRARS AND DISTRICT JUDGES IN THE HIGH COURT TO HIGH COURT JUDGE

From Masters in the High Court

If permission to appeal was needed and is given, or if it was not needed,

the appeal may be heard by a

- Group A Judge or a
- Group B Judge authorised to hear the appeal by the Judge in Charge of the Queen's Bench List or the Chancellor of the High Court.

From Registrars in the High Court

If permission to appeal was needed and is given, or if it was not needed

the appeal must be heard by a Group A Judge.

From District Judges in the High Court

If permission to appeal was needed and is given, or if it was not needed

the appeal may be heard by either a

- Group A Judge
- Group C Judge sitting in the High Court or
- in exceptional circumstances, a Group D Judge authorised to hear the appeal by the Appropriate Presiding or Supervising Judge.

APPLICATIONS WITHIN APPEALS TO THE HIGH COURT AND WITHIN THE COUNTY COURT

Applications within appeals other than applications for permission to appeal but including applications for a stay of execution, may be heard and directions in the appeal given, by any judge who may hear the appeal, could be authorised to hear the appeal, or to whom the appeal could be allocated.

EM: grounds on which appeals may succeed - continued

Contents of the appeal bundle for filing and serving include:

- sealed copy of Appellant's notice including copy LC judgment transcript
- sealed copy of the order being appealed
- skeleton argument of A's Counsel [may be filed after the rest of the bundle, but within 14 days of the filing of the AN] (cost sanctions if don't); PDs to Part 52 set out the required contents of skeleton arguments. In addition please cross refer to your advocacy training
- relevant statements of case
- other matters that A considers reasonably necessary as set out in the PDs to Part 52.

Following service on R, as per the final diagram in this Chapter, there will be either a paper exercise or a hearing (both are referred to as hearings) to either grant or refuse permission to appeal.

Where the AC refuses permission to appeal

Where the lower appeal court refuses an application for permission to appeal, a further application for permission may be made to the appeal court. The order refusing permission will specify which is the appropriate AC and the level of judge who should hear it.

Where the AC grants permission to appeal

EM: respondent's notice

- A respondent **may** file and serve a respondent's notice.

- If the Respondent wishes to ask the appeal court to uphold or vary the order of the lower court for reasons different from or additional to those given by the lower court, the Respondent **must** file an appeal notice **(Respondent's Notice, form N162)** setting out those different/additional reasons or the grounds for variation. (This notice is not needed if the Respondent wishes the decision to be upheld for the same reasons as in lower court).

- Where the respondent seeks permission from the appeal court it must be requested in the respondent's notice.

- A respondent's notice must be filed within such period as may be directed by the lower court, or where the court makes no such direction, 14 days after one of the following
  - the date A's notice was served on her where
    - permission to appeal was given by the lower court; or
    - permission to appeal is not required;
  - the date the respondent is served with notification that the appeal court has given the appellant permission to appeal; or
  - the date the respondent is served with notification that the application for permission to appeal and the appeal itself are to be heard together.

  Should this be done out of time, any application for relief from a sanction, e.g. not to allow it, is governed by CPR 3.9 and Denton (see end Chapter 19).

- Unless the appeal court orders otherwise, The Respondent must serve it as soon as practicable, at the latest 7 days after it is filed, on the Appellant and on any other Respondent.

- This rule on respondent notices does not apply where the appellant is not required to serve the appellant's notice on the respondent or an appellant seeks permission to appeal against a decision to refuse to grant an interim injunction under section 41 of the Policing and Crime Act 2009.

- A must add the following documents to the appeal bundle for the appeal itself
  - R's notice and skeleton argument (if any)
  - the parts of transcript evidence directly relevant to the question at issue on the appeal
  - the order granting permission to appeal (or the transcript or note of the judgment where it was given at oral hearing)
  - any documents that A and R have agreed to add as a result of amendments agreed between A and R.

Where permission to appeal is refused on a particular issue A must remove documents relevant only to that issue from the bundle.

Transcripts at public expense

The lower court or the appeal court may direct, on the application of a party to the proceedings, that an official transcript of the judgment of the lower court, or of any part of the evidence or the proceedings in the lower court, be obtained at public expense for the purposes of an appeal.

Before making the direction the court must be satisfied that the applicant qualifies for fee remission or is otherwise in such poor financial circumstances that the cost of obtaining a transcript would be an excessive burden; **and** it is necessary in the interests of justice for such a transcript to be obtained.

Stay

Unless the appeal court or the lower court orders otherwise; or the appeal is from the Immigration and Asylum Chamber of the Upper Tribunal,

an appeal shall not operate as a stay of any order or decision of the lower court.

EM: routes of appeal

Tables 1, 2 and 3 appeal destinations tables in the White book may be depicted as in the following tables created by the author. In addition, they show

- a compilation of the routes for all proceedings, including family and insolvency proceedings,
- remind you to consider whether or not permission to appeal is needed,
- show to what type of Judge an application for permission to appeal may be made and
- by which type of Judge an appeal will be heard.

The appeal will take the form of a review of the decision, unless the court considers it would be in the interests of justice to hold a full hearing.

Final decisions

A final decision is a decision of a court that would finally determine, subject to any possible appeal or detailed assessment of costs, the entire proceedings whichever way the court decided the issues before it.

A decision is to be treated as a final decision for destination of appeal purposes where it is made at the conclusion of part of a hearing or trial which has been split into parts and would, if it had been made at the conclusion of that hearing or trial, have been a final decision.

The following are examples of final decisions
- a judgment on liability at the end of a split trial
- a judgment at the conclusion of an assessment of damages following a judgment on liability.

The following are examples of decisions that are not final
- a case management decision

- a grant or refusal of interim relief
- summary judgment
- striking out a claim or statement of case
- a summary or detailed assessment of costs
- an order for the enforcement of a final decision.

The tables which follow are in relation to first appeals and are set out in the order, of the contents of this Chapter so far.

ROUTE OF FIRST APPEAL

WITHIN THE COUNTY COURT

From DISTRICT JUDGE IN THE COUNTY COURT

to CIRCUIT JUDGE (OR EXCEPTIONALLY RECORDER) IN COUNTY COURT

Appeals from the lower court [20]	Need to apply for permission to appeal? **Yes** **Unless** against – a committal order – habeas corpus – Children secure accommodation	Decision under appeal	to the (appellate) [higher] court
→	Please read →	across the rows →	

District judge in the County Court	Need permission?	Except for • Non-insolvency proceedings brought THROUGH the COMPANIES ACTS • Individual insolvency • Corporate insolvency • Family	**Circuit Judge (or exceptionally Recorder) in County Court** Will be by way of a review of the decision (unless the court considers it would be in the interests of justice to hold a full hearing).
	Application heard by The Designated Civil Judge in consultation with the Presiding Judge has responsibility for allocating appeals from decisions of district judges to circuit judges.	**ANY**	Appeal heard by The Designated Civil Judge in consultation with the Presiding Judge has responsibility for allocating appeals from decisions of district judges to a Circuit Judge.

[20] Note than all rows of boxes shaded in this light colour, all contain the same information.

ROUTE OF FIRST APPEAL From DISTRICT JUDGE IN THE COUNTY COURT to HIGH COURT JUDGE OR REGISTRAR			
Appeals from the lower court	Need to apply for permission to appeal? **Yes** **Unless** against – a committal order – habeas corpus – Children secure accommodation	Decision under appeal	**to the higher (appellate) court**
→	Please read →	across the rows	→

District Judge in the County Court	**Need permission?** **Application heard by** Group C Judge Or Group A Judge allocated to Business and Property Courts or authorised by the Chancellor to hear appeals.	**Non-insolvency** proceedings brought **THROUGH** the **COMPANIES ACTS**	**High Court Judge** If permission to appeal was needed and is given, or if it was not needed Appeal heard by **Group A Judge** where Group A Judge is allocated to BP courts or authorised by the Chancellor to hear appeals **Or** **Group B Judge** (note that a Group B Judge is automatically a Group B Judge if s/he is already a Group C or D judge)

District Judge in the County Court (or in the District Registry) From an ICC Judge	<u>**Need permission?**</u> **Application heard by** Group A Judge hears any application for permission to appeal unless the appeal centre is the RCJ - e.g. if it is an appeal from an ICC Judge,- when must be heard by a salaried Registrar in Bankruptcy.	**Individual insolvency**	**High Court Judge** If permission to appeal was needed and is given, or if it was not needed Appeal heard by **Group A Judge** **Or** in exceptional circumstances **Group D Judge** authorised to hear the appeal by the Appropriate Presiding or Supervising Judge. unless RCJ appeal, which must be heard by a **Registrar in Bankruptcy**
	Ditto	**Corporate insolvency**	Ditto **Except** where appeal is from District Judge in District Registry, Supervisors in Business and Property Courts may then allow it to be heard by a Circuit Judge acting as a judge of the High Court.
	Group A Judge	**Family**	**HCJ (Family Division)**

ROUTE OF FIRST APPEAL From CIRCUIT JUDGE OR RECORDER IN THE COUNTY COURT to HIGH COURT JUDGE			
Appeals from the lower court	Need to apply for permission to appeal? **Yes** **Unless** against – a committal order – habeas corpus – Children secure accommodation Please read	Decision under appeal across the rows	**to the higher (appellate) court**

Circuit judge in the County Court	**Need permission?** **Application heard by** Group A Judge hears any application for permission to appeal	**ANY**	**High Court Judge** If permission to appeal was needed and is given, or if it was not needed Appeal heard by **Group A Judge** **Or** in exceptional circumstances **Group D Judge** authorised to hear the appeal by the Appropriate Presiding or Supervising Judge.
Recorder in the County Court	Ditto	**ANY**	**High Court Judge** If permission to appeal was needed and is given, or if it was not needed Appeal heard by **Group A Judge** **Or** in exceptional circumstances **Group C Judge** authorised to hear the appeal by the Appropriate Presiding or Supervising Judge.

ROUTE OF FIRST APPEAL From MASTER, REGISTRAR OR DISTRICT JUDGE IN THE HIGH COURT to HIGH COURT JUDGE			
Appeals from the lower court ⟶	Need to apply for permission to appeal? **Yes** **Unless** against – a committal order – habeas corpus – Children secure accommodation Please read ⟶	Decision under appeal across the rows ⟶	**to the higher (appellate) court**

From Master, Registrar or District Judge in the High Court	**Need permission?** **Application heard by** Group A Judge hears any application for permission to appeal	**ANY**	**High Court Judge** If permission to appeal was needed and is given, or if it was not needed
From Master			Appeal heard by **Group A Judge** or a **Group B** Judge authorised to hear the appeal by the Judge in Charge of the Queen's Bench List or the Chancellor of the High Court.
From Registrar			**Group A Judge**
From District Judge in the High Court			**Group A Judge** **Group C Judge sitting in the High Court** Or in exceptional circumstances, a **Group D Judge** authorised to hear the appeal by the Appropriate Presiding or Supervising Judge.

ROUTE OF FIRST APPEAL From HIGH COURT JUDGE to COURT OF APPEAL			
Appeals from the lower court	Need to apply for permission to appeal? **Yes** **Unless** against – a committal order – habeas corpus – Children secure accommodation	Decision under appeal	**to the higher (appellate) court**
→	Please read →	across the rows →	

High Court judge	**Permission needed?**	**ANY**	**Court of Appeal** **Remember to refer to how requests for permission are considered. This is in the grey boxes in the tree diagrams following the box on second appeals.**

In addition

Assignment of appeals to the Court of Appeal – (leap-frogging) [Note that the tables above in relation to first appeals, do not (as neither to Tables 1, 2 and 3 in the White Book) relate to the situation known as leap-frogging].

As regards those appeals flash-circled in the diagram below, the court can, either as the lower court or as the higher court, where it considers that appeals would **make an important point of principle or practice or if there is some other compelling reason** for the Court of Appeal to hear it, order a transfer to the Court of Appeal or the Master of Rolls can so direct. The Court of Appeal or the Master of the Rolls may also remit it back!

Diagram to show leapfrogging

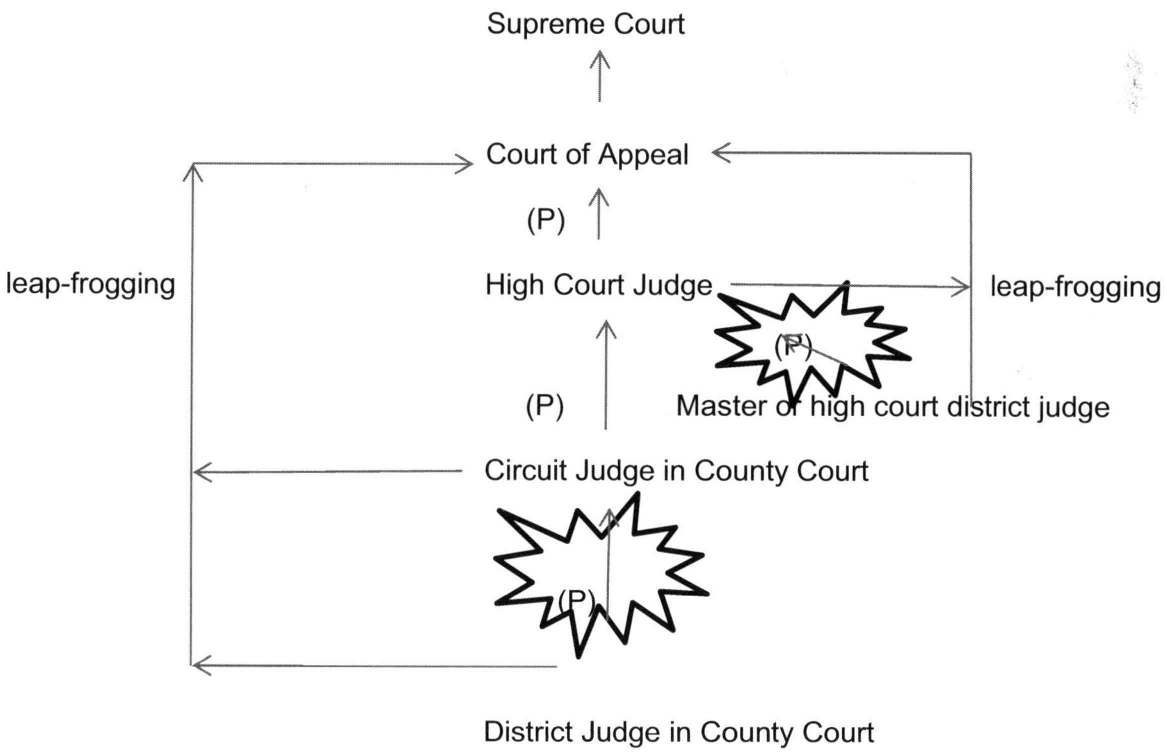

Second Appeals

Where you wish to appeal the result of a first appeal, you can, with court permission where require, make a second appeal.

Second Appeals		
From the lower court	→	**To the higher (appellate) court**
Circuit judge in County Court	**Need permission** Except when appealing against • a committal order • refusal to grant habeas corpus • a Children Act secure accommodation order so A simply notifies R. Permission is **only from the Court of Appeal on the grounds that there is** • an important point of principle or practice; or • SOCR for CA to hear it.	**Court of Appeal** **Remember to refer to <u>how</u> requests for permission are considered. This is in the grey boxes in the tree diagrams following the box on second appeals.**
High Court judge		
Court of Appeal	→	Supreme Court

There follows on the next two pages, the earlier contents of this Chapter on appeals in diagram form.

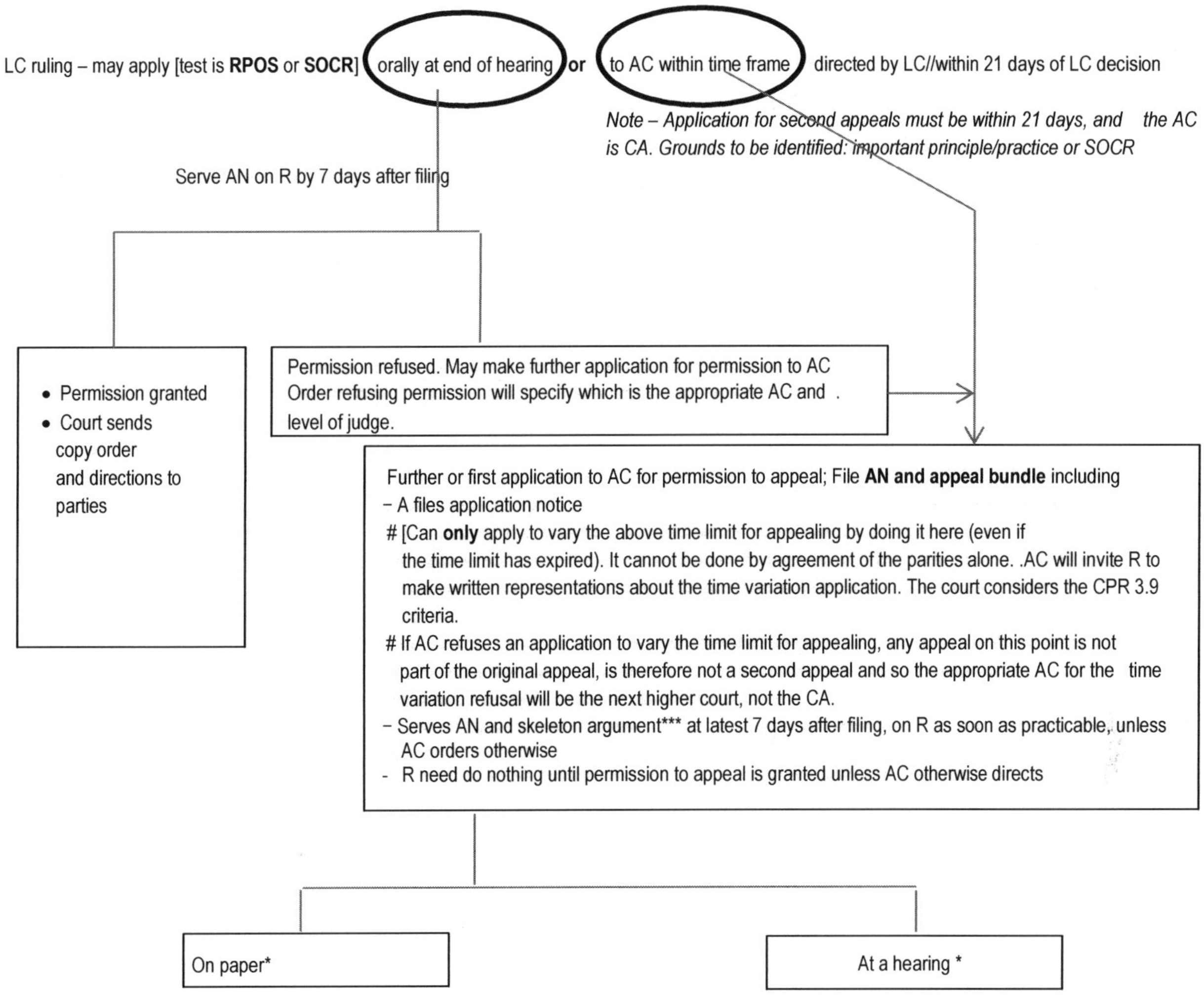

* Remember that these are both referred as hearings (even though one is a paper exercise).

This diagram is continued on the next page.

.

Continued from the previous page

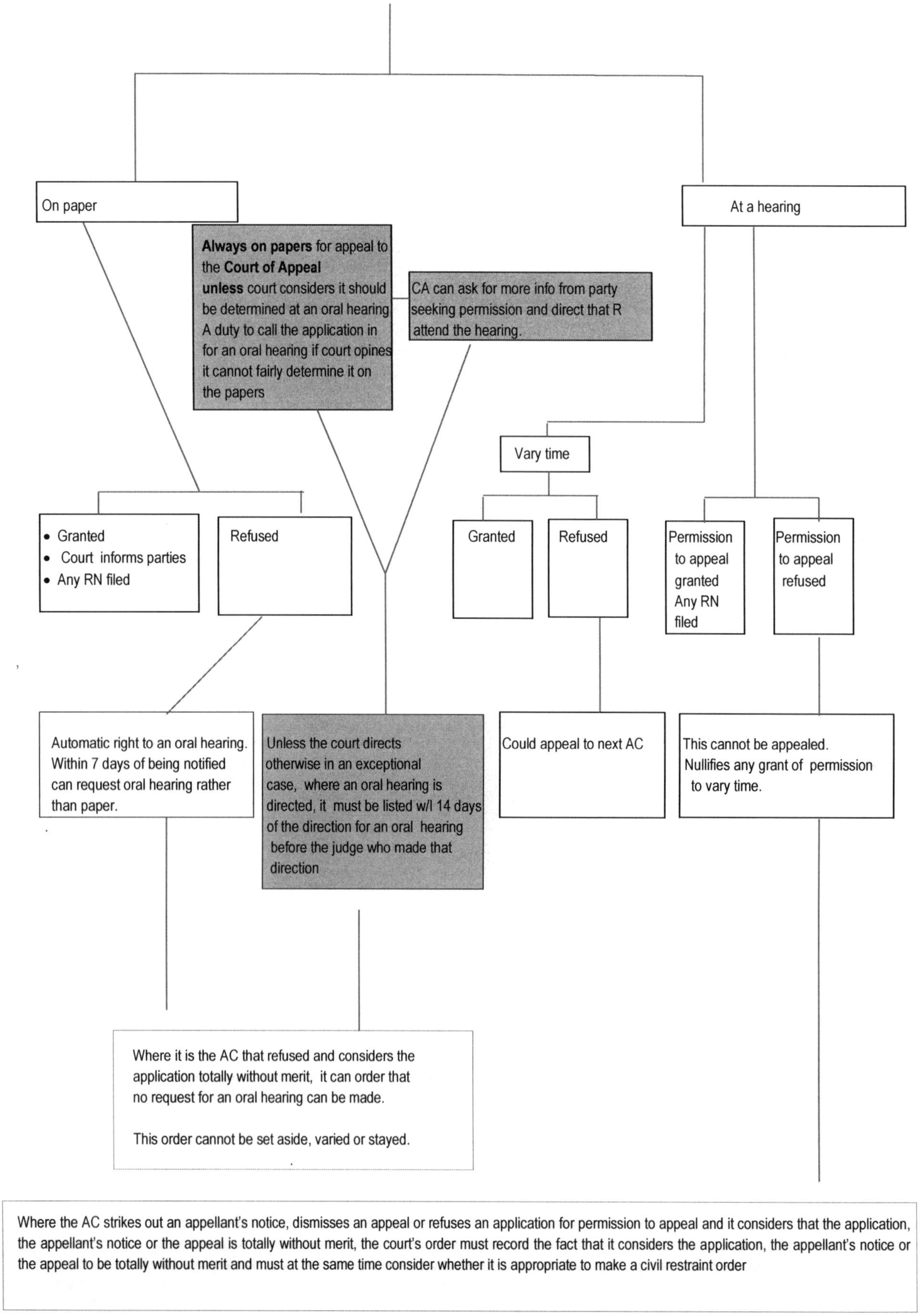

EM: skeleton arguments

The purpose of a skeleton argument is to assist the court by setting out as concisely as practicable the arguments upon which a party intends to rely.

A skeleton argument must

- be concise
  - not normally exceeding 25 pages (excluding front sheets and back sheets)
  - be printed on A4 paper in not less than 12 point font and 1.5 line spacing (including footnotes)
  - be labelled as applicable (e.g. appellant's PTA skeleton, appellant's replacement skeleton, respondent's supplementary skeleton), and be dated on its front sheet.
    - Where it does not so comply it will be returned to its author by the Civil Appeals Office and may not be re-filed unless and until it complies with those requirements; and
    - If it is re-filed out of time it must be served on all other parties to the appeal; but the party re-filing it must make an application under Part 23 to obtain the permission of the court in advance of the hearing in order to rely on it.
- both define and confine the areas of controversy
- be set out in numbered paragraphs
- be cross-referenced to any relevant document in the bundle
- be self-contained and not incorporate by reference material from previous skeleton arguments
- not include extensive quotations from documents or authorities.

Documents to be relied on must be identified.

Where it is necessary to refer to an authority, a skeleton argument must state the proposition of law the authority demonstrates and identify the parts of the authority that support the proposition.

If more than one authority is cited in support of a given proposition, the skeleton argument must briefly state why.

The cost of preparing a skeleton argument which does not comply with these requirements , or was not filed within the time limits will not be allowed on assessment except as directed by the court.

The parties should consider what other information the appeal court will need. This may include a list of persons who feature in the case or glossaries of technical terms. A chronology of relevant events will be necessary in most appeals.

Any statement of costs must show the amount claimed for the skeleton argument separately.

Where an appellant has filed a skeleton argument in support of an application for permission to appeal, the same skeleton argument may be relied upon in the appeal or the appellant may file an appeal skeleton argument.

At the hearing the court may refuse to hear argument on a point not included in a skeleton argument filed within the prescribed time.

EM: hearing of appeals

At the appeal hearing
The AC
- is limited to reviewing the LC decision unless
  - a practice direction makes different provision for a particular category of appeal or
  - the court considers it would be in the interests of justice to hold a re-hearing
- will not receive oral evidence or evidence which was not before the lower court, unless it orders otherwise
- will allow an appeal where the decision of the lower court was wrong, or unjust because of a serious procedural or other irregularity in the proceedings in the lower court
- may draw any inference of fact which it considers justified on the evidence.

At the hearing of the appeal a party may not rely on a matter not contained in his appeal notice unless the appeal court gives permission.

Activity

Remember to make notes on the relevant case law authorities in paragraphs 52.21.1 and 52.21.3 the commentary in the White Book.

You may find it useful to add in references to the case law NOW at the appropriate points of this Chapter.

When approaching final revision time, remember to add in the salient findings of the cases at the relevant point in any 'mental crib sheet' into which you have distilled the main points of your learned knowledge.

EM: Fresh evidence in appeals.

There is no oral evidence and no evidence that was not before LC unless the court orders otherwise.

Applications to adduce fresh evidence need to be in a separate bundle.

AC may admit fresh evidence (rare) if AC thinks it's in the interests of justice to actually rehear; this discretion is exercised by consideration of the Ladd v Marshall principles (and the overriding objective). The principles are
- reasonable diligence could not have obtained the evidence for use at LC trial; and
- the evidence would probably have an important influence on the result; and
- the evidence was apparently credible

Chapter 26

Elements of the syllabus which you have now covered

- A cell with heavy outlining means that that area of the syllabus was covered in this Chapter;
- A darkly shaded cell with a tick √ means that the whole of that syllabus element has now been covered;
- A lightly shaded cell means that part of that element of the syllabus has been covered in a previous Chapter; and
- An unshaded cell means that element of the syllabus has not yet been covered.

1.1 √	1.2 √	1.3 √	2.1 √	2.2 √	3.1 √	3.2 √	6.1 √	6.2 √	6.3 √
6.4 √	7.1 √	7.2 √	8.1 √	8.2 √	8.3 √	9.1 √	9.2 √	9.3 √	10.1 √
10.2 √	11.1 √	11.2 √	12.1 √	12.2 √	12.3 √	13.1 √	13.2 √	13.3 √	13.4 √
13.5 √	13.6 √	13.7 √	13.8 √	14.1 √	14.2 √	14.3 √	14.4 √	14.5 √	14.6 √
15.1 √	15.2 √	15.3 √	15.4 √	16.1 √	16.2 √	17.1 √	17.2 √	17.3 √	17.4 √
18.1 √	18.2. √ 16.3 √	16.4 √ 18.5 √	19.1 √	19.2 √	19.3 √	20.1 √	20.2 √	20.3 √	21.1 √
21.2 √	21.3 √	22.1 √	22.2 √	23.1 √	23.2 √	23.3 √	21.4 √	**24.1√**	

Elements of the syllabus which you have now covered for **ADR**

- A cell with heavy outlining means that that area of the syllabus was covered in this Chapter;
- A darkly shaded cell with a tick √ means that the whole of that syllabus element has now been covered;
- A lightly shaded cell means that part of that element of the syllabus has been covered in a previous Chapter; and
- An unshaded cell means that element of the syllabus has not yet been covered.

1.4 √	1.5√	3.3 √	4.1√	4.2√	5.1√	5.2√	18.1 √	22.3 √ record	22.3 √ enforce

Books, webinars, private coaching & work mentor

Suzanne Reece, BA (Hons),CPE, PGCE, Solicitor [NP].

Suzanne is an education coach. She is a solicitor [non-practising] who worked in legal firms for over 17 years. She later moved into education teaching post-graduate law students on the Bar Training Course (previously BPTC) at City, University of London for nearly 10 years.

A message from Suzanne

My Mum believed there was only one standard you worked to and her advice was always the same whatever task I was tackling, "**Suzanne, do your best**." I am sure you know someone who has given you wise advice.

I understand how much hard work and dedication it takes to achieve professional excellence. No less is required on the road to academic excellence as a law graduate hoping to train as a future barrister or solicitor. Developing the legal and professional skills to be an exceptional lawyer is a path I have travelled.

Having taught on the BTC [previously BPTC] for nearly 10 years, I understand that working long hours should produce success, but this is not always the case. Law is a difficult and competitive profession.

- A little guidance and support from an experienced lawyer can go a long way to helping you navigate the new skills you need.
- In my books, webinars, workshops and private coaching sessions you work on your advocacy, drafting and opinion writing skills so you can pass your assessments and move on to the next stage of your legal career.

10 Reasons you didn't write an outstanding opinion by Suzanne Reece

Opinion writing students said:

- "I cannot speak highly enough of how helpful Suzanne is as a tutor and as a person... she managed to make me feel optimistic. Indeed, thanks to her words of wisdom and advice I felt reassured. When she began helping me, she made me realise that opinion writing would be easy thanks to her methodical and systematic approach. As a result, I started enjoying writing opinions..."

- "The subject I was really concerned about is the opinion writing. The improvement is obvious from the fact that two mocks I had were both marked below pass, and having had a couple of sessions, I have achieved VC in the final assessment. How to write an opinion is quite clear to me now, but this was not clear till Suzanne explained to me how to approach the questions on a step by step basis, which came to me as a light bulb."

- "I bought your book, '10 reasons: you didn't write an outstanding opinion'. This book was amazing, it helped me a lot during BPTC and my final result for opinion writing was an 'outstanding'. I went from a 'competent grade' in my mocks to achieving an outstanding in this subject. I always found it quite hard as I used to think there is one answer but I used your book as guidance and ended up doing extremely well. I would strongly recommend this book to all BPTC students out there."

- "This book is an excellent companion when reviewing your Opinion Writing drafts to see where you could improve. It encourages you to think through your opinion and again, to understand the tactical purpose behind drafting an opinion. It is a great book and really helped me. Unfortunately, Opinion Writing has proved to be a very challenging exam for many BPTC students (me included) so hopefully in the future it will become a take home assessment rather than in timed conditions. Either way, cut through Opinion Writing stress by using this book."

- After two failed attempts at the opinion writing exam and a year of thinking I was never going to 'get it' - I passed. Passing the exam was all down to this book and Suzanne's guidance. Suzanne writes in a simplistic form making a complex and difficult skill easier to understand. This book is a step by step guide to successful opinion writing, that every BPTC student should consider using. Thank you Suzanne.

- "Hi Suzanne, I hope you are well! I recently ordered 10 Reasons You Didn't Write An Outstanding Opinion and it's awesome!"

- "I have bought that book, it's really helpful and effective for opinion writing."

Read more reviews on Suzanne's LinkedIn testimonials https://www.linkedin.com/in/suzannereece/

How to maximise marks for your Practice Focused Dissertation by Suzanne Reece

In this easy to read book Suzanne will explain the essential tasks you need to consider BEFORE choosing your dissertation title. She will then give you the tools to start planning your dissertation. By the end of the book you will have a:

- clear and specific law topic
- legal thesis
- clear list of the issues you want to explore in your dissertation
- clear practical application of your area of law for your dissertation
- plan for your research method

Dissertation students said,

“I began reading Suzanne's book 'LLM Dissertation' once I decided to embark on my LLM. The book provided me with a solid foundation upon which to build and much needed clarity on what I was actually required to do. The book provides very helpful advice and tips to aid your focus and narrow the issues you will face when conducting your research and drafting your project. I greatly recommend this book to anyone contemplating their LLM or for those who are currently on the journey but require added guidance.”

“Suzanne’s LLM Dissertation manual was instrumental to my success at City Law School. Taking the LLM alongside the BPTC was no easy task, but I was lucky enough to be recommended her manual early in the year. With this I was able to manage my time and work on my pro-bono portfolio efficiently, without disrupting the much needed focus on the BPTC.”

Webinars

The Confidential Notes Series

The Introduction. This webinar will give you Suzanne's top tips for preparing for the BTC courses in advocacy, drafting, opinion writing and how to use the CPRs.

Drafting –A series of webinars to help you draft particulars of claims, defences and skeleton arguments.

Opinion Writing- A series of webinars to help you write opinions in contract, negligence and breach of statutory duties.

Advocacy – A series of webinars to help you understand how to use the CPRs to present a civil submission and the essentials of witness handling.

Each recorded webinar costs £19.98

FREE Live webinar recordings covering a range of topics from How to be confident at law school to Skills for Future Lawyers . Free to sign up and watch at www.inspiredtostudy.org

Private Coaching

Suzanne provides coaching in study skills to help law students understand how to use case analysis and their understanding of the law, evidence and Civil Procedural Rules to construct legal arguments for advocacy, drafting and opinion writing. In addition she provides support for LLM students who need supervision and guidance with their dissertation.

Book your 20 minutes study skills consultation at www.inspiredtostudy.org or email enquiries@inspiredtostudy.org

Work Mentor

Work Mentor for Graduates

Graduates and law graduates who have successfully passed their BPC or SQE exams find that the next stage can be as stressful as you navigate the world of work. It is easy to become overwhelmed managing tasks, your workload, performance targets and professional relationships. This is the very time when an experienced and confidential mentor can help to guide you through these complex stages.

Are You

- Working in a new job?
- Overwhelmed by your job?
- Disappointed with the way your work is perceived?
- Confused on how to get ahead?

Want help?

Suzanne works with you to develop your confidence, spoken and written skills so you are better prepared for:

- Interviews
- Working in a team
- Working with challenging people
- Better organised
- Better at communicating your needs
- Focused on achieving your work goals
- Focused on your promotion

One of Suzanne's work mentees said of our work together:

➢ "Suzanne is a warm and engaging person… has a wealth of knowledge and experience that is beneficial to those looking to change careers or to build confidence for your next steps. Suzanne effectively identified what help I needed and provided this through our sessions. I would definitely recommend coaching by Suzanne and I hope to use her services myself again in the future."

You may book your 20 minutes work skills consultation at www.inspiredtostudy.org or email enquiries@inspiredtostudy.org

Warmest wishes to all those sitting the Bar Training Course or the Bar Transfer Test centrally set assessments from December 2020.

Gillian Woodworth

October 2020

Printed in Great Britain
by Amazon

64082170R00221